On the State of Democracy

This stimulating new international study of the state of democracy today contributes towards improving and deepening our understanding of the democratic process, both in new and old democracies. A particular concern of the book is to identify and evaluate policies aimed at securing improvements in democratic practices.

In many countries the state of democracy is a cause of concern. Countries that have recently become democratic are often unable to satisfy the elementary social and economic aspirations of their citizens and many continue to restrict basic civil and political freedoms. Meanwhile, voter apathy, distrust of politicians, media manipulation and corruption are issues that also trouble citizens in old established democracies.

This book was previously published as a special issue of *Democratization*.

Julio Faundez is a Professor of Law at Warwick University. He has written extensively on governance and legal and judicial reform in developing countries. He has advised the Governments of South Africa and Namibia on affirmative action legislation and the Republic of South Korea on Free Trade Agreements. He has acted as consultant for several international organizations and international law firms.

"With impeccable timing this valuable volume takes the measure of the complex, troubled state of contemporary democracy. A diverse array of first-rate scholars draw on cases spanning established and new democracies alike to cover a host of critical topics in the democracy domain, from media development and political parties to the relationship of economic and political development. The result is a wealth of insights that call attention to central areas of concern as well as pressing issues for further inquiry."

Thomas Carothers, Carnegie Endowment for International Peace

"This collection of highly original essays combines breadth and depth. Artfully organized around the subjects of politics, markets, law and empowerment, it gives us a thought provoking overview of the state of democracy in old and new regimes. Its many insights on the challenges to citizenship in established and emerging regimes make the book useful for scholars and policy makers alike."

Nancy Bermeo, Professor of Politics, Princeton University

On the State of Democracy

Edited by
Julio Faundez

Routledge
Taylor & Francis Group

First published 2007 by Routledge
2 Park Square, Milton Park, Abingdon, Oxon, OX14 4RN

Simultaneously published in the USA and Canada
by Routledge
270 Madison Ave, New York, NY 10016

Routledge is an imprint of the Taylor & Francis Group, an informa business

© 2007 Taylor & Francis Ltd

Typeset in Times Roman by Techset Composition Limited
Printed and bound in Great Britain by Antony Rowe Ltd, Chippenham, Wilts

British Library Cataloguing in Publication Data
A catalogue record for this book is available from the British Library

Library of Congress Cataloging in Publication Data
A catalog record for this book has been requested

ISBN 10: 0-415-37130-9 (hbk)
ISBN 10: 0-415-41420-2 (pbk)
ISBN 13: 978-0-415-37130-8 (hbk)
ISBN 13: 978-0-415-41420-3 (pbk)

Contents

Democratization Studies
(Formerly Democratization Studies, Frank Cass)
Series Editors: Peter Burnell and Peter Calvert

Democratization Studies combines theoretical and comparative studies with detailed analyses of issues central to democratic progress and its performance, all over the world

The books in this series aim to encourage debate on the many aspects of democratization that are of interest to policy-makers, administrators and journalists, aid and development personnel, as well as to all those involved in education.

Democratization and the Media
Edited by Vicky Randall

The Resilience of Democracy
Persistent practice, durable idea
Edited by Peter Burnell and Peter Calvert

The Internet, Democracy and Democratization
Edited by Peter Ferdinand

Party Development and Democratic Change in Post-communist Europe
Edited by Paul Lewis

Democracy Assistance
International co-operation for democratization
Edited by Peter Burnell

Opposition and Democracy in South Africa
Edited by Roger Southall

The European Union and Democracy Promotion
The case of North Africa
Edited by Richard Gillespie and Richard Youngs

Democratization and the Judiciary
Edited by Siri Gloppen, Roberto Gargarella and Elin Skaar

Civil Society in Democratization
Edited by Peter Burnell and Peter Calvert

The Internet and Politics
Citizens, voters and activists
Edited by Sarah Oates, Diana Owen and Rachel Gibson

NOTES ON CONTRIBUTORS

Susanne Brandtstädter, Lecturer in Chinese Anthropology, Department of Anthropology, University of Manchester.

Sir Bernard Crick, Professor of Politics (Emeritus) Birkbeck College, University of London.

Andrea Cornwall, Fellow, Institute of Development Studies, University of Sussex.

Donatella Della Porta, Professor of Sociology, Department of Political and Social Sciences, European University Institute, Florence, Italy.

Julio Faundez, Professor of Law, University of Warwick.

William E. Forbath, Professor of Law and Professor of History, University of Texas (Austin).

Anne Marie Goetz, Fellow, Institute of Development Studies, University of Sussex.

Mushtaq H. Khan, Professor of Economics, Department of Economics, School of Oriental and African Studies, University of London.

Adrian Leftwich, Senior Lecturer, Department of Politics, University of York.

John F. McEldowney, Professor of Law, University of Warwick.

Gunter Schubert, Professor of Greater China Studies, Institute of Chinese and Korean Studies, University of Tübingen, Germany.

Donna Lee Van Cott, Assistant Professor, Department of Political Science, Tulane University.

Aidan White, General Secretary, International Federation of Journalists, Brussels, Belgium.

Paul Webb, Professor of Politics, Department of International Relations and Politics, University of Sussex.

On the State of Democracy: Introduction

JULIO FAUNDEZ

A majority of states in the world today, some 60 per cent, are governed by democratic regimes; that is, by regimes where political authorities are selected through competitive elections in which opposition parties have a realistic chance of attaining power. This is vastly different from the situation that prevailed five decades ago, when the number of democratic regimes in the world was just over ten per cent.[1] Indeed, today, after the collapse of the Soviet Union and the end of the Cold War, democracy has emerged as the only internationally accepted political regime. As such, it is actively promoted and encouraged by development agencies of industrialised countries and by international organizations, including the European Union and various United Nations agencies.

The spread of democracy has had many positive consequences. It has strengthened the view that citizens should have equal voice in political affairs. It has reaffirmed the principle that civil and political rights should be universally guaranteed and respected. It has invigorated civil society organizations. It has made politicians more aware that domestic and international public opinion are effective devices to monitor, evaluate and influence government policy. It has focused countries' attention on the importance of constitutional design as one of the means of securing more effective systems of accountability and achieving judicial independence. It has brought about the establishment of constitutional courts designed to ensure government compliance with constitutional standards. Perhaps the single, most important consequence of the current resurgence of democracy is that new democracies have become increasingly capable of managing serious crises through political means, rather than by resorting to the military. Thus, in recent years, vigorous popular protests in Ukraine, Ecuador, Georgia and Bolivia brought about major political changes, but did not destroy either the democratic process or the constitution.

These positive developments are offset, however, by awareness that the quality of governance in many regimes currently classified as electoral democracies is poor. Indeed, many countries that have recently embraced democracy continue to restrict important civil and political freedoms. As a consequence, citizens are either retreating from politics or, worse still, becoming sceptical about the value of democracy. One of the factors triggering political disaffection is, arguably, the failure of new democratic regimes to resolve pressing social and economic problems of vast sections of their population. Although democracy aims mainly at guaranteeing political and civil equality, pervasive economic inequalities have a negative impact on the capacity of citizens to exercise their democratic rights. The danger posed by this situation is that populist leaders or sectarian groups could take advantage of democracy's freedom to undermine, discredit or overthrow its institutions. It is not easy, however, for governments in new democracies to design strategies that re-engage citizens because, as a consequence of development in the international economy, they do not fully control their political agenda. Indeed many of their public policies often originate in decisions taken by multilateral banks or by international organizations in which their influence is negligible. Moreover, even when governments manage to formulate their own public policies, their implementation is often hampered by rampant corruption or, as is more generally the case, by their weak institutional capacity.

The retreat from politics, however, is not confined to new democracies. It is also a matter of concern in old established democracies, where electoral participation is in decline, trust in politicians low and much of the media is more concerned with trivia and sensationalism than with the promotion of informed discussion on public affairs. The responses to international terrorism in the wake of the September 11 (9/11) attacks on the United States have raised numerous issues that have a direct bearing on democracy. The implementation of measures designed to meet the terrorist threat has revived the debate about the balance between state security and democratic rights. Moreover, the US-led global war on terror and its progeny, the military intervention in Iraq, has, unexpectedly, invigorated international efforts to promote democracy. Yet, in this new context democracy promotion has become selective and increasingly tainted with foreign-policy objectives that are hard to reconcile with the democratic ideal of self-government.

The foregoing suggests that while the spread of democracy is a cause of celebration, democratic regimes, both new and old, are today confronting numerous issues. The aim of this collection is to contribute towards informing and stimulating the debate on democracy. It covers key themes that have a bearing on the quality and sustainability of democratic practices in specific countries or regions. It is organized into four sections; politics, markets, law and empowerment. The contributors are experts in a variety of fields, including politics, economics, sociology, history, journalism, anthropology and law.

Section I addresses political topics. The opening essay by Bernard Crick notes that populism is a spectre that haunts modern democracy. Populist leaders, Crick reminds us, are impatient with political procedures, have a tendency to rush to decisions and appeal directly to the people in order to avoid parliamentary scrutiny, conceal party divisions or placate public opinion. To dispel the threat of populism he proposes a revival of the tradition that populists are keen to denounce – politics itself. Politics, according to Crick, is 'the activity by which the differing interests and values that exist in a complex society are conciliated'. But if the spectre of populism, as Crick acknowledges, is prompted by structural features such as the media's tendency to dumb down political issues and citizens' obsession with consumption, it is not easy to envisage how politics could be revived. Intriguingly, however, Crick suggests, that perhaps populism should be stirred when 'a purely pragmatic, purely compromising practice of politics lacks any sense of vision or moral purpose'. From this perspective, the emergence of populism could be seen as a symptom that democratic institutions are not in good working order. This observation is especially appropriate to understanding the plight of democracy in some developing countries where regimes are not inclusive and do not respond to the needs and demands of its citizens, or where a restricted conception of democracy limits the scope for political action. In such countries the emergence of populist tendencies often constitutes a warning that there is a need for urgent institutional reforms to enable the political process effectively to channel citizens' interests and aspirations.

Any effort to stimulate political activity must take into account the role of political parties. Yet, there is evidence that political parties are facing difficulties. As Paul Webb notes in 'Political parties and democracy', surveys carried out in advanced industrial democracies identify several problems that have an effect on the efficacy of political parties: increased electoral volatility, party fragmentation, low electoral turnout, decline in partisan loyalty, reduction of party membership and significant levels of anti-party sentiment. Given the political and social diversity of interests in contemporary industrial societies, political parties find it hard to fulfil their traditional interest aggregation function. As a consequence, they tend to offer bland political programmes that fail to excite citizens' imagination. Since these bland programmes often resemble each other, differences among parties are blurred, thus furthering citizens' indifference towards political parties and bringing about the emergence of social movements that focus on single issues. While Webb acknowledges that political parties face serious problems, he questions whether they are facing a crisis. He points out that, although they may have difficulties aggregating diverse interests, there is no better mechanism to perform this function. He also notes that parties continue to have a major impact on government policy and retain control over an important reservoir of patronage. Those who argue that parties are facing a crisis appear to have unrealistic expectations about their role in a democracy. As Webb notes, it is wrong to assume that there was a golden age when parties exercised an overwhelming influence over government policy. Parties have always had to compete for political influence with interest groups and the media. They have never been more than one among several actors that influence and shape public policy. He thus concludes that the argument that political parties are facing a crisis is based on ambiguous evidence.

In 'Truth, Honesty and Spin' Aidan White focuses on the role of the media. He is a journalist and, at present, general secretary of the International Federation of Journalists. He offers a personal perspective and analysis on two crucial issues: first, on the way media ownership and technological changes are affecting working conditions and professional standards of journalists; and secondly, on the impact that political spin by governments is having on free speech and on the quality of public debate.

White points out that, although recent changes in technology and the proliferation of media outlets hold the promise of a golden age for truth and understanding, in reality we are living in an age of uncertainty. Competition among media outlets has not led to an overall increase in the availability of good-quality news and information. Instead, what prevails in the media is trivial, trite and one-sided. Media outlets do not invest in professional training, and investigative journalism is not encouraged. Moreover, in some large media markets journalists do not enjoy job security, as more than 50 per cent of journalists are freelance or on short-term contracts. These alarming developments are compounded by the tendency of governments increasingly to rely on political spin to persuade, manipulate and often misrepresent public policies. Although spinning information and even concealing the truth are as old as politics, what is disturbing is that the current obsession of political leaders with what White describes as 'the alchemy of public relations and spin' is creating a special relationship between governments and large media outlets so that governments are now able directly to influence public opinion without having to bother with the procedural niceties of democracy. Moreover, this special relationship often enables media barons, and through them, corporate interests, to exercise a disproportionate influence on public policy. White does not purport to offer solutions to the many complex issues raised by his essay. He does nonetheless call for a return to the practice of scrupulous journalism based upon solid professional standards, carried out by decently paid and fairly treated reporters and news editors.

Section II explores the relationship between democracy and economic processes, both global and national. In her essay Donatella della Porta considers the impact of globalization on democracy. She explores this complex issue by focusing, in turn, on the economic, cultural and social dimensions of the process of globalization. This approach enables her to identify and assess its positive and negative consequences. Thus, while she points out that globalization has shifted decision-making power from the national to the international level, she also notes that globalization has prompted the emergence of new forms of political action and has encouraged the establishment of social movements that open up interesting new horizons in the efforts to enhance democracy. Della Porta asks whether it is possible to democratize the process of globalization. This is an important question since globalization has significantly enhanced the power of international economic organizations, such as the World Trade Organization, the International Monetary Fund and the World Bank. Today, these organizations have acquired enormous capacity to control and influence the behaviour of states. Thus, it is natural to ask whether democratic procedures can be devised to ensure that international agencies promoting globalization take into account the interests of citizens' worldwide, instead of solely reflecting the priorities of powerful industrialised countries or large multinational companies. Della Porta explores this issue and examines in detail a proposal that advocates introducing democratic practices and procedures at the international level, while retaining and reinforcing democracy at the national level. She acknowledges that while this and similar proposals may seem unrealistic or utopian, it is urgent to consider their feasibility, given the rapidly changing international environment

After Della Porta on globalization and democracy, Adrian Leftwich examines the relationship between democracy and development. In the 1960s and early 1970s, theories of political and economic modernization raised doubts as to whether democracy could take root in countries that did not have well-established market systems, strong civil societies, efficient civil services and legal institutions that could be effectively deployed both to regulate and defend basic civil and political rights.[2] The current wave of democracy has exposed the shortcomings of these theories. Today, newly established democracies in developing countries are attempting to consolidate democratic regimes in economic environments hitherto regarded as hostile to democracy and are simultaneously seeking to establish modern legal institutions and practices that old democracies achieved only after a long and arduous evolution. Thus, not surprisingly, it has been argued that the old theories of political development, with their list of conditions and prerequisites for democracy, are not reliable guides to action.[3] But, even if today democracy is 'the only game in town',[4] the question that remains is whether or not democratic institutions do in fact facilitate economic development. Leftwich's response is unequivocally negative. In his view, there is an institutional incompatibility between democracy and development. Democracy, in his view, is profoundly conservative and demands compromises based on the expectation that losers in the democratic game will accept unfavourable outcomes and that winners will show restraint in the exercise of power. Because of these features, the democratic process is incompatible with development, which he defines as a radical process of social, political and economic transformation that brings about a more equitable distribution of resources. Given this definition of development, it is not easy to dispute the view that democracy and development are incompatible. Yet, if democratization is regarded as a process that involves enhancing the capacity of citizens to participate in public affairs on an equal footing, thus enabling them to hold political authorities to account and to mobilize in support of their interests, then it would appear that the goal of enhancing democracy and achieving equitable development outcomes are not incompatible, but complementary. Moreover, development projects that are not subject to democratic scrutiny rarely achieve their objectives and often cause widespread misery and suffering.[5]

Mushtaq Khan also examines the relationship between democracy and economic processes, but focusing on countries where the market is not yet dominant and where the political process is characterized by patron–client relations. In these societies, political competition is personalised and the main political asset of faction leaders is their ability to dispense favours to their followers. Faction leaders, however, do not derive their legitimacy from traditional deference or charisma, but from their capacity to offer pay-offs to those who support them. This capacity, in turn, derives from the fact that they control or have predominant influence over informal economic networks, which are beyond the reach of the regulatory powers of the official political system. Some scholars and policy-makers argue that to break the dominance of patron–client relations it is necessary to strengthen democratic institutions and to enhance the states' governance capacity. Khan describes this approach as neopatrimonial and rejects it on the ground that it is based on the erroneous assumption that the flaws of the political systems stem from moral weaknesses of their leaders (such as their proclivity for corruption), rather than from the economic conditions that support the structures of political competition.

If, as Khan argues, democratization is unlikely to overturn patron–client relations since they are underpinned by a complex web of formal and informal economic processes, is there any hope for democracy in these countries? Khan's response to this question is that while democratization is desirable, it is unlikely to deliver any real benefits unless and until a minimum level of economic development is achieved. This response might suggest that Khan's argument is an attempt to revive old modernization theories that claim that developing countries are unable to sustain democracy. Khan, however, does not endorse modernization theories, especially the strand that regards authoritarianism as an inevitable step towards economic transformation. Instead, he calls upon policy-makers to pay close attention to patterns of patron–client competition to identify those that are compatible with the emergence of a capitalist sector. This approach requires a detailed understanding of the operation and interaction of formal and informal political and economic processes.

There is general agreement that law is an important component of any democratic regime. Law establishes rules that allow citizens to plan their lives with a degree of certainty and security; enables citizens to hold government to account and protects them from arbitrary action by the government. But law is also a complex mechanism that can be used both to further and restrain the process of democratization. The contents of Section III explore different aspects of the relationship between law and democracy.

First, William Forbath examines the evolution of social rights in the United States from the New Deal to the present. He traces the development of legal doctrine, placing it firmly within the historical and political context of the welfare rights movement of the 1960s. Forbath's essay shows the remarkable impact of the Supreme Court on the elaboration of the notion of welfare as a right owed by the state to all needy individuals. As he explains, the Supreme Court's approach in this area involved a bold interpretation of statutory texts and legislative history. Indeed, so bold was it that the Court came close to endorsing the view of welfare rights as a form of property that would enjoy the same safeguards as property in general. This line of reasoning, however, was abruptly reversed when President Nixon appointed three new members to the Supreme Court.

Forbath, though sympathetic to the Supreme Court's progressive approach to the interpretation of welfare rights, acknowledges the conceptual and doctrinal shortcomings of the Court's reasoning. He also notes that the limitations of the welfare rights movement of the 1960s stemmed from the failure of the US Congress in the 1940s to endorse the vision of social citizenship embodied in President Franklin Delano Roosevelt's second bill of rights. This vision involved a conception of social life in which all citizens would be brought into the world of work and opportunity. The rejection of this vision by the Congress in the 1940s severely narrowed the terms of the agenda of the War on Poverty, which President Lyndon Johnson launched in the 1960s in response to social ferment at the grass-roots. Instead of attempting to develop a policy on social rights as a device to achieve social inclusion, the War on Poverty delivered welfare rights that came to be regarded as mechanisms designed to compensate the poor for their exclusion. Though aware that the current political mood in the United States is not conducive to a revival of the debate on social rights, Forbath believes that courts continue to have a role in the elaboration of social rights and he proposes a conceptual framework that distinguishes between welfare rights and social citizenship.

The turbulent evolution of the law on social rights in the United States raises important questions for countries that lack the resources to provide for the basic needs of the poor. If, as Forbath suggests, even in a country as rich as the United States the absence of robust social policies is a barrier to the exercise of rights of poor and marginal citizens, how does democracy fare in countries that lack the resources to satisfy the basic needs of its citizens? Is it realistic, or feasible, in such countries to expect that law can further the process of democratization? In 'Democratization through Law', Julio Faundez addresses these questions in relation to the experience of two Latin American countries, Chile and Colombia. Until General Augusto Pinochet's military coup in 1973, Chile was universally regarded as a model of legality and stability. A close inspection, however, shows its political and legal systems had fundamental flaws. On the one hand, constitutional stability was achieved at the cost of excluding large sections of the population, mainly peasants and the urban poor. On the other hand, the independence of the judiciary was achieved largely at the cost of excluding courts from any involvement in controlling the legality of government action. Thus, when in the 1960s progressive politicians attempted to build a more inclusive polity, the fundamental weakness of the political and legal system was exposed. Courts, which hitherto had refused to venture into controversial areas of public policy, were called upon to adjudicate matters of fundamental constitutional and political importance. Unsurprisingly, their decisions, instead of resolving the underlying conflict, exacerbated it, thus accelerating the collapse of democracy.

The experience of the Constitutional Court in Colombia stands in sharp contrast to the case of Chile. Against the odds and defying the notion that courts in civil law countries are formalistic, the Constitutional Court in Colombia has adopted a bold approach to constitutional interpretation, which has forced the government to assume responsibility for the needs and interests of the poor and vulnerable groups in society. The experience of the Constitutional Court in Colombia also demonstrates that where courts are open and not excessively formalistic, citizens respect and trust them. It would be foolish to expect that constitutional litigation could resolve the intractable problems of a developing country with a highly stratified society such as Colombia. Yet, the achievements of the Constitutional Court should not be underestimated: it has made an important contribution to the development of social rights in critical areas such as housing and health; it has contributed to the stability of the political system and has enhanced the legitimacy of the legal system and legal institutions.

The 9/11 attacks on the United States and the subsequent terrorist attacks on major cities both in developed and developing countries have resulted either in the amendment to state security laws or in the enactment of the new anti-terrorist legislation. This flurry of legislative activity has generated, in most countries, a lively and often bitter debate. In general, anti-terrorism legislation – or any other legislation designed to defend the integrity of the state or the constitutional order – authorises governments to take measures that suspend or restrict basic civil and political rights such as, for example, personal liberty, freedom of assembly, freedom of movement and freedom of speech. In a democracy, the expectation is that emergency measures are carefully tailored so that the expansive powers given to the government and the police are effectively controlled. In 'Political Security and Democratic Rights', John McEldowney offers a comprehensive account of the legal and political debate arising from recent anti-terrorism legislation in the United Kingdom. His discussion is informed by a detailed analysis of the emergency measures taken by the government against terrorism in Northern Ireland. A crucial lesson emerging from this experience is that emergency measures designed to meet a specific threat often spill over into other areas of the law to become permanent fixtures of the legal system. Thus, as McEldowney notes, 'the "normal rules" of criminal justice have been gradually eroded in terms of the protection of the accused through increasing pressure to increase the efficiency in the criminal justice system'. There are no easy solutions for ensuring that emergency legislation is proportionate to the nature of the threat and that due process safeguards and mechanisms of accountability remain effective. The experience of the UK confirms that continuous open debate and rigorous judicial scrutiny by courts are indispensable safeguards to ensure that emergency legislation fulfils its objective without eroding either the rule of law or the integrity of the democratic process.

The inquiries in Section IV all ask whether democratic institutions and practices can serve as vehicles to empower citizens, especially those who have suffered systematic discrimination or are victims of social exclusion. In recent years an increasing number of women have entered into the political arena as elected representatives. The importance of this development is reflected in the fact that the third Millenium Development Goal identifies the number of women in politics as an indicator of women's empowerment. In 'Democratizing Democracy', Andrea Cornwall and Anne Marie Goetz acknowledge that the goal of enhancing women's access in politics is desirable, but note that achieving it does not automatically redress historically embedded disadvantages. Their review of affirmative action measures designed to increase the presence of women in politics confirms that merely increasing the number of females in elected posts does not necessarily lead to policy changes in their favour. Indeed, they argue, that increasing the number of women in elected offices has, often, unintended consequences such as reinforcing ruling parties' bias against women, neglecting important domains of political activity of special interest to women and even undermining democratic institutions, as is the case where women representatives are drawn to form alliances with religious groups that have political agendas inconsistent with the ideals of democracy.

Aware that the formal political institutions are not necessarily receptive to the goal of engendering democracy, women often concentrate their political efforts in civil-society organizations. This approach is, on the surface, promising as community-based organizations provide women with a suitable vehicle to defend their interests and to gain experience in political leadership. Yet, as Cornwall and Goetz explain, it is not always easy for women to transfer the skills acquired in community-based organizations onto the national political stage. Also, community-based organizations are often unsuitable as political training ground either because they are not democratic or because they lack mechanisms of accountability. More troubling still is the fact that international donors often cast community-based organizations as partners of state institutions, thus eroding their capacity as mechanisms for political mobilization and contestation. Cornwall and Goetz recognize the importance of increasing the number of women in elected offices and also acknowledge the need for creating spaces for female political participation. Yet, they caution that both in traditional and in new political spaces, women should have the opportunity effectively to articulate their political agendas.

Susanne Brandtstädter and Gunter Schubert then examine the political impact of village elections in China. Although China is not a democracy, its recent shift towards market-based policies has prompted a lively debate as to whether these changes constitute a prelude to a democratic transition. Against this background, Brandtstädter and Schubert examine the political consequences of a 1987 Act giving village-dwellers the right to elect representatives to village committees. On the surface, it is difficult to regard this measure as a genuine move towards democracy since the government showed no signs of easing its authoritarian grip on society and was, and still is, unwilling to allow private ownership over agricultural land. Indeed, the government regards village elections as means for improving governance rather than a way of spreading democracy. The Communist Party retains control over the appointment of party secretary at the local level and those running for elections do so as individuals and not as representatives of groups or parties. Yet, as Brandtstädter and Schubert show, the political and social impact of village elections has been far from negligible. Although the electoral process does not meet the standards of free elections, it has brought about important changes in the way peasants view their relationship with the state. Elections, according to Brandtstädter and Schubert, have introduced among villagers a discourse of rights, as well as the notion, albeit incipient, that party functionaries are accountable to local communities.

This process, however, is not without contradictions, as the introduction of village elections has been accompanied by a revival of local traditions around temples and ancestral halls. The revival of distinctly undemocratic traditional institutions enables peasants to compare the prevailing political mismanagement and often corruption at the local level with the purity of traditional village life. Brandtstädter and Schubert argue that village elections are bringing about a new 'moral contract' between villagers and the state. The wider implications of this emerging contract are uncertain. So far, it seems that it has reinforced the authority of the central government. Yet, it has also served to legitimise unprecedented acts of popular resistance. Thus, while it is unclear whether history will regard village elections as a first step towards democratization, it is undeniable that the introduction of this measure has transformed the political consciousness and behaviour of peasants in ways that the government could not have envisaged.

Finally, Donna Lee Van Cott examines the impact of constitutional design on the integration and empowerment of ethnic minorities and indigenous peoples. After reviewing and assessing several approaches proposed by scholars and policy-makers, she concentrates on the recent experience of Latin American countries and explains how these countries have adapted their institutions to take into account the rights and interests of indigenous peoples and ethnic minorities. Until the current wave of democratization, Latin American countries pursued a policy of cultural assimilation, thus ignoring diversity and tolerating discrimination against ethnic minorities and other vulnerable groups. The policy of import substitution, which prevailed in the region until the late 1970s, reinforced the policy of cultural assimilation. Indeed, import substitution, which assigned a pre-eminent economic role to the state, paid scant attention to land rights, traditional practices and institutions of ethnic minorities or indigenous peoples. Although the shift to neo-liberalism did not bring about a gentler approach to economic policy, the advent of democracy did provide the opportunity to enact either new constitutions or new legislation recognising the rights of indigenous peoples and ethnic minorities. These rights include collective land rights, the right to self-government, the reservation of seats in representative assemblies and the right to bilingual education. Perhaps it is too early to gauge whether the recognition of these rights will translate into effective action and empowerment. There are signs, however, as Van Cott notes, that privileged elites and powerful business interests, especially in extractive industries, are reluctant to allow prompt implementation. Yet, whether or not the political elites honour their commitments these constitutional and legal provisions have already had practical consequences, as evidenced by the political resurgence of indigenous movements in Mexico, Guatemala, Ecuador and Bolivia.

ACKNOWLEDGEMENTS

I am very grateful to Peter Burnell, joint editor of *Democratization*, for his advice and encouragement. Without his valuable help this project would not have materialised. I would like to thank the British Council for its financial support. I am especially grateful to Sital Dhillon, former Head of Governance at the British Council, who first floated the idea of this project and with unremitting enthusiasm and optimism ensured that funding was made available. I am also grateful to Farah Kabir and Stephen Shaw for their support. I am very grateful to Celine Tan for her expert and efficient editorial assistance. I would also like to extend my gratitude to Mrs Marilyn Field, who assisted with the financial management of the project.

NOTES

1. Freedom House, *Freedom in the World 2004* (www.freedomhouse.org/research/survey2004.htm).
2. Edward Shils, 'Political Development in New States: II', *Comparative Studies in Society and History*, Vol.2, No.4 (1960), pp.379–411; Seymour Martin Lipset, 'The Social Requisites of Democracy Revisited: 1993 Presidential Address', *American Sociological Review*, Vol.59, No.1 (1994), pp.1–22.
3. Myron Weiner, 'Empirical Democratic Theory and the Transition from Authoritarianism to Democracy', *PS*, Vol.20, No.4 (1987), pp.861–6.
4. Juan J. Linz and Alfred Stepan, 'Toward Consolidated Democracies', in Takashi Inoguchi, Edward Newman and John Keane (eds), *The Changing Nature of Democracy* (Tokyo: United Nations University Press, 1998), pp.48–67.
5. James C. Scott, *Seeing Like a State* (New Haven, CT: Yale University Press, 1998).

Populism, Politics and Democracy

SIR BERNARD CRICK

One of the most famous speeches ever made about democracy was that given in the public square in Athens 2,500 years ago by Pericles to his fellow citizens:

> Let me say that our system of government does not copy the institutions of our neighbours. It is more the case of our being a model to others, than of our imitating anyone else. Our constitution is called a democracy because power is in the hands not of a minority, but of the whole people. When it is a question of settling private disputes, everyone is equal before the law; when it is a question of putting one person before another in positions of public responsibility, what counts is not membership of a particular class, but the actual ability which the man possesses. No one, so long as he has it in him to be of service to the state, is kept in political obscurity because of poverty ...
>
> Here each individual is interested not only in his own affairs but in the affairs of the state as well: even those who are mostly occupied with their own business are extremely well informed on general politics – this is a peculiarity of ours: we do not say that a man who takes no interest in politics is a man who minds his own business; we say that he has no business here at all. We Athenians, in our own persons, take our decisions on policy or submit them to proper discussions: for we do not think that there is an incompatibility between words and deeds; the worst thing is to rush into action before the consequences have been properly debated.

That is an immortal statement. But historians now tell us that Pericles was in fact a demagogue, flattering the people, telling them what they wanted to hear, but doing so above the heads of his fellow politicians and magistrates, asking them in effect to ignore the normal slow traditional – we would say constitutional – procedures of decision-making. He wanted them to trust him with power in their name for the period of a wartime crisis. In other words, he was not just a demagogue, he was a populist. He claimed to understand directly and to embody the will of the people. Perhaps he really believed that he was inspired by the popular will, or perhaps he was just damned clever and unscrupulous. Even with great men of our own time perfectly well known to us, it is sometimes difficult to tell which, especially though the filter of the media.

For there to be a populist leader, there has to be a people – a widespread belief that at the social base of society there is a collective will and not simply a variety of individuals, interests or fragmented indifference. This is what, in the eighteenth century, Jean Jacques Rousseau believed, and also those members of the Jacobin club who put his bust upon their table. In the modern world populist orators commonly couple the sacred names of 'nation' and 'people'. Populists are impatient of procedures. The one procedure today that populists favour and demand is referendum, even when there is no constitutional provision or established precedent for such. The president or prime minister may decide to broadcast directly to the nation to support his war aims; and this perhaps above the heads of the Congress or Parliament, or certainly before they have had time to consider or to ask for more information. Sometimes governments themselves initiate or promise referenda because of splits in their party, or to avoid parliamentary scrutiny, or to placate an aroused public opinion. Perhaps sometimes they have to do so in what they may think to be the national interest. Every different circumstance is debatable. But such acts are a kind of populism nonetheless. They exhibit what Pericles hypocritically called 'the worst thing', that is 'to rush into action before the consequences have been properly debated'.

Two Aspects of Populism

Some years ago the American sociologist Edward Shils suggested that populism has two aspects: the supremacy of the will of the people and its endeavour to create a direct relationship between people and government. Such an attempt usually blames intermediary institutions for frustrating the will of the people. At various times, and, in various places, these intermediary and divisive institutions have appeared as the landlords, the bankers, the bureaucrats, the priests, the elite, the immigrants and, most popular of all for populists to denounce, the politicians. Sometimes, of course, there are good reasons to denounce one or more of these entities. The populist style can sometimes restore or reinvigorate democratic processes. But when all intermediary institutions are denounced, especially the politicians, there are great dangers to liberty and democracy. Someone must say to the populist leader, 'By all means denounce particular politicians, but do not denounce or discredit the political process'. I see a fundamental contradiction between populism and politics. But before elaborating this point, we must understand in broad terms when populism can arise.

Sometimes spasmodically, sometimes for longer periods, large numbers of people possess an intense and shared feeling that their common interests are being ignored by rulers and politicians or addressed too slowly out of respect for traditional or complex legal procedures. Typically these intense feelings of common grievance have arisen among peasant populations (as in nineteenth-century South America and in Tsarist Russia, even in pre-modern China and Japan); but today newspaper editors as well as populist leaders can articulate, stir, sometimes create, but most certainly shape widespread anxieties over immigration, race relations, crime, poverty or simply taxation. Populists always simplify such issues, and usually have a single magic solution: 'expel the foreigners', 'give the banks to the nation', 'restore our lost national glory', and so on, and so on. Often a leader emerges from outside the traditional elites – like Jean-Marie Le Pen in contemporary France, or William Jennings Bryan or Huey Long in American politics of the last century – or sometimes a renegade breaks from the ruling class, as happened towards the end of the Roman Republic.

'The politics of the future', said Napoleon Bonaparte, 'will be the art of stirring the masses.' He himself did quite well at that at the time. For he was the first ruler able to trust the common people with guns, and could therefore for the first time institute universal rather than selective military conscription, the *levée en masse*. He could do so because he could still invoke – dictator and then Emperor though he became – the spirit of the French Revolution, and use and augment the intense and popular nationalism it had created. 'A patriot', Robespierre had said, 'supports the Republic en masse; he who fights about details is a traitor. Everything that is not respect for the people and you [the Jacobin Convention or Assembly] is a traitor.' The Jacobins claimed to embody the will of the people.

Again, for a populist to stir the masses, there have to be masses – both in social fact, to some degree, and certainly in popular psychology. There has to have been a centralization and standardization – in broad terms brought about nowadays by both industrialization and nationalism – in states of the size of France, Japan or the United Kingdom. Such states were once highly decentralized with strong regional or provincial popular cultures; even if there was a central state, it was far less powerful than in industrial or post-industrial societies. But what is wrong with populism? Is it not for some the very spirit of democracy: lack of deference and contempt for elites? The pre-modern world had believed universally that only the well educated should have an influence on affairs of state. Even John Stuart Mill in nineteenth-century England held that a democratic franchise must first involve compulsory secondary education. No philosopher before Rousseau had formulated any argument why all men (and soon even women), even if equal spiritually or in the eye of God, should have an equal voice in affairs of state. No religions had said anything about that.

For Rousseau, it is not our powers of reasoning or possession of educated knowledge that gives us civic equality; it is our uniqueness as individuals. No two natural species are more alike than one man is to another – the brotherhood of man; but each of us is also more distinct from another than any other animal is to one of its same species. And individuals were soon to be seen as unique and authentic personalities. But, of course, Rousseau famously avoided anarchism, or an uncontrolled individualism, advocating only the moral imperative that each man, however unique, must will the best for all others. If we exercise our will in that manner, if we 'will' simply, innocently even, and discard elitist knowledge, superstition and tradition, we must in fact all agree. That is his theory of the 'General Will'. The true will of each is the will of all. Some such belief is the necessary basis for democracy, but it is not a sufficient basis for what most of us understand by democracy. We know all too well that the actual will of a majority can deprive both individuals and minority groups of freedom and what we have come to construct and conceive as human rights. Scholars have long realized that Rousseau's populist theory of the General Will has been a necessary condition for totalitarianism as well as for liberal democracy.

Beatrice Webb once said, socialist and Fabian though she was, 'Democracy is not the multiplication of ignorant opinions.' I quoted that recently on BBC television in a discussion on immigration. Speaking to the editor of a popular newspaper opposed to immigration, I reminded him that most people in opinion surveys believed the numbers of immigrants to be some three times greater than the actual numbers, and I asked him why he did not correct such fake beliefs among his readers. He replied that it was his duty as an editor to reflect – not to presume to correct – the well-known beliefs of his readers. That is when I quoted Beatrice Webb: 'Democracy is not the multiplication of ignorant opinions.' I got dozens of angry e-mails denouncing me as 'elitist', although almost an equal number praising me for courage. Not being a politician, it had not occurred to me that it was particularly courageous to draw a distinction between opinion and knowledge. Nor does it seem courageous to suggest that even 'democracy' needs some qualification or limitation, especially at a time when political leaders tend to speak in emotive 'sound bites' or slogans on a level seemingly set by the great dis-educator of our times (certainly in Britain and the United States), the populist tabloid press.

We need to stipulate some limitations on democracy if it is seen simply as majority opinion. Morality is, I suppose, the most general such limitation; laws of general applicability figure too (so long as they are reasonably just); and there is now almost a craze for the idea of human rights. Let me never be heard to mock the idea of human rights, yet I agree with the eighteenth-century Scottish philosopher David Hume that all ideas of rights – whether called natural, human or civil – are human achievements and artefacts and are not natural endowments. I simply want to draw a distinction between human rights that lay upon each of us the responsibility, obligation even, to respect the rights and needs of others, and that modern idea of individual rights which can actually work against social responsibility. Some modern formulations of rights can lead to both former Prime Minister Margaret Thatcher's 'there is no such thing as society' and to the current outbreak of litigiousness, once called Californian but now spreading rapidly among us British. If you follow much of the media regularly, you will soon learn that there is no such thing as an accident, a natural disaster or a risk reasonably taken: someone must be held responsible; the optimistic belief is even propagated that all death must somehow be put at the doctors' door. I want to argue that there is a concept of citizenship, called 'civic republicanism' by scholars, that should mediate both common views of the primacy of democracy and even some liberal views of the primacy of individual rights. Rights imply civic duties and duties imply civil rights.

Politics Itself

Now if Rousseau was right to search for some justification for everyone to be a citizen regardless of rank or education, yet he was wrong to suggest in his theory of the General Will that all intermediary groups and institutions between the individual and 'the Legislator' (his selfless and benign state) are divisive of the general interest.

Alexis de Tocqueville, without mentioning Rousseau, in fact answers him in his great two volume work *Democracy in America* (1835; 1840). The famous chapter entitled 'The Danger of the Tyranny of the Majority' is immediately followed by 'The Causes that Mitigate the Tyranny of the Majority'. These mitigations were the dispersal of central power to the States, the importance of local government and democracy, and, more fundamentally, the presence of intermediary institutions of commerce, of culture, of voluntary bodies, of different churches, and what we would now call pressure groups or interest groups, all standing between the individual and the state. These are essential for freedom and provide the cornerstones of the school of active citizenship.

Now in the Western tradition of political thinking, there is a formidable alternative tradition to populism, and it turns upon the very concept or process that populist leaders so often denounce – politics itself. How do we civilize ourselves? Aristotle said that we must enter into the *polis* as citizens, enter into political relationships with other citizens. By politics and citizenship I mean what I take Aristotle to have meant. Politics is an activity among inhabitants living as citizens in a state or *polis*, which through public debate decides how they govern themselves.[2] But political rule was not necessarily, at any given time, democratic. A *polis* should have a democratic element in it, but Aristotle advocated mixed-government: the wise and the able rotating and governing in turn with the consent of the many (to him, that many – whom Romans called *populus* – excluded slaves, foreigners and, of course, women, all of whom were to enter the polity much later; but this, I think, is as an extension, not a refutation of his thinking).

A pure democracy, Aristotle said, would embody the fallacy that because men are equal in some things, they are equal in all. However, the special sense of *polis* or civic state was to him a conditional teleological idea: both a standard and a goal to which all states would naturally move if not impeded – as well they might be impeded, by folly, unrestrained greed and power-hunger by leaders lacking civic sense, or by conquest. Aristotle brings out the intense specificity of the political relationship (and soon I will say its inherent secularity) when, in the second book of *The Politics*, he examines and criticizes schemes for ideal states. He says that his teacher Plato in *The Republic*, made the mistake of trying to reduce everything within the polis to an ideal unity. Rather it is the case that:

> there is a point at which a polis, by advancing in unity, will cease to be a polis; there is another point, short of that, at which it may still remain a polis, but will nonetheless come near to losing its essence, and will thus be a worse polis. It is as if you were to turn harmony into mere unison, or to reduce a theme to a single beat. The truth is that the polis is an aggregate of many members.[3]

Politics then, according to Aristotle, arises in organized societies that recognize themselves to be an aggregation of many members, not a single tribe, religion, interest or even tradition. That is why in my book *In Defence of Politics*, first published in 1962, I defined politics as the activity by which the differing interests and values that exist in any complex society are conciliated. There is no necessary General Will (except to decide issues politically), nor do we need to invent one. Thus politics arises out of a perception of differences as natural. This perception has both an empirical and an ethical element. The empirical element is the generalization that all advanced, complex or even just large societies contain a diversity of interests – whether moral, social or economic, and in fact usually a complex blending of each, hard to disentangle. The ethical component, whatever its precise nature, always sets limits beyond which a government should not go in attempting to enforce consensus or unity. Perhaps no general limits can be demonstrated. They may all be specific to time and place – here the relativist is half right. But the relativist is also half wrong because the principle of limitations is general and the empirical distinction is usually clear, allowing for deceit, rhetoric and muddle between constitutional regimes that strive to limit power and thus to govern politically, and those regimes whose rulers strive after total or at least unchallengeable power. That my definition of politics, or rather Aristotle's, is not an empty truism, can be seen at once if one remarks sadly that most regimes even in the modern world are not political: they hunt down or suppress politics rather than encouraging it as a civic cult. And even the most dictatorial and oppressive regimes – say North Korea – claim to be doing it in the name of 'the people'. If they act politically at all, then it is only between these four palace walls or else when facing a superior rival power. They allow no public politics – the Roman *res-publica*.

Aristotle certainly held that to be himself at his best a man must be a citizen. But he did not believe that was all a man should do: he could be a philosopher or a merchant – why not? Nor did he hold that to be an active citizen ensured that one would act rightly, act ethically. To be an active citizen was a necessary condition for the good life, but not a sufficient one.

Democracy Not By Itself

In a modern democracy the politician must, of course, always be aware of the dangers of trying to ignore strong public opinion. But he must also be aware of the dangers of simply trying to flatter and follow it if he thinks public opinion at a given moment is acting against its own longer term best interests. He must have the courage to stand up and argue back when the public is being urged by populist leaders (whether politicians, preachers or press lords) to break laws or conventions democratically legitimated and designed to mediate compromises between the different interests and values that are characteristic of a modern state and a complex society. Pericles had said in his praise of democracy, 'the secret of liberty is courage'.

To recall another bold saying, Oliver Wendell Holmes, a famous United States Justice of the Supreme Court, once said ironically, 'Democracy is what the crowd wants.' He was defending his view of constitutional guarantees of freedom of speech against some repressive but popular anti-socialist legislation by a state legislature. Well, sometimes democracy is 'what the crowd wants', but sometimes not. On the one hand, populism can arise from the failure of intermediate institutions to consider ordinary opinion, when a political class, one party or a president or prime minister appears to treat the bureaucracy and local government as their own property, rather than as a public trust. Perhaps populism even can be stirred – even should be stirred – when a purely pragmatic, purely compromising practice of politics lacks any sense of vision or moral purpose. As Margaret Canovan has written, '[when] too great a gap opens between hallowed democracy and the grubby business of politics, populists tend to move onto the vacant territory, promising instead of the dirty world of party manoeuvring the shiny ideal of democracy renewed'.[4]

Somewhat similarly, Jack Hayward has seen the recent rise of populist politics in many countries of the European Union as a response to 'the democratic deficit' and remote elitism, even corruption, at high levels.[5] It is this very gap between doctrine and practice that makes me so positively concerned, not just with a revival of serious political thinking (which unhappily rarely penetrates beyond the academy nowadays) but with a new type of citizenship education in schools that can discuss real issues, concentrate on problem-solving, and learn participative skills as well as realistic knowledge about how the political system works. (A new subject in the English national curriculum attempts all this in the name of 'the active citizen', not just 'the good citizen').[6] Over time, this could help people become more knowledgeable and more realistic about political and economic possibilities, and encourage political leaders to engage with the voters through more rational persuasion and less populist sound bites and dumbing-down of issues.

So I conclude that there is a basic tension between the political or Aristotelian way of looking at the world – whereby politics only arises because of differing interests and values that we must endure, harmonize or compromise creatively and educatively – and a Rousseau-like way which always looks for a united general will or popular sovereignty. But in modern democracies, the sociologist Peter Worsley was perhaps right to suggest that we should regard populism, not as something wholly distinct, but as 'an emphasis, a dimension of political culture in general, not simply a particular kind of overall ideological system or type of organisation'.[7] He might better have said 'movement' rather than 'organisation'; but the point still stands. And if we think of Abraham Lincoln, Georges Clemenceau, Lloyd George, Winston Churchill or Nelson Mandela, we have examples of statesmen who were able to challenge public opinion and opposition successfully - sometimes even within their own party - precisely because they had 'the common touch'. They had at least as many of the techniques of a populist leader as are needed to achieve great political compromises. But it is surely more common for populist leaders to be opportunistic and exploitative of grievances and prejudices.

Populism is indeed a spectre haunting democracy from which it is hard, perhaps impossible, to escape entirely in modern conditions of a consumption-driven society and a populist free press. Democracy itself, as Tocqueville realised, can have two aspects: individual liberties for all and equality before the law but also the ability of the state to mobilize and control the people en masse.[8] But populism needs to be, and can be, kept in check by leaders earning public respect for the political processes of compromise by being willing and able to explain and justify them publicly, in reasonable and reasoning terms, and not, as so often, by practicing a glib, cynical and usually quite transparent populism. Refusal to state publicly hard but necessary truths can, whether through folly, deceit, cowardice or neglect, exacerbate the contempt in which populist leaders so often hold not just particular politicians, but the political process itself. Rival political leaders who when faced with popular concerns, whether (for example) the reasons for going to war or the options in pensions policy always have a glib rhetorical answer of the 'we-were-right-all-along-so-trust-us-now' kind, never admitting reasonable doubt or that solutions to most problems are problematic. They should not be surprised that the electorate distrust them. Then their own smart populism – having debased the level of public debate and thus popular understanding of the complexities of government and policy – is perpetually threatened by being outbid in plausible simplicities by new populist leaders from outside the traditional political classes.

NOTES

1. R.V. Rieu, (ed.), *Thucydides, The Peloponnesian War*, trans. Rex Warner (London: Penguin, 1954), pp.117–19.
2. Bernard Crick, *In Defence of Politics*, 5th ed. (London: Continuum, 2000), first published in 1962. The last edition admits that the first edition can now appear overly optimistic in only considering politics within states rather than among states.
3. *The Politics of Aristotle*, trans. and intro. Ernest Barker (Oxford: Oxford University Press, 1946), p.51.
4. Margaret Canovan, 'Trust the People! Populism and the Two Faces of Democracy', *Political Studies*, Vol.47, No.1 (1999), pp.2–16. Canovan has been a notable commentator on Hannah Arendt.
5. Jack Hayward, 'The Populist Challenge to Elitist Democracy in Europe', in J. Hayward (ed.), *Eliticism, Populism and European Politics* (Oxford: Clarendon Press, 1996).
6. Bernard Crick, *Essays on Citizenship* (London: Continuum, 2001) and the report of an advisory group I chaired: *Education for Democracy and Citizenship in Schools* (London: Department of Education, 1998).
7. Peter Worsley, 'The Concept of Populism', in G. Ionescu and E. Gellner (eds), *Populism: Its Meaning and National Characteristics* (Basingstoke: Macmillan, 1969), p.245. Ionescu and Gellner's book is still one of the best modern accounts.
8. See Bernard Crick, *Democracy: A Very Short Introduction* (Oxford: Oxford University Press, 2003). Margaret Canovan (note 4) ends her fine article on populism by pointing to 'the inescapable ambiguity of democracy' (p.15). See also her *Populism* (London: Junction Books, 1981). But Benjamin Arditi, 'Populism as a Spectre of Democracy: a Response to Canovan', *Political Studies*, Vol.52, No.1 (2004), pp.135–43, offers 'a friendly interrogation' that (following a distinction of Michael Oakeshott's) puts more stress on the politics of faith than on the politics of scepticism.

Manuscript accepted for publication August 2005.

Address for correspondence: Professor Sir Bernard Crick, 8A Bellevue Terrace, Edinburgh EH7 4DT, Scotland. E-mail: <Bernard.Crick@ed.ac.uk>.

Political Parties and Democracy: The Ambiguous Crisis

PAUL WEBB

Introduction

Political parties are universally regarded as essential components of democratic regimes and key vehicles in the process of securing effective political representation, mobilizing voters, organizing government and shaping public policy. Yet, across the established democracies[1] today, parties are often perceived in very negative terms: among other things, they are said to be self-interested, untrustworthy, corrupt, challenged by interest groups, social movements, the media and the Internet as forms of political participation or communication, and incapable of providing accountable and effective governance. How justifiable are such claims? Do they really lie at the heart of a generalized crisis of representation? Are parties redundant, obsolete or pathological, as some critics would claim? This study will review the existing evidence and argue that it is not at all clear that such conclusions can always be safely inferred. Much of the evidence is drawn from closed-ended surveys of citizens, and based on questions which are not even designed primarily to gauge attitudes towards parties and democracy. Thus, we are dealing with sometimes highly imperfect instruments of measurement, which present researchers with difficulties of interpretation. As a result, there is an urgent need for research that clarifies the present ambiguity in much of the evidence, and which rests on a deeper understanding of citizen attitudes towards democratic institutions and processes. This would help create the conditions for a more sustained and sharply defined debate about the state of democracy today.

The Dimensions of Party Crisis

Parties have long figured prominently in the canon of Western political science, and concern about the role they play within a democratic context has been evident almost from the start, as illustrated by the work of well-known observers such as Ostrogorski and Michels.[2] In the 1960s, Jack Dennis noted that 'anti-party norms and images are present as a living part of the political culture' in many Western political systems, while Anthony King suggested 'we are entitled, at the very least, to a certain scepticism . . . concerning the great importance attached to parties in large segments of the political science literature'.[3] In the same decade, Otto Kirchheimer's seminal contribution to comparative scholarship suggested that 'the political party's role in Western industrial society today is more limited than it would appear from its position of formal pre-eminence'.[4] Driven by evidence of the partisan de-alignment and electoral instability that began to afflict Western democracies in the 1970s, these concerns developed into a fully-fledged debate about the alleged 'decline of party'. Hans Daalder has characterized the variety of critiques articulated in this debate in the following terms: first, a persistent body of thought which denies a legitimate role for party and sees parties as a threat to the good society (the normative *denial of party*); second, the selective *rejection of certain parties* that are regarded as normatively bad, but not of party per se; third, the selective rejection of certain party *systems* which are regarded as pathological for democracy and/or effective governance; and finally, the contention that parties are becoming increasingly irrelevant to democratic politics as other actors and institutions take on their functions (an empirically based assertion of the *redundancy of party*).[5]

Loss of Popular Legitimacy?

While the academic literature on decline has tended to be framed in terms of the last of these categories by focusing on the challenge which parties supposedly face from functional 'competitors', such as interest groups, social movements and the media, political activists and critics have often expressed a normative rejection of parties or party systems. By the early 1990s, developments in a number of countries were stimulating a fresh round of speculation about the decline of party. For instance, in Germany, it became commonplace to refer to the phenomenon of *Parteienverdrossenheit*, or a crisis of party legitimacy. Survey data in that country produced much evidence to suggest that citizens were disillusioned with the motivations, true concerns and effectiveness of the parties. This attitudinal trend reflected a mixture of the sentiments outlined above: while some citizens reacted against particular parties (typically the major established players in the system such as the Social Democrats, Christian Democrats or Free Democrats[6]), others took against the role and nature of parties in general.[7] Some commentators have conflated analytical statements of functional redundancy with a clear normative accusation against party.

This was implicit, for instance, in the position of the critic Hans Magnus Enzensber-ger, who argued that the country's true political innovators now lay outside the orthodox domain of the governing parties, and claimed that Germany could 'afford an incompe-tent government, because ultimately the people who bore us in the daily news really do not matter'.[8] At the same time, a similar, though far more intense, rejection of party was apparent in Italy. The roots of this ran deep, stemming from longstanding public scepti-cism about the immobilism that had characterized post-war governments in the country, but it was transformed into a fully fledged systemic crisis by the collapse of the Berlin Wall in 1989 and the widespread corruption among party elites which the *Tangentopoli* (bribesville) scandals of the early 1990s brought to light.[9]

Criticism of party was by no means the exclusive preserve of countries experien-cing overt crises. In most other advanced industrial democracies, parties were subject to allegations of weak performance, often from a left-wing or radical democratic perspective. Such observers of party life brought with them two major accusations in respect of party politics. First, parties were deemed to be failing when it came to fostering democratic political participation. Typically, the decline of participation in and through parties would be contrasted with burgeoning non-partisan forms of associative life though single-issue groups and new social movements.[10] Second, the prominence of neo-liberal political economy in the 1980s and a growing con-sciousness of the alleged effects of economic globalization in the 1990s served to con-vince some on the Left that a political convergence was developing which undermined the ideological distinctiveness of party governments.[11]

Attempts to assess the putative crisis of party in the established democracies have certainly revealed a good deal of plausible evidence. First, there is a body of public opinion research which seems to point to widespread popular dissatisfaction with parties, and related data which broadly suggest the erosion of linkages between parties and society at large. To be sure, this dimension of analysis raises significant issues about the appropriateness and true meaning of the evidence employed, a theme that will be returned to in due course, but it is hard to dispute that a prima facie case exists.

A helpful cue for research into the popular standing of political parties is provided by Poguntke's suggested indicators of *anti-party sentiment*.[12] These comprise survey-based evidence of popular disaffection with parties in general, the erosion of partisan identification and affinity, declining electoral turnout, the growth of 'uncertainty' or 'hesitancy' within the electorate (in practice, a direct counterpart of the decline of par-tisan affinity) and declining party membership. While these indicators do not necess-arily constitute evidence of active hostility towards parties, they are all consistent with a weakened sense of 'partyness' in society. Recent comparative studies of the popular legitimacy of parties in these terms reveal a good deal of evidence that appears to be consistent with the theme of 'party decline'.[13] Among the key findings of one of these studies are:

- An increase in *electoral volatility* in 12 out of 16 countries over time since 1960, and an increase in the *effective number of parties* in 13 out of 16 cases.[14] It should be said that neither of these indicators unambiguously taps antipathy towards party. Voting behaviour at the individual level may become more volatile and a party system may fragment at the aggregate level without necessarily implying the weakening legitimacy of parties: both these measures might fluctuate over time according to short-term contingencies of party competition and electoral change. However, it is interesting to observe that both indicators seem to have changed across the vast majority of cases surveyed across recent decades, which suggests the possibility that some more systematic cause may underlie these developments, denoting the loss of party anchorage in society.

- *Electoral turnout* – another variable which could fluctuate over time for quite contingent reasons – has dropped in 12 of the 16 cases, a development that would seem quite damning for parties which have played a historical role in mobilizing the masses.
- A *decrease in the proportion of voters claiming strong partisan affinities* in each of the 13 countries for which broadly comparable data are available. This more clearly signifies a loss of party penetration of society, perhaps. Moreover, in 11 cases we find *a combination of weakening partisan identification and increased volatility*, which is not surprising since we would expect voting behaviour to become less stable as people's partisan loyalties wane.
- A striking reduction in *party membership*, in all cases except one (Spain), both in terms of absolute numbers and relative to the size of the electorate. Again, this strongly suggests the erosion of direct party links with society.
- Similarly, in all cases bar one (Spain again),[15] *survey based evidence of apparently significant levels of anti-party sentiment can be identified.* Indeed, in two cases – Italy and Belgium – the level of popular dissatisfaction recorded might be said to be somewhat more than merely 'significant' and has to be understood as part and parcel of a full-blown crisis of the political system.

In summary, it is undeniable that there exists evidence consistent with the view that the popular standing of parties has been weakened in most Western democracies. However, it is frequently not easy to know how to interpret the detail of this evidence. For instance, we cannot automatically infer that parties and party politicians are viewed with active hostility by many citizens, though the well-known phenomenon of partisan de-alignment has undeniably served to weaken party penetration of society and to leave the average voter more indifferent towards parties than his or her counterpart of 40 years ago. It may be important, however, that in almost all of the countries for which we have data, the erosion of partisan identification coincides with definite evidence of significant (and usually increasing) levels of anti-party sentiment. Circumstantially at least (though this can only be confirmed by detailed individual-level analysis with data which are not always available), this suggests the possibility that significant minorities in most established democracies are more than merely 'de-aligned' in the sense of lacking an underlying partisan affinity: they are also actively critical of, or hostile towards, parties in general. If so, this would seem to have quite profound implications for party legitimacy. Uncovering the exact truth of this remains a challenge for political scientists working in this field of inquiry, a point that will be returned to in more detail later.

Weak Performance?

What of the claims made by critics who adopt a functionalist perspective? Although functional approaches to parties have sometimes been criticized,[16] there is a very long tradition of paying attention to 'what parties do, what function, what role, or what purpose is served' by them.[17] It is intuitive to ask these questions, and certainly very hard to overlook them when trying to assess the question of a generalized party crisis. If parties really are in crisis, as might seem to be indicated by the signs of widespread public disaffection with them, then must it not reflect their failure to perform adequately some or all of the key tasks normally imputed to them? Perhaps. This is an intrinsically demanding part of the inquiry. For one thing, it is not at all easy to measure functional performance over time. Inevitably, analysis tends to fall back on somewhat impressionistic interpretation. For another, it is important to understand that parties have probably never really dominated all of the functions claimed for them.[18] Thus, the degree of party crisis which some observers claim might derive from the misperception that there was once a 'Golden Age' in which parties monopolized these systemic requirements. In truth, parties have always had to share the performance of, say, the representative functions with actors such as interest groups and the mass media, and they have never been more than one of a number of factors which influence the governing process.

Which functions should we examine? While Theodore Lowi counsels against assuming an inventory of agreed functions of party 'as though these were as regularly a part of the political process as stages in the passage of a bill', it is clear from the considerable overlap between writers that something very like an 'agreed inventory' does in fact exist.[19] True, they do not always use the same terminology, but frequently, they are interested in the same phenomena. The evidence from the established democracies points to a number of conclusions about most of the frequently cited party functions.[20]

First, and perhaps foremost, there is the task of *governance*. One of the central purposes of political parties in a representative democracy is to organize accountable and effective government. Yet parties in contemporary democracies have often seemed to struggle to impose distinctive and effective policy solutions when in government. In part, this is because they often find it difficult to 'make a difference' to policy outcomes given the legacies of previous incumbents in office.[21] Furthermore, it is well recognized that a variety of macro-social developments can seriously constrain party governments' scope for autonomous action, including technological changes, demographic and social trends, and economic cycles. These factors help us understand why parties (particularly since the end of the long post-war boom) have suffered from the widespread perception of policy ineffectiveness; the apparent failures of government to resolve persistent national policy problems are bound to undermine the popular status of parties – especially when these failures are associated with more than one major party in a system. It is not surprising to discover, for instance, that British voters who perceive a long-term weakening of the national economy are significantly more likely to express anti-party sentiment or indifference.[22] Moreover, the lack of autonomy has only been exacerbated by the growing globalization of economic processes, which further incapacitates national governments so that 'they cannot always respond to domestic demands in a way which fully satisfies the local interests on which they depend for their legitimacy and authority'.[23] Supra-national integration may offer the long-term prospect of political agencies regaining a degree of control over the international economy in Europe, but this does not necessarily imply a greater role for party unless a meaningful and accountable role for transnational parties can be introduced into the EU's decision-making processes, something powerfully advocated by some critics, but far from easy to establish.[24]

Nevertheless, two key points should be borne in mind about the record of parties in government. First, those of the 'declinist' persuasion need to reflect on the undoubted fact that parties have never really dominated the governmental function to the exclusion of all other factors. They have always acted under a variety of often powerful constraints, but in democratic polities have nevertheless generally been located at the heart of key policy-making networks, and by and large they continue to be so situated. Second, and concomitantly, there is a good deal of systematically presented evidence to suggest that party effects on governmental policy outputs are far from negligible.[25] Thus, while government in the democratic world is never *exclusively* party government, it is virtually always *party-influenced* government. This implies that voters are required to reflect very carefully about what parties and their leaders may and may not reasonably be held to account for, but it does not mean that these vital elements in the democratic mix are beyond any form of meaningful accountability.

Then there are the key representative functions of *interest articulation* and *aggregation* which political parties have traditionally been expected to fulfil. These are absolutely central to any concept of 'representation', of course, and there would seem to be at least two significant problems for parties as mechanisms of effective representative linkage. In the first place, the capacity of the party system to articulate interests may be seriously undermined if there exists a widespread sense that parliamentary representation is inadequate for certain social or political groups, Britain being an obvious case in point. British Election Survey data suggest that one-third or more of the electorate want electoral reform and two-fifths feel that the country would be better served by the introduction of coalition government to replace the single-party model that has been so characteristic of post-1945 Britain; other estimates suggest that dissatisfaction with the electoral system may be still higher than this.[26] More broadly, a number of countries suffer from the perception that their parliamentary parties fail to provide adequate representation for certain key social groups such as women and ethnic minorities.[27] Still, while debates about electoral reform are not uncommon, they are rarely highly salient across the advanced industrial democracies.

Of generally greater significance for parties as mechanisms of representative linkage is the widespread perception that they are challenged by alternative sources of interest articulation. As we have already observed, evidence of burgeoning single-issue group activity suggests that, in the eyes of many citizens at least, other organizations are better at articulating demands now. In part, this preference for non-partisan modes of articulation is often thought to reflect the growing difficulties that parties face in aggregating interests. With the erosion of traditional cleavages, it is less common for parties to be closely tied to particular social groups or communities (be they defined by class, religious denomination, regional affiliation or ethnicity). Consequently, contemporary parties – especially the major vote-winners – are increasingly obliged to compete for the votes of very heterogeneous blocks of supporters, and the task of aggregating this diversity of interests is bound to be daunting. One consequence is that contemporary parties tend to be accused of offering electors blandly 'catch-all' policy programmes, thus depriving them of meaningful choices. The irruption onto the agenda of new issues which cut across old lines of conflict may offer a possible way out of such blandness, but it further complicates the task of aggregation.[28] Consequently, as the parties struggle to aggregate interests effectively, the task of interest articulation can become individualised, with citizens preferring to participate in single-issue groups or social movements.

That said, care must be taken not to exaggerate the threat to party in all this, for while it is true that the decline of partisan orientations has coincided with the rise of interest group activism, research also suggests that commitment to group activity can be a stimulant rather than a hindrance to partisanship.[29] Moreover, while interest groups or media actors might be equally, or more, effective in articulating sectional demands and placing issues on the political agenda, the fact remains that it is only the political parties (or individual candidates in candidate-centred systems of politics) that can legitimately perform the key function of aggregating demands into more or less coherent programmatic packages in democratic contexts. While this task is undoubtedly increasingly difficult, parties remain central to it.

A third function for which European parties have traditionally taken responsibility is that of *political communication*; once again, however, things appear increasingly challenging, for few would deny that citizens rely far more on non-partisan forms of media for political information and comment than hitherto. Seldom now do major parties in Europe continue to run their own press organs, accepting instead the need to compete for favourable coverage in the independent (though admittedly not always apartisan) media. This implies that the agenda-setting capacity of political parties has most probably been squeezed. An example of the way in which the style of media treatment of party politics affects the public perception of parties can be provided by the coverage of election campaigns. It is apparent from research conducted in the United States and Britain that this focuses increasingly on the conduct of campaigns rather than substantive issues of policy or leadership. Thus, by 1997, two-thirds of the broadcast media's election campaign coverage focused on party strategies and the electoral process itself– that is, on the 'horse race' rather than the substance of polices. The print media's concentration on the campaign rather than the issues was even greater.[30] There is something doubly dangerous about this for party legitimacy.

First, it carries the potential to leave citizens frustrated with politics in general, since the media's obsession with the process of political competition clearly runs contrary to the public's own preferred agenda of substantive issue concerns.[31]

Second, the intimate and constant exposés of party strategies and news management techniques leave little to the public imagination, and surely serve to foster a growing – and possibly exaggerated – cynicism about parties and politicians. Not that parties are entirely blameless in this: while they can hardly be faulted for losing control of the agenda-setting process, there is evidence that the growing inclination of parties to adopt 'negative' styles of political communication has further soured public perceptions of elite-level politics, and may even have served to depress election turn-out.[32] I believe that this is potentially a very serious point for parties, and indeed, for democracy as a whole – indeed, the point will be revisited in the conclusion.

The fourth central function of parties is one on which their recent record seems to increasingly disappointing – that of *fostering political participation*. There is incontrovertible evidence, already alluded to, of the decline of European party memberships and activism.[33] A variety of reasons for membership decline have emerged in the literature and are neatly summed up by Susan Scarrow as either 'supply-side' (stemming from the social changes which make citizens less willing to join parties) or 'demand-side' (reflecting the organizational reasons why party strategists might no longer seek to recruit members) in nature.[34] Of these two approaches, the supply-side model seems more plausible, since there is little hard evidence to suggest that parties have reduced their demand for members. Notwithstanding the undoubted impact of developments such as the communications revolution and the growth of public funding available to them, parties still seem to believe that ordinary members constitute a valuable resource in certain ways – to help run election campaigns, the raise money, to legitimize party standing, to act as 'ambassadors in the community', and so on. Thus, it is very likely an exaggeration to claim, as Kirchheimer once put it, that parties have come to regard memberships as little more than a 'historical relic'.[35]

Even so, it is from the participationist perspective that political parties are most likely to be regarded as 'failing'; hence, for instance, Geoff Mulgan's lament about the 'centralised, pyramidal, national (party structures) with strictly defined rules of authority and sovereignty'.[36] That said, an overall assessment of the importance of parties for political participation in Western Europe demands that we bear in mind at least two points: first, clear majorities of voters still turn out to vote for one party candidate or another (at least at national elections); and second, the incentives to participate in party politics are often significantly greater now than hitherto, given both the introduction of various reforms by which many major parties have sought to democratize their internal procedures, and the generally participatory ethos of a number of newer parties, especially the Greens. These reforms have been designed to afford ordinary members new rights of participation and influence in areas such as candidate selection, leadership election and policy-making.[37]

In one sense, parties are hardly threatened in respect of the final major function, namely *political recruitment*. National parliamentarians in most advanced industrial democracies are still overwhelmingly likely to bear party labels; moreover, the parties in most countries maintain control over important – sometimes vast – reservoirs of patronage, from the British *quangocracy* to the Italian system of *lotizzazione*.[38] Thus, recruitment of candidates for representative office at both national and sub-national levels remains virtually inconceivable without political parties. On the other hand, even here the reputations of parties have often foundered, for in a number of countries citizens have become deeply cynical about the corruption which attends some of these patronage networks (for instance, in the Italian and Belgian cases).

This brings us back to the issue of popular disaffection with parties, one aspect of which is the widespread perception that they are self-interested, unduly privileged and inclined to corruption. Nothing is more likely to generate a sense of cynicism about party elites than the feeling that politicians are narrowly utilitarian and prepared to exploit their situations for partisan or personal gain. This point incorporates, but takes us well beyond, the domain of the patronage scandals associated with political recruitment. Indeed, it is not hard to think of a wide variety of examples from the democratic world over the past 20 years or so; national parties in Italy, Germany, France, Spain, Belgium and Britain, not to mention a host of less celebrated local party elites, have all been tainted by the whiff of corruption. These cases are by no means all essentially identical, but they are likely to have similarly disillusioning effects on ordinary citizens. Moreover, it is possible that party legitimacy has been eroded through perceptions of self-interest even when parties have not been involved in any illegitimate activity. This is a point made well by Richard Katz and Peter Mair in respect of their concept of the 'cartel party',[39] which holds that leading parties across various Western European states, whether currently in government or not, effectively collude to establish institutional rules of the game favouring their dominant positions within the system. In particular, they exploit the resources available from the state (such as financial subventions or subsidies-in-kind) in order to ensure their organizational survival and even growth. This leaves us with a paradox which may be acutely relevant to the problems of waning popular legitimacy:

> On the ground, and in terms of their representative role, parties appear to be less relevant and to be losing some of their key functions. In public office, on the other hand, and in terms of their linkage to the state, they appear to be more privileged than ever.[40]

The combination of public privilege and waning functional relevance is precisely the thing, according to Mair, most likely to stimulate popular distrust and resentment of parties.

Overall, while this brief review of the systemic functions reveals a set of significant challenges which confront parties in contemporary democracies, a balanced judgement should not overlook the ways in which they remain central to the operation of these political systems. Thus, we have observed that parties have always faced a variety of constraints as governmental actors, and while these external pressures may be increasing, they nevertheless remain vital cogs in the machinery of government. Similarly, while parties undeniably face very significant challenges in respect of interest articulation, communication and participation, it would be an exaggeration to claim that they have been rendered insignificant in these roles. The pressures they face here reflect the nature of advanced industrial society, which is more affluent, leisured, privatist and cognitively mobilized (through the joint impact of education and the communications revolution) than the industrialized democratic world of 40 years ago. As a consequence, citizens are less closely bound to parties through old social group identities and less dependent on parties for their cognitive cues about public affairs. And finally, while we have observed that such developments render the aggregation function more complex, it is crucial to understand that parties continue to play a vital and indeed irreplaceable systemic role in this regard.

Organizational Resilience and Adaptation

The case for the party crisis interpretation which we have encountered so far can be summarized briefly in the following terms: there is undeniable evidence of the erosion of the sort of linkages with society that typified mass parties in the era of stable class or denominational alignments; although this pattern of de-alignment should not simply be regarded as a loss of popular regard for parties, there is nevertheless evidence from a variety of disparate survey indicators to suggest that a significant degree of mass disaffection may exist in many democracies. Further, there is also a good deal of somewhat impressionistic evidence implying that parties are challenged in respect of some of the classic political functions they perform, especially interest articulation and aggregation, facilitating political participation and communication, and governance.

Yet we have seen, particularly in reviewing the evidence on functional performance, that to speak of a fully fledged 'crisis' of party may be to exaggerate. Indeed, we may go further: an alternative interpretation could be that the passing of the mass party has demonstrated the adaptive capacity of modern parties. This is perhaps most apparent if one focuses on a dimension of party life that the discussion has largely so far bypassed: organization. The resilience and adaptability of party organizations has long been a theme in studies of parties in the United States,[41] and in the 1990s an exhaustive comparative survey of three decades' worth of organizational material confirmed that in many other countries parties had succeeded in enhancing the supply of resources at their disposal in spite of weakening social linkages.[42] A recent survey[43] reveals that this pattern has been maintained and is consistent across most countries. For instance, in 14 of the 15 countries for which we have evidence, the average incomes of parties have increased in real terms in recent decades, and in 11 out of 12 cases average central party staffing levels have grown. It should be said that these findings need to be set in the context of other variables for which it is harder to gather systematic data, but which seem to be less positive for parties' organizational strength. Thus, we know that in many places local party organizations are far less healthy than central party headquarters due to factors like the decline of membership activism: this is evident in the UK, Italy, the United States and New Zealand. But it can reasonably be said that central party resources are especially critical with the advent of televisual, capital-intensive and professionalized forms of political communication and campaigning.[44]

For the same reason, the decline of party-controlled presses and publications has probably not been as significant as it might initially seem. In essence, it is clear overall that parties have adapted and survived as organizations, re-modelling themselves to the needs of an era in which patterns of linkage and communication between parties and social groups have been transformed. As already noted, it is now widely acknowledged this process of adaptation has been achieved on the back of the public subvention of party organizations – though this might be something which might in itself pose problems for party legitimacy, for it creates the impression of privilege at the very time that party links with society are eroding.[45]

The Ambiguity in the Evidence

Thus, the evidence for party crisis is somewhat mixed. Party links with society have been weakened and the challenges in respect of the representative and communication functions have been especially pronounced. But parties remain particularly important to processes of aggregation, political recruitment and governance, and have adapted organizationally to the needs of modern communication, often sustaining themselves on the back of their continued centrality to the governing process. As Mair says:

> as the mass party model has passed away, the functions which parties can – or do – perform in contemporary polities have also been rebalanced, such that they now lay much more emphasis on procedural functions alone. This process goes hand in hand with the concurrent move of parties from society to state.[46]

This is important, for it contextualizes the evidence we have encountered on public opinion of parties. If parties have 'retreated from society' in various ways (as demonstrated by the loss of members and partisan affinities), making it harder for them to perform the representative functions (articulation and aggregation), while nevertheless leaving them as important as ever to the governing function, it is hardly surprising that public attitudes towards them might shift. But this begs important questions: just how clearly do citizens really comprehend what is happening in respect of parties? For that matter, how clearly do political scientists comprehend citizens? From the perspective of the citizenry, what is the appropriate role for parties in the context of modern democracy, and how far do they seem to achieve it? What do citizens really expect of parties? Of course, we have pointed to evidence of popular disaffection with parties in many democracies, but on closer examination this evidence is often far from incontrovertible. For one thing, the significance of some of the aggregate-level indicators is open to more than one interpretation. This is also true of the some of the individual-level indicators, which have generally been culled from surveys that are seldom designed with the express purpose of gauging anti-party sentiment in mind.

For instance, falling turnout, the erosion of partisanship and the growth of voter 'uncertainty' (that is, long prevarication about the voting decision) could all be explained by temporary processes of ideological convergence between the major parties in a political system, rather than by active disillusionment with parties. Under such circumstances, deciding between the alternatives on offer becomes a more difficult but less consequential task for many citizens; equally, partisan loyalty and voting simply do not matter so much when the perceived differences between parties are not so great. Should the perception of ideological convergence prove a purely transient phenomenon, however, it is possible that partisanship and turnout would increase once more, while voter uncertainty could be expected to decline. Of course, the fact that we find consistent developments across these indicators in most advanced industrial democracies gives the impression that an underlying long-term process might be at play, rather than something which is merely transient. Nevertheless, one is left with a sense of not getting directly to the heart of the matter.

Further, the survey data indicators are frequently problematic. Juan Linz makes this case persuasively. He points out that even when people appear to be critical of parties, they usually agree that parties are nonetheless important for democracy. But despite this widespread acceptance of the functional need for parties, citizens tend to hold opinions which are ambiguous, contradictory or downright unreasonable. Linz cites several examples: for one thing, people resent the bluster and acrimony of competitive party politics, and yet dislike 'all parties being the same'; it seems that people have a sense of the need for parties to represent plural interests in society, while nevertheless finding distasteful the conflict that goes with it. Or again, people expect parties to articulate the interests of 'people like me', but may be critical of party links to other groups on the grounds that these are 'special interests'. And with respect to the vexed question of party funding, while people generally agree that parties are necessities of democratic political systems, they seem unwilling to accept any of the major forms by which parties might be resourced: party money should not be mine, not from my taxes and not from interest groups, as Linz puts it! Thus, we are left to ponder how far these confusing evaluations of parties are 'based upon unreasonable expectations or a lack of understanding of the complexities and cross-pressures that parties are subjected to in performing their many roles in democratic politics'.[47]

Underlying the ambiguity in the evidence is a fundamental question about how the citizens of democratic nations see democracy and what they expect of it. For instance, it is not uncommon for critics to argue that the solution to the perceived problems of contemporary democratic systems lies in an injection of more participatory forms of democracy. Among other things, this approach proposes that, given the particular weakness of parties in terms of representative and participatory linkage, citizens are becoming disaffected and disengaged. Give them more and better forms of democratic linkage, goes the argument, with an emphasis on greater participation, and the disaffection will evaporate. Germany is an example of a country which has implemented direct democratic reforms at the sub-national level in response to the perceived problem of voter disengagement, albeit with little clear evidence of the intended effects as yet.[48]

The claims on behalf of greater participation often derive from a civic orientation[49] which contends that democracy cannot be fully realized until citizens express their shared interests as members of a community, a theme which goes all the way back to Jean-Jacques Rousseau in the eighteenth century. Participation in the democratic process is seen as vital to the political education of citizens if they are to develop this civic orientation. From this perspective, the role of contemporary political parties is simply too limited. Indeed, some would argue that parties are downright pathological, in that they too often articulate and foster narrow group interests to the detriment of the wider community, that is to say, of the general will. Not all advocates of participatory democracy would necessarily go this far, but deliberative democrats, for instance, would certainly champion participation in terms of the benefits of better-informed decision making, greater social tolerance and cohesion.[50]

But do the citizens of contemporary democracies really want more participation? There is a quite different tradition of democratic theory, of course, which is far more sceptical of the supposed benefits of participatory democracy. Advocates of elitist representative democracy, such as Joseph Schumpeter (1883–1950), regarded the popular control requirement of democracy as satisfied by little more than the electorate's capacity to remove leaders when they are no longer wanted. Parties are useful in facilitating this. This is a relatively undemanding criterion for assessing party performance, which implies that anti-party sentiment might be based mainly on the ignorant and unreasonable expectations of citizens. In any case, representative democrats would argue, more participation is not the answer to the problem. A powerful reassertion of this position has been made recently by John Hibbings and Elizabeth Theiss Morse in their research on American voters. They offer a stark challenge to the participatory visionaries:

> The last thing people want is to be more involved in political decision-making: They do not want to make political decisions themselves; they do not want to provide much input to those who are assigned to make these decisions; and they would rather not know the details of the decision-making process … This does not mean that people think no mechanism for government accountability is necessary; they just do not want the mechanism to come into play except in unusual circumstances.[51]

Those attempting to get an intellectual grip on what citizens think about and want from political parties need to understand which of these approaches is fundamentally more in tune with popular sentiment: participatory or representative democracy. In order to achieve this, it is important to make use of a blend of quantitative and qualitative opinion research. Closed-ended surveys have their uses, but these need to be complemented by qualitative focus groups in order to get a more subtle and clear-sighted sense of how people regard the political system, democracy in general and parties in particular. Reliance on quantitative surveys alone leaves us with the ambiguities that Linz highlighted. In-depth qualitative opinion research should provide a more profound understanding of how people think the systems works (or fails to work), and how they feel it ought to work.

Conclusions: Understanding the Citizen–Party–Media Nexus

With a clearer understanding of how citizens in democratic polities actually conceive of democracy, we will be in a far better position to consider the implications for parties. Moreover, we will be more able to judge what, if anything, needs to be done. For instance, evidence of widespread frustration at lack of citizens' voice, or at the shortage of opportunities for meaningful involvement might justify the implementation of more deliberative modes of democratic participation.[52] On the other hand, evidence to the contrary might lead us to rule out such options, although we should be alive to the possibility that citizens could prove to be at once essentially passive and yet disaffected with political parties and elites: 'we don't rate the politicos, but neither do we actually want to sully our own hands with political involvement'. Such an outcome would point to a cynical and disengaged electorate, which would be worrying. This is essentially what Hibbings and Theiss Morse discovered in America, where voters often held naive and unrealistic views about the nature of the political process. In effect, people were found to believe that Americans generally shared similar basic goals, but were betrayed by elites beholden to the 'special interests'. This was seen to create a cacophonous power struggle based on the pursuit of self-interest, whereas it was felt that an impartial technocratic elite should be able to make policies based on the public interest. As Hibbings and Theiss Morse point out, however, 'people's perception seems to be that the common good is not debatable but rather will be apparent if selfishness can be stripped away'.[53]

This will strike many as naively Rousseauean, to say the least. The notion of some kind of 'stealth' arrangement, whereby citizens know that democracy exists, but expect it to be barely visible on a routine basis, is simply unfeasible and smacks of civic flabbiness. Clearly, democracy needs to be actively nurtured and sustained and not just appreciated in the abstract if it is to remain healthy. This does not necessarily mean that an extensive programme of participatory or deliberative policy-making must be introduced to all corners of state and society for democracy to flourish. But it does require a sensible appreciation of the nature of plural democracy and the challenges confronting parties and politicians. To that end, any reform measures deemed appropriate to the enhancement of democracy might need to involve elements of better education designed to improve popular understanding of democracy and the roles played by parties and elites.

This leads us to an important issue, which should not be overlooked in the final analysis. Whence do citizens derive their views of democratic processes and elites? If the *Stealth Democracy* findings from America do indeed approximate those we find in other established democracies then how can this state of affairs have come about? Doubtless the parties and their leading lights should carry a portion of the blame, for it is not difficult to uncover egregious examples of bad faith and self-regarding or corrupt behaviour by party politicians in most countries. Yet was it not ever thus? If so, then why is it only in recent decades that we should so often hear of the rise of anti-party sentiment and citizen disaffection with political systems? People gain their understanding of politics and public affairs largely from the media, of course, and this raises the issue of whether the media has come to play a role in distorting popular perceptions of the democratic process and its leading actors.

Certainly, this is the view propounded in a recent and acerbic analysis of the way in which the British media operate, by John Lloyd (himself a journalist, it should be noted). Lloyd argues that the media in the UK have ceased to function simply as a vital cog in the democratic process, a restraining check on the elites and a vital means of accountability. Instead, they have increasingly come to propagate distrust of politicians, parties and institutions in general, something which has produced mass cynicism about politics and indifference to the intricacies of policy-making.[54] Lloyd suggests that the media are at the height of their power and that their 'master narrative' is one of political rottenness – 'the cynical assumption that politicians are born liars and rogues'. Typically, aspiring reporters and commentators (and note that the line between comment and news reportage has become increasingly blurred) 'hunt for prey' in a joust with politicians which serves to spread 'anomie and distrust within civil society'. His contention is that:

> the goal of developing informed citizens need not be served by acts of constant aggression or attitudes of constant suspicion towards politicians and public officials. It could also be served – and better served – by understanding and taking seriously official and representatives' stated aims, indeed by seeking an understanding of the public world which is richer than that attempted by most media organizations now.[55]

Lloyd's claims seem to me to be plausible and certainly serious enough to warrant closer examination. If he and the authors of *Stealth Democracy* are right, then it suggests that a disturbing syndrome of afflictions characterizes contemporary democracies. We have citizens who are ill informed about the nature of public affairs and the difficulties of policy-making; who do not desire more knowledge of or participation in public affairs, but are frequently cynical about the motives of those who are active, be they elected representatives or state officials; who are susceptible to a naive myth about the possibility of conflict-free policy-making, which is ruined only by the self-interested machinations of party politicians; and who are brought to this impoverished view of the democratic process by a mass media that is self-serving and largely unaccountable. This is a depressing prospect, sure enough, and perhaps it is an exaggerated one. It is to be hoped so. To know whether or not this is the case requires more extensive and subtle research than has hitherto been conducted across the democratic world. To remedy this pathology of democracy, should it prove to be well-founded, would be an infinitely greater challenge.

NOTES

1. I define 'established' democracy operationally as any country which has enjoyed unbroken competitive democratic rule since 1945, or which has made a successful transition since then in so far as few would suggest any foreseeable prospect of authoritarian rule. In effect, we are talking about Organization for Economic Cooperation and Development (OECD) countries enjoying high per capita incomes; such countries are often referred to as 'advanced industrial', 'post-industrial' (see, for instance, Russell J. Dalton, and Martin Wattenberg, *Parties Without Partisans: Political Parties in Advanced Industrial Democracies* (Oxford: Oxford University Press, 2000), or even 'post-modern' in nature (Ronald Inglehart, *Modernization and Post-Modernization: Cultural, Economic and Political Change in 43 Societies* (Princeton, NJ: Princeton University Press, 1997)). Geographically, this more or less equates to Western Europe, North America, Japan and Australasia.
2. M. Ostrogorski, *Democracy and the Organisation of Political Parties, Volume 1* (London: Macmillan, 1902); R. Michels, *Political Parties: A Sociological Study of the Oligarchical Tendencies of Modern Democracy* (New York: Free Press, 1962; first edition, 1915).
3. Jack Dennis, 'Support for the Party System by the Mass Public', *American Political Science Review*, Vol.60, No.3 (1966), p.613; Anthony King, 'Political Parties in Western Democracies: Some Sceptical Reflections', *Polity*, Vol. 2, No.2 (1969), p.140.
4. Otto Kirchheimer, 'The Transformation of West European Party Systems', in J. LaPalombara and M. Weiner (eds), *Political Parties and Political Development* (Princeton, NJ: Princeton University Press, 1966), p.200.

5. Hans Daalder, 'A Crisis of Party?', *Scandinavian Political Studies*, Vol.15, No.4 (1992), pp.269–70; see also Hans Daalder, 'Parties: Denied, Dismissed or Redundant? A Critique', in Richard Gunther, Jose Ramon Montero and Juan. J. Linz (eds), *Political Parties: Old Concepts and New Challenges* (Oxford: Oxford University Press, 2002), pp.39–57.
6. The SPD is the German Social Democratic Party, the CDU is the Christian Democratic Union, and the FDP is the Free Democrat (or Liberal) Party.
7. Thomas Poguntke, 'Explorations into A Minefield: Anti-Party Sentiment', *European Journal of Political Research* Vol.29, No.3 (1996), pp.319–44; Susan Scarrow, 'Politicians Against Parties: Anti-Party Arguments as Weapons of Change in Germany', *European Journal of Political Research* Vol.29, No.3 (1996), pp.297–317.
8. Cited in Anthony Giddens, *The Third Way: The Renewal of Social Democracy* (Cambridge: Polity Press, 1998), p.51.
9. Paul Ginsborg, 'Explaining Italy's Crisis', in S. Gundle and S. Parker (eds), *The New Italian Republic: From the Fall of the Berlin Wall to Berlusconi* (London: Routledge, 1996), pp.19–39.
10. See Jeremy Richardson, 'The Market for Political Activism: Interest Groups as A Challenge to Political Parties', *West European Politics*, Vol.18, No.1 (1995), pp.116–39; Kay Lawson and Peter H. Merkl., *When Parties Fail: Emerging Alternative Organizations* (Princeton, NJ: Princeton University Press, 1998); Geoff Mulgan, *Politics in an Anti-Political Age* (Cambridge: Polity Press, 1994).
11. See, for example, S. Ahmin, *Capitalism in the Age of Globalization* (London: Zed Books, 1997).
12. See Poguntke (note 7), pp.325–38.
13. The findings cited here are summarized from Paul Webb, David M. Farrell and Ian Holliday, *Political Parties in Advanced Industrial Democracies* (Oxford: Oxford University Press, 2002), pp.438–42. See also Russell J. Dalton and Martin Wattenberg, *Parties Without Partisans: Political Parties in Advanced Industrial Democracies* (Oxford: Oxford University Press, 2000).
14. The effective number of parties is a classic indicator of party system fragmentation. See M. Laakso and R. Taagepera, 'Effective Number of Parties: A Measure with Application to Western Europe', *Comparative Political Studies*, Vol.12, No.1 (1979), pp.3–27.
15. That Spain is the exception should not be surprising in view of the fact that this is the most recently transitional democracy among the cases surveyed; it is to be expected that the early years of democratization and party system formation will be associated with volatile electoral behaviour, but that volatility will gradually reduce as the party system consolidates into a stable competitive pattern. Similarly, Spanish citizens' appreciation of parties is likely to derive from their relatively recent memories of competitive party politics as heralding the advent of democracy. In general, these findings suggest that citizens' attitudes are shaped by a country's stage of democratic development rather than by the 'contagious' influence of neighbouring states.
16. W.R. Shonfeld, 'Political Parties: The Functional Approach and the Structural Alternative', *Comparative Politics*, Vol.15, No.4 (1983), pp.477–99.
17. Howard Scarrow, 'The Function of Political Parties: A Critique of the Literature and the Approach', *Journal of Politics*, Vol.29, No.4 (1967), p.770.
18. A point made a surprisingly long time ago by some observers. See, for example, Frank J. Sorauf, *Political Parties in the American System* (Boston, MA: Little Brown, 1964).
19. Theodore J. Lowi, 'Toward Functionalism in Political Science: The Case of Innovation in Party Systems', *American Political Science Review*, Vol.57, No.3 (1963), p.571.
20. See Webb *et al.* (note 13), pp.444–50, for further detail.
21. Richard Rose, *Do Parties Make a Difference?* (London: Macmillan, 1980; 2nd edition, 1984); Francis G. Castles, *The Impact of Parties: Politics & Policies in Democratic Capitalist States* (London: Sage Publications, 1982).
22. Paul Webb, 'Apartisanship and Anti-Party Sentiment in the UK: Correlates and Constraints', *European Journal of Political Research*, Vol.29, No.3 (1996), pp.376–7.
23. Peter Mair, 'Political Parties, Popular Legitimacy and Public Privilege', *West European Politics*, Vol.18, No.3 (1995), pp.43–5.
24. See, for instance, Mark Leonard, *Politics Without Frontiers: The Role of Political Parties in Europe's Future* (London: Demos, 1997).
25. Ian Budge and Hans Keman, *Parties and Democracy: Coalition Formation and Government Functioning in Twenty States* (Oxford: Oxford University Press, 1990); Michael Laver and Ian Budge, *Party Policy and Coalition Governments in Western Europe* (London: Macmillan, 1993); Hans-Dieter Klingemann, Richard Hofferbert and Ian Budge, *Parties, Policies and Democracy* (Boulder, CO: Westview Press, 1994).
26. Paul Webb, *The Modern British Party System* (London: Sage Publications, 2000), p.271.

27. Pippa Norris, *Passages to Power: Legislative Recruitment in Advanced Democracies* (Cambridge: Cambridge University Press, 1997).
28. Kay Lawson and Thomas Poguntke, *How Political Parties Respond: Interest Aggregation Revisited* (London: Routledge, 2004).
29. Kees Aarts, 'Intermediate Organizations and Interest Representation', in H.-D. Klingemann and D. Fuchs (eds), *Citizens and the State* (Oxford: Oxford University Press, 1995), p.251.
30. Pippa Norris, John Curtice, David Sanders, Margaret Scammell and Holli Semetko, *On Message* (London: Sage Publications, 1999), pp.93, 97.
31. Ibid., p.127.
32. Stephen Ansalobehere and Shinto Iyengar, *Going Negative: How Political Advertisements Shrink and Polarize The Electorate* (New York: Free Press, 1995).
33. P. Mair and I. van Biezen, 'Party Membership in Twenty European Democracies, 1980–2000', *Party Politics*, Vol.7, No.1 (2001), pp.5–22.
34. Susan E. Scarrow, *Parties and Their Members* (Oxford: Clarendon Press, 1996).
35. Otto Kirchheimer, 'The Transformation of West European Party Systems', in J. LaPalombara and M. Weiner (eds), *Political Parties and Political Development* (Princeton, NJ: Princeton University Press, 1966), pp.177–200. The reasons why parties might continue to demand members are set out in Susan E. Scarrow, 'The Paradox of Enrolment: Assessing the Costs and Benefits of Party Membership', *European Journal of Political Research*, Vol.25, No.1 (1994), pp.41–60, and Webb, *The Modern British Party System* (note 26), pp.221–7.
36. Geoff Mulgan 'Party-Free Politics?', *New Statesman*, 15 April 1994.
37. S.E. Scarrow, P.D. Webb and D.M. Farrell, 'From Social Integration to Electoral Contestation: The Changing Distribution of Power within Political Parties', in R.J. Dalton and M.P. Wattenberg (eds), *Parties Without Partisans: Political Change in Advanced Industrial Democracies* (Oxford: Oxford University Press, 2000), pp.129–53.
38. *Quangocracy* is literally rule by 'quasi-autonomous non-governmental organizations'. Also known as 'non-departmental public bodies', quangos are 'bodies that are either entirely or partly financed by government departments, and which act with a large degree of independence from government' (Dan Lewis, *The Essential Guide to British Quangos 2005* (London: Centre for Policy Studies, 2005), p.4). There are now estimated to be some 529 quangos in the UK, which provide appointive positions for approximately 60,000 individuals. Many of these positions are in the gift of the political parties. *Lotizzazione* refers to the practice of allotting the spoils of office according to the electoral returns of the parties in parliament (or even of the various factions within the old Christian Democratic Party). This approach to distributing public sector jobs clearly undermined placement and promotion through merit, and although Italians came to accept this as so normal that the fine-tuned percentages, ministry by ministry, were actually published in a regularly revised booklet, critics nevertheless saw it as a cause of weak performance by a bloated public sector.
39. Richard S. Katz and Peter Mair 'Changing Models of Party Organization and Party Democracy: The Emergence of the Cartel Party', *Party Politics*, Vol.1, Vol.1 (1995), pp.5–28.
40. Mair, 'Political Parties, Popular Legitimacy' (note 23), p.54.
41. Cornelius P. Cotter, and John F. Bibby, 'Institutional Development of Parties and the Thesis of Party Decline', *Political Science Quarterly*, Vol.95, No.1 (1980), pp.1–27; John F. Bibby,. 'Party Organizations, 1946–1996', in Bryon E. Shafer (ed.), *Partisan Approaches to Postwar American Politics* (New York: Chatham House, 1998), pp.142–85.
42. See Katz and Mair, 'Changing Models' (note 39); Richard S. Katz and Peter Mair, *Party Organizations: A Data Handbook on Party Organizations in Western Democracies, 1960–1990* (London: Sage Publications, 1992); Richard S. Katz and Peter Mair, *How Parties Organize: Change and Adaptation in Party Organizations in Western Democracies* (London: Sage Publications, 1994).
43. For a summary of trends in party organizational resourcing, see Webb *et al.* (note 13), pp.442–4.
44. D.M. Farrell and P.D. Webb, 'Political Parties as Campaign Organizations', in R.J. Dalton and M.P. Wattenberg (eds), *Parties Without Partisans: Political Change in Advanced Industrial Democracies* (Oxford: Oxford University Press, 2000), pp.102–28.
45. Mair, 'Political Parties, Popular Legitimacy' (note 23), p.54.
46. Peter Mair, 'Democracy Beyond Parties', paper presented to European Consortium of Political Research Workshop on Political Parties and Democracy, Granada, 14–19 April 2005.
47. Juan J. Linz, 'Parties in Contemporary Democracies: Problems and Paradoxes', in Gunther *et al.* (note 5), p.294.

48. Susan E. Scarrow, 'Party Competition and Institutional Change: The Expansion of Direct Democracy in Germany', *Party Politics*, Vol.3, No.4 (1997), pp.451–71.
49. Alan Ware, *Citizens, Parties and the State* (Cambridge: Polity Press, 1987), p.13.
50. Carole Pateman, *Participation and Democratic Theory* (Cambridge: Cambridge University Press, 1970); Benjamin Barber, *Strong Democracy: Participatory Democracy for a New Age* (Berkeley, CA: University of California Press, 1984); James S. Fishkin, *Democracy and Deliberation* (New Haven, CT: Yale University Press, 1991).
51. John Hibbings and Elizabeth Theiss-Morse, *Stealth Democracy: Americans Beliefs About How Government Should Work* (Cambridge: Cambridge University Press, 2002), pp.1–2.
52. For an example, see Clare Delap, *Making Better Decisions: Report of an IPPR Symposium on Citizens' Juries and other Methods of Public Involvement* (London: Institute for Public Policy Research, 1997).
53. Hibbings and Theiss-Morse (note 51), p.9.
54. In similar, though somewhat more academic, vein see Steven Barnett, 'Will a Crisis in Journalism Provoke a Crisis in Democracy?', *Political Quarterly*, Vol.73, No.4 (2002), pp.400–408.
55. John Lloyd, *What the Media Are Doing to Our Politics* (London: Constable, 2004), p.22.

Manuscript accepted for publication August 2005.

Address for correspondence: Professor Paul Webb, Department of International Relations and Politics, University of Sussex, Brighton, BN1 9SJ, UK. E-mail: <P.Webb@sussex.ac.uk>.

Truth, Honesty and Spin

AIDAN WHITE

Introduction

This should be a golden age for truth and understanding. We live in a time of unprecedented access to information sources; when ideas, opinions and facts about the world we live in circulate the globe in seconds in a technological landscape that, in theory at least, empowers confident and engaged citizens to exercise their freedom and democratic rights more effectively than ever before. In reality, however, this is a new age of uncertainty. There is deep anxiety in society. Many people, unsure about their future, have lost trust in political institutions. They see that democracy is not the open, freedom-inspiring process of exercising choice, but is narrowly defined in a prudent manner by governments who are increasingly resentful of dissidence and opposition. Their free press turns out to be free only to those who own one.

All we want is the truth, but instead all we get is the mendacious art of mass deception whereby public opinion is shaped and manipulated by singular powers – political and corporate.

Most democrats hate the word 'propaganda'. It smacks of deception, censorship and, even, outright lying. People would rather not believe they are either the victims of it or their governments are guilty of it, but most of us are increasingly aware that in many of the world's leading democracies very little happens without some degree of tampering with the information we receive.

Media machinations, public relations and political image-making today play a significant role in shaping popular and political culture and the ideas which drive the democratic process. There is too little truth and honesty and too much spin. When the voters of France and, shortly after, the people of the Netherlands, decisively rejected the Constitutional Treaty of the European Union in the summer of 2005, they took part in a remarkable event. Not only did they deal a fatal blow to the latest phase of the European project, they exposed how detached political leaders have become from the people they claim to represent. When an all-party political establishment, buttressed by the best media money can buy, and armed with a 'consensus' of smartly dressed business leaders, trade unionists and do-gooders, all of them skilled in the art of telling people what is good for them, are routed by their citizens, people are sending a message not just about their attitude to a wordy, poorly drafted and vague political statement about the future. They are also expressing a deeply felt anxiety about their place in the world.

Put simply, people have become overwhelmed by a communications culture over which they have little influence and which treats them with little respect.

Democracy in the post-war consensus was built around a notional set of values – articulated by democratic rights and standards – that were well understood and tested routinely by democratic institutions, a reasonably free press, and the push and shove of politicians jostling for power with clearly defined policies and ideological messages that voters could understand. Today that has all changed.

What are the origins of this crisis? And, more importantly what is needed to reassert the values of open government, media quality and democratic pluralism beyond the pursuit of narrow self-interest? Unless these questions are answered and acted upon, the disaffection of many in society, already evident in the growth of intolerance, the isolation and disenchantment of many young people, and the collapse of confidence in political structures and democratic institutions such as media will only intensify. What follows looks at the role of media in this process and examines how free speech has been increasingly constrained by political and business interests. It highlights how media themselves play a role in the decline of public confidence in democratic institutions, considers how some are fighting back, and offers some thoughts on what needs to be done to reverse the current trend.

Political Spin in War and Peace

For democracy to have any meaning for citizens, they need free and open access to accurate, reliable and timely information. But that is not enough. In a democracy, information must be useful. It must reflect the expression of a wide variety of different opinions, including ideas and views we might find troubling, outrageous, and even dangerous.

However, modern politics is carefully filtered and treated through the alchemy of public relations and spin to create a political discourse which, when reported in the newspapers and on television is far from honest, fair or delivered with a sense of duty to the public.

When it comes to war, governments have to mobilize their people and build support for their policies, even when they are sometimes painful in terms of anticipated loss and suffering. Inevitably, rulers rely upon the patriotism of democratic institutions, including the press, to get their message across. Sometimes, this is not so difficult. During the Second World War, the mobilization of democracies in the United Kingdom and the United States was built upon the cooperation, decency and professionalism of journalists, who understood their role well and who recorded failures as well as successes in a carefully controlled information environment. Few complained. After all, many lives were at stake and the cause was just and the public well informed about the issues at the root of the conflict. However, the same could not be said for the war in Iraq in 2003.

Even less so could it be said about the 'war on terror' launched by the United States in the wake of the terrorist attacks of 11 September 2001 (9/11). Both of these developments relied heavily upon the shaping and manipulation of public opinion. Whether this war was, as many now argue, a grotesque fabrication in response to the tragedy of 9/11 and based upon an agreement between the US president and the British prime minister to go to war if necessary without United Nations (UN) approval and in the face of widespread international opposition, is still not clear, but it is undeniable that, on both sides of the Atlantic, a ferocious campaign was waged in the run up to the invasion to shield policy-makers and the public from the truth about the situation. The monstrous failure of the United States media to challenge the spin and dishonesty of the White House information machine and, particularly, the two lines of deceit that were fed into the public consciousness – that Saddam Hussein had weapons of mass destruction and that his regime was linked to al-Qaeda and Osama Bin Laden – has provoked an unprecedented bout of hand-wringing and self-doubt among journalists working within the world's most constitutionally free media.

In the weeks and months prior to the war, the media in the United States were remarkably acquiescent. Statements and suggestions from the Bush administration about the need to confront Saddam – the policy of 'regime change' – were hardly questioned at all. In some respects this was hardly surprising, for the US media were still cowed by the harsh crackdown on dissenting voices which had followed the attacks on New York and Washington. Administration officials in Washington were sharply critical of attempts to explain the origins of the attacks. Commentators who suggested that American policies in the Middle East for example, may have contributed to this drift towards extremism and terror were isolated. Some were sacked. Any argument that even hinted at rational justification or excuse for what the government identified as an incomprehensible, inexcusable act of mindless terror was swiftly stifled.[1]

As a result, people were starved of reliable background information. The true picture of the Middle East was obscured by the political and strategic objectives of the political establishment. One primary reason why people did not get any answers was because media did not ask the right questions. The population at large, anxious and destabilized by the appalling assault of 9/11, followed the lead of their president and his key advisors who planted seeds of intolerance and fear into this ignorant pasture. These have taken root and may not be dislodged for some time.

Even today, in spite of Michael Moore's film *Fahrenheit 9/11*, Seymour Hersh's brilliantly executed expose of torture by US soldiers at the Abu Ghraib prison in Baghdad, and vivid daily reporting revealing that the plight of Iraqis has worsened considerably since the invasion, many Americans cling stubbornly to the view that Saddam was somehow linked to 9/11, that his government was developing new and horrifying nuclear and chemical weapons, and that the invasion was justified in the name of peace and democracy. In the US, dissident journalists were harried and intimidated while mainstream media were, on the whole, willing accomplices in a government strategy of mass deception. Sometimes, though, the relationship between journalists and politicians is dangerously cosy leading to self-inflicted wounds that weaken public trust in media.

There is no better example of how the grace and favour, back-scratching world of media and politics is dangerous for democracy than the extraordinary events in Spain following the series of bomb attacks on Spanish commuter trains which killed 192 people and left 1,400 injured in March 2004. It was a horrifying terrorist assault, carried out only days before the Spanish general election and was, predictably, a massive media story. It stunned the country and sent shock waves through Europe, already jittery of terrorist threats following the 9/11 attacks on the United States and the Bali (Indonesia) bombings of September 2003.

Within hours, Spanish politicians, led by Prime Minister Jose Maria Aznar, conscious of the controversy over his government's support for the war in Iraq, were spinning a story to the media about the origins of the attack. Those responsible, said Aznar in a series of telephone calls to Spanish editors and media chiefs, were members of the Basque terrorist group ETA (Euzkadi ta Azkatasuna). An ETA attack would play better with the voters who were generally supportive of Aznar's tough line against the Basque militants.

Press conferences were called and media were told, with heavy hints, if not directly, that those responsible were the country's home-grown terrorists – the ETA separatists in the Basque country of Spain, even though there was much head scratching about the scale of the attack which went far beyond anything ETA had ever carried out in its 30-year campaign of violence. Furthermore, ETA was emphatic and instant in its denial of responsibility. Aznar and his followers, increasingly desperate, played every media card in their hands. They cajoled and persuaded leading media organizations to accept their version of events, even as the evidence began to emerge that the perpetrators could indeed be linked to the al-Qaeda terrorist network.

The government's desperation to keep voters 'on message' was understandable, but that some of Spain's leading newspapers should go along with it was unconscionable. Within hours, the people of Spain were to go to the polls in an election where government support for the war in Iraq was an issue. Clearly, if it was acknowledged that the bombings were a reprisal for Spanish support of the US invasion, that could have an impact on government support, but equally a vigorous 'we will not be intimidated' defence of democracy could have played well. What did not go down at all, however, was a blatant attempt by government and their media friends to fool the voters.

The failure to recognize that telling the truth might have provided a basis for a swift political counter-punch was catastrophically exposed by the government's decision to try to deceive the people. Within hours, as rumour and speculation increased, millions of text (Short Message Service or SMS) messages circulated about the truth being suppressed. Thousands of demonstrators took to the streets, forcing the authorities to come clean about the attack. And there was, of course, a tremendous backlash at the polls as voters turned the government out of office, delivering what some commentators mistakenly supposed was a victory for terrorists – the overthrow of a democratic government.

However, calmer judgement suggests that this sort of analysis fails utterly to comprehend the capacity for indignation in a democracy when the government is widely believed to be deliberately misleading the people. The Spanish case illustrates the dangers when journalists are tempted to succumb to the line of a government determined to pursue its political objective. Those newspapers that were taken in by their political friends woke up quickly to the realization that a story as dramatic, as tragic and as momentous as the Madrid bombings needed to be reported straight – with facts, more facts, question marks over everything that could not be explained, and good old-fashioned scepticism about the strategy, arguments and evidence behind the government's claims.

If the Spanish media learned a good lesson the hard way, the British media, and particularly the BBC, learned that a government that lives by spin and misinformation can be a vicious and ruthless opponent. Unlike their colleagues in the US, British journalists were more alert to the consequences of the war and the arguments surrounding it. They were not burdened by the mood of tragedy and loss that constrained US journalism. In Britain media were divided into 'for' and 'against' camps with lively public debates about the issues. The normal antagonism between government and media erupted into a series of pitched battles fought over strategy and evidence that would justify going to war. This culminated in the infamous gladiatorial struggle between the prime minister's office in Downing Street and the BBC over its coverage of the Iraq story. This battle, which led to the suicide of David Kelly, a personable source for journalists covering the intelligence story, was a vivid drama in which a government's natural wish to spin information in favour of its own strategic interests came up against journalism which resented political pressure and bullying.

The row erupted over an early-morning radio broadcast (prime time listening for politicians, as it happens) stating that the government had deliberately manipulated intelligence information to support its contentions about the existence of weapons of mass destruction in Iraq in order to justify going to war. In fact, this broadcast had been preceded by weeks of low-intensity conflict between the BBC news management and Downing Street during which government officials consistently complained about the BBC's lack of support. The broadcast, part of which was acknowledged as a mistake at the time and was corrected for later reports, led to bitter exchanges between the two sides, both publicly and in parliament, and the subsequent public identification of David Kelly as the BBC source. When he committed suicide, a further investigation, the Hutton Inquiry – led by a former Lord Chief Justice of Northern Ireland – found that the BBC had made mistakes, and this led to the resignation of Greg Dyke, the director-general of the BBC, and Gavyn Davies, the head of the BBC Board of Governors.

However, a further inquiry, carried out by the former top civil servant Lord Butler, into the origins of the decision to go to war, provided another view. It criticized the government for its policy-making in this area and noted the interference and role of Downing Street in dealing with the reports from intelligence officials.

The suspicions of many that governments in both London and Washington were engaged in a sophisticated strategy of massage and manipulation of information related to the Iraq conflict were further reinforced in May 2005 when the *Sunday Times*, only days before a general election in the United Kingdom, revealed details of the 'Downing Street Memo'. This was a confidential record of a meeting in 2002 of Prime Minister Tony Blair with his advisers in which it was reported that the United States strategy was to go to war with Iraq, but needed to 'fix' the intelligence information to justify this objective. While this story was well reported in the UK and throughout the rest of Europe, it was hardly reported in the United States media, even though some members of Congress see it as a basis for a new inquiry into the reasons for going to war and whether the President had committed impeachable offences.[2]

Today, the people closest to this affair at the BBC, including Richard Sambrook, head of news at the time, and now head of BBC World News, have little doubt that the original report about government 'sexing up' intelligence information over weapons of mass destruction was nearer the mark than they thought at the time. The failure to find any such weapons damaged not only the image of intelligence services, for whom hard facts are the raw material for detached judgement, but also illustrated how a government driven by political imperatives and intent upon careful and strategic management of information, will do anything, including hounding journalists, to ensure that its message takes precedence over the people's right to know the truth.

The Iraq War is a prime example, and the early years of the twenty-first century have seen renewed political pressure on journalism from governments everywhere, much of it based upon the United States-led 'war on terror', which has led to the introduction of new rules in many countries of the world that chip away at freedom of expression and other civil liberties. Journalists feel these pressures acutely. The rush to legislate and, particularly, the adoption of rules in the US and Europe that monitor the Internet and electronic communications, and increases surveillance of citizens, inevitably has consequences for journalism.[3]

In some countries, of course, such as Zimbabwe, Russia, Ukraine and China, there is already undue pressure from politicians and state authorities, exercised directly by regimes that display contempt for the simple virtues of freedom of expression and opinion as set out in Article 19 of the Universal Declaration of Human Rights. But the evidence of journalism as a plaything of political interests in the democratic world, particularly during times of peace, is less well known. In early 2005, the *New York Times* gave a rare insight into the routine nature of political manipulation when it exposed how US government-sponsored propaganda and the compliance of big media had reached levels that should be shocking to any democrat or professional journalist.[4]

The US administration under George Bush has become its own news and spin machine and has been spectacularly successful in selling government propaganda as genuine news. Federal agencies have been buying so-called 'independent' columnists and making their own 'news' videos disguised as genuine journalism and then circulating them to the news media. News networks – including major players such as Fox and ABC – have been using these fake news clips and some have even been altering them slightly to give them a home-made look. According to the *New York Times*, more than 20 federal agencies, including the State Department and the Defense Department, make up their own news, all of which extol the virtues of the Bush regime and its policies. The White House under George Bush has spent US$254 million over the past four years on contracts with public relations firms, twice as much as was spent under the Clinton administration.

The media have gone along with this process because the material is slickly produced, simple to use and it is easy to pretend it is real news produced by your own people. It is also a money-saving device. Free, off-the-peg programmes from the government are a life-saver for cash-strapped editors, but they only work, of course, if the viewers remain ignorant of the process.

Developments like this and the failure to maintain standards have provoked a crisis of confidence among many of the world's leading daily newspapers – the *New York Times*, *Le Monde* and the *Daily Mirror*, for instance have either lost editors or endured crises in recent years as journalism has declined into a cult of mass production, dominated by people glued to their screens in offices they never leave, plagiarizing stories from rivals or the Internet, and vulnerable, above all, to the machinery of public relations, political confidence tricksters and the spin merchants of special interest groups.

Media and Journalism in Crisis

The emergence of more interventionist, muscular politics in dealing with media comes as media organizations and journalism worldwide are undergoing, according to a recent report, an 'epochal event, as momentous probably as the invention of the telegraph or television'. Journalism is on the move towards a fast-paced and fragmented future in which the hallmarks of good journalism, context and thoughtfulness, are fading, both in print and broadcast media.[5]

Changes in the media industry, including new fears over media concentration, attacks on public service broadcasting and the impact of technological and structural change have themselves led to increased internal pressure on journalistic standards. These led the International Federation of Journalists, in November 2002, to launch a quality campaign aimed at reinvigorating the mission of media. It is a move that reflects the anxiety of journalists over the decline in the quality of their work in recent years.

The latest research information indicates that in the world's most developed media markets, the dominant mass media of the last century, newspapers and terrestrial network television, are in decline. A major 2004 study in the United States, a market that gives direction to the future of media elsewhere, reveals that most American news outlets are significantly cutting their investment in staff and resources in the face of falling newspaper sales and a shrinking audience for prime time television news.[6]

The fall in the United States is dramatic: daily newspaper circulation down 11 per cent since 1990; television evening news viewers down 28 per cent since 1993; only three out of eight media sectors see audience growth: ethnic, alternative and online media.

As the numbers have fallen, so have the jobs in the newsroom and the quality of work in journalism. According to this report, there are 2,200 fewer people in newspapers this year than there were in 1990, the number of network television correspondents is down by a third and the number of full-time radio news staff slumped by 44 per cent between 1994 and 2001.

Reports carried out in Europe reveal that the employment profile of journalism has changed equally dramatically, with more than 50 per cent of journalists in some of the most developed media markets such as Germany now working to freelance, casual or short-term contract arrangements.

Converging media technology, increased competition and media concentration are having an impact: there is internal pressure on editorial budgets and increasing use of freelance journalism as a proportion of editorial content in all forms of media; there is less investment in professional training, less investigative journalism and a reduction in scope of editorial coverage, particularly foreign affairs; and there is pressure to integrate advertising and commercial objectives into editorial work.

The news is not all bad. The US report also reveals an expansion of the media advertising market, an explosion of new media outlets, and an upsurge in the circulation and audience reach of minority media (Spanish language newspaper circulation in the US has quadrupled in just 13 years). But the overwhelming evidence from all sides is that journalism is in the midst of turbulent restructuring in which good quality news and information are available, perhaps more than ever, but so are the trivial, the trite, the one-sided and the false. There has never been a more important moment than now for journalists to identify with quality, with standards and with sound ethical practice.

While there needs to be a more robust and vigorous debate about how independent journalism survives the process of globalization of the media economy and the resurgence of political authority over fundamental liberties, the media do not play their role very well. The poor performance of many media outlets undermines the traditional watchdog role of media and weakens the credibility of journalism. In the fragmented, less-filtered world of 24-hour rolling news programming, the priority is speed and convenience, sometimes at the expense of accuracy. The problem is that while society and journalism are in the midst of moving from a print culture (including traditional broadcasting, which has its news-gathering roots deep in the traditions of newspaper journalism) to a multimedia culture, not enough thought is being given to the quality and accuracy of information on offer. And in the online world, traditional journalistic systems of checking and verification are becoming sidelined. This adds an extra dimension to the concern over the circle of deceit created by political spin doctors and the public relations industry.

Although this account is concerned primarily with the growth of external pressures on journalism it would be absurd not to recognize that media and many journalists are hardly innocent bystanders in the crisis currently enveloping the profession. It has always been the case that everyone associated with public information – from advertisers and politicians to media owners, journalists and the patchwork of interest groups in civil society – has an agenda. There is nothing new about this, of course. The man who is recognized as the father of spin is Edward Bernays, who died in 1995 at the age of 103, and who spent most of the twentieth century developing the craft that is today called public relations. Thanks to him, national and global public relations agencies today play a dominant role in helping politicians, corporations and powerful interest groups manipulate public opinion. This trade encourages people to smoke, to buy cars, to support wars and to vote for politicians they have never heard of and it uses the media to do its bidding. The hand of public relations is everywhere in the newsroom of modern media.[7]

But journalists, editors and owners also play a key role in shaping public opinion. They have their stories to follow, often initiated by publishers with their own clear ideas about what makes news and how it should be reported. Media work in a very competitive environment, more cut-throat than ever before, and news executives are driven by at least three powerful impulses – the punishing demands of owners who want profits and political influence in equal measure; the pressure from advertisers and sponsors for audience and sales; the aspirations of journalists to deliver exclusives on time, more dramatically and more effectively than the opposition. For journalists, 'news' is what sells, impresses your rivals and has an impact on the readers or viewers. It normally comes in one of three forms – controversy (which can be positive or negative), emotion in the guise of 'human interest' stories, or the reporting of events.

In television, for instance, the presentation of news is about vivid, emotional context and slick bite-sized chunks of dramatic footage squeezed into the time-critical spaces between the mix of light entertainment, style, soap and chat-show mosaic that fills the 24-hour television agenda.

The explosion of information over the past ten years has opened our eyes to a new landscape full of opportunities for health, education and human development. It has also revealed, for all our whimsical notions of democracy, how we live in a world of lies, and evasion, while many, if not most of us are addicted to banality, trivia and mindless entertainment. The expansion of new communications technologies has exposed the frailties of journalism and the world of information to everyone with access to a personal computer and the Internet.

In spite of grandiose declarations which underscore the industry's honourable traditions, particularly from the likes of the United Nation's cultural agency United Nations Educational, Scientific and Cultural Organisation (UNESCO) and the Council of Europe, as well as genuine commitment by journalists and many other media professionals, journalism today suffers as much from internal threats as it does from those outside the newsroom. One critical reason is the impact of dramatic changes in the international media market, which is more competitive and turbulent than it has been for decades.

Modern media corporations are less interested in the truth and public-interest journalism and much more interested in the commercial opportunities presented by entertainment, glamour and lifestyle, and they see many more opportunities to focus on that in the multi-media environment of converging information technology. They publish stories and broadcast programmes that further their business interests and fawn over politicians who favour them, while pouring scorn on political opponents and interest groups that challenge their own world view, such as trade unions or human rights groups that harp on about curbing the power of global capitalism or provide alternative views about everything from social exclusion to the environment.

Even today, in arguably the freest age humanity has ever enjoyed, political censorship – the use of the big lie – is still at work. In China, for instance, there are no books or films or articles published which expose the man-made famine between 1958 and 1962 in which 30 million people died. This crime against its own people, committed by the Communist Party of China, and grotesquely described as 'The Great Leap Forward', is now mentioned in bashful terms and skimmed over in national history books as 'three years of hardship'. Today, most young Chinese are left completely ignorant of what happened when the Communist Party leadership sent the tanks into Tiananmen Square to confront unarmed protesters in 1989.

It is unacceptable that a new generation of Chinese are fed propaganda about the world they live in while the past is shrouded in secrecy and censorship, but the fact that Western media corporations, anxious for a slice of the country's lucrative information market, cravenly reinforce Chinese cynicism about democracy by their own acts of self-censorship is equally deplorable.

In 1993, Rupert Murdoch, who a few years earlier had boasted about changes in information technology sounding the death knell for the tyranny of state control of media and information, set the pace. His companies eliminated the BBC from the package of satellite channels he beamed into China because the Communist leadership was angry at BBC coverage of Tiananmen Square. The distinguished correspondent of *The Times*, Jonathan Mirsky, resigned from his flagship daily because the paper refused to run his articles about dissidents in China; and Murdoch's book publisher, Harper Collins, under instructions from the owner, terminated the publishing contract of Chris Patten, former and last Governor of Hong Kong, because of his book's criticism of China.

Dictatorship and state monopoly are not repellent to the modern media providing they can make the deals they want to gain access to the world's biggest market. News International and other major media conglomerates provide much evidence that despite emphatic statements from international organizations and human rights groups that media products are not like other economic products because they have a social, cultural and democratic value, the treatment of news and information as a commodity continues to override or interfere with the duty of journalists to inform their audience.[8]

Much can be blamed on competition and heavy concentration within the industry. While most large countries jealously guard their national media treasures from undue concentration, many small countries – particularly the transitional states of Europe –

have seen their major newspapers and private electronic media bought up by major foreign media companies. The consequences for local democracy and pluralism have already sparked major concern within European journalism.[9]

The major players in the expanding global media market are a handful of powerful corporations which are laying siege to one of democracy's prize possessions – the tradition of public service values in media. They lobby ferociously for the elimination of state aid to national systems of public broadcasting, even when these are acknowledged leaders in the field of quality, internal pluralism and editorial independence. The persistence of private sector attacks on the BBC and public service systems in France, Spain, Italy and other countries suggests that the market-led transformation of media and information services, which many already blame for declining standards, will lead to the destruction of viable public broadcasting, and will further reinforce the crisis of quality in journalism.

The most dramatic example of the threat to pluralism posed by concentration is found in Italy, where the closeness of media with political power structures has reached its ultimate stage. Italian Prime Minister Silvio Berlusconi, owner of the country's largest private media business, now exercises control over the public television system RAI and effectively runs the country's entire media system.[10]

Media organizations are increasingly international in nature. They are driven by the political and economic imperatives of a global market place in which the impulse to increase circulation or audience and to satisfy the needs of advertisers and sponsors is ever stronger. The resulting pressure on the quality of journalism is evident to all. There is a built-in pressure on journalists to reach for the attention-grabbing stories for sensationalism. Newsroom budgets around the world have been slashed, investment in journalism training has fallen and, in the age of rolling 24-hour news coverage, there is less time and less money for investigative journalism and effective background research. Pictures offend good taste, stories intrude upon privacy, and questionable methods are used to get information.

In the United States, opponents of media concentration point out that media giants Viacom and Clear Channel Communications, the country's largest radio network with more than 1,250 stations, have been fined for indecent radio broadcasts much more than other networks. Since 1999, Clear Channel, for instance, which owns 11 per cent of America's 11,000 commercial stations, has received around 52 per cent of the fines imposed by regulators. Viacom's 180 Infinity stations, about two per cent of all stations, have received 28 per cent of the fines; all other stations account for the remaining 20 per cent.

The clash of interests between independent journalism and powerful media corporations was dramatically exposed in Canada in 2001 when the country's largest media conglomerate, CanWest Global Communications Corporation, tried to centralize its control over opinion journalism and then tried to stifle internal opposition by gagging and censorship.

In December 2001, CanWest announced that all its newspapers must print the same editorial produced from its Winnipeg headquarters. Half a continent away, journalists working in the independently minded region of Quebec staged an immediate revolt. Reporters at the company's flagship title in Montreal, the English-language

Gazette, warned that this action in Canada, where regional diversity is the cornerstone of the country's democratic culture, was a prime example of how quality journalism is at risk from powerful monopolies.

Subsequently, the company banned its journalists in newspaper and television newsrooms across Canada from taking part in editorial protests at the *Montreal Gazette* and *The Leader Post* in Regina, where four *Leader Post* reporters were suspended for five days for talking to outside media and another six were given letters of reprimand after they withdrew their bylines in protest over an incident of censorship at the newspaper. Management at the *Leader Post* censored a story to tone down criticism of CanWest for pulling articles by some of its columnists who expressed views the company did not like.

In the event, protesting journalists won their case, securing a landmark arbitration verdict in which the company gave way – gag orders were lifted and the journalists' right to defend their independence were reaffirmed. In a similar way, protests by news staff at radio stations in Detroit and St Louis in the United States in 2003 exposed an editorial/advertising deal between companies with links with two of the world's largest media conglomerates. Infinity Broadcasting, a part of the media giant Viacom, owns 180 radio stations in the United States and reached an agreement with AOL (America Online) for Broadband whereby the online service (a subsidiary of AOL Time Warner, at the time the world's biggest media company) pays Infinity US$15 million in the coming year for radio airtime.

The internal documents indicate that the deal required journalists to promote AOL for Broadband in their normal editorial work. On-air broadcasters were instructed to follow news stories with reminders that streaming video or audio or online chatter on the subject at hand could be had through AOL. They were told to do this six times a day. Listeners remained blissfully ignorant of the deception. Journalists called in their union, the American Federation of Radio and Television Artists (AFTRA), to challenge the move. Yet the incident appears to be a violation of Federal Communication Commission rules which state that listeners and viewers are entitled to know by whom they are being persuaded. Thus an audience must be clearly informed that it is hearing or viewing matter which is being paid for when such is the case, and the person paying for the broadcast of matter must be clearly identified.

Media Ethics and Democratic Values

The game of lying, both commercial and political, may be a part of journalistic life, but, in the end, it never provides anything other than short-term gain for those who play it.

Without a notional attachment to something like the truth, the exercise of business or politics is impossible. Telling lies can buy time, as *Daily Mirror* proprietor Robert Maxwell recognized when he fooled his gullible bankers and investors. The promotion of incomplete and misleading intelligence information may also prove useful in achieving a political objective, as was the case in the United Kingdom when the government persuaded Parliament to endorse the decision to invade Iraq. But in a democracy these lapses are nearly always found out.

As most governments and corporate leaders eventually learn, in both the intelligence and the business communities, there is one rule, one law, and that is to do with the objective truth. Business leaders and politicians alike are constantly tempted by spin-doctors, mercenaries and speculative fabricators ready to tell them something they think the former want to hear, but they play a dangerous game when they go along with it. Being caught out in a lie is death to confidence in the markets and it will hasten political destruction at the polls come election time.

Can media provide a counter to the massive forces of self-interest that populate the board rooms and the corridors of political power? Despite all the problems, freedom of media has improved, but it is not because traditional media have become better, but rather that new communication technologies see the introduction of new sources and dialogues, ideas and opinions that have been, until recently, outside the vision of traditional media. The modern newsroom is multi-media and traditional divisions are already a memory in most parts of the world. Journalists working on online editions and media websites are an integral part of the media structure. There is a proliferation of new outlets for information.

However, this new landscape brings challenges to media, old and new. In a world that demands news instantly and has dozens of places to look for it, public confidence in media may have fallen to dangerous levels, but people have not abandoned as futile the search for reliable, accurate reporting. Nor have journalists given up the fight.

In January 2004, journalists at the *Daily Express* group in London protested at the 'confrontational racist hatred' in the newspaper's coverage of asylum seekers, which was being driven by the owner's belief that these sensational stories were adding thousands to the newspaper's daily circulation. The journalists, all members of the National Union of Journalists in Great Britain and Ireland, expressed their anger after the *Express* had splashed on asylum stories for six consecutive days. The journalists passed a resolution expressing 'disapproval of the sustained campaign against asylum seekers . . . the media has an important role to play in a democratic society and should not distort or whip up confrontational racist hatred, in pursuit of increased circulation'.

Nevertheless, the day after the meeting, proprietor Richard Desmond insisted that the *Express* lead on a refugee story again. He claimed these stories had added 20,000 to the circulation. The journalists decided to complain about this interference to the Press Complaints Commission after a senior finance journalist at the group spoke out publicly against the editorial interference of Richard Desmond. City Correspondent David Hellier, who edits the Media Uncovered section and is a member of the union committee at the newspaper, claimed to be sickened by the continual interference of the proprietor in allegedly objective reporting and above all in the inflammatory hate-stirring headlines on asylum seekers. His frustration is understandable, but it raises the question once again about how journalists regulate themselves and have effective mechanisms for maintaining quality against the interference of others, including owners.

Journalists' groups argue that, rather than blunt instruments of control, journalists require a better social and professional environment in which to make their daily ethical judgements. Most remain convinced that self-regulation is key to the supervision of ethical conduct, even if it lacks the legal authority and hard edge of enforcement that comes with a legal code. But in the face of the current media crisis, caused by excessive commercialization which is driving down standards, is this voluntary approach still a viable option to restore respect for editorial independence, ethical journalism and democratic values?

The debate within journalism is difficult and divided on this question and centres upon difference over how journalism should function in a democracy. One approach is the laissez-faire doctrine of free-market media employers who define press freedom as the right to publish without interference from anyone, including government, outside interests and even journalists in their employment. Most reporters and editors on the other hand argue that some form of editorial independence, expressed through the right of journalists to act according to their conscience, irrespective of the views of owners, governments or others, is equally important in defining the scope of press freedom in a democracy.

Some libertarians are obsessively opposed to any form of regulation – rejecting press cards, for instance, or any official or professional registration of journalists as forms of licensing that may permit governmental or other external 'control' of journalism. Some even argue that trying to enforce professional codes of conduct or allowing any state engagement in media – even public broadcasting – leads to unacceptable pressure. Many others, even in journalism, argue that in an industry which shows wanton disregard for social responsibility, journalists and media organizations should be obliged to engage with the authorities and the public to actively promote free expression through a free and responsible press, with respect for a codified set of standards. This may include such ideas as a clause of conscience for journalists, which operates in France, for instance, or the development and promotion of independent ownership models that apply at media houses such as *Le Monde*, in France, *The Guardian* in London or *Corriere Della Sera* in Italy.There is much discussion about how this is done, not least of which concerns the limits to be set on what government can and cannot do.

Over the years, these ideas have been debated vigorously in the public policy arena, most notably during the late twentieth century when arguments over a New World Information and Communication Order split the United Nations. Twenty years on, with globalization and corporate social responsibility high on the international agenda, the debate is back, but in a very different world of converging information systems, new online services that owe no allegiance to traditional values in the media, muscular and intrusive political attitudes to the press, and a vigorous and volatile media market.

It is now highly questionable whether journalists themselves and their media are able to set editorial standards and to create credible structures of accountability that protect the interests of citizens and consumers. New initiatives – codes of good practice, the introduction of readers' editors and readers' panels, the creation of a global network of news ombudsmen – are useful but they are no substitute for empowering journalists through editorial independence to confront internal as well as external pressures on their work. Laws are not needed to define ethics, but press councils or other national voluntary panels that regulate media may need the backing of law to enforce their rulings, as long as these same laws keep the dead hand of political control out of the newsroom.

Journalists themselves are taking up these questions at national and international levels and at the core of the discussions are the three cardinal principles which underpin an ethical framework – respect for the truth, the need to be independent and the need to be aware of the consequences of what media publish.

But the debate is not made easier by divisions within journalism. Many editors and executives who willfully ignore public concerns about falling standards appear foolishly complacent. They reinforce an image of arrogance and distance as well as give an uncritical endorsement of the notion that commercial interests should prevail above all in journalism. But there are welcome signs of resistance too. As some of the examples in this account illustrate, there are many unions and journalists ready to take the fight to those who are running down the industry.

Beyond the media industry, too, there is also an awakening among consumers and the public at large that they have muscles to flex. In the United States, for instance, media industry lobbyists have spent enormous sums lobbying for reform of media rules that limit concentration of ownership. Since the Telecommunications Act of 1996 was passed, a small number of media corporations have moved into dominant positions by acquiring chunks of the US media. Deregulation has boosted both the commercial power of companies like AOL Time Warner, Viacom, Disney, but it also gives them political power. They have demanded even greater relaxation of rules on media ownership, spending freely – more than US$1 billion, according to the Center for Public Integrity, an investigative journalists' group in Washington – on political donations and lobbying key politicians. They thought they had succeeded when the Federal Communications Commission adopted new regulations that permitted cross ownership in the media market.

However, unprecedented public protests in major metropolitan centres over extending media consolidation to the point where any single corporation could dominate the local television and local newspaper markets forced policy-makers in Congress to think again. Although some of the rules, increasing the right of a single company to hold up to 35 per cent in a single market were upheld, for instance, plans which permitted monopolies in local markets were finally withdrawn in January 2005. It was a remarkable victory for local campaigners and for pluralism.[11]

Conclusion

It is difficult not to conclude that, within Western democracies, we are seeing the institutionalization of lying and, with it, the destruction of public trust in democracy. The dishonesty of the political elite, the military and judicial institutions of state, and the corporate framework of globalization is being exposed daily by the information society with its capacity to denounce corruption as never before.

The tendency of the media to follow government-generated consensus, whether over war in Iraq as in the United States, and to a certain extent in Britain, or at moments of profound national crisis, as in Spain after the train bombings of March 2004, reveals a systematic bias within media in favour of the official line, that marginalizes dissent. It suggests to the public that wholesale deception and misinformation have become a way of life, both within politics and among those who promote the interests of global capital.

Some commentators might argue that these were historical aberrations that would not be repeated, but this point of view lacks any credibility. When a British government press officer sent a memo on September 11 to colleagues suggesting that events in New York and Washington made it a perfect day for putting out any 'bad news' announcements (presumably because they would be lost in the media frenzy over the terrorist attacks) she was following to the letter the rules of engagement of a communications strategy based upon evasion and deception. The fact that she was the subject of an unconvincing chorus of indignation within government circles did not flow from a rejection of the communications culture that led to her action, but simply because she was found out.[12]

The only solution to this is for a return to scrupulous journalism based upon experience and professionalism and carried out by reporters and editors who are treated fairly, decently paid and able to resist the pleadings of the liars and charlatans who currently influence much of the news agenda. Above all, journalists and media should take responsibility for their work. They must admit and correct their mistakes. They must avoid exaggeration, intolerance and cloying emotionalism. They must take advantage of the Internet and access to faster, easier means of communication it brings to ensure that the information they put out is more reliable and of better quality.

These are by no means unrealistic objectives, even if they are easy to write on the page. They can be achieved. It will just take more investment, braver and more conscientious journalism and editing, and political will to recognize that open government is, more often than not, first and foremost about telling the truth. The urge to manipulate and spin is strong, and will always be there, but playing it straight in politics should be the first principle in any democracy worthy of the name. At the same time, editors, broadcasters and writers would do well to remember that informed, honest and reliable journalism is part of the renewable energy of democracy. It discourages passivity and low morale within society and it challenges the pompous self-righteousness and malevolence of people in power. Without it, democracy would be diminished.

NOTES

1. For details of the extensive difficulties faced by journalists in the United States see the information provided by The Newspaper Guild-CWA (available at <http://www.newsguild.org>).
2. See *Sunday Times*, 1 May 2005, and *The Nation*, 6 June 2005.
3. See the report 'Journalism, Civil Liberties and the War on Terrorism', International Federation of Journalists and Statewatch, May 2005 (available at <http://www.ifj.org>).
4. Reported in detail by the *New York Times*, 16 March 2005.
5. Report from the Project for Excellence in Journalism, March 2004 (available at <www.journalism.org>).
6. Ibid.
7. Larry Tye, *Edward L Bernays: The Father of Spin and the Birth of Public Relations* (New York: Henry Holt, 1998).

8. There are a number of sources that develop this theme very effectively, including Ben Bagdikian, *The Media Monopoly* (Boston, MA: Beacon Press, 2002) and Robert McChesney, *Rich Media, Poor Democracy: Communication Politics in Dubious Times* (Urbana: University of Illinois Press, 1999).

9. See the European Federation of Journalists report of on foreign media ownership and the crisis of media concentration in countries of central and eastern Europe, *Foreign Ownership in Central and Eastern European Media: Ownership, Policy Issues and Strategies* (Brussels: European Federation of Journalists: Brussels, 2003) (available at <www.ifj.org/default.asp?index=1690&Language=EN>).

10. See International Federation of Journalists,' Crisis', 6 January 2004 (available at <www.ifj.org/default.asp?index=2176&Language=EN>).

11. This victory came after a coalition of public interest groups, including trade unions and media campaign groups, organized a national campaign against media consolidation. Further information is available from <www.TNG-CWA.com or http://www.moveon.com>.

12. This refers to Jo Moore, a departmental press officer, who survived an initial storm created by an infamous September 11 'bury bad news' e-mail which shocked the public but, to press officers, was merely the unfortunate exposure of one of the oldest tricks in the handbook. She eventually resigned on 15 February 2002 along with another official, Martin Sixsmith, amid allegations about another e-mail to 'bury bad news', this time during the funeral of Princess Margaret (*The Guardian*, 16 February 2002).

Manuscript accepted for publication August 2005.

Address for correspondence: Aidan White, General Secretary, International Federation of Journalists, IPC Residence Place, Rue de la Lois, B-1040 Brussels, Belgium. E-mail: <Aidan.White@ifj.org>.

Globalizations and Democracy

DONATELLA DELLA PORTA

Globalizations, Concept-Stretching and Democracy

Globalization has been seen as a factor in increasing democratization, but also as one of the main challenges to democracy. In the last few decades, the number of countries with elected governments has increased–from 39 in 1974, to 117 in 1995, to 193 at the start of the new millennium.[1] The growing influence of international governmental organizations (IGOs) has been seen as supportive of democratic transitions, if not of the consolidation of democracy.[2] But, at the same time, terms such as 'post-democracy' have emerged to define the reduced capacity for intervention by elected politicians, as well as citizens' growing dissatisfaction with their performance.[3] Scholars warn that the 'third wave' of democratization risks ending in a globalized economic war, with an increase in armed conflicts and violence with significant impact on the civic population.[4] As David Held aptly summarized,

> There is a striking paradox to note about the contemporary era: from Africa to Eastern Europe, Asia to Latin America, more and more nations and groups are championing the idea of democracy; but they are doing so at just that moment

when the very efficacy of democracy as a national form of political organization appears open to question. As substantial areas of human activity are progressively organized on a regional or global level, the fate of democracy, and of independent democratic nation-state in particular, is fraught with difficulties.[5]

Disagreements about the effects of globalization are due, in part, to the imprecise definition of the concept itself. Globalization is associated with the large transformations involved in 'the increasing scope and intensity of commercial, communicative and exchange relations beyond national borders'.[6] Quite a 'stretched' concept, it has been applied to define economic, social, political, and cultural phenomena with quite different characteristics and effects.[7] Indeed, social scientists have often declared their preference for more specific concepts, such as transnationalization[8] or complex internationalism,[9] which specify the arenas where global conflicts take place. In political debate, globalization has been praised or stigmatized, in turn, as free trade and cosmopolitan values, market dominance and global governance, hierarchical processes 'from above' and the development of civil society 'from below'. The distinction in the French language between the more threatening 'globalization' and the more benign 'mondialisation' testifies to these cognitive tensions.

Whatever the definition of globalization, challenges to democracy arise from the necessity to adapt conceptions and practices developed at the national level to a reality in which transnational actors and global events have an increasingly larger influence. The normative conceptions and empirical implementation of democracy developed in and about the nation-state are not easily applied at the supra-national level. Indeed, 'democracy as we know it within countries does not exist in a Globalized Space. More accurately, to the extent that Globalized Space is marked by conventional democratic procedures, these are ad-hoc, non systematic, irregular and fragile.'[10] Not only do IGOs usually have no electoral accountability (the European Parliament is an exception), but a transnational conception of citizenship and citizenship rights is difficult to develop. The fundamental principles of nation-state democracy – such as territoriality, majority principles, and use of coercive power – 'have to be reformulated, if they are to be applied globally'.[11] As Habermas observed, 'one alternative to the forced cheerfulness of a "self-dismantling" neoliberal politics would consist in finding the *appropriate forms* for the democratic process to take beyond the nation-state' (emphasis added).[12]

As will be argued in what follows, the various phenomena that have been included in the unfocused definition of globalization present challenges but also opportunities for democracy. In this vein, the account will discuss the potential effects of globalization in its economic, cultural, social and political components, focusing on both the risks and the opportunities that the heterogeneous processes mentioned under the label of 'globalization' represent for democracy and democratization. It concludes with some remarks on reforms and good practices in the area of global governance.

Economic Globalization and Democracy

Several scholars have defined globalization as mainly an economic phenomenon.[13] Although opinions diverge on the historical origins of economic globalization, as well as its periodization, the last few decades are seen as characterized by increasing exchanges in the traditional forms of trade in industrial goods and capital investments, as well as in the more innovative forms of financial flows and investment in services.[14] In fact, in the economic system, globalization has been defined as a growing internationalization of financial capital in particular, with an increase in international trade and investment.[15] In the last two decades, the liberalization of the capital market has been reflected in an increasingly integrated financial system – some speak of an 'economy without borders'.

The material aspects of globalization are indeed visible in intensified flows of money, goods and people.[16] Growing interdependence has meant production being transferred to countries with lower wages (in economic theory, the 'de-localisation of production processes'). Economic global interdependence has been a factor in transforming the division of international labour, not only by de-industrializing the North (where the economy is increasingly service oriented) and industrializing some areas of the South (in particular in Latin America and Central Asia and, now, in Eastern Europe), but also by pushing large numbers of people from the south and east of the world to its north and west. It has also meant the growth of multi-national corporations that in the late 1990s controlled 20 per cent of world production, 70 per cent of global trade, and 80 per cent of direct foreign investment.[17]

While the process of global interdependence has its roots in the distant past,[18] the technological revolution of the 1980s contributed to intensifying 'both the reality of global interdependence, and also the awareness of the world as one single unit'.[19] As Manuel Castells notes, 'a technological revolution, centred around information technologies, is reshaping, at accelerated pace, the material basis of society. Economies throughout the world have become globally inter-dependent, introducing a new form of relationship between economy, state, and society, in a system of variable geometry.'[20]

The effects on democracy of these intensified economic flows are debated in the social sciences. A main assumption presented by neo-liberal approaches, especially in economics, is that the moving of capital to poor countries and the opening-up of Western markets to their products spur economic development, and, with it, the pre-conditions for liberal democracy. Private investments are presented as an alternative to state intervention and its potential for corruption. The main hypothesis is that, as in Western democracies, free markets would produce economic development and, in turn, democracy, with a convergence of standards of income and welfare in the North and South.

Sociologists have been more sceptical about the potentially positive effects of globalization as global free market. Economic globalization as 'return to the market' has certainly reduced the potential for state intervention in economic inequalities, challenging the model (previously dominant in Europe, but also in Keynesian political economy) of the need for state involvement to insure economic development, but also social justice. In Habermas's words,[21] 'increased capital mobility makes the state's access to profits and monetary wealth more difficult, and heightened local competition reduces the state's capacity to collect taxes' – reducing the effectiveness of public administration, but also the legitimacy of state institutions. In the last two decades, the deregulation of financial markets, reduction of taxes, and privatization of public services have indeed been common trends in advanced democracies, although with some differences between European countries and the United States.[22] Globalization as devolution of power from the state to the market has reduced the relevance of territorial control.[23] And, 'as markets drive out politics, the nation-state increasingly loses its capacities to raise taxes and stimulate growth, and with them the ability to secure the essential foundations of its own legitimacy'.[24] Lacking a conception of positive international integration, 'national governments, terrified of the implicit threat of capital flight, have let themselves be dragged into a cost-cutting deregulatory frenzy, generating obscene profits and drastic income disparities, rising unemployment, and the social marginalization of a growing population of the poor'.[25]

Indeed, globalization does not seem to have resolved global inequalities: according to an often quoted report of the United Nations Development Programme (UNDP),[26] member countries of the Organization for Economic Cooperation and Development, with 19 per cent of the world's population, control three-quarters of the internal income, 71 per cent of trade, and 58 per cent of foreign investment. At the turn of the century, there were still 30 million unemployed or under-employed individuals.[27] Globalization has indeed been seen as increasing the polarization between the globalized rich and the localized poor.[28] According to various measures of quality of life, inequalities have also increased within both rich and poor countries with growing numbers of the working poor and severe exploitation of child labour.[29] The turbulence of financial markets and irrational exploitation of natural resources are also viewed as free-market globalization effects that weaken and destabilize democracy.

In the most pessimistic views, politics and governments lose ground or are conquered by privileged elites, and the welfare state – as the product of the mid-century compromise between capital and workers – falls victim to a new, anti-egalitarian conception.[30] With neo-liberalism, a drastic decline of altruism would have undermined the moral basis of capitalism and with it the capacity to define a general interest.[31] Therefore, economic globalization, in this neo-liberal version, challenges a conception of democracy as development of social rights that is deeply rooted in sociological theory.[32] In these interpretations, the effect of deregulation is not a competitive market, but the growth of multi-corporations and oligopolies. Globalization, in these terms, means 'the involution of the state – in other words, the regression to a penal state concerned with repression and progressively abandoning it social function of education, health, welfare'.[33] With economic 'globalization' the state renounces its social role, keeping only its repressive powers.[34]

Cultural Globalization and Democracy

Globalization has also been identified with significant *cultural* changes, the fundamental point being the growing interdependence in today's world. As Giddens suggested, globalization implies the creation and intensification of 'worldwide social relationships which link distinct localities in such a way that local happenings are shaped by events occurring miles away and vice versa'.[35] The shortening of space and time in communication processes affects the production and reproduction of cultures. Indeed, globalization has been defined as 'a process (or set of processes) which embodies a transformation in the spatial organization of social relations and transactions – assessed in terms of their extension, intensity, velocity and impact – generating transcontinental or interregional flows and networks of activity'.[36] The new channels of communication lead us to a 'global village' in which we are targeted in real time by messages sent from far away. The spread of satellite television and the Internet has made possible instantaneous communication that easily crosses national boundaries.

In terms of democratic values, globalization has been welcomed as a confirmation of democracy as the only legitimate regime. A human rights regime has developed in the international system, providing support for democratization processes.[37] However, we also see the increasing dominance of a liberal model of democracy based upon an elitist conception of electoral participation for the mass of the citizens and free lobbying for stronger interests, along with low levels of state intervention.[38] It is also debated whether the intensification of transnational communication will bring about homogeneity or fragmentation, increasing tolerance for the diverse or producing a clash of civilizations. According to some scholars, the emerging global culture is cosmopolitan and rich; for others, it is the most developed form of imperialism – according to Pierre Bourdieu, a 'politics of de-politization imposed by international organizations which base their policies on the individualistic, neo-Darwinist historical tradition, embedded in the United States of America'.[39]

One of the perceived dangers of cultural globalization is the predominance of a 'single way of thinking' emerging triumphant from the defeat of 'real socialism'. The international system had been tied to a bipolar structure in which each of the two blocs represented a different ideology. The fall of the Berlin Wall in 1989, which symbolically marked the demise of the Eastern bloc, made Western capitalism seem the only, dominant model. The lack of a concurrent world power has certainly curtailed, at least in the short term, the need for the United States and its allies to enact policies to mitigate the inequalities of the capitalist model, and has also limited the number of strategic options open to countries in the south of the world. In cultural terms, 'modernization' processes promoted by science and the leisure industry have paved the way for what Serge Latouche has called 'the westernization of the world'[40] – in other words, the spread of western values and beliefs on a global scale.[41]

Although the scenario of a single 'MacDonaldized' world culture[42] is an exaggeration, there has been an undeniable increase in cultural interaction with the export – albeit filtered through local culture – of Western cultural products and values.[43] Globalization is not Americanization, but glocalization: homologous values within infinite variations of specific activities in different contexts.[44] While territorial identities remain strong, the impact of values from other cultures and the rise in interactions between cultures tend to increase the number of identifications that interweave into and compete with those anchored in the territory. Globalization is not only 'out there', but also 'in here':[45] it transforms everyday life and leads to the defence of cultural traditions against the intrusion of foreign ideas and global issues.

In particular, globalization challenges the grounding of democracy in the 'community of fate' of the nation-states, increasing transversal and multiple territorial identifications. Intensified interactions favour the emergence of a new ethic with global responsibility for inequality. In David Held's words, 'our world is a world of overlapping communities of fate, where the fate of one country and that of another are more entwined than ever before'.[46] According to Beck,[47] in late modernity, the state survives by overcoming the merely national definition of the political community (beyond but not without the state). A cosmopolitan solidarity develops 'through feelings of indignation over the violation of rights, i.e. over repression and injuries to human rights committed by states'.[48] Since the global risks (environmental pollution, wars and so on) are indivisible, collective destinies emerge as tightly connected,[49] and 'global self' develops on the basis of the acknowledgement of shared risks,[50] together with the implementation of universalistic values (and therefore responsibility). The mobilization on global issues has been linked to the development of a reflexive global consciousness which designs global futures and global utopias.[51]

The development of supra-national identities, however, is a process that challenges the established conception of liberal, representative democracy: 'the notion that consent legitimizes governments, and that the ballot box is the appropriate mechanism whereby the citizen body as a whole periodically confers authority on government to enact the law and regulate economic and social life, becomes problematic as soon as the nature of a "relevant community" is contested'.[52]

The Social Dimension of Globalization and Global Movements

Globalization also has social effects that impact upon the construction and development of civil society.[53] It represents a challenge also for the emerging conflicts and available resources for social movements as important components of democracy. The initial debate on globalization was, in fact, dominated by concern regarding its potentially negative impact on the survival of social movements. Concentrated in the north of the world and focusing on the processes of institutionalization (or normalization) of movements, social scientists were slow to perceive the emergence of a global protest movement. Globalization was indeed blamed for hindering the formation of collective actors:

> social movements tend to be fragmented, localistic, single-issue oriented, and ephemeral, either retrenched in their inner worlds, or flaring up for just an instant around a media symbol ... The implicit assumption is the acceptance of full individualization of behaviour, and of society's powerlessness over its destiny.[54]

Market sovereignty appeared without an alternative, resulting in a belief 'that there is little we can change – singly, severally, or all together – in the way the affairs of the world are running or are being run'.[55] The diminution of trade unions' membership and power has been considered an unavoidable consequence of capital hyper-mobility.

Nevertheless, globalization – in its different meanings and understandings – has also produced increasing conflicts at both the local and the transnational levels. Economic globalization has raised specific problems that mobilize actors, both old and new. Signs of emerging political opposition to the consequences of a forced convergence of socio-economic models of development were noted as early as the first part of the 1990s.[56] In the North, the increase in unemployment and especially in job insecurity and unprotected working conditions brought about frequent mobilizations of both industrial and peasant workers. In the South, unions seemed capable of taking advantage of globalization, strengthening workers' rights in countries where capital was now invested – as Beverly Silver observes, 'the deep crisis into which core labour movement fell in the 1980s was not immediately replicated elsewhere. On the contrary, in the late 1980s and 1990s, major waves of labour militancy hit "showcases" of rapid industrialization in the Second and Third Worlds.'[57] As with Fordism, initially considered a source of unavoidable defeat for the working class, post-Fordism could also present both challenges and opportunities for the workers' organizations. Globalization tends to favour, if not a homogeneous and self-conscious global working class, at least, growing contacts between workers in different countries.[58] The unions have since the 1980s been the main protesters in some southern countries against the negative social effects of the substantial cuts in social spending imposed by the major international economic organizations. Urban movements and groups of unemployed have joined with them in Latin America as well as in Asian and African countries.[59]

Also in the South, native populations have often mobilized against the destruction of their physical habitat through the private exploitation of natural resources, and against development projects with major environmental impact.[60] The resurgence of forms of nationalism, ethnic movements, religious mobilizations and Islamic (and other forms of) fundamentalism are, in part, a reaction to the intrusion of different cultures and values. At the same time, in the North, solidarity-based movements are mobilizing proactively on 'distant' issues not directly connected with their own national context. While cultural globalization may endanger national identity, new technologies also provide a formidable array of tools for global mobilization, easing communication between worlds once distant, via new media that defy traditional censorship. Increased perception of issues as global also heightens people's willingness to mobilize at the transnational level. Local traditions become delocalized and re-adapted to new contexts through the presence of transnational networks of ethno-cultural communities.[61]

Fifteen or more years after the fall of the Berlin Wall, the various actors engaged in the conflicts mentioned above have become increasingly networked, spawning common mobilizations. If globalization is the challenge, it seems also to be the resource of protesters who may not oppose it outright, but aim towards changing its content. Indeed, globalization has consistently transformed the conditions for collective action, and, along with its limits, brought occasions and resources for protest. In the economic, political, and cultural systems, the intensification of interaction has generated new conflicts and, also, opportunities for expressing these conflicts at multiple territorial levels.

Although protest activity is still mainly based at the local and national level, in the last decade transnational campaigns have often targeted international organizations (see below). Environmentalists have protested against the World Trade Organization's (WTO) Appellate Body decision that found that the United States in breach of free-trade principles because it had prohibited the importation of shrimps caught in nets that endangered sea turtles. Protesters have also targeted other decisions such as Japan's block on importing products treated with pesticides; Europe's laws against importing meat from animals fed with hormones; and Canada's ban on petrol containing a methanol additive. Consumer-protection organizations mobilized against supranational agreements such as North American Free Trade Agreement (NAFTA), the General Agreement on Tariffs and Trade (GATT) and the WTO for allegedly lowering consumer protection standards in the name of free trade, and so did trade unions, fearing the worsening of workers' rights. At United Nations (UN) conferences on women's rights, feminist groups from the North of the world met their counterparts from the South. Development non-governmental organizations (NGOs) pressed for a rise in aid to Third World countries and even called for reparations for the historical social and environmental debts the North of the world imposed on the South. Supported by religious and other groups, the Jubilee 2000 campaign called for the cancellation of poor countries' foreign debt. Pacifist and human rights organizations added their voices, calling for freedom of movement for migrants and denouncing anti-personnel mines. Over the last decades, transnational protest campaigns have multiplied, in particular on issues such as environmental protection, gender discrimination and human rights.[62]

During these campaigns, common themes developed around global justice and global democracy.[63] One common theme of transnational mobilizations is the criticism of globalization as free market. In particular, national and international elites are accused of strengthening market freedom at the expense of social rights which, at least in the North, had become part and parcel of the very definition of citizenship. Criticism of neo-liberal forms of globalization and demands for 'another globalization' entered the public sphere with the protests against the WTO summit in 1999 – as the American weekly *Newsweek* wrote, 'one of the most important lessons of Seattle is that there are now two visions of globalization on offer, one led by commerce, one by social activism'.[64] After Seattle, it was said that, if nothing else, protests had had the immediate impact of bringing international summits out from the shadowy world of reserved agreements between diplomats and technocrats and into the media spotlight: 'Never before had the beginning of multilateral trade negotiations been at the centre of the international public sphere'.[65] Since then, protest on the issue of globalization has continued in dozens of countries and gained increased visibility through systematic transnational mobilization in counter summits, challenging the official summits of major IGOs, among them, not only, the International Monetary Fund (IMF) and the World Bank, but also the European Union (EU).[66]

Global themes have been fostered by transnational organizations. The various dimensions of globalization have been reflected in the emergence of a 'global civic society' – a much-used and much-debated term to indicate a civil society that 'increasingly represents itself globally, across nation-state boundaries, through the formation of global institutions'.[67] The organization of a global civil society is inevitably linked to globalization processes in economics, culture and politics.[68] The shift of decision-making to the supra-national level has, in turn, encouraged the birth of international non-governmental organizations (INGOs), whose numbers, members and availability of material resources have grown.[69] The concept of 'transnational social movement organizations' (TSMOs) was coined to define INGOs active within networks of social movements.[70] While social movements developed with the growth of national politics, the formation of TSMOs has been seen as a response to the growing institutionalization of international politics.[71] Some NGOs have been credited with having not only increased in size, but also with having strengthened their influence in various stages of international policy-making.[72] Their strengths include their increasing credibility in public opinion and consequent availability of private funding,[73] as well as their roots at the local level. Their specific knowledge, combined with useful contacts in the media, make many NGOs seem particularly reliable sources. With a professional staff on hand, they are also able to maintain a fair level of activity even when protest mobilization is low. Independence from governments, combined with a reputation built upon solid work at the local level, enable some NGOs to perform an important role in mediating inter-ethnic conflict.[74]

Finally, NGOs enhance pluralism within international institutions by representing groups who would otherwise be excluded[75] and by turning the spotlight on transnational processes, increasing the transparency of the governance process.[76] Studies on INGOs found that many had become increasingly institutionalized, in terms of both their professionalism and their forms of action (more lobbying than marching).[77] However, the global movement that emerged in Seattle managed to involve many of these organizations, via informal, flexible networks, in highly visible mass mobilizations.

Political Globalization: A Global Governance?

Globalization cannot be identified with the ideology and practice of a global free market. The hypothesis of a technologically driven convergence and the forced passivity of the nation-state has been criticized and rejected by many sociological studies.[78] As many scholars have observed, globalization does have a strong political component: it is not the perverse effect of natural phenomena, but is – at least in part – the result of specific economic policies implemented by major superpowers and international institutions.[79] The widely accepted maxim of the 1990s – that capital mobility favoured by technology erodes the political capability to govern markets – has been questioned, and decreased state intervention in market policies, lower taxation and the consequent dismantling of the welfare state have been defined as conscious political choices. Susan Strange has spoken of a 'corporation empire', namely an imperial bureaucracy headed by the US Treasury and multinational corporations which, together, control the leadership of international financial organizations:

> Authority in this non-territorial empire is exercised directly on people – not on land. It is exercised on bankers and corporate executives, on savers and investors, on journalists and teachers. It is also of course exercised on the heads of

allied and associated governments, as successive summit conferences have clearly shown.[80]

According to this interpretation, the liberalization of trade and particularly of financial markets is driven by political actors within single states (and in particular within the most powerful state, the United States) – as well as by international actors, first and foremost, the international financial institutions: the World Bank, the International Monetary Fund and the WTO. Market deregulation and the privatization of public services are seen not as a 'natural' effect of technological development, but as a strategy adopted and defended by international financial institutions and by the governments of the most powerful nations (in particular through the Group of Seven (G7) and the Group of Eight (G8)) to the advantage of multinational corporations. As Colin Crouch has observed, the establishment of the (ideology of a) free market has clearly been facilitated by the WTO, whose 'post-democratic' aim is the liberalization of international exchanges of goods and services.[81]

Globalization, therefore, is not only a matter of new technologies and modes of production, but also of the *political* tools set in place to regulate and reproduce this social structure through, among others, the proliferation of international governmental organizations (IGOs). Globalization has indeed been defined as the growing size and intensity of international relations.[82] Some IGOs have simultaneously served as tools for economic globalization, through policies that liberalize trade and the movement of capital, and attempts to govern processes that can no longer be handled at the national level.

From this perspective, the international system based on sovereign nation-states seems to have evolved into a political system composed of overlapping multi-level authorities with little functional differentiation and scant democratic legitimacy. While 'the discovering of inter-dependence reduces sovereignty',[83] globalization brings about a 'transnationalization' of political relationships. If the national political context still cushions the impact of international shifts on national politics, growing economic interdependence goes hand in hand with 'a significant internationalization of public authority associated with a corresponding globalization of political activity'.[84] Globalization has indeed increased the awareness of 'global commons' that cannot be defended only at the national level and challenges a hierarchical model of territorial control.[85]

Recent research into international relations has indeed highlighted a pluralization of relevant actors.[86] Since the Second World War, and increasingly in recent years, there has been a growth in the number of IGOs with a worldwide scope of action (such as the United Nations) or a regional one (such as the European Union, but also Mercosur in Latin America and the NAFTA), with military objectives (such as the North Atlantic Treaty Organization (NATO) or the now-defunct Warsaw Pact), or with the declared aim of fostering economic development (such as the IMF, the World Bank or the WTO). The number of international organizations rose from 37 to 309 between 1909 and 1988,[87] and the number of IGO-sponsored conferences grew from a couple per year in the nineteenth century to close to 4,000 annually at the end of the twentieth century.[88] As seen in Figure 1, while the growth of

FIGURE 1
NUMBER OF NGOS AND IGOS (A = FORMAL; B = INFORMAL), 1909–97

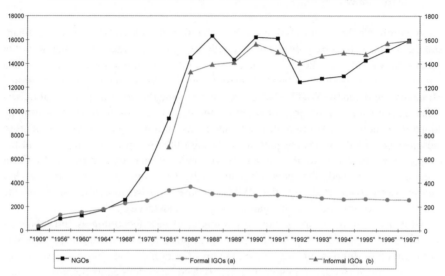

Note: The values for the number of NGOs by year refer to the scale from 0 to 18,000 (left axis); the values for the number of IGOs refer to the scale from 0 to 1,800 (right axis).
Source: Deutscher Bundestag 2002, p.427.

conventional intergovernmental organizations has levelled out over the last decade, there has been an increase in the number of international groups of a more informal character, from 702 in 1981 to 1,592 in 1997.[89]

If global governance implies the development of global norms, the area covered by international *public* law is still limited (notwithstanding the growing presence of IGOs, whose competence are, however, often limited to 'soft' power of influence); but particularly in the economic sphere, a *private* law based on contracts is instead proliferating. Law, in the European tradition, is seen as command of political power; the international juridical order is instead based on the ideology of contract law.[90] A new *lex mercatoria* emerges with the increasing role of law firms specializing in corporate law, but also with societies of bond rating and debt security, arbitrations and similar methods of dispute resolution.[91] Growing numbers of law-makers necessitates the opacity of rules, with the development of a 'law *à la carte*' designed on the basis of the needs of global firms.[92] In this transnational private legal regime, norms are reactive, ad hoc, often unwritten, and always negotiated.[93] Globalization implies, therefore, increasing fragmentation and opacity of sovereignty power, along with alternative legalities, either overlapping, complementary or antagonistic.[94]

Furthermore, while the majority of inter-governmental organizations function mainly as meeting places and discussion fora where decisions are taken unanimously and then ratified by national organs, there are a growing number of 'supra-national' organizations in which decisions, binding for all member states, are made on a majority basis – the European Union being the most outstanding example.[95] More generally, parallel to the acquisition of power by numerous IGOs, criticism has, in particular, been centred on their manifest 'deficit of democracy'.

First, the debate on the democratic deficit stresses the lack of democratic accountability and even transparency of many IGOs with powers extending beyond the negotiation of treaties. Unlike its predecessor, the GATT, the WTO expanded its mandate to focus on new areas of economic activity (agriculture, services, investment, and protection of intellectual property rights) and strengthened the legal structure of the organization.[96] Dispute settlement procedures moved from a system of negotiation to one of adjudication, with decisions approved unless rejected by consensus.[97] The World Bank and IMF – accused, during the Cold War, of defending Western interests, through distributing help according to political loyalty[98] – have increased their power through the negotiation of structural adjustment programmes with debtor governments. With its growing involvement in liberalization policies (in Eastern Europe in particular), the IMF has relied upon long-term loans given under conditional approval of its plans for liberalization, deregulation, privatization and fiscal reform.[99] As for the World Bank, whose stated objectives include poverty reduction, the move from financing development projects to supporting structural adjustment has, since the late 1970s, brought about an attempt at re-organizing domestic economies, with 'considerable influence on the daily lives of the world's population'.[100] At the end of the 1990s, half of the world's population and two-thirds of its countries were subject to the influence of the International Monetary Fund or the World Bank.[101]

In addition to the lack of elected officials, critics have noted the unequal balance of power in some IGOs. In the United Nations, the role of the superpowers is evident in the composition of Security Council membership and their veto power in the Council. As for the World Bank, each of the five largest shareholders (the United States, Japan, Germany, France and the United Kingdom) appoints an executive director. In both the World Bank and the IMF, moreover, the influence of the most powerful countries is recognized according to the principle of 'one dollar-one vote'.[102] The G7 and G8, although lacking formal structures and competence, have contributed to coordinating and strengthening the power of a few nation states.

The many economic crises of the last decade have also shaken the legitimacy of these institutions, whose aims are to promote economic and social development.[103] Among other issues, the continued reliance of as many as 50 countries on financial support from the IMF and World Bank for the last 20 years does not reflect success.[104]

Democratizing Globalization? Some Conclusions

In summary, the term 'globalization' has been used to indicate various and heterogeneous types of phenomena, all of them producing challenges for the traditional, nation-state-based models of democracy. Economic globalization as free trade, with a devolution of power from the state to the market, challenges the welfare state model of tempered capitalism that has been dominant, especially in European democracies, and, with it, the social dimension of democracy as a political regime which aims to reduce economic inequalities. Cultural globalization, with intensified communication over borders, and the related risk of homogenization, but also with the promise of increasing cosmopolitanism, challenges the idea of democracy as based upon a pre-political community of destiny. The social dimension of globalization brings about a fragmentation of social groups and identities, but also a growing transnationalization of civil society organizations and protest campaigns. In the political system, the economic, cultural and political dimensions of globalization reverberate in the complexity of the structure of international organizations and international regimes.

The various instances of globalization all challenge the power and competence of the nation-state. As Habermas remarked, 'In contrast to the territorial form of the nation state, "globalization" conjures up images of overflowing rivers, washing away all the frontier checkpoints and controls and ultimately the bulwark of the nation state.'[105] Indeed, although with different accents and nuances, social scientists have reflected on the need and possibilities for intertwining the nation-state-based institutions of democracy with some additional institutions at the transnational level. International organizations and norms, multinational corporations, and transnational movements all limit the sovereignty of the nation-state, introducing a new level of politics.

Normative theories of democracy suggest the need to create new political institutions that take into account the reduced power of nation-states and the changing definition of the 'relevant political communities'. In the communitarian approach, democracy is seen as difficult to apply in culturally heterogeneous communities.[106] For others, the weakening of the reference to a 'pre-political community of shared destiny' makes political participation all the more important. In Habermas's words,

> the strength of the democratic constitutional states lies precisely in its ability to close the holes of social integration through the political participation of its citizens ... Basic human rights, and rights to political participation, constitute a self-referential model of citizenship, insofar as they enable democratically united citizens to shape their own status legislatively.[107]

This makes the democratization of the post-national constellation relevant and urgent.

However, scholars also agree that the supra-national level of democracy must take different forms from national democracy. Again according to Habermas, the post-national constellation cannot be organized in a 'world state': 'Rather than a state, it has to find a less demanding basis of legitimacy in the organizational form of an international negotiating system ... In general, procedures and accords require a sort of compromise between independent actors who have the ability to impose sanctions to compel consideration of their respective interests.'[108] In fact, this presents the 'dynamic picture of interferences and interactions between political processes that persist at national, international, and global levels'. If a federalist model has been suggested at the transnational level,[109] its format has nevertheless to be adapted to the complexity of international institutions.

A normative proposal has developed around the concept of 'cosmopolitan democracy', defined as a political project that 'aims to engender greater public accountability in the leading processes and structural alteration of the contemporary world'.[110] Cosmopolitan democracy implies:

the development of administrative capacity and independent political resources
at regional and global levels as a necessary complement to those in local and
national politics ... A cosmopolitan democracy would not call for a diminution
per se of state power and capacity across the globe. Rather it would seek to
entrench and develop democratic institutions at regional and global levels as
a necessary complement to those at the level of the nation-state.[111]

As a project oriented to the development of democracy within and among states, but
also aimed at the global level, cosmopolitan democracy implies the existence of
global institutions where citizens are seen as individual 'inhabitants of the world'
rather than as part of a nation-state. The basic assumption is that 'if some global questions are to be handled according to democratic criteria, there must be political representation for citizens in global affairs, independently and autonomously of their
political representation in domestic affairs'.[112] Global institutions should therefore
enable 'the voice of individuals to be heard in global affairs, irrespective of their resonance at home'.[113]

In this proposal, cosmopolitan democracy requires democratic states, but also
democratic supra-national institutions. Suggestions for short-term reforms of existing
IGOs include the re-organization of leading UN institutions, such as the Security
Council, in order to increase the power of developing countries; the creation of a
second UN chamber as a space for the participation of representatives of the civil
society; the use of transnational referenda; direct individual access to the jurisdiction
of an International Human Rights Court; and the establishment of an effective and
accountable international military force. Other proposals have addressed the presence
in the UN General Assembly of delegates of both national governments and opposition groups, as well as directly elected delegates; limitation or abolition of veto
power; opening to regional organizations; consultative vote to representatives of
NGOs and elective parliamentary assembly with consultative power.[114] The subordination of international financial institutions to the UN General Assembly has been
suggested, as well as the reform of international governmental organizations on the
basis of the principle of one-state-one-vote. In the long term, proposed reforms
include the creation of a global parliament, the strengthening of international legal
systems embracing criminal and civil laws, and a charter of global rights and
obligations.[115]

These proposals may appear too moderate to some, too utopian to others; they
signal, however, the perceived need to respond to the challenges of globalization
with a democratization of international institutions. More generally, they indicate
that the economic, cultural, and social processes of globalization produce political
conflicts, the results of which will affect the legitimacy and efficacy of democratic
institutions.

NOTES

1. Freedom House, *Freedom in the World* (New York: Freedom House, 2002); Klaus Mueller, *Globalisierung* (Frankfurt/Main: Campus Verlag, 2002), p.27.
2. Mueller (note 1), p.41.

3. Colin Crouch, *Post Democracy* (Oxford: Blackwell, 2004); also Pippa Norris, *Democratic Phoenix: Reinventing Political Activism* (New York: Cambridge University Press, 2002).
4. Charles Tilly, *Social Movements 1768–2004* (Boulder, CO: Paradigm, 2004).
5. David Held, 'Democracy and Globalization', in Daniele Archibugi, David Held and Martin Kohler (eds), *Re-imagining Political Community: Studies in Cosmopolitan Democracy* (Cambridge: Polity Press, 1998), p.11.
6. Jürgen Habermas, *The Postnational Constellation* (Cambridge: Polity Press, 2001), p.66.
7. Donatella Della Porta and Lorenzo Mosca, 'Movimenti sociali e globalizzazione: una introduzione', in idem (eds), *Movimenti sociali e globalizzazione* (Rome: Manifestolibri, 2003).
8. Alessandro Pizzorno, 'L'ordine giuridico e statale nella globalizzazione', in Della Porta and Mosca (note 7).
9. Donatella Della Porta and Sidney Tarrow (eds), *Transnational Protest and Global Activism* (New York: Rowman & Littlefield, 2005).
10. James Rosenau, 'Governance and Democracy in a Globalizing World', in Archibugi, Held and Kohler (note 5), p.39.
11. Daniele Archibugi, 'Cosmopolitical Democracy', in Daniele Archibugi (ed.), *Debating Cosmopolitics* (London: Verso, 2003), p.7.
12. Habermas (note 6), p.61.
13. Luciano Gallino, *Globalizzazione e diseguaglianze* (Roma-Bari: Laterza, 2000).
14. Mario Pianta, *Globalizzazione dal basso* (Rome: Manifestolibri, 2001), p.11.
15. David Held and Andrew McGrew, *Globalismo e antiglobalismo* (Bologna: Il Mulino, 2000).
16. Andrew McGrew, 'Il grande dibattito sulla globalizzzione', in Elisabeth Batini and Rodolfo Ragionieri (eds), *Culture e conflitti nella globalizzazione* (Firenze: Leo S. Olshki, 2002); Gerald Lafay, *Comprendre la mondialisation* (Paris: Economica, 1996).
17. Held (note 5), p.17.
18. Immanuel Wallestein, *The Modern World System* (New York: Academic Press, 1974).
19. Roland Robertson, *Globalization, Social Theory and Global Culture* (London: Sage Publications, 2000), p.8.
20. Manuel Castells, *The Rise of the Network Society* (Oxford: Blackwell, 1996), p.1. Indeed, globalization waves tend to coincide with discoveries in communication technologies. Robert Gilpin, 'Attori nell'economia globale', in Batini and Ragionieri (note 16), pp.31–62).
21. Habermas (note 6), p.699.
22. Crouch (note 3); also Mueller (note 1).
23. Susan Strange, *States and Markets* (London: Pinter, 1994).
24. Habermas (note 6), p.79.
25. Ibid.
26. United Nations Development Programme, *Human Development Report 1999: Globalization with a Human Face* (New York: Oxford University Press, 1999), pp.18–19.
27. International Labour Office (ILO), *World Labour Report 1997–98* (Geneva: ILO, 1997); ILO, *World Employment Report* (Geneva: ILO, 1999).
28. Zygmunt Bauman, *Globalization: The Human Consequence* (Cambridge: Polity Press, 2000).
29. Gallino (note 13), p.70ff; Pianta (note 14).
30. Crouch (note 3), p.9.
31. Ronald Dore, 'A chi giova la convergenza ?', in Susan Berger and Ronald Dore (eds), *Differenze nazionali e capitalismo globale* (Bologna: Il Mulino, 1998), p.244.
32. T.H. Marshall, 'Citizenship and Social Class', in T.H. Marshall and Tom Bottomore, *Citizenship and Social Class* (London: Pluto Press, 1992); Tilly (note 4).
33. Pierre Bourdieu, *Acts of Resistance: Against the New Myths of Our Time* (Cambridge: Polity Press 1998), p.34.
34. Ibid. p.75.
35. Anthony Giddens, *The Consequences of Modernity* (Cambridge: Polity Press, 1990), p.64.
36. Held and McGrew (note 15), p.16.
37. Margaret Keck and Katryn Sikkink, *Activists Beyond Borders* (Ithaca, NY: Cornell University Press, 1998).
38. Crouch (note 3), p.5.
39. Pierre Bourdieu, *Coutre-feux 2: Pour movement social européen* (Paris: Libre, 2001), p.25.
40. Serge Latouche, *L'occidentalizzazione del mondo: saggio sul significato: la portata e I limiti dell'uniformazione planetaria* (Turin: Bollati Boringhieri, 1992).

41. Davis Strange and John W. Meyer, 'Institutional Conditions for Diffusion', *Theory and Society*, Vol.22, No.4 (1993), p.500ff.
42. G. Ritzer, *The McDonaldization of Society* (London: Sage, 2000).
43. Robertson (note 19).
44. John Boli and George M. Thomas, *Constructing the World Culture: International Nongovernmental Organizations since 1875* (Stanford, CA: Stanford University Press, 1999), p.18.
45. Giddens (note 35), p.22.
46. Held (note 5), p.25.
47. Ulrich Beck, *What is Globalization?* (Cambridge: Polity Press, 2000).
48. Habermas (note 6), p.108.
49. Anna Lorentoni, 'Per un'analisi critica della globalizzzione', in Barbara Henry (ed.), *Modi globali. Idetitá, sovranitá, confini* (Pisa: Edizioni ETS, 2000), p.93.
50. Elena Pulcini, 'L'io globale: crisi del legame sociale e nuove forme di solidarietá', in Dimitri D'Andrea and Elena Pulcini (eds), *Filosofie della globalizzazione* (Pisa: Edizioni ETS, 2001).
51. John A. Guidry, Michael D. Kennedy and Mayer N. Zald (eds), *Globalization and Social Movements: Culture, Power, and the Transnational Public Sphere* (Ann Arbor: University of Michigan Press, 2000).
52. Held (note 5), p.22.
53. Laura Leonardi, *La dimensione sociale della globalizzazione* (Rome: Carocci, 2001).
54. Castells (note 20), pp.3–4.
55. Bauman (note 28), p.1.
56. Susan Berger, 'Introduzione', in Berger and Dore (note 31), p.37.
57. Beverly Silver, *Forces of Labor: Workers' Movements and Globalization since 1870* (Cambridge: Cambridge University Press, 2003), p.164.
58. Ibid. p.10.
59. John Walton and David Seddon, *Free Markets and Food Riots: The Politics of Global Adjustment* (Oxford: Blackwell, 1994); Mounia Bennani-Chaibri and Olivier Fillieule, *Résistances et protestations dans les societies musulmanes* (Paris: Presses de Sciences, 2003).
60. Florence Passy, 'Supranational Political Opportunities as a Channel of Globalization of Political Conflicts: The Case of Rights of Indigenous People', in Donatella dell Porta, Hanspeter Kriesi and Dieter Rucht, *Social Movements in a Globalizing World* (London: Macmillan Press, 1999).
61. John B. Thompson, *The Media and Modernity* (Cambridge: Cambridge University Press, 1995).
62. Donatella della Porta and Hanspeter Kriesi, 'Social Movements in a Globalizing World', in Donatella della Porta, Hanspeter Kriesi and Dieter Rucht (eds), *Social Movements in a Globalizing World* (London: Macmillan, 1929).
63. Massimiliano Andretta, Donatella della Porta, Lorenzo Mosca and Herbert Reiter, *Global, NoGlobal – Newglobal: Idetität und Strategien der Antiglobalisierungsbewegung* (Frankfurt and New York: Campus Verlag, 2002, 2003); Donatella della Porta, *I new global* (Bologna: Il Mulino, 2003).
64. *Newsweek*, 13 December 1999, p.36
65. Andreas Pfeil, 'Lehren aus Seattle', *Blätter für deutsche und internationale Politik*, Vol.45, No.1 (2000), pp.15–28.
66. See Mario Pianta and Federico Silva, *Globalizers from Below: A Server on Global Civil Society Organisations* (Rome: GLOBI Research Report, 2003).
67. Martin Shaw, 'Civil Society and Global Politics: Beyond a Social Movement Approach', *Millennium*, Vol.23,No.3 (1994), pp.647–67.
68. Helmut Anheier, Mary Glasius and Mary Kaldor, *Global Civil Society* (Oxford: Oxford University Press, 2001).
69. From 1909 to 1988, the number of INGOs grew from 176 to 14,518, and to 15,965 in 1997 (Deutscher Bundestag, *Schlussbericht der Enquete-Kommission Globalisierung der Weltwirtschaft – Herausforderungen und Antworten.* (Berlin: Deutscher Bundestag, 2002), p.427).
70. Jackie Smith, Ron Pagnucco and Winnie Romeril, 'Transnational Social Movement Organisations in the Global Political Arena', *Voluntas*, Vol.5, No.2 (1994), pp.121–54; Charles Chatfield, Ron Pagnucco and Jackie Smith (eds), *Solidarity Beyond the State: The Dynamics of Transnational Social Movements* (Syracuse, NY: Syracuse University Press, 1997).
71. Jackie Smith, 'Transnational Political Processes and the Human Rights Movement', *Research in Social Movements, Conflict and Change*, Vol.18 (1995), pp.187–221.
72. Kathryn Sikkink and Jackie Smith, 'Infrastructures for Change: Transnational Organizations 1953– 1993', in S. Khagram, J.V.K. Riker and K. Sikkink (eds), *Reconstructing World Politics: Transnational Social Movements, Networks and Norms* (Minneapolis, MN: University of Minnesota Press,

2002); John Boli, 'Conclusion: World Authority Structures and Legitimations', in John Boli and George Thomas (eds), *Constructing World Culture: International Nongovernmental Organizations since 1875* (Stanford, CA: Stanford University Press, 1999).

73. As an example, Amnesty International – which has often supported anti-globalization protests – could in 2000 count on the backing, including funding, of 1,300,000 members organized in 53,000 sections in 56 nations. See Volker Schneider, 'The Global Social Capital of Human Rights Movements: A Case Study of Amnesty International', in Kaster Ronit and Volker Schneider (eds), *Private Organizations in Global Politics* (London: Routledge, 2000), pp.146–64.

74. Mats Friberg and Bjorn Hettne, 'Local Mobilization and World System Politics', *International Social Science Journal*, Vol.40, No.3 (1998), pp.341–60.

75. Elizabeth Riddel-Dixon, 'Social Movements and the United Nations', *International Social Science Journal*, Vol.47, No.2 (1995), pp.289–303.

76. Hilmar Schmidt and Ingo Take, 'Demokratischer und besser ? Der Beitrag von Nichtregierungsorganisationen zur Demokratisierung internationaler Politik und zur Lösung globaler Probleme', *Aus Politik und Zeitgeschichte*, Vol.43 (1997), pp.12–20.

77. Donatella della Porta and Mario Diani, *Movimenti senza protesta?* (Bologna: Il Mulino, 2004).

78. Berger (note 56), p.20; Robert Wade, 'La globalizzazione e i suoi limiti', in Berger and Dore (note 31); Geoffrey Garret, *Partisan Politics in the Global Economy* (New York: Cambridge University Press, 1998).

79. Gallino (note 13), pp.21–8

80. Susan Strange, 'Toward a Theory of Transnational Empire', in E.O.Czempiel and J.N. Rosenau (eds), *Global Change and Theoretical Challenges* (Lexington, MD: Lexington Books, 1989), p.170.

81. Crouch (note 3), p.95.

82. Iain Clark, *Globalization and Fragmentation: International Relations in the Twentieth Century* (Oxford: Oxford University Press, 1997).

83. Betrand Badie, *Une monde sans souveraineté* (Paris: Fayard, 1999), p.297.

84. Held and McGrew (note 15), p.27.

85. Badie (note 83), p.301.

86. M. Nicholson, *Introduzione allo studio delle relazioni internazionali* (Bologna: Il Mulino, 1998), p.131ff.

87. Thomas Princen and Matthias Finger, 'Introduction', in Thomas Princen and Martin Finger (eds), *Environmental NGOs in World Politics: Linking the Local and the Global* (London: Routledge, 1994), p.1.

88. Held (note 5), p.20.

89. Deutscher Bundestag (note 69), p.427.

90. Maria Rosaria Ferrarese, *Le istituzioni della globalizzazione: Diritto e dirritti nella societá transnazionale* (Bologna: Il Mulino, 2000); see also Umberto Allegretti, *Stato e diritti nella mondializzazione* (Troina: Oasi, 2002).

91. Saskia Sassen, 'Fuori controllo? Lo Stato e la nuova geografia del potere', in Dimitri D'Andrea and Elena Pulcini (eds), *Filosofie della globalizzazione* (Pisa: Edizioni ETS, 2001), pp.111–40.

92. Yves Dezalay and Bryant G. Garth, *Dealing with Virtue: International Commercial Arbitration and the Construction of a Transnational Legal Order* (Chicago. IL: University of Chicago Press, 1998).

93. Ferrarese (note 90), p.138.

94. Ibid. p.62.

95. Ibid.

96. Robert O'Brien, Anne Marie Goetz, Jan A. Scholte and Marc Williams, *Contesting Global Governance* (New York: Cambridge University Press, 2000), p.11.

97. Ibid. p.71.

98. S.C. Thacker, 'The High Politics of IMF Lending', *World Politics*, Vol.51, No.1 (1998), pp.39–75.

99. O'Brien *et al.* (note 96), p.162. By the end of the 1990s, 84 states had borrowed for at least ten years from the IMF, whose staff increased from 750 in 1960 to 2,660 in 1997.

100. O'Brien *et al.* (note 96), p.11.

101. Ute Pieperm and Lance Taylor, 'The Revival of the Liberal Creed: the IBM, the World Bank and Inequalities in a Globalized Economy', in Dean Baker, Gerry Epstein and Robert Podin (eds), *Globalization and Progressive Economic Policy* (Cambridge: Cambridge University Press, 1998).

102. Traditionally, the presidency of the bank went to the United States, that of the IMF to Europe; but international relations scholar Gilpin recognizes the influence of the United States on both institutions, see Gilpin (note 20), p.48.

103. Mueller (note 1), p.109.

104. Ibid. p.113.
105. Habermas (note 6), p.76.
106. Archibugi, 'Cosmopolitical Democracy' (note 11), p.206.
107. Habermas (note 6), pp.76–7.
108. Ibid. pp.109–10.
109. Raffaele Marchetti, 'Consequentialist Cosmopolitanism and Global Political Agency', in D. O'Byrne (ed.), *Global Ethics and Civil Society* (Aldershot: Ashgate, 2004).
110. Archibugi *et al.* (note 5), p.4.
111. Held (note 5), p.24.
112. Archibugi, 'Principles of Cosmopolitan Democracy', in Archibugi *et al.* (note 5), pp.211–12.
113. Archibugi, 'Cosmopolitical Democracy' (note 11), p.8.
114. Archibugi, 'Principles of Cosmopolitan Democracy' (note 112), p.221.
115. Held (note 5), p.25.

Manuscript accepted for publication August 2005.

Address for correspondence: Donatella Della Porta, Department of Political Sciences, European University Institute, Badia Fiesolana, Via dei Roccettini 9, 50016 San Domenico di Fiesole, Firenze, Italy. E-mail: <Donatella.DellaPorta@iue.it>.

Democracy and Development:
Is There Institutional Incompatibility?

ADRIAN LEFTWICH

Context

Since the end of the Cold War, official Western overseas development and aid concerns have become increasingly focused on poverty, inequality and political instability. For instance, high up on the United Nations' list of Millennium Development Goals (MDGs) is the commitment to halve poverty in the developing world by 2015.[1] Growth, and pro-poor growth in particular, has become a stated policy objective of major bilateral and multilateral Western development agencies. And as the more extravagant claims of the 1980s and early 1990s for the all-round developmental advantages of neo-liberal 'free' markets have been shown to be somewhat excessive, especially in the African context,[2] research interest has turned to the role of institutions in promoting or hindering growth and in the distribution of its benefits.[3]

Associated with this has been the recognition that political instability *within* countries (the dominant form of conflict today[4]) is most commonly associated with poverty, inequality and the unequal access to resources, influence and power. While fragile and failed states account for only 14 per cent of the global population, they contain a third of the world's poor and account for over 40 per cent of all child deaths.[5] Moreover, some of the more 'unstable', 'rogue', 'collapsed', 'fragile' or 'failed' states are not only profoundly poor, but are also characterized by weak governance, the absence of consensus about the rules of the political game, by rent-generating natural resources (oil, diamonds) and sharp political cleavages between regional, ethnic, religious or class groups (and often a lethal mixture of them all) – all of which serve to undermine or obstruct the emergence of stable and consolidated democratic polities.[6] And, thus, if growth and development can help to reduce instability (and hence threats to regional and global security) by providing people with a greater stake in their economies and societies, then the case for growth and development is not only moral and economic, but is also profoundly political, as three recent and very significant reports from both sides of the Atlantic suggest.[7] Indeed, one of the key policy implications of these reports, as spelled out by the UK's Department for International Development (DFID), in its report on *The Causes of Conflict in Africa*, has been for there to be 'greater coherence between foreign policy, security and development objectives'.[8]

Democratization

But democratization, too, has been a dominant concern of Western governments and international agencies since the early 1990s, after the end of the Cold War, and its promotion has become part of the wider package of conditions often attached to both bilateral and multilateral loans.[9] As with the arguments for economic growth and development, both moral and economic arguments are pressed into service for the promotion of democracy. Democratic polities on the liberal model are inextricably linked with capitalist or mixed economies, and thus the pursuit of democratization needs also to be seen as part and parcel of the wider economic dynamic which has driven globalization. But there are also urgent political and security arguments for the promotion of democratic polities which have come to the fore in the past decade. For not only is it clear that 'full democracies are least likely to undergo significant political upheaval and instability',[10] and that they are generally more effective in promoting good governance,[11] the evidence is also overwhelming that liberal democracies do not go to war with each other.[12]

Fragile States

Taken together, and for all these reasons, the dual objectives of promoting economic development (especially pro-poor growth as part of that) and democratization constitute the essence of the post-Cold War (and increasingly post-11 September 2001) political economy of foreign policy of most Western governments and the international institutions, such as the World Bank and the International Monetary Fund, which they dominate. In particular, the increased concern for 30 'low-income countries under stress' (LICUS),[13] as they are called by the World Bank, or 'fragile states', as they are called by the UK's DFID and the United States Agency for International Development (USAID), has been driven primarily by *political* rather than economic or moral considerations.

Politics

All this reflects a much deeper and more open appreciation of the role of politics, governance and institutions in development – and not before time. Indeed the contrast between the 1980s and early 1990s, when neo-liberalism was in its ascendancy, could not be more stark. In its *World Development Report* of 1991 entitled 'The Challenge of Development', the World Bank prescribed a very limited role for the state and its institutions. But by 1997, when many structurally adjusted economies had not achieved what had been intended, the *World Development Report* of that year, 'The State in a Changing World', began to acknowledge a far more sympathetically realistic, but still cautious, role for the state in development. And when, in 2002, the Bank produced its annual *World Development Report*, 'Building Institutions for Markets', it was clear that the bank had begun to recognize the centrality of politics much more openly (though seldom saying as much) in not only making, but also breaking institutions, something which was to become increasingly prominent in the bank's research output.

Whether this presages a return to a more positive view of the role of the state in development, or merely a refinement of neo-liberalism, is not yet clear. However a close investigation of the various research themes, working papers and research reports produced by the bank from the late 1990s gives some indication because it reveals a much more thoughtful appreciation of the role of politics and especially institutions in development – and the presence of more political scientists in the bank.[14] The bank and the IMF (but not the European Bank for Reconstruction and Development, which also has 'multi-party democracy and pluralism' as its goals for Eastern Europe[15]) are both forbidden in their Articles of Agreement from pursuing 'political' goals, such as democratic reform. Inevitably, they therefore still find it difficult to discuss politics explicitly, for fear of infringing their articles or the sovereignty of their members (though that has never applied to IMF loan conditionality or the recent World Bank's more explicit attachment of both economic and governance conditions to its loans). Nonetheless, it was becoming clear to them by the early years of the twenty-first century that both structural adjustment processes and functioning market economies required strong, efficient and stable states, delivering 'good governance', which could avoid 'capture'[16] by special interests and which could establish and maintain a system of legitimate institutions to encourage and safeguard economic growth and development.

Institutional Incompatibility?

But are the institutions of development and the institutions of democracy structurally compatible? Or, at the very least, can they only coexist in tension with each other? If so, this may well mean that, in the context of many developing societies, and in Africa in particular, this tension will make the *simultaneous* progress towards democratic stability and developmental progress very difficult. This is not to enter the debate about whether development should precede democracy, or vice versa, or whether development (certainly rapid and catch-up development) is attainable under democratic procedures: there have been a number of recent studies which have concluded on the basis of statistical and econometric analyses that there is no historical case for arguing that democracy should be 'sacrificed on the altar of development', or that authoritarian dictatorships necessarily are better at promoting development.[17] Rather, if and where such tensions and trade-offs do exist, the purpose here is to explore why that may be: the explanation is framed in terms of an institutional approach to politics and political economy. In essence the argument that follows is that the institutional characteristics and requirements for development and for democracy pull in opposite directions. In order to build that argument, an assessment of the role and centrality of institutions in human societies must come first.

Institutions, Societies and Politics

It is a central axiom of the social sciences in general (and political science in particular) that human societies cannot endure, prosper or – especially – develop without broadly agreed and appropriate rules and conventions governing the conduct of social, economic and political affairs, and about how human and other resources are to be used and distributed. This is because we are a social species and have to live together. In order to do so we need to have agreed understandings as to how we do things, how we deal with each other, how collective decisions (or decisions *for* the collective) are taken, how rules and decisions are implemented and how transgressions are dealt with. Such sets of rules are what we mean when we talk about *institutions*. In essence, institutions are collections of (broadly) agreed norms, rules, procedures and routines – whether they are formally established and written down, in law or by decree, as with constitutions, or whether they are informal understandings embedded in the practices of culture.[18] And, usually and crucially, such institutions – whatever domain they govern – express and sustain relations of power.

This is not a view confined to political science. Building on an older tradition in economics,[19] the 'new institutional economists' have made a strong and persuasive bid to insist – especially in the field of development – that institutions are the 'humanly devised constraints that shape human interaction' and which therefore 'structure incentives in human exchange', especially (but not only) economic exchange.[20] A slightly different perspective on this is taken by the World Bank when discussing 'public institutions' which 'create the incentives which shape the action of public officials'.[21] But the point is essentially the same: institutions are best thought of as rules, and rules shape the way we behave. This is not to suggest that rules do not or cannot change: that would be absurd, for clearly people make and change rules for their collective purposes and inevitably these reflect different (and commonly changed) distributions of power. Rather, it is to argue that, once established and consolidated, institutions – whether social, cultural, economic or political – have a powerful effect on human behaviour and are not easy to change. To illustrate, if the electoral system in the United Kingdom were to be changed to one of proportional representation, political behaviour in the form of democratic party politics would be radically different from what it now is. But it is also clear that assembling the coalition of interests which would support such a change would not be easy because dominant (or potentially dominant) parties see no incentives for changing.[22] Consequently, electoral political behaviour remains bound by the institutions (and rules) which shape it.

However, because institutional contexts (both formal and informal) vary enormously from society to society (for example Chile or China, Brazil or Bangladesh), it is naive to believe, for example, that the same kind of economic or developmental policies will have the same outcomes in all societies.[23] In no small measure, this realisation – that institutions matter – has been influential in taming some of the wilder excesses of neo-liberal political economy and in steering policy research in development agencies to look at the provenance, development, maintenance and change of the institutions of development, the institutions which may promote or hinder growth.[24]

Social scientists thus recognise that there are different institutional spheres, which often overlap (and are sometimes in conflict to produce undesired or unintended outcomes), such as social institutions (governing social interaction and behaviour – for instance between genders), economic institutions (the rules and procedures governing economic behaviour, ranging from silent barter to rules pertaining to stock market behaviour) – and political institutions (defining and governing the relations of power and decision making). And it is the manner of their *interaction* which is so decisive in shaping the political economy – that is the creation and distribution of wealth – of any given society, in the context of its history and endowments.

Students of politics, at least since the nineteenth-century formation of the modern discipline of politics, have always been interested in institutions. However, with its intellectual and disciplinary roots in law and history (and constitutional history in particular), the main focus of political science was, traditionally, somewhat narrow – typically involving the national or comparative study of constitutions, parties, elections, legislatures and the relations of executives, legislatures and judiciaries.[25] It was no doubt this narrowness that, in part, led Michael Oakeshott to observe in 1961 that British students of politics had 'imposed upon them, a curriculum of study of unimaginable dreariness in which they learned the structures of the current constitutions of the world and whose anatomical studies were enlivened only by some idle gossip and some tendentious speculation about current policy'.[26]

New Institutionalism

In recent years, however, a much broader view of institutions has been adopted. Political scientists (and economists) are increasingly interested in the way in which different institutions (sets of rules), both formal and informal, national and international, interact with each other, within and between societies, through the broad and over-arching set of processes which we understand as 'governance', which has been usefully defined recently as 'the formation and stewardship of the formal and informal rules that regulate the public realm, the arena in which state as well as economic and societal actors interact to make decisions'.[27]

If the public realm, therefore, is the arena in which formal rules of the state interact with those of the 'social' and 'economic' spheres, then such interactions can either be between compatible or incompatible institutional practices, or both. To illustrate, Robert Price has brilliantly shown how the institutions (social rules) of loyalty, mutual support and obligation governing relations between members of descent groups (extended families and lineages) in southern Ghana had very powerful effects on how Ghanaian bureaucrats discharged their administrative duties: given the conflicting pulls of institutional norms and practices between those of kin and those of bureaucracy, the effect was to undermine the 'proper' functioning of Weberian governance.[28]

Likewise, and despite the many trenchant criticisms of the concept,[29] the considerable body of work in the field of 'social capital' has shown how norms of trust and varying institutions of cooperation in different societies (or regions within them) have affected not only political institutions and practices, but levels and forms of development, too. As Robert Putnam, has pointed out, 'there is mounting evidence that the characteristics of civil society affect the health of our democracies, our communities, and ourselves'.[30] In short, the institutions (norms, rules and practices) of cooperation in the social sphere impact decisively on political institutions and practices which in turn have implications for economic and social institutions and practices through these multiple interactions.[31]

Moreover, comparative studies of 'corruption' in developing countries have shown that some forms of corruption are precisely that: the directly dishonest use of public office for private and personal gain. This is what Gordon White referred to in relation to China as 'Class A' corruption.[32] However, it is useful to understand and explain other forms of the phenomenon in terms of the manner in which traditional institutions of patron–clientelism or other relationships (such as *guanxi*, or personal trust and reciprocity, in China[33]) have permeated the relations between economy, society and the formal institutions of government and the state, thereby shaping the practices of parties, politics and systems of governance.[34] The functioning of legislatures, too, everywhere, can be profoundly affected by the broader informal institutional context in which they exist. This is particularly noticeable in the developing areas – Africa provides depressingly many examples of legislative decay and constitutional disintegration after independence – where the evolution of such institutions has not occurred as an indigenous process, but has come about by external imposition and insertion.[35] The *Fiji Times* illustrated this point more generally when it asked, in a leader article on 3 September 1992, whether democratic institutions were perhaps not a 'foreign flower', unable to 'take root in South Pacific soil'.[36]

Political Institutions and the Modern State

Political scientists have always taken a special interest in the evolution and forms of one of these institutional spheres: the political sphere and, especially, the institutions of the *modern state* with particular respect to the forms of politics and power which gave rise to it and which it both expresses and reflects.[37] We are also interested in the *processes and practices of rule*, of *governing*, or the many forms of *institutionalized domination* which the state takes and the changing balance of relations between state and society, state and citizens – for example in relation to the complex bargaining between voters and governments over the exchange between taxation and the provision of public services.[38] Quite unlike anything before it, the nation-state, and the formal political institutions of the modern state, became the dominant template for political systems, or polities, at least from the eighteenth century onwards, initially in Europe and then progressively through conquest, empire and unavoidable replication (for instance in Japan after 1868) in the wider world.

Challenges to the State

However two fundamental challenges have faced modern states from the nineteenth century onwards. The first was the challenge of 'development', or how to promote rapid and often (catch-up) economic growth, initially in the light of the mid-nineteenth-century dominance of Great Britain and, subsequently, in the light of more general and widespread Western dominance.[39] While the key driver for this was often the need to promote national defensive capability,[40] economic growth and prosperity was a necessary condition for this.[41] And, in the course of the nineteenth and twentieth centuries, following the French and American revolutions, the second challenge which the modern state had to face was the demand for greater voice and participation by citizens in the processes of decision-making, that is in the form of democratic demands, especially as the state, for its part, increased its demand for taxes from the society.

These two challenges to the modern state were at the core of many of its problems as it came to consolidate and spread in the nineteenth century, and remain core problems in the new states of the developing world. Moreover, the institutional requirements for stable and consolidated democracy are structurally different to the institutional requirements for rapid and transformative growth and, especially, development.

The Institutions of Development

The concept of 'development' is highly contested and a variety of meanings attach to it.[42] But for the purposes of this account Joseph Stiglitz's approach is adopted: he argues that it involves a 'transformation of society'.[43] And this transformation will inevitably occur across all main institutional spheres – social, economic, political and legal. This involves the application of technical and 'scientific' ways of thinking across a wide swathe of institutions in order to increase productivity with a view to enhancing human welfare and potential by the reduction of infant mortality, the extension of life expectancy and the improvement of education and health-care.

In addition to such material aspects of development, others, like Amartya Sen, would argue that development entails the expansion of freedom and choice – involving political and social aspects.[44] So, while there has clearly not been (nor is there) one single path to its achievement, the central idea of development needs to be understood in two critical senses. First, it needs to be understood as a *process*, a transformative process, involving (at least initially in relatively low income, or highly unequal, economies) quite radical and rapid *change* in the social, economic and political institutions and, inevitably, in the social (class and other) structure and in the underlying distributions of wealth and power which they express. Second, what crucially distinguishes 'development' from 'growth' is the issue of the distribution of the benefits of growth. Rapid growth is possible without development, as occurred in

Brazil in its 'miracle years' after 1965 and in South Africa during and after the Second World War. In both cases, large majorities of the population were left 'out' of development, a condition which is still reflected in their grossly unequal distributions of income (in Brazil the top 10 per cent still take almost 47 per cent of income and in South Africa the figure is 46 per cent).[45] But where the benefits of growth are being more rather than less evenly distributed, development can be said to be occurring, particularly (as Dudley Seers insisted many years ago) where the impact with respect to poverty, employment and inequality is positive.[46]

Change in Economic Institutions

Understood in this 'transformative' sense, laying (or re-starting) the foundations for development, and sustaining the processes once in motion, will impact on many extant institutions. For example, in the economic sphere, any path to development requires at its core 'the production and distribution of a surplus',[47] and hence the institutional arrangements to encourage and manage the process (in relation to savings, taxation and especially investment, for example). Where deeply entrenched values and institutions impede this, development will be compromised. For example, the institutions of generalized reciprocity and egalitarianism which have characterized many hunting and gathering societies,[48] however admirable and extreme an example, are clearly a case in point. More generally, the problem is that development is both by definition and in practice a radical and commonly turbulent process which is concerned with often far-reaching and rapid change in the structure and use of wealth, and which – if successful – must transform it and the structures of wealth and power. Moreover, it is inevitable that non-consensual steps will have to be taken, especially where a new developmentally committed regime comes to power facing a legacy of immense inequality in wealth and opportunity which requires urgent attention.

This is illustrated dramatically by the cases of post-revolutionary China in 1949 and Cuba in 1959, where almost all old economic institutions were overturned and new ones established and consolidated. This happened, too, under very different circumstances in non-democratic South Korea (especially after the military coup of 1960) and in formally democratic Singapore, after its independence from Malaysia in 1965. By contrast, the political inability or unwillingness to do this in most of sub-Saharan Africa – either on a full-blooded socialist or on a capitalist model[49] – in large part explains the depressing condition of much of the continent.

Land reform is a good example of the kind of non-consensual change in the economic institutions often regarded as a necessary condition for rural and more general development. Even with compensation, land reform is rarely consensual as landowners in general do not agree to it, especially where (as is the norm) the purpose is to reduce poverty (and hopefully promote growth) by altering the structure of rural power and wealth.[50] As in Latin America and Asia, the landowners have often constituted a very powerful interest with intimate connections to dominant parties, the military or the state, or with the capacity to subvert land reform programmes.[51] In consequence, Third World regimes (whether democratic or not) have seldom been effective in overcoming such vested rural interests to reform successfully the institutions of both rural wealth and power. Land reform failed in the

Philippines under President Ferdinand Marcos,[52] and proved impossible in Pakistan under the Ali Bhutto regime in the 1970s.[53] Indian democracy, too, has had very little success in pushing through national land reforms (though some states, such as Kerala, have been more successful) and the slow pace of land reform in South Africa after 1994 (less than two per cent of the land had been transferred by 2001) is further illustration of this.[54]

Change in Political Institutions

Development has also inevitably required often radical transformations in the political institutions of a country, directly reflecting (and helping to bring about) a changed distribution of power of a more or less radical kind. Obvious and more dramatic examples are the revolutionary changes, in recent times, as in China and Cuba, where the institutional structures of politics and governance of the old order have been totally replaced. Dramatic changes occurred, too, in the political institutional structure of Japan, after the Meiji Restoration of 1868 – a 'revolution from above'[55] – as well as in Turkey under Kemal Atatürk after 1923, and in Thailand after 1932.[56] These transformations in the institutional arrangements of politics, power and governance also occurred in South Korea, first under Japanese rule and then, later, after its independence in 1945, especially during the intense developmental drive initiated by General Park after the coup of 1960. These changes in Korea (as elsewhere) involved considerable centralization of power under the central executive within a set of bureaucratic institutions (especially the Economic Planning Board) which were created specifically in order to promote, manage and monitor rapid rural, industrial and financial development.[57] In Botswana, a comparable institution, the Ministry of Finance and Development Planning was established but, at the same time, the power of the traditional authorities, the Tswana chiefs, was radically scaled down – and kept down – after independence in 1966, with power being ceded to the new parliament and new developmental institutions in the central bureaucracy.[58]

The fundamental point here, which all these examples illustrate, is that economic growth and development is a turbulent and transformative process, challenging (and often defeating) old interests and creating new ones. The institutional changes which it requires and generates, both in the economic and political spheres (especially where attempts are made to make growth into development) have commonly been radical and far-reaching, bringing with them cognate changes in social, cultural and ideological institutions (notably in the class structures and in the general trend to secularism). These changes, at their inception, have seldom been achieved consensually (as amply demonstrated in the course of the industrial revolution in Britain), and have most commonly been associated with opposition, conflict and violence which may take religious, regional, ethnic or class-based forms.

And, as growth (if not developmental) processes begin to take root, instability is common, as illustrated by the conflicts in Europe between 1850 and 1950 and by the way in which both Turkey and Thailand, and much of South and Central America, have vacillated between military and civilian rule, with periods of intense and violent rural and urban unrest. This is hardly a new observation – the point was made effectively in Huntington's classic study, nearly 40 years ago.[59] But, equally, sustained growth and development has almost everywhere required a coherent, consistent and continuous policy path which has normally only been achieved by strong states through either non-democratic authoritarian rule or dominant-party democracy.[60] Where this has not been the case, again in either democratic (say, India) or non-democratic (say Haiti or Zaire) contexts, the result has been slow or negative growth which has seldom achieved developmental status. The point has been well made by Ronald Herring in his assessment of India where, for almost 30 years, the attempt by the dominant Congress Party to organize the development of what was, in effect, a 'continental political economy, more empire than nation', was undertaken 'with one arm tied behind its back by its commitment to liberal democracy',[61] producing limpingly slow development, once described by Raj Krishna as 'the Hindu rate of growth'.[62]

The processes of development have both required and engendered radical, transformative and pervasive change in the formal and informal socio-political and economic institutions of societies, but these changes are very different to those required for democracy. For, as I shall now suggest, democracy is essentially a conservative system of power, geared to stability, not change.

The Institutions of Democracy

Formal Institutions for Democracy

For my purposes here, democracy is best thought of as a set of institutions, rules, by which the political game is played out (though it is also often thought of normatively, as a good thing, which it may, of course, be too). However, like 'development', the concept of 'democracy' is highly contested: Collier and Levitsky found more than 550 sub-types in recent treatments of the topic.[63] Likewise, institutional forms of democracy vary widely.[64] But whether federal or unitary, presidential or parliamentary, whether based on proportional or majoritarian electoral systems, or whether dominant-party, two-party or multi-party patterns of competition predominate, there appear to be certain irreducible, *formal* institutions which define the minimal operational requirements for electoral democracy.

Taking the Freedom House approach, these formal institutional characteristics of *electoral* democracy, in essence, are: (1) a competitive (and multiparty) political system; (2) universal adult suffrage for all citizens; (3) regularly contested, free and fair elections with secret ballots; and (4) effective public access by political parties to the electorate through the media and through generally open political campaigning.[65] In a liberal democracy, these electoral characteristics are supplemented, in general, by a wide range of institutionalized civil rights and liberties for citizens, including freedom of expression, association and religion; the rule of law; individual rights and autonomy (including, significantly, property rights). It would also hardly be a liberal democracy without institutions which seek to constrain the behaviour of the state and to ensure and its transparency and accountability.

Detailed comparative research has consistently shown that for these formal institutions of electoral and liberal democracy to survive and prosper, it is necessary for there to be a strong state, a *rechtsstaat*, capable of applying the rules, and an independent legal system that enforces the laws predictably and fairly. For just as 'development' requires an effective state, so too does democracy.[66] But the problem is that the *types* of effective state required are different. An effective state *for democracy*, that is one which is capable of maintaining the institutions of competitive democracy, presupposes a particular kind of consensual competitive politics that generates and sustains the legitimacy of the state.[67] It must allow and encourage the fullest possible range of interests and preferences (whether economic, political or social) to jostle and argue for advantage, to strike deals, form coalitions and accept compromises, within the formal rules of the game and in relation to the state. Without such a state, the formal institutional requirements for democracy will not be sustained and will be quickly corrupted. The kind of state required for development, on the other hand, as argued earlier, requires the power and authority to be able to take on some of such sectional interests at various times (whether landlords or trades unions), and to favour some and sideline others, if it is effectively to promote and achieve its national developmental objectives.

The distinguished American political scientist, Adam Przeworski, has theorized democratization as 'a process of institutionalizing uncertainty, of subjecting all interests to uncertainty'.[68] Strictly speaking this is true: by definition, no-one can know the outcomes of electoral politics. But while this may be the case in theory, and while the formal rules (above) certainly allow for this, it is seldom true in practice. To understand why this is so, it is necessary to look at the informal institutions of democracy which act to reduce uncertainty and to instil a necessarily conservative bias into democratic politics.

Informal Institutions of Democracy

There are two crucial informal institutions which are necessary for stable and consolidated democracy, and which (unlike development) make it hostile to rapid change and, especially, the radical transformative change which is inherent in development (understood here as growth plus distribution). Moreover, these two balancing, binary and informal operational institutions of democratic politics make it almost certain that democracy will be a conservative system of power. The first, as a rule, is simply that losers must accept the outcome of the political game, knowing that they have the right to participate again, within a given and constitutionally stipulated period of time. If democracy is to be established, and to survive, losers cannot and must not return to the gun, the *foco* or the bomb (if that is what they did before democratization). In short, democracy – as understood in terms which Sir Bernard Crick made explicit for politics more generally – 'is a distinctive form of rule whereby people act together through institutionalised procedures to resolve differences, to conciliate diverse interests and values and to make public policies in the pursuit of common purposes'.[69]

But, in typical developing country contexts, poverty and inequality (regional or social) are often intense; long-standing tensions and (ethnic, religious or regional) conflicts are neither dead nor forgotten; and (historically speaking) control of the state enabled winners to feather their own or their followers' nests (as in Zaire,

Haiti, Pakistan). So why would any party or group wish to abide by the institutions of electoral democracy if it knew or feared that losing could mean that anything might happen – for instance that it, or the interests it represents, would lose *too* much, if not everything? If – at least in theory, as Przeworski points out – democracy involves the institutionalization of uncertainty, no group or interest would participate in democratic institutions if it believed or feared that one possible outcome of the uncertainties of electoral defeat would result in its effective elimination, politically or otherwise. In short, where the stakes for winning or losing are high, who would want to risk such uncertainty?

This is where the second of the two informal and balancing operational institutions for stable consolidated democracy enters the picture. Simply stated, the quid pro quo for the first rule (the losers' acceptance of defeat) is that winners must agree to exercise restraint. They cannot, as it were, take all. Democratic electoral victory is not the same as a licence for the winners to undermine, attack or eliminate the vital interests or resources of the losers; on the contrary, there must be significant limits to what they can do with their newly-won power, and they must agree to that. This rule means that sustained and sustainable democratic politics therefore depends on victorious parties exercising restraint when in power, although the temptation (and sometimes the developmental or egalitarian need) may often be to re-write the policy book. That is to say, new or born-again democracies are more likely to consolidate and prosper if their new governments do not pursue highly contentious policies too far or too fast, especially where these policies seriously threaten other major interests, whether such policies are economic (such as land reform, expropriation or nationalization), distributional (such taxation and social expenditure), social (perhaps with regard to issues of religion, language or gender). Indeed, such agreed limits on policy change are often established *before* democratization can be completed, in the course of negotiations about the rules of the game, and are thus part of that process itself.[70]

The case of Venezuela aptly illustrates this. In 1958, two extraordinary 'pacts', the Worker–Owner Accord and the Pact of Punto Fijo, were concluded between the three main parties, excluding the Communist Party.[71] These pacts (hence 'pacted' democracy) framed the directions and limits of policy change and effectively tied the major parties into a consensus on the broad limits of developmental policy choice. They also provided for a sharing of power which, for almost 30 years, sustained democracy in Venezuela, something rare in Latin America during the period. They did so by guaranteeing that the main parties would all have a stake in the government and that neither they nor their supporters would ever lose too much through electoral defeat. Sometimes these limits to what governments can do are inscribed in the constitution. Indeed, the negotiated agreement which brought the new constitution into being in South Africa in 1994 did precisely that. Although *political* power in the institutions of the state was transferred, there was clear agreement that the fundamental structure of wealth and ownership would not be challenged – a strategy confirmed in the African National Congress government's policy and programmes after 1994 and which, as some argue, may have had valuable implications for political democracy but worrying ones for development and the reduction of the legacies of inequality inherited from the apartheid era.[72] By contrast, as Mushtaq Khan has pointed out, the consensus which has underpinned the (sometimes) democratic process in Pakistan has been between loose coalitions of factions from the 'intermediate classes', which (as in many developing countries) have sought to use state power for purposes of often corrupt and primitive accumulation, not for developmental purposes.[73]

One thing should now be clear. Without the formal institutions, and a strong state to enforce them, there will be no democracy. But where such a state is established which can maintain the *formal* democratic institutions, the *informal* rules which underpin these – acceptance of loss by losers and restraint by winners – will undermine the possibility of active developmental initiative by the state, precisely because if the state were to act transformatively, it would almost certainly damage some of the interests involved, thereby possibly provoking withdrawal from the democratic process, or worse.

Although it is common now for most of the member countries of the Organization for Economic Cooperation and Development (OECD) to have democratic politics that are well established, and where most major political parties share a broadly consensual view about the appropriate institutions for capitalist democracy, this kind of consensus about the formal and informal institutions of democracy is not easy to achieve in developing countries. In its absence, the institutions of *both* development and democracy are impeded. The necessary consensus is difficult to achieve not only because of the deep cleavages that exist with respect to class, region, religion or ethnicity, but also because of the proliferation of political parties. In many parts of Africa, for instance, in the new formally democratic context that prevails, the number of registered parties range from 91 in Mali to 10 in Egypt, and from 73 in Chad to 30 in Nigeria. Though many are very weak, highly personalized, unfunded and transient, their strength in numbers and the variety of discrete interests they represent make achieving agreement about rules very difficult indeed.[74]

The situation in Afghanistan is certainly worse. There, given the grip of the warlords, the absence of any established and functioning national institutions, the power of strong regional autonomy (and military forces) and local institutions of governance, not to mention the continuing 'reliance on violence to settle disputes',[75] it is inconceivable that the kind of institutions (both formal and, especially, informal) that would establish and sustain even the loosest federal democracy will emerge for some time. The prospects of a strong (and not necessarily democratic) developmental state are even slimmer until a political order can be established 'based not on the private provision of violence, but rather the public provision of force'.[76] Much the same could be said for the on-going crises in Somalia, Sudan and the Democratic Republic of Congo to mention but a few of the many depressing African examples.[77]

Conclusions

While it is an uncomfortable thesis, it is now possible to see why I argue that democracy (especially, but not only, in its inherently limited, but also in its almost universally practised representative form that follows the model posited by Joseph Schumpeter) is a *conservative system of power*. Democracies, to be sure, are radical and progressive in that they have established the principle and practice of many valued personal freedoms, as well as civil and political rights. But, as I have suggested above, democracy may be considered 'conservative' in a perhaps more fundamental and troubling sense, at least from a developmental point of view. Why?

Given the nature of the formal and, especially, informal institutions which underpin them, democracies have great difficulty in taking *rapid and far-reaching steps* to reduce structural inequalities in wealth which new democratic governments (as in post-apartheid South Africa) or born-again (and again) democratic governments (as in Brazil or the Philippines) may have inherited, whether they be based on class, colour, ethnicity, religion or a combination of them. In short, the institutions and system of power which democratic politics both require and represent seldom promote the politics of radical change in the control, accumulation, distribution or use of wealth which is normally vital, early on, for establishing developmental momentum, *especially in late developing societies*, where the problems are most acute.

That is to say, given the initial range of often sharply conflicting interests, the new democracies have few of the characteristics of what David Apter referred, long ago, to as 'mobilization' systems, as opposed to 'reconciliation systems'.[78] Indeed, the expansion of democratic space in the last decade may well exacerbate the problem. And this is one of the key reasons why the relationship between the institutions of democracy and the institutions of development is so problematic, and often tense. For while development requires institutions that promote more or less radical accumulation, change and transformation, the institutions which are required to sustain and consolidate democracy are characteristically the ones that promote the politics of accommodation, compromise and the centre. The political logic of democracy is generally, therefore, necessarily consensual, conservative and incremental in the change it brings about. For many, that is the virtue of democracy: for others, that is its vice.

NOTES

1. For details see World Bank, 'Millennium Development Goals', at <www.developmentgoals.org/Poverty.htm>.
2. Nicolas van de Walle, *African Economies and the Politics of Permanent Crisis* (Cambridge: Cambridge University Press, 2001).
3. Dani Rodrik (ed.), *In Search of Prosperity* (Princeton, NJ: Princeton University Press, 2003).
4. Stockholm International Peace Research Institute (SIPRI), *SIPRI Yearbook 2004* (Oxford: Oxford University Press, 2004), ch.3 (available at <www.editors.sipri.se/pubs/yb04/aboutyb.html>).
5. Department for International Development (DFID), *Why We Need to Work More Effectively in Fragile States* (London: DFID, 2005), p.5. States which in recent times have fallen into the collapsed and failed state categories include Somalia, Sudan, Afghanistan, Angola, Democratic Republic of Congo, Sierra Leone and Liberia. Failing or fragile states is a larger category and includes states ranging from Haiti to Tajikistan, and Chad to Burma.
6. Robert I. Rotberg (ed.), *State Failure and State Weakness in a Time of Terror* (Washington, DC: Brookings Institute Press, 2003); Robert I. Rotberg (ed.), *When States Fail* (Princeton, NJ: Princeton University Press, 2004); Robert H. Bates 'Political Insecurity and State Failure in Contemporary Africa', Working Paper 115, Center for International Development, Harvard University, January 2005 (available at <www.cid.harvard.edu/cidwp/115.htm>).

7. The first is the report of the National Intelligence Council, *Global Trends 2015* (Washington, DC: National Intelligence Council, 2000) and the second is the report of the Prime Minister's Strategy Unit, of the Cabinet Office, *Investing in Prevention. An International Strategy to Manage Risks of Instability and Improve Crisis Response* (London: The Strategy Unit, 2005). But see also DFID (note 5). See also 'From Chaos, Order', *The Economist*, 3 March 2005.

8. DFID, *The Causes of Conflict in Africa* (London: DFID, 2001), p.20.

9. G. Crawford, 'Foreign Aid and Political Conditionality: Issues of Effectiveness and Consistency', *Democratization*, Vol.4, No.3 (1997), pp.69–108; O. Stokke, 'Aid and Political Conditionality: Core Issues and State of the Art', in O. Stokke (ed.), *Aid and Political Conditionality* (London: Frank Cass, 1996), pp.1–87; Larry Diamond, *Developing Democracy: Towards Consolidation* (London: Johns Hopkins University Press, 1999); Michael Bratton and Nicolas van de Walle, *Democratic Experiments in Africa* (Cambridge: Cambridge University Press, 1997).

10. Nick Donovan, M. Smart, Magui Moreno-Torres, Jan Ole Kiso' and George Zachariah, 'Countries at Risk of Instability: Risk Factors and Dynamics of Instability', Prime Minister's Strategy Unit, Background Paper (London: The Cabinet Office, 2005), p.3.

11. United Nations Economic Commission for Africa, *Striving For Good Governance in Africa* (Addis Ababa: UNECA, 2004), p.3.

12. Michael W. Doyle, 'Kant, Liberal Legacies and Foreign Affairs', *Philosophy and Public Affairs*, Vol.12, No.3 (1983), pp.205–35.

13. See <http://siteresources.worldbank.org/INTLICUS/Overview/20313429/LICUSpercent20Brief.doc>, and World Bank, *World Bank Group Work in Low Income Countries Under Stress: A Task Force Report* (Washington, DC: The World Bank, 2002); DFID (note 5).

14. See, for instance, Daniel Kaufmann, Aart Kraay and Pablo Zoifo-Lobató, 'Governance Matters', Policy Research Working Paper 2196 (Washington, DC: The World Bank, 1999); and see the particularly interesting paper by Joel S. Hellman, Geraint Jones and Daniel Kaufmann, '*Seize the State, Seize the Day': State Capture, Corruption and Influence in Transition*, Policy Research Working Paper 2444 (Washington, DC: World Bank Institute, 2000); Philip Keefer, *Democratization and Clientelism: Why Are Young Democracies Badly Governed?* (Washington, DC: Development Research Group, The World Bank, 2003); Philip Keefer, 'What does Political Economy tell us about Economic Development – and Vice Versa?', *Annual Review of Political Science*, Vol.7 (2004), pp.247–72.

15. *Agreement Establishing the European Bank for Reconstruction and Development1990*, Article 1. The clear political goals of the EBRD indicate how far Western governments had moved in the direction of recognizing and pushing for political aspects of development.

16. Hellman, Jones and Kaufmann (note 14).

17. Adam Przeworski, Michael E. Alvarez, José Antonio Cheibub and Fernando Limongi, *Democracy and Development. Political Institutions and Well-Being in the World, 1950–1990* (Cambridge: Cambridge University Press, 2000), pp.269–78.

18. James March and Johan P. Olsen, *Rediscovering Institutions. The Organizational Basis of Politics* (New York: The Free Press, 1989), pp.21–6. See, especially, Douglass C. North, 'Institutions', *Journal of Economic Perspectives*, Vol.5, No.1 (1991), pp.97–112; see also Douglass C. North, *Institutions, Institutional Change and Economic Performance* (Cambridge: Cambridge University Press, 1990) and a host of papers, particularly North's 'Institutions and Economic Growth: An Historical Introduction', *World Development*, Vol, 17. No.9 (1989), pp.1319–32.

19. Geoffrey M. Hodgson, *How Economics Forgot History* (London: Routledge, 2001).

20. North, *Institutions, Institutional Change* (note 18), p.3.

21. The World Bank, *Reforming Public Institutions and Strengthening Governance* (Washington, DC: World Bank, 2000), pp.xii and 2.

22. John Kingdom, *Government and Politics in Britain*, 3rd edn. (Cambridge: Polity Press, 2003), pp.264–76.

23. Dani Rodrik, 'Growth Strategies', unpublished manuscript.

24. Ibid. p.5. But see also Christopher Clague (ed.), *Institutions and Economic Development. Growth and Governance in Less-Developed and Post-Socialist Countries* (Baltimore, MD: Johns Hopkins University Press, 1997). Both the United Kingdom's DFID and the International Monetary Fund (IMF), for instance, are currently funding significant research into how institutions are established and changed.

25. For an account of this 'old institutionalism' see B. Guy Peters, *Institutional Theory in Political Science* (London: Continuum, 1999). For a more detailed account of the history of political science in the United States, see David M. Ricci, *The Tragedy of Political Science* (New Haven, CT: Yale University

Press, 1984) and for a rather bleak view of the discipline in Britain, see Jack Hayward, 'British Approaches to Politics: the Dawn of a Self-Deprecating Discipline', in Jack Hayward, Brian Barry and Archie Brown (eds.), *The British Study of Politics in the Twentieth Century* (Oxford: Oxford University Press, 1999).

26. Michael Oakeshott, 'The Study of Politics in a University', in Michael Oakeshott, *Rationalism in Politics and Other Essays* (London: Methuen, 1967), p.323.

27. Goran Hyden, Julius Court and Kenneth Mease, *Making Sense of Governance. Empirical Evidence from Sixteen Developing Countries* (Boulder, CO and London: Lynne Rienner, 2004).

28. After the writings on state and bureaucracy of the famous German sociologist Max Weber. See Robert M. Price, *Society and Bureaucracy in Contemporary Ghana* (Berkeley, CA: University of California Press, 1975).

29. John Harriss, *Depoliticizing Development. The World Bank and Social Capital* (London: Anthem Press, 2002).

30. Robert D.Putnam and Kristin A. Goss, 'Introduction', in Robert D. Putnam (ed.), *Democracies in Flux. The Evolution of Social Capital in Contemporary Society* (New York and Oxford: Oxford University Press, 2002), p.6.

31. David Halpern, *Social Capital* (Cambridge: Polity Press, 2004).

32. Gordon White, 'Corruption and the Transition from Socialism in China', *Journal of Law and Society*, Vol.23, No.1 (1966), pp.149–69.

33. Ibid. p.159; Hongying Wang, 'Informal Institutions and Foreign Investment in China', *The Pacific Review*, Vol.13, No.4 (2000), pp 525–56.

34. Two brilliant analyses of this phenomenon and its historical provenance may be found in Peter Ekeh, 'Colonialism and the Two Publics', *Comparative Studies in Society and History*, Vol.17, No.1 (1975), pp.91–112; and Bruce Berman, 'Ethnicity, Patronage and the African State: the Politics of Uncivil Nationalism', *African Affairs*, Vol.97, No.388 (1998), pp.243–61.

35. Joel Smith and Lloyd D. Musolf (eds.), *Legislatures in Development: Dynamics of Change in New and Old States* (Durham, NC: Duke University Press, 1979).

36. Peter Larmour, 'Democracy without Development in the South Pacific', in Adrian Leftwich (ed.), *Democracy and Development* (Cambridge: Polity Press, 1996), p.230.

37. No better example of this can be offered than Charles Tilly, *Coercion, Capital and European States, AD 990–1992* (Cambridge, MA: Blackwell, 1992).

38. A fine recent contribution to this is Mick Moore, 'Revenues, State Formation and the Quality of Governance in Developing Countries', *International Political Science Review*, Vol.25, No.3 (2004), pp.297–319. But for a different perspective on the question, see also Margaret Levi, *Of Rule and Revenue* (London: University of California Press, 1989).

39. Ha-Joon Chang, *Kicking Away The Ladder* (London: Anthem Press, 2002).

40. Adrian Leftwich, 'Theorising the State', in Peter Burnell and Vicky Randall (eds.), *Politics in the Developing World* (Oxford: Oxford University Press, 2004), pp.139–54. 'Rich Country. Strong Army' was the Meiji formulation for this in Japan after 1870.

41. Tilly (note 37).

42. Adrian Leftwich, *States of Development* (Cambridge: Polity Press, 2000), chs 2 and 3.

43. Joseph Stiglitz, 'Towards a New Paradigm of Development', in John H. Dunning, *Making Globalization Good* (Oxford: Oxford University Press, 2003), pp.77ff.

44. Amartya Sen, *Development As Freedom* (Oxford: Oxford University Press, 1999).

45. World Bank, *World Development Report 2002* (New York: Oxford University Press, 2002), Table 2, pp.234–5.

46. Dudley Seers, 'The Meaning of Development', *International Development Review*, Vol.11, No.4 (1969), pp.2–6.

47. Barbara Harriss-White, *India Working. Essays in Economy and Society* (Cambridge: Cambridge University Press, 2003), p.1.

48. R.B.Lee and I. de Vore (eds.), *Man the Hunter* (Chicago: Aldine, 1968); Lorna Marshall, *The !Kung of Nyae Nyae* (Cambridge, MA: Harvard University Press, 1976). Richard Lee observes of the !Kung San of the Kalahari that the '!Kung are a fiercely egalitarian people, and they have evolved a series of important cultural practices to maintain this equality, first by cutting down to size the arrogant and the boastful, and second by helping those down on their luck to get back in the game'. R.B. Lee, *The !Kung San* (Cambridge: Cambridge University Press, 1979), p.244.

49. Robert Bates, *Markets and States in Tropical Africa* (Berkeley, CA: University of California Press, 1981), p.121; Richard Sandbrook, *The Politics of Africa's Economic Stagnation* (Cambridge: Cambridge University Press, 1985); Richard Sandbrook, *The Politics of Africa's Economic Recovery*

(Cambridge: Cambridge University Press, 1993), p.23; Paul Collier and Jan Willem Gunning, 'Explaining African Economic Performance', *Journal of Economic Literature*, Vol.37 (March 1999), pp.64–111.

50. Michael Lipton, 'Towards a Theory of Land Reform', in David Lehman (ed.), *Peasants, Landlords and Governments* (New York: Holmes & Meier, 1974), pp.269–315.

51. Solon Barraclough, *Land Reform in Developing Countries: the Role of the State and Other Actors* (Geneva: UNRISD, 1999).

52. B.J. Kerkvliet, 'Land Reform in the Philippines since the Marcos Coup', *Pacific Affairs*, Vol.47, No.3 (1974), pp.286–304.

53. Ronald J.Herring, 'Zulfikar Ali Bhuto and the "Eradication of Feudalism" in Pakistan', *Comparative Studies in Society and History*, Vol.21, No.4 (1979), pp 519–57.

54. Stuart Corbridge and John Harriss, *Reinventing India* (Cambridge: Polity Press, 2000), pp.62–6; W.D. Thwala, 'Land and Agrarian Reform in South Africa' (Johannesburg: National Land Committee, 2003) (available at <www.nlc.co.za/pubs.htm>).

55. Ellen Kay Trimberger, *Revolution from Above* (New Brunswick, NJ: Transaction Books, 1978); and see also K M. Panikkar, *Asia and Western Dominance* (London: George Allen & Unwin, 1959), pp.153–62.

56. Çağlar Keyder, *State and Class in Turkey. A Study in Capitalist Development* (London: Verso, 1978); Fred Riggs, *Thailand: The Modernization of a Bureaucratic Polity* (Honolulu, HI: East-West Center Press, 1966).

57. Atul Kohli, 'Where Do High Growth Political Economies Come From? The Japanese Lineage of Korea's "Developmental State"', *World Development*, Vol.22, No.9 (1994), pp.1269–94; Jung-en Woo, *The Race To the Swift* (New York: Columbia University Press, 1991); and Peter B. Evans,'Transferable Lessons? Re-examining the Institutional Pre-Requisites of East Asian Economic Policies', *Journal of Development Studies*, Vol.34, No.6 (1998), pp.66–86; Hyuk-Rae Kim, 'Korea's Economic Governance in Transition: Governance Crisis and the Future of Korea Capitalism', *Korea Observer*, Vol.31, No.4 (2000), pp.553–77.

58. Ian Taylor, 'Work for Development: Botswana as a Developmental State', in Graham Harrison (ed.), *Global Encounters. International Political Economy, Development and Global Governance* (Basingstoke: Palgrave, 2004), pp.41–62.

59. Samuel P. Huntington, *Political Order in Changing Societies* (New Haven, CT: Yale University Press, 1968).

60. I have elaborated this point at some length in Adrian Leftwich, 'Forms of the Democratic Developmental State: Democratic Practices and Development Capacity', in Mark Robinson and Gordon White (eds.), *The Democratic Developmental State* (Oxford: Oxford University Press, 1998), pp.52–83.

61. Ronald J. Herring, 'Embedded Particularism: India's Failed Developmental State', in Meredith Woo-Cumings (ed.), *The Developmental State* (Ithaca, NY: Cornell University Press, 1999), pp.306–34.

62. Corbridge and Harriss (note 54), p.173.

63. David Collier and Steven Levitsky, 'Democracy With Adjectives: Conceptual Innovation in Comparative Research', *World Politics*, Vol.49, No.3 (1997), pp.430–51.

64. Arend Lijphart, *Patterns of Democracy* (New Haven, CT: Yale University Press, 1999).

65. Freedom House, *Freedom in the World 2004* (Washington, DC: Freedom House, 2004) (available at <www.freedomhouse.org/Research/Survey2003.htm>).

66. Adam Przeworski *et al.*, *Sustainable Democracy* (Cambridge: Cambridge University Press, 1995), p.110; Larry Diamond, *Developing Democracy. Toward Consolidation* (Baltimore, MD: Johns Hopkins University Press, 1999), pp.12–13.

67. I have discussed these forms of legitimacy in more detail in 'A Contradiction in the Politics of Economics', *New Political Economy*, Vol.7, No.2 (2002), pp.269–73.

68. Adam Przeworski, 'Some Problems in the Study of the Transition to Democracy', in G. O'Donnell, *et al.* (eds), *Transitions from Authoritarian Rule: Comparative Perspectives* (Baltimore, MD: The Johns Hopkins University Press, 1986), p.58.

69. Bernard Crick, 'Politics as a Form of Rule: Politics, Citizenship and Democracy', in Adrian Leftwich (ed.), *What is Politics?* (Cambridge, Polity Press, 2004), p.67.

70. S.P. Huntington, 'How Countries Democratize', *Political Science Quarterly*, Vol.106, No.4 (1991/2), pp.609–15.

71. Jennifer McCoy, 'The State and the Democratic Compromise in Venezuela', *Journal of Developing Societies*, Vol.4, No.2 (1988), pp.85–133.

72. Edward Webster and Glenn Adler, 'Towards a Class Compromise in South Africa's "Double Transition": Bargained Liberalization and the Consolidation of Democracy', *Politics and Society*,

Vol.27, No.3 (1999), pp.347–85. Detail is elaborated in Patrick Bond, *Elite Transition: From Apartheid to Neo-Liberalism in South Africa* (London: Pluto Press, 2000).

73. Mushtaq Husain Khan' 'Fundamental Tensions in the Democratic Compromise', *New Political Economy*, Vol.7, No.2 (2002), pp.275–7.

74. Economic Commission for Africa, *Striving For Good Governance in Africa* (Addis Ababa: Economic Commission For Africa, 2005), p.5.

75. Alexander Their and Jarat Chopra, 'The Road Ahead: Political and Institutional Reconstruction in Afghanistan', *Third World Quarterly*, Vol.23, No.5 (2002), p.906 and passim.

76. Robert H.Bates, *Prosperity and Violence. The Political Economy of Development* (New York: W. W. Norton, 2001), p.69.

77. Rotberg, *State Failure* (note 6).

78. David Apter, *The Politics of Modernization* (Chicago, IL: University of Chicago Press, 1965).

Manuscript accepted for publication August 2005.

Address for correspondence: Adrian Leftwich, Department of Politics, University of York, Heslington, York YO10 5DD, UK. E-mail: <AL23@york.ac.uk>.

Markets, States and Democracy: Patron–Client Networks and the Case for Democracy in Developing Countries

MUSHTAQ H. KHAN

Democracy is a system of rules for electing the executive and the legislature that constitutes the government of a society through a process of competitive and contested elections. The relationship between democracy and the developmental performance of markets and states, particularly in the developing world, has been at the heart of some of the most intense debates in economics, political science and development studies. On the one hand, the evidence is overwhelming that rich countries can sustain viable democracies, while poor countries often cannot. The data that show that more developed economies have more sustainable democracies are about as conclusive as data in social science can be. The debate has instead been over the extent to which *democracy* allows or is even necessary for economic development. On this critical question, political opinion has swung dramatically away from the modernization theories that held sway till two decades ago, but on many substantive questions, the jury is still out.

The historical evidence can be interpreted in various ways depending on the samples chosen and the period examined, but taken as a whole, the evidence on the impact of democracy on development is inconclusive. There are enough exceptions on both sides of the argument to suggest that neither democracy nor authoritarianism is a precondition for development. We can find examples of rapid growth in the set of countries that were democratic as well as in the set that was authoritarian. Similarly, we can find (unfortunately even more) examples of economic stagnation in the set of countries that were democratic as well as in the set that was authoritarian. Since most people would agree that democracy is better than its absence, this evidence can be interpreted as an argument for democracy. However, the evidence can also be interpreted to mean that democracy is not necessarily a *precondition* for economic development. It follows that the policy priority given to democratization in recent years may be diverting us from more important priorities that may be necessary to achieve the prosperity required for making democracy both more sustainable and capable of delivering real decision-making powers to societies.

This study, then, examines some important but often neglected aspects of the two-way relationship between democracy and economic development by looking at how democracy affects and is affected by the operation of markets and states in developing countries. This, in turn, leads us examine the implications of these observations for political reform strategies in developing countries.

To understand how democracy operates in developing countries, our starting point will be to argue that we need to look more closely at why political contestation in developing countries is organized through the mobilizations of patron–client factions, rather than through the mobilization of class or economic interest groups. In reality these political features of developing countries are intimately connected to the underdevelopment of economies, the limited scope of viable capitalist economies in developing societies, and the inevitable social transformations that these societies are experiencing. The factional mobilizations that are characteristic of this period can, and often do, have negative effects on economic development and political stability. This could explain not only why democracies are vulnerable in developing countries, but also why economic growth is often so fragile.

However, factional conflicts and contests over resources do not necessarily have to lead to either economic stagnation or the breakdown of democracy. In some cases, democracy may be a viable mechanism of managing these conflicts, and factional conflicts can drive economic growth in some contexts. The economic outcomes of democratic management of factional conflicts are therefore not well-defined without a further examination of the specific patron–client networks and factions that are involved in particular countries. The example of India demonstrates how factional politics operating through democratic institutions can allow a country to continue its transition to a specific type of capitalist economy. While some countries such as India have done well with democracy, the bigger policy question is about the viability of the democratization reforms that are being promoted across the world by international agencies. Here, by not understanding the role of patron-client factions in the politics of developing countries, programmes of democratization are often missing the point, even from the narrow perspective of deepening the entrenchment of democracy.

The first of the following sections reviews a number of conventional theories linking democracy to development and points out how these theories are undermined by the presence of factional politics in developing countries. The next section presents some of the extensive evidence showing that developing country democracies are in fact characterized by intense patron–client politics and are quite different in their operation from advanced country democracies. The third section presents an alternative way of explaining the dominance of patron-client politics in developing countries based on structural features of their economies. This analysis has significant implications both for the debate between modernization theory and its opponents and for the support for democratization coming from theories of neo-patrimonialism that have become very influential as part of the good governance agenda. The final section summarizes some of the conclusions.

Conventional Theories of Democracy and Development

Conventional theories of democracy and development present abstract arguments linking democracy with economic outcomes. Their general argument, however, is undermined if we bring into the analysis specific features of developing countries, in particular, as will be explained below, the issues of patron–client networks and factional politics. The case for democracy has to be built on other grounds, and the policies that are required for making democracy viable need to be identified using other more appropriate theories. It is therefore useful to begin with a brief review of the main types of arguments that are conventionally presented about the links between democracies on the one hand and the operation of markets and states on the other.

There are three major arguments linking democracy to the more efficient operation of markets and states, which consequently has a positive effect on developmental outcomes. The first argument focuses on the better use of information in democracies. This, in turn, allows for better preference identification, better policy and project choice or simply disaster avoidance. The second argument focuses on the procedural advantage of democracy in allowing more rapid institutional change in the direction of greater efficiency. The third argument focuses on the advantage of democracy in maintaining the stability of the political system and of property rights, both essential for economic development. The account summarises each argument in turn and considers how the patron–client political characteristics of developing countries can undermine them. A later section considers a fourth, neo-Weberian argument, which claims that democracy is essential for overcoming patron–client politics.

Information-based Arguments for Democracy

The most obvious argument linking democracy with development is that the competition for office reveals information for current and future policy-makers that could not otherwise have been generated. We have to distinguish here between information that allows preference identification (what do the 'people' want), information that enables better policy and project choice, and information that allows governments to avoid major catastrophes.

The preference identification argument is the least convincing. It is not at all clear, even in theory, what democracy can do to identify 'social' preferences. The problem is that a single set of social preferences may not exist, so that there is no simple sense in which we can discover them. Different groups and classes in society may have incompatible preferences, and the outcome of voting may depend on the details of voting procedures, or differences in the organizational power of different groups and their ability to set agendas.[1] The distribution of organizational abilities is a particularly important factor. The superior organizational power of patron–client factions in developing country democracies can help to explain why electoral competition does not in general result in government preferences being set by the poor even though they constitute huge majorities. There are, of course, exceptions. Economic policy in some developing country democracies is more decidedly pro-poor. Some arguments about the desirability of democracy extrapolate from specific examples of pro-poor state policies in democracies (the state of Kerala in India is a particular favourite) to the general conclusion that democracy empowers the poor to influence or even determine state policies in ways that help to develop the capabilities of the poor to participate in development.[2] But in fact, a comparison of Kerala with equally democratic neighbouring Indian states suggests that the emergence of pro-poor economic policies depends on many contingent features of the factional politics of particular states rather than on democracy in general. Equally, far less democratic states like China (under Mao) or South Korea (in the 1960s) achieved higher scores on health and education relative to their comparators at similar per capita incomes. Thus, while policy preferences that reflect majority interests can emerge through democracy, the latter is neither necessary nor sufficient for this result.

The second type of information argument is that democracy provides greater scrutiny for policy and project choices and therefore results in better economic outcomes. This is theoretically a more plausible argument, but even here, the linkage is ambivalent. Clearly, bureaucrats in charge of project selection need to have incentives for making the right choices and should be accountable if they make mistakes, but democracy (as a system for selecting and rejecting politicians) may not be either necessary or sufficient to achieve this. Even from a narrow information perspective, having more points of scrutiny does not necessarily lead to better policy or project choices. In particular, if the cost of collecting and assessing information is high, increasing the degree of scrutiny could result in bad outcomes.[3] If we add to this information perspective the observation that the scrutiny in real developing country democracies is effectively being practised by political factions who are likely to have sectional interests, the outcomes of democratic scrutiny clearly depends on specific local factors. This qualified scrutiny can often be better than the alternative, but need not necessarily be so.

The most powerful variant of the information argument is that democracy produces information about impending disasters, and therefore, major disasters can be avoided. Drèze and Sen famously argued that famines never happen in democracies because the press and the opposition ensure that even the most self-interested government takes steps to avert major disasters.[4] But major disasters need to be defined. Many democratic developing countries can live with festering poverty and high numbers of deaths due to nutrition deficiency as a 'normal' state of affairs. Nor is it strictly true that no democratic country has suffered from a famine. The 1974 famine in Bangladesh happened under a democratic regime, which turned increasingly authoritarian as it failed to manage the economy and polity. Nevertheless, disaster avoidance is arguably the most convincing information-based argument in favour of democracy.

Democracy as a Regime that Ensures Efficient Institutional Change

A somewhat more sophisticated but, ultimately, unconvincing set of arguments in favour of democracy comes from the transaction cost analysis of Douglass North. The argument here is that economic efficiency requires the evolution of economic institutions and property rights to reduce transaction costs in the market. All institutional changes involve winners and losers. Institutional changes that are efficient from the perspective of economics are those where the winners gain more than the losers lose. If our political institutions ensured that only this type of institutional change could happen, these political institutions would promote economic efficiency.

North argues that for all its imperfections, a democratic system with low political transaction costs (the costs of organizing coalitions and reaching compromises between them) is most likely to achieve this. By reducing the cost of political negotiation, a democracy could assist in negotiating compensations to losers that would allow their opposition to efficient policy or institutional changes to be overcome.[5] Equally, inefficient institutional changes or policies would be rapidly blocked by coalitions of losers because their loss would be greater than the potential gain of the proposers of the inefficient policies. Democracy would allow potential losers to offer enough to proposers of bad policies to stop these policies being implemented. The possibility that democracy can assist in introducing efficient policy and institutional change and to stop bad policies being implemented is one of the underlying arguments in support of democratization in the good governance reforms that developing countries are being encouraged to undertake.[6]

However, as North himself points out, even the most democratic political institutions are unlikely to approach zero transaction costs. When transaction costs remain high, the cognitive models of participants and their relative bargaining power will matter very much in determining the types of institutional changes that are negotiated and these outcomes need not enhance efficiency.[7] In fact, the qualification is even stronger than North admits. Given very large differences in the political power of factions, there is no necessity for winners to offer compensation to losers. Indeed, historically, winners have rarely compensated losers, and democracy has never really functioned as an efficient institutional system to organize compensation. Rather, both democracy and authoritarianism have functioned as mechanisms for managing conflicts and suppressing losers.[8] Occasionally, democracies have achieved efficiency-enhancing institutional changes in developing countries, but when they have, this was not achieved through the efficient compensation of losers, but rather through ruling factions using a combination of obfuscation and divide and rule tactics against the opponents of reform to achieve their objectives.[9] More often, democracies in developing countries have found it difficult to organize efficiency-enhancing institutional changes because losers could organize resistance through alliances with powerful factions. But authoritarian regimes did not necessarily perform better either. Some authoritarian regimes did find it easy to override resistance to efficiency-enhancing institutional changes, but many others found institutional change just as difficult to organize as democracies. Nevertheless, we can conclude that if we are not close to a world with zero political transaction costs, there is no reason to expect democracies to achieve efficiency-enhancing institutional changes faster than authoritarian regimes.

Democracies as Systems that Ensure Political and Economic Stability

A recent restatement of the argument that democracies are inherently stable has come from Olson, who introduced the metaphor of stationary and roving bandits to analyse the predatory tendencies of states.[10]

In Olson's stylization, the worst conditions of rule are those where societies face the predation of rulers behaving like roving bandits. Roving bandits by definition take a short-term view and have no incentive to limit their plunder. Development outcomes are dire. Things improve markedly when rulers who are roving bandits settle down and become stationary bandits. Although still predatory, these rulers take a longer-term view because they will remain in place for a long time, and consequently they have an incentive to moderate their extraction. A high rate of extraction can shrink the economy to the extent that the rulers' 'tax' take over time actually falls. Since stationary bandits will want to maximize their tax take over time, they have an incentive to *reduce* the rate of taxation so that social output can rise, and the *total* tax they collect is maximized. While the higher social output is a great improvement, the rule of stationary bandits suffers from periodic crisis due to the absence of rules to deal with succession. The transition from one ruler to the next is marked by uncertainty and the frequent outbreak of civil war.

Democracies end this uncertainty and provide rules for the smooth transfer of power. In addition, democracies can result in a further reduction of taxation. Even though the majority can tax the minority, since the tax benefit has to be spread across the majority, each individual within the ruling group get very little and the incentive to organize taxation falls. The result is an even greater stability of property rights and political systems. An inherent problem with Olson's approach is that taxation is always seen as predatory above a minimum level required to provide basic public goods, so that it is always assumed that less taxation is better. Nonetheless, even in terms of Olson's own logic, there are limitations to his argument.

While Olson supported the emergence of democracies in developing countries, he was less sanguine about the role of democracy in advanced countries where democracies have matured. In the advanced countries he was more familiar with, Olson recognized that although democracy can theoretically limit the predation of the state, it could also create opportunities for *non-state* interest groups to increase their rent-seeking activities. Thus, in the United States, Olson saw democracy as a much more problematic system through which interest groups lobbied for special benefits to the detriment of the collective interest. He argued that the longer democracy operates, the higher the number of these special interest groups and the more sclerotic mature democracies become. Democracies occasionally require a shake-up to destroy the growing power of these special interest groups.[11] Indeed in Olson's view, the destruction of special interest groups in Germany and Japan before, during, and after the Second World War through a number of very undemocratic processes helped to explain the subsequent dynamism of these two economies in the post-war period.

Whatever we make of this particular explanation for the post-war successes of Germany and Japan, Olson is wrong to think that interest group-driven redistribution is a problem faced only by mature democracies. In fact, the factional competition that characterizes developing country democracies is, if anything, more intense than the interest group competition in advanced country democracies. The choice in developing countries is in fact between different combinations of predation, factionalism and clientelism. Movements towards or away from greater democratization can therefore have net effects that are very specific to the factional structures of particular countries. In some cases, democratization could reduce wasteful predation, in others it could result in greater waste by increasing factional rent-seeking activities. Moreover, Olson has no satisfactory explanation for why South Korea or Taiwan achieved economic and political stability in the 1960s and 1970s apart from the observation that they were stationary bandit states. However, other stationary bandit states failed to achieve this degree of success. Thus, in the case of developing country states no less than in advanced ones, we need to look more closely at the structure of interest groups and factions to be able to explain how democracy or authoritarianism worked to enhance or diminish economic and political stability.

The Evidence

From the very large body of evidence and empirical work in this area, the following presents some of the evidence that justifies questioning conventional wisdom. The first type of evidence comes from cross-sectional data on the economic characteristics of democratic and authoritarian countries. The one uncontested piece of evidence in an area where much of the empirical evidence and analysis is highly contested is that richer countries are more likely to be democratic than poorer ones. This has been emphatically demonstrated in many cross-sectional studies, including the extensive statistical study of 141 countries over the period 1950–1990 conducted by Przeworski *et al.* and by Barro in his work on economic growth.[12] Przeworski *et al.* show that, in the long run, per capita income is the best predictor of democracy, and that other possible variables, including, in particular, dominant religions, colonial and political history, and ethno-linguistic and religious fractionalization do not add much to the power of per capita income to predict the likelihood of democracy. Statistically, we are also more likely to observe high per capita incomes leading to democratization rather than the other way around.[13] However, when it comes to explaining why richer countries are more likely to be democratic, statistical analysis on its own offers much more limited insights. Przeworski *et al.* reject the simplistic modernization thesis that argues that democracy will follow once economic development has been achieved. Their argument against this position is based on the observation of a significant number of relatively rich countries that remain authoritarian. These contrary examples show there is no consistent internal mechanism that ensures a transition to democracy as countries become richer.

Instead, they propose a statistical selection mechanism that is more consistent with the historical observations. They suggest that when rich countries become democratic (through whatever mechanism) they have a higher probability of remaining democratic, while poorer countries who make an early transition to democracy are more likely to revert to authoritarianism.[14] This can explain why poor countries are statistically more likely to be authoritarian and rich countries more likely to be democratic, even without any mechanism to ensure that economic development will lead to a transition to democracy. Nevertheless, even if we say that rich countries are more likely to remain democratic regardless of how they become democratic, we still need to identify the factors that can explain why this should be the case. While the authors do not suggest specific mechanisms, they suggest that this could be because greater prosperity reduces the severity of distributive conflicts (which undermine democracy) and higher levels of education makes it easier to operate democratic procedures. But they agree that the mechanisms that make democracies in rich countries stable and democracies in developing countries vulnerable are not easy to identify with statistics alone.[15]

A second and very different type of evidence about the operation of democratic systems in developing countries is provided by comparative case studies. This kind of evidence does not allow the inclusion of every country for which we have data, in the way that cross-sectional regression analysis does. But what they lack in breadth, these case studies make up in depth. In particular, they allow hypotheses to be identified and tested using 'analytical induction', a method used to good effect in the work of Barrington Moore and his followers on the conditions enabling the emergence of democracies in different contexts.[16] Applied to contemporary developing countries, this approach suggests a very different set of issues affecting the interaction between democracy, markets and states that determines the nature of the relationship between democracy and development. Contemporary case study approaches to the study of democracy in developing countries provide a number of critical observations that define the starting point of our analysis.

First, they provide very consistent evidence that the politics of developing countries is dominated by patron–client factions. This is true for both democratic and authoritarian developing countries, implying that democracy in developing countries has features that are in general quite different from democracies in advanced countries. These features need to be understood if we are to elaborate the relationship between democracies in developing countries and the operation of markets and states relevant for understanding the prospects of development. Internal political stability in developing countries is maintained not primarily through fiscal policy, but through the largely off-budget and selective accommodation of factions organized along patron–client lines. Neither democracy nor authoritarianism appear to do away with the factional politics that underlie these processes but serve only to modify the processes of accommodation, the numbers of factions that are accommodated, the terms of accommodation, and the ways in which factional competition is organized.

The common features of this type of politics have been collectively described as patrimonialism, clientelism, patron–client politics, and factional politics. The common features include the personalization of politics by faction leaders and the organization of politics as a competition between factions. The personalization of leadership is not based on traditional deference or the greater susceptibility of developing country societies to charisma, but is a rather 'modern' phenomenon in that faction leaders offer payoffs to those who support them. In turn, they capture the resources for making these payoffs by mobilizing their supporters in factions. In India, arguably the most successful democracy in a developing country, the deep inter-penetration of formal politics with informal structures of networks and factions has been powerfully described by Harriss-White and by Jenkins.[17] In Africa, it used to be argued that neo-patrimonialism was due to the absence of democracy, and authoritarianism allowed the continuation of personalized politics and the use of informal sources of power by the 'big men'.[18] However, it is now more commonly recognized that neo-patrimonialism and patron–client networks have survived the transition to democracy in Africa, and they continue to operate with relatively slight modifications.[19]

Second, parallel to these 'informal' political features of developing countries are economic characteristics that set them apart from advanced economies. These characteristics include a larger 'informal' economy, widespread non-market accumulation processes (often described as primitive accumulation), and the use of state power to create a large range of rents that directly benefit the factions in power.[20] These economic characteristics of developing countries set them apart from advanced countries. While democracy or authoritarianism can modify some of these characteristics, democratic and authoritarian developing countries are not significantly different in terms of these characteristics.

The 'informal economy' describes activities that are not formally regulated by the state. These activities comprise as much as 80 per cent of the economy of the relatively highly regulated (and democratic) India.[21] This does not mean that large chunks of the economy are not regulated; it simply means that these areas are not regulated through the *formal* institutions of the state. These are precisely the areas where the regulatory and enforcement capacities of informal networks operating within and outside the state become critical for determining the types of economic activities that are viable and the ways in which rents are shared between producers, political factions and the formal state. This allows us to explain why entrepreneurs in developing countries are so willing to invest in factional political networks as an ongoing part of their normal commercial activities.

The use of political power in these ways to sustain accumulation in developing countries has attracted much attention from conventional economists who see this as evidence of rent-seeking and political corruption. However, these activities are so systematic and widespread that we should look for structural reasons that may explain these features of developing countries. Once again, democracy or authoritarianism appears at best to modify the nature of these relationships and the ways in which political power is exercised. But democracy does not result in a significant change in these economic characteristics – in particular, it does not ensure the elimination of property rights instability, rent-seeking, or political corruption in developing countries.[22]

Patron–Client Factions and Democracy in Developing Countries

Given the prevalence of patron–client politics in developing countries, we need to investigate the factors that could explain the dominance and the implications for democratization. The analysis of patron–client politics in developing countries has drawn heavily on the German sociologist Max Weber (1864–1920) in his analysis of modern bureaucratic states as a foil against which to compare and assess developing country realities. Weber saw bureaucratic rule as the most rational form of organizing the social order, paralleling capitalism as the most rational form of organizing the economy. Bureaucratic rule and capitalism are therefore complementary forces that drove the secular rationalization that Weber saw as the most significant trend in contemporary history. We will see later that the appropriateness of Weber's conception of capitalism for understanding the emerging capitalisms in contemporary developing countries is questionable.[23] But interestingly, even in terms of his own analysis, Weber saw a permanent tension between the logic of bureaucratic rule, which was inherently rational, and the logic of political leadership and charisma operating through democratic processes. This tension was unavoidable, and even necessary. It was indeed periodically necessary to revitalize bureaucratic rule by questioning and changing its objectives, without which it would have a tendency to ossify.[24] Weber's analysis is therefore deliberately 'antinomical', showing the inner contradictions within his ideal types.

Neo-Weberians looking at developing countries have often ignored these subtleties and concentrated instead on the checklist of ideal-typical characteristics that a modern state should possess, characteristics that are most strikingly absent in developing countries. These ideal-typical Weberian characteristics of the modern bureaucratic state include a formal, meritocratic bureaucratic structure that adheres to rules, is impersonal in its dealings with individual citizens, and represents a sharp separation of the private and public spheres. The operations of the typical developing country state in contrast are based on personalized exchanges between rulers and their factions, bureaucratic rules are regularly broken, and private interests are deeply penetrated in the public sphere represented by the bureaucracy. It appears that this could provide a compelling explanation of why a rational organization of social order does not appear to be taking place in developing countries. The absence of a rational bureaucratic structure could in turn explain why the development of capitalism has been impeded, as capitalism (in the Weberian conception) was the rational organization of the economic sphere. If the state was 'irrational' in its interventions in society, the development of capitalism could not but be affected.

The Neo-Patrimonial Analysis

The question that arises is why developing countries across the board should fail to meet the criteria of a Weberian bureaucratic state? Weber lived long before modern post-colonial developing countries emerged. His analysis was not about these countries at all, but rather about the contrast between 'rational' bureaucratic forms of governance seen in modern capitalism and *traditional* forms of authority in pre-capitalist societies. He identified patrimonial rule as one of the most important of these pre-capitalist forms of governance, where allegiance to a leader is based on personal loyalty and traditional legitimacy.[25] However, it has become clear that in modern developing countries, patrimonial rule is not based on traditional legitimacy but rather on modern forms of exchange between patrons and clients, where clients agree to provide political support to the patron in exchange for pay-offs that the patron can deliver by using political power to capture public resources. Based on this observation, Eisenstadt, Médard and others have developed the analysis of *neo-patrimonialism*, which seeks to explain the persistence of pre-modern state structures in developing countries, particularly in Africa.[26]

The key characteristic of the neo-patrimonial state is the personalization of power. The state is treated as an extension of the property of the leader, and the leader rules with the help of clients who get a pay-off for their support. Clearly, formal rules are now less important than the informal networks upon which the leader's power is based. Indeed, formal rules are regularly flouted and corruption is widespread. In this sense, the neo-patrimonial state is the antithesis of bureaucratic rationality. In contrast to Weber's analysis of patrimonialism based on traditional legitimacy, the theorists of neo-patrimonialism argue that the basis of this new form of rule is the ability of leaders to personalize their power and avoid accountability. The democratic process now acquires a significant and very different role in the new analysis that it did not have in Weber's original analysis. Far from political leadership (expressed through the democratic process or otherwise) periodically coming into conflict with norms of bureaucratic rule, democracy in the neo-patrimonial model is the mechanism for undermining personalized rule and thereby allowing the emergence of rational bureaucratic forms of rule. The latter is in turn necessary for the deepening of the rational capitalist form of economic organization. Democracy thus emerges as the process that drives the emergence of capitalism in a way that was never suggested by Weber. Variants of this mechanism also appear in good governance models that have become popular in policy circles in the post-Cold War period.[27]

The problem with the neo-Weberian analysis is that it assumes that patron-client politics in developing countries is based on the *intention* of rulers and factions to personalize politics and that these intentions do not have significant *structural* factors supporting them. Only if this assumption were true would it make sense to believe that subjecting the selection of rulers to greater transparency and competition would result in a weakening of personal political fiefdoms and the faction-based exercise of power. But, in fact, all the evidence of democratization in developing countries show that competition, transparency and electoral contests do very little to undermine the dominance of patron–client politics and of informal networks mediating the exercise of power. And since states remain informal, the extension of democracy does little to further the Weberian goal of constructing rational bureaucratic forms of rule.

Thus, the puzzle of patron–client politics remains to be explained, particularly since most neo-patrimonial analysts rightly argue that political relationships in contemporary developing countries are 'modern' in the sense that leaders and followers are recognizably rational, and neo-patrimonialism is not based on traditional deference or culture. Deference for leaders is rarely more than superficial in most developing countries, and in addition, wide variations in culture appear to have little effect on the salience of patron–client networks. Thus, the evidence, some of which we have referred to earlier, requires us to look for other factors that could explain the dominance of variants of patron–client political organizations in developing countries, both democratic and authoritarian.

At the general level, political competition involves political organizations and interests competing to achieve distribution of income and assets that favour them. But the nature of the competing political organizations and the types of political strategies they employ appear to be significantly different between advanced and developing countries and this needs to be explained. I argue that without resorting to the functionalism of modernization theory, we can identify powerful *economic* factors that ensure that patron–client politics is rational for both leaders and organizationally powerful constituencies in developing countries. The difference between this and modernization theory will be discussed later, but a little reflection on the structural differences between advanced and developing capitalist countries tells us why the strategies of democratic political players are likely to be very different in the two. In advanced countries, structural factors encourage the representation of generalized economic and class interests and the formulation of redistributive political demands within narrow bounds set by the limits of economic viability. In contrast, in developing countries, incentives favour the construction of pyramidal patron–client factions that compete for the capture of public resources in ways that are relatively unconstrained by economic viability considerations.

Political Competition in Advanced Capitalist Countries

The economic characteristics of advanced capitalist countries have systemic effects on the types of political organizations that are likely to develop and the redistributive strategies they are likely to follow. These characteristics include the following. First, the level of economic development of advanced capitalist countries means they have a dominant capitalist sector, and this has significant implications for politics. In these economies, the welfare of most people, even if they are not capitalists, depends on the health of the capitalist sector. If they are workers, their employment and wage growth depends directly on the growth of the capitalist sector. If they are private sector professionals, the purchasers of their services are most often capitalists, or workers whose spending power depends on the health of the capitalist sector. And if they are public sector workers or professionals, their wages and salaries come from taxation, which again depends on how well the capitalist sector is performing. Thus, even though the substance of democratic politics is necessarily about achieving a different distribution of income and consumption from the one that the market might otherwise have produced, parties and interest groups soon come to understand that their success in mobilizing their constituents and delivering to them depends on maintaining the viability of the capitalist economy.

Within these limits, there is, of course, much room for variation. But the self-interest of class and interest groups in advanced country democracies tends to ensure that their political competition does not damage the viability of the capitalist system. As a result, democratic politics remains broadly pro-capitalist even though capitalists are necessarily in a minority. This does not mean that the process of politics in these countries is always smooth. There may be serious disagreements about what is feasible, and occasionally there may be deep crises when economic viability is adversely affected. But since all groups and classes suffer from policies that result in a shrinkage of the capitalist sector, and since the latter has a shared set of requirements for profitability and viability, powerful feedback mechanisms set in to constrain the demands of political groups when they exceed the tolerance of the capitalist sector. This feedback is particularly constraining when thoroughly anti-capitalist political movements in advanced countries are weak or absent, as they have been for most of the post-Second World War period, and even more so in the post-Cold War period.

Second, a high degree of economic development in advanced countries also means that politically active groups can address their redistributive concerns by seeking to influence or control the significant fiscal budget and/or by amending the state's considerable regulatory powers (for instance in regulating the financial sector or through health and safety regulations). In practice, this has meant that redistributive goals have been pursued through marginal changes in tax and subsidy rates, and marginal changes in regulatory structures, subject to the constraint of maintaining capitalist viability. Given the significant share of national income that is taxed in advanced countries and the very large national incomes, as well as the considerable scope and enforcement capacities of state regulation, these strategies have offered big rewards to groups engaging in political activity. At the same time, since fiscal and regulatory policies benefit everyone who shares these interests (whether class, regional or sectoral), a public case can always be made for the proposed changes.

These characteristics ensure that redistributive agendas in advanced economies are likely to be organized around broadly based organizations that represent the economic interests of large groups of individuals, who, in turn, share common economic interests or perspectives due to similar class positions in production, regional locations, or occupations. The actual delivery of subsidies and the implementation of regulations through the bureaucracy can then be achieved through impersonal, transparent, and bureaucratic processes in the Weberian sense. This does not mean that violations of these norms do not happen in advanced countries. There are always going to be incentives for corruption, theft and nepotism. These violations can be dealt with by enforcing bureaucratic norms and allowing open and transparent political competition.

Third, and very importantly, while economic development allows certain types of redistributive goals to be achieved through the budget and through regulatory reform, it also rules *out* certain types of redistributive activity. This is because economic development means that most people who own assets or earn an income do so from economic activities that are viable. This means that not only do they produce economic surpluses, but that the surpluses are large enough to pay for the protection of the assets or the economic activities in question. This protection is typically organized not just through the employment of private protection for assets and activities (such as in the form of guards and lawyers). In addition, the protection of assets in advanced countries is primarily ensured through the state, which collects significant taxes from asset owners and income earners and uses these resources to provide an effective protection of valuable assets and activities.

Economists typically describe advanced countries as having stable property rights and a rule of law, with relatively low expropriation risk.[28] While the statistical link between these variables and economic development is strong, the direction of causality is difficult to establish using statistics alone. The interesting question is whether property rights in advanced countries are stable because redistributive coalitions are sufficiently responsible not to cross the line between redistribution and expropriation, or are attempts at expropriation prevented by advanced country states because they have the effective power to enforce property rights and protect activities as a result of collecting significant amounts of taxes? In reality, both are likely to be true, but the voluntary responsibility of redistributive coalitions is unlikely to be sustained if coalitions knew they could get away with expropriation. Indeed, the economic ability of the state to enforce property rights and prevent expropriation is likely to be more important the more open the competition for redistribution. Rich countries can afford to have open democracies because the limits to expropriation are set not only by the self-interest of most coalitions (as discussed earlier) but also by the strong enforcement capacities of well-funded states.

Political Competition in Developing Countries

In contrast, the conditions that enable transparent and impersonal redistributive political activity in advanced country democracies are almost entirely absent in developing countries. The less developed the country, the more significant is its divergence from the advanced country characteristics described earlier. In upper middle-income developing countries, a growing number of characteristics of advanced country economies begin to emerge and in these countries, the structural differences that affect politics are less stark compared to advanced countries. In our discussion, we will not distinguish between poorer and more advanced developing countries, although there is clearly a grey area between the two, taking into account the moderately high levels of economic development in middle-income countries.

The first contrast is that in developing countries, capitalism is not (yet) the dominant economic system and so the feedback mechanisms from the economic requirements of this sector to the organization of political demands are much weaker. While in the very long-term a decline in the growth prospects of the capitalist sector will impinge upon the income prospects of most people, in the short or even medium-term, a decline in the capitalist sector may not even be perceived by most people. This is because the majority of the population continue to live in subsistence agriculture or to survive through informal activities like petty production and trade, and their dependence on the performance of the capitalist sector is indirect at best. There are, therefore, much weaker constraints on the organization of mass movements based on populist demands as the participants in these movements do not see any direct effect on themselves of an immediate decline in the country's economic prospects.

Second, economic underdevelopment means that not only is the size of the national income small, the share of the formal capitalist sector is also small. Therefore, compared to advanced countries, the fiscal regime of the typical developing country taxes a smaller share of a much smaller national income. Indeed, in poorer developing countries, the budget is in deficit after paying the salaries of public employees, and even in the relatively more developed of the developing countries, the budget is in deficit after paying for the essential infrastructural investments. In most cases, much of public investment is financed by borrowing or by aid. Not surprisingly, the budget is usually not the primary focus of redistributive political activity in developing countries. Nor do redistributive coalitions primarily seek to achieve their goals by modifying the state's regulatory rules since much of the economy is in fact unregulated given the limited scope of the modern (capitalist) sector.

It is therefore not at all surprising that redistributive strategies in developing countries are typically not defined in terms of the interests of broad economic groups that could be met by transparent changes in fiscal or regulatory rules. Rather, political entrepreneurs in developing countries who want to achieve redistribution in their favour will rationally have to look for other strategies. Political entrepreneurs in most countries are likely to come primarily from the middle classes, but middle classes in developing countries have some special characteristics. Unlike their equivalents in advanced countries, who are mostly professionals and whose economic interests are closely tied to the capitalist sector, middle classes in developing countries consist of a collection of classes that can collectively be described as the 'intermediate' classes.[29] Political entrepreneurs from different sections of the intermediate classes are unlikely to share common interests or to be constrained by the fate of the capitalist sector. The only viable redistributive strategy for developing country political entrepreneurs in the absence of any fiscal or regulatory space is to organize enough organizational muscle to be able to capture resources through a combination of fiscal, off-budget and even illegal means.

The intermediate classes include the educated classes with college or university education, the petty bourgeoisie, particularly those in the informal sector, and middling to rich peasants. This middle strata may be numerically small (possibly 10 to 30 per cent of the population) and economically weak (compared to emerging capitalists), but in terms of legitimacy and organizational power, they are collectively the most powerful political group in most developing countries. This group produces the political entrepreneurs who lead both organized and informal politics in developing countries. Authoritarian regimes have to deal with them and accommodate the most powerful and vociferous groups. Equally, without their leadership and participation, electoral politics would be impossible. In practice, what we see most frequently in the democratic domain are contests between factions led and dominated by members of the intermediate classes. And even authoritarian regimes have to include enough factions led by intermediate class leaders within the ruling coalition to achieve political stability.

The economic structure of developing countries can also help explain the typical pyramidal structure of the factions led by the intermediate classes that emerge to participate in redistributive politics. As we have already pointed out, the intermediate classes consist of a vast group of people of differing social and economic status. Many of them are underemployed but organizationally powerful. Political entrepreneurs constructing factions can be expected to prefer faction members lower than themselves in social and economic status as these individuals will expect less in terms of payoffs for participating in the faction and lending their organizational weight to it. At the same time, faction leaders want to maximize their organizational power by including the most aggressive individuals and sub-factions, without whose support faction leaders will be unable to achieve their objectives.

Pyramidal patron–client networks are then likely to emerge as the most rational form of organization for faction leaders at all levels of the social structure. Faction leaders promise rewards to their clients based on their organizational support, who in turn mobilize those below them, all the way down to foot soldiers who may only be mobilized during elections, strikes, riots and other political events, in return for very small pay-offs. But factional membership and activity is rational at all levels of the faction since the pay-offs available from the faction are always higher than those available from alternative types of political activity given the non-existence of budgetary resources and other economic features of the developing country economy referred to earlier. The difference between democratic and authoritarian regimes in this respect is the number of factions that the ruling coalition needs to accommodate for achieving the minimum political stability and the types of competition through which insiders and outsiders are selected. The ruling coalition is always a coalition of many different sub-factions, and irrespective of the type of regime, the ruling group has to make calculations of who to include and exclude using the same logic of cost and benefit as individual faction leaders.[30]

What political factions seek is not the construction of a coalition that can mobilize votes to allow a transparent renegotiation of taxes and subsidies, but a coalition that can mobilize organizational power at the lowest cost to the faction leader, to achieve a redistribution of assets and incomes using a combination of legal, quasi-legal, or even illegal methods. The organizational power of the faction is then used either directly to capture state power or to force an accommodation in the form of payoffs from the factions who are currently controlling the state. The faction's access to economic resources either in the form of revenue or in the power to grab valuable economic resources legally or otherwise is then used to benefit faction members all the way down the pyramid, though the pay-offs may be very unequal for different levels of the faction.

While factions may use generalized arguments based on class, region or interest in its public discourse, no one in society is under any illusion that the faction is out to look after itself at the least cost in terms of paying off voters and others who need to be mobilized occasionally. When factions do not deliver on these generalized aims, broader social constituencies may grumble but they do not really expect anyone to deliver on the publicly stated general social goals. However, if factions cannot deliver acceptable pay-offs to faction members, the leaders are likely to get into serious trouble. Factions rarely fear a general public revolt, given that no other political organization can deliver what the public wants. What factions actually fear is that their sub-factions may be bribed away by other factions and that the coalition may crumble. Indeed, this often happens and accounts for the frequent changes of government in developing countries that usually lead to no discernible changes in government policies, but do lead to different sets of individuals making money in turn. Given the opportunistic nature of factional membership and the shifting offers and counter-offers made by different factional leaders, it is possible to explain the extreme volatility in the factional politics of developing countries in a context where government policies are often remarkably constant.

Finally, developing countries are also different from advanced countries in a very significant respect: most of the economic assets and activities of a developing country (land, or traditional economic activities in the informal sector) are barely viable in that they produce very small surpluses, and, in general, do not produce enough to pay for their effective protection. It is difficult to explain why property rights are uniformly weak in every developing country if we ignore the fact that the effective protection of property rights is very expensive, and developing countries typically have pre-modern economic systems that do not use existing assets in ways that can generate large surpluses to pay for their protection. This has significant implications for the strategies that our pyramidal patron–client factions are likely to employ in pursuit of their redistributive agendas. If property rights and economic activities are not in general effectively protected in developing countries, they can easily become targets for the redistributive activity of coalitions seeking redistribution.

If we combine these observations, we find a list of developing country characteristics that are very different from advanced countries. First, compared with the coalitions in advanced countries, redistributive coalitions in developing countries enjoy much greater latitude in the redistributive strategies they can follow because there is much weaker political feedback from the capitalist sector. Given this weak feedback from the productive sector, the strategies employed by redistributive coalitions in developing countries can vary very widely, from growth-enhancing strategies in some cases to growth-destroying strategies in others.

Second, redistributive coalitions in developing countries have strong incentives to try and achieve redistribution through means that go well beyond marginal changes in taxation, spending, or regulation. This is because the relatively limited taxes paid by the small capitalist sector and the limited role of economic regulation cannot accommodate redistributive demands, however limited. Since public resources for accommodating broadly defined interests simply do not exist, political entrepreneurs seek to organize powerful groups that can assist their political accumulation and redistribution strategies. Given the structure of the intermediate classes, these groups are most likely to be the pyramidal patron–client factions that we observe.

Third, developing countries invariably have weak protection for property rights across the economy, which opens up a wide range of activities and assets to expropriation attempts. Even if assets are not totally expropriated by powerful redistributive coalitions, owners of assets, as well as many income earners, find they have to purchase protection from powerful factions if they are to continue gainful economic activities. Developing countries can thus range from situations close to anarchy, where neo-patrimonialism acquires characteristics quite similar to warlordism, to the relatively more normal variety of factionalism where property rights are unstable but are protected by patron–client coalitions at a price.

Thus, the economic structures of developing countries create strong incentives for the emergence of the very phenomenon that neo-Weberians identify as the variable explaining underdevelopment, namely the proliferation of patron–client networks, and the domination of personalized politics, variously described as clientelism, patrimonialism, and neo-patrimonialism. To that extent, the neo-Weberian argument stands reality on its head. The argument that neo-patrimonialism has to be addressed *first* in order to assist development sets developing countries an impossible target. To then argue that *democratization* will assist in achieving the weakening of neo-patrimonial relationships is even more problematic as a policy prescription because the presence or absence of democracy has very little to do with the powerful incentives that drive the organization of patron–client politics. Indeed this approach can explain why patron–client politics continues to survive and thrive in *democratic* developing countries, an observation that has been referred to earlier in the section on evidence.

Conclusion

To sum up, both states and markets operate somewhat differently in advanced and developing countries. Developing country states are significantly penetrated by patron–client factions characterized by personalized leadership and the objectives of factional rent capture. Developing country markets are characterized by the underdevelopment of the capitalist sector, and the use of factional political power to protect assets and to support accumulation strategies based on the capture of assets using political power. These empirical observations are relevant for explaining the vulnerability of democracies in developing countries, for analysing the conditions under which democracies can survive and where it faces serious constraints, and for discussing the implications of democratic processes for economic development.

In contrast to the functionalist aspects of modernization theory, our analysis of the economics of developing countries suggests that while democracy is vulnerable in developing countries and is likely to operate very differently from advanced countries, democracy is not the *cause* of underdevelopment. Conversely, authoritarianism is not functionally required for development. In this sense, our analysis is fundamentally different from modernization theory. Instead, the argument advanced here is that variants of patron–client politics are likely to characterize both democratic and authoritarian regimes in developing countries. If regime change in a particular country is observed to result in a change in performance, the causes have to be sought in the structure of patron–client factions in the particular country and the ways in which patterns of accommodation and competition are affected by democracy or its absence. The effects of democratization can therefore vary from country to country. In some countries, democratization could boost development, in others the reverse.[31] But general results about the effects of democratization are certain to be misleading.

This analysis also challenges some of the core results of the neo-patrimonial analysis developed by neo-Weberians, and adopted in different forms in the good governance approach. In contrast to that analysis, this argument suggests that democratization does not undermine patrimonial politics. This is because the organization of personalized patron–client factions is driven not by the absence of democracy but, rather, by structural features of the economies of developing countries that make modern welfare-driven redistributive politics unviable. Nevertheless, it could be argued that since democracy is an end in itself, the support for democratization from the neo-Weberian analysis is desirable. However, this does not necessarily follow. We are not just referring to the selective way in which democratization is likely to be used by Western countries to target some developing country regimes and not others depending on their own geo-political interests. There is a much more serious concern.

While democratization is very desirable, the economies of developing countries are such that democratization is unlikely to deliver real benefits to a broad range of social groups till a minimum level of economic development has been achieved. The developmental challenge is how to accelerate that transition, and democratization, however desirable in even the most unpromising contexts, has little to do with accelerating the social transformations that developing countries require. The pace of the necessary social transformation depends on how the competition between factions affects the emergence of a capitalist sector, the acquisition of advanced technologies by that sector, and its ability to begin to compete in global markets. Historical examples show that a number of different patterns of patron–client competition are compatible with the rapid emergence of such a capitalist sector, while many other patterns of factional competition act as a brake on this transformation.[32] If accelerating the transformation was our objective, these patterns of factional politics should have been the target of analysis and of internal policy since they do not correlate in any simple way with the democracy–authoritarianism divide. The danger is that by prioritizing a series of reforms that have little to do with accelerating the development of a productive economy, policy-makers in developing countries are being encouraged to expend scarce reform capacities in areas that are unlikely to deliver results in the years to come.[33] The outcome is likely to be not only slow growth in living standards in very poor economies, but also a much more serious disenchantment with what democracy has to offer, and a possible return to equally unpromising strategies of authoritarianism. A more realistic analysis of the operation of democracy in developing countries is necessary to counter both the excessive faith on democratization as well as to challenge the functionalist defence of authoritarianism coming from variants of modernization theory.

NOTES

1. Kenneth J. Arrow, *Social Choice and Individual Values*, rev. ed. (New York: John Wiley, 1963), Dennis C. Mueller, *Public Choice II: A Revised Edition of Public Choice* (Cambridge: Cambridge University Press, 1989).
2. Jean Drèze and Amartya K. Sen, *India: Economic Development and Social Opportunity* (New Delhi: Oxford University Press, 1995).
3. Raaj K. Sah and Joseph Stiglitz, 'Committees, Hierarchies and Polyarchies', *Economic Journal*, Vol.98, No.391 (1988), pp.451–70.
4. Jean Drèze and Amartya K. Sen, *Hunger and Public Action* (Oxford: Oxford University Press, 1989).
5. Douglass C. North, *Institutions, Institutional Change and Economic Performance* (Cambridge: Cambridge University Press, 1990), esp. pp.107–10.
6. Mushtaq H. Khan, 'State Failure in Developing Countries and Strategies of Institutional Reform', in Bertil Tungodden, Nicholas Stern and Ivar Kolstad (eds), *Toward Pro-Poor Policies: Aid Institutions and Globalization* (Oxford: Oxford University Press and World Bank, 2004).

7. North (note 5), pp.48–51.
8. Mushtaq H. Khan, 'State Failure in Weak States: A Critique of New Institutionalist Explanations', in John Harriss, Janet Hunter and Colin M. Lewis (eds), *The New Institutional Economics and Third World Development* (London: Routledge, 1995).
9. Rob Jenkins, *Democratic Politics and Economic Reform in India* (Cambridge: Cambridge University Press, 2000).
10. Mancur Olson, 'Dictatorship, Democracy and Development', in Mancur Olson and Satu Kähkönen (eds), *A Not-so-Dismal Science: A Broader View of Economies and Societies* (Oxford: Oxford University Press, 2000).
11. Mancur Olson, *The Rise and Decline of Nations* (London: Yale University Press, 1982).
12. Adam Przeworski, Michael E. Alvarez, José Antonio Cheibub and Fernando Limongi, *Democracy and Development: Political Institutions and Well-Being in the World, 1950–1990* (Cambridge: Cambridge University Press, 2000), pp.78–88; Robert J. Barro, *Determinants of Economic Growth: A Cross-Country Empirical Study* (Cambridge, MA: MIT Press, 1997), pp.61–2.
13. Ross Burkhart and Michael Lewis-Beck, 'Comparative Democracy: The Economic Development Thesis', *American Political Science Review*, Vol.88, No.4 (1994), pp.903–10.
14. Przeworski *et al.* (note 12), pp.92–117.
15. Ibid., p.101.
16. Barrington Moore, *Social Origins of Dictatorship and Democracy* (Harmondsworth: Penguin, 1991); Dietrich Rueschemeyer, Evelyne H. Stephens and John D. Stephens, *Capitalist Development and Democracy* (Oxford: Polity, 1992).
17. Barbara Harriss-White, *India Working: Essays on Society and Economy* (Cambridge: Cambridge University Press, 2003); Jenkins (note 9).
18. Jean-François Médard, 'Corruption in the Neo-Patrimonial States of Sub-Saharan Africa', in Arnold J. Heidenheimer and Michael Johnston (eds), *Political Corruption: Concepts and Contexts*, 3rd ed. (New Brunswick, NJ: Transaction Publishers, 2002).
19. Patrick Chabal and Jean-Pascal Daloz, *Africa Works: Disorder as Political Instrument* (Oxford and Indianapolis: James Currey and Indiana University Press, 1999).
20. Mushtaq H. Khan and K.S. Jomo (eds), *Rents, Rent-Seeking and Economic Development: Theory and Evidence in Asia* (Cambridge: Cambridge University Press, 2000); Harriss-White (note 17).
21. Harriss-White (note 17), pp.3–16.
22. Ibid., particularly pp.43–71 and 239–47.
23. For more on this see also Mushtaq H. Khan, 'State Failure in Developing Countries and Strategies of Institutional Reform', and idem, 'Rent-seeking as Process', in idem and K.S. Jomo (eds), *Rents, Rent-Seeking and Economic Development: Theory and Evidence in Asia* (Cambridge: Cambridge University Press, 2000).
24. Wolfgang J. Mommsen, *The Political and Social Theory of Max Weber* (Oxford: Polity Press, 1989), esp. pp.109–20.
25. Max Weber, *Economy and Society: An Outline of Interpretive Sociology*, ed. Guenther Roth and Claus Wittich, Vol. II (Berkeley, CA: University of California Press, 1978), pp.1006–1110.
26. Médard (note 18); Samuel N. Eisenstadt, *Traditional Patrimonialism and Modern Neo-Patrimonialism* (London: Sage, 1973).
27. See Mushtaq H. Khan, 'Evaluating the Emerging Palestinian State: "Good Governance" versus "Transformation Potential"', in Mushtaq H. Khan, George Giacaman and Inge Amundsen (eds), *State Formation in Palestine: Viability and Governance during a Social Transformation* (London: RoutledgeCurzon, 2004), particularly pp.18–35 and Khan, 'State Failure in Developing Countries' (note 23), for discussions of the good governance and neo-patrimonial models.
28. Christopher Clague, Philip Keefer, Stephen Knack and Mancur Olson, 'Democracy, Autocracy and the Institutions Supportive of Economic Growth', in Christopher Clague (ed), *Institutions and Economic Development: Growth and Governance in Less-Developed and Post-Socialist Countries* (Baltimore, MD: The Johns Hopkins University Press, 1997); North (note 5).
29. Intermediate classes are classes that are not asset-rich to the extent that their incomes are primarily from rents, profits, interest or other components of the economic surplus, nor are they so asset-poor that their incomes primarily come from labour. See Mushtaq H. Khan, 'Class, Clientelism and Communal Politics in Bangladesh', in K.N. Panikkar, Terence J. Byres and Utsa Patnaik (eds), *The Making of History: Essays Presented to Irfan Habib* (New Delhi: Tulika, 2000) for a discussion and contrast with the definition of intermediate classes coming from the economist Michal Kalecki (1899–1970). The intermediate classes dominate the politics of developing countries because of their organizational power and social legitimacy. Their roots can usually be traced back to colonial strategies of developing

a local administrative class to manage the colony. See also Atul Kohli, 'Where Do High Growth Political Economies Come From? The Japanese Lineage of Korea's "Developmental State"', *World Development*, Vol. 22, No. 9 (1994), pp.1269–93.

30. See Mushtaq H. Khan, 'Fundamental Tensions in the Democratic Compromise', *New Political Economy*, Vol.7, No.2 (2002), pp.275–7 and Khan, 'Class, Clientelism' (note 29), for more details on the rational choices that faction leaders and followers are making.

31. For a more detailed analysis of the effects of different types of patron-client structures see Khan, 'Rent-seeking as Process' (note 23).

32. Ibid. pp.89–104.

33. For a detailed analysis of what this social transformation entails, see Khan, 'State Failure in Developing Countries' (note 23).

Manuscript accepted for publication August 2005.

Address for correspondence: Mushtaq H. Khan, School of Oriental and African Studies, University of London, Thornhaugh Street, Russell Square, London, WC1H 0XG, UK. E-mail: <MK17@soas.ac.uk>.

Social Rights, Courts and Constitutional Democracy: Poverty and Welfare Rights in the United States

WILLIAM E. FORBATH

Most of the world's constitutions include three kinds of rights: civil, political and social. You will find all three kinds in the charter documents of the United Nations. But the US Constitution sets out no 'social rights'. Consult the US Supreme Court; it will confirm that the constitution's 'majestic generalities', like 'liberty' and 'equal protection of the laws' confer no 'affirmative rights', no right to welfare or housing, no right to a minimally adequate education. No less than other nations, however, the United States needs social rights to make good on the promises of constitutional democracy. Constitutional democracy is impossible without some limits on social and economic inequality. Poverty, chronic joblessness, a renaissance of sweat shops, a lack of education and basic social goods like health care and housing: Americans thus afflicted cannot participate on anything like a roughly equal footing in the political community nor in the world of work and opportunity. The 'consent of the governed' is a hoax in a system that allows such savage inequality as ours. Yet 'social rights' and 'social citizenship' sound oxymoronic to Americans today. Public social provision stands outside the dignifying aura of citizenship. 'Welfare' is seen as a ground of disrespect, a threat to citizenship and equal standing, not their realization.

Americans forget. Thanks to Franklin Roosevelt and the New Deal, the vocabulary of social and economic rights was an American export in the 1940s, dispatched
from Washington to influence post-war international charters and European constitutions. Again in the 1960s and1970s, American courts were in the vanguard of judicial elaboration and enforcement of social rights. Today's US Supreme Court would
have you think that social rights and the solicitude for them in several of the world's
great constitutional courts are foreign to American constitutional experience. That is
wrong. Hundreds of social rights cases were decided in the 1960s and 1970s and
beyond, producing remedial schemes comparable to many now under construction
abroad. What is true, though, is that the current federal courts' hostility reflects the
broader disillusionment with the New Deal and the welfare state, as these are understood in the United States today.

What is to be done? What can Americans and others learn from the career of
social and economic rights in twentieth-century American constitutional theory and
practice? Only by situating past thinking and practice in the context of the institutional constraints, social movements, and political moments that shaped them can
we appreciate their distinctive insights and achievements – and their limitations
and blind spots. This account briefly offers such a situated account of the intellectual,
judicial, and grass-roots adventures of the 'welfare rights movement' of the 1960s and
1970s, with an eye to current debates about the possibilities and limits of courts and
constitutionalism as vehicles for promoting social rights. It engages with two programmatic alternatives. Call the first a right to welfare or to a basic income or a guaranteed social minimum; and call the second a right to decent work or employment-
based social citizenship. This essay offers some reflections about the practical and
moral promises and pitfalls of these two alternatives, with particular attention to
the role of courts and legal advocacy.

Welfare and the War on Poverty

Background: The New Deal

The welfare rights movement was a product of President John Kennedy's and President Lyndon Johnson's 1960s War on Poverty, the first social movement of poor
Americans deliberately spawned by a national administration to assail state and
local government policies and agencies. The Office of Economic Opportunity was
the command centre of the national War on Poverty. It created Community Action
Agencies, and alongside them, it created the Legal Services Organization (LSO). In
addition to law offices in the inner cities, the LSO funded a handful of law school-
based back-up centres. A great portion of the work of these agencies and inner-city
law offices involved getting poor people to apply for welfare and attacking the
social and legal barriers to their receiving it. Centuries-old restrictions were broken
down by a combination of civic unrest and federally funded organizing and litigation.

Constitutional scholars see the origins of the constitutional welfare rights idea in
the 1960s Supreme Court's case law and that Court's new solicitude toward the
nation's poor. But why was 'welfare' the terrain on which 1960s community activists,

federal policy-makers, and legal advocates and scholars came to wage their 'War on Poverty'? The answer lies in the constraints and opportunities created by inherited statutory, institutional, and ideological frameworks – the results of the victories and defeats of earlier efforts to forge a more substantive and 'social' array of citizenship rights.

Put baldly, it was the defeat of key New Deal reforms in the 1940s that deprived 1960s advocates of broader channels down which to try to nudge the Court's solicitude for the poor. Franklin Roosevelt's famous 1944 'second Bill of Rights' set forth not welfare but decent work and universal social insurance as the economic rights essential to free and equal citizenship in the twentieth century, but Roosevelt's vaunted rights met defeat at the hands of Jim Crow – the American South's subjugation and disenfranchisement of its black citizens. Measures instituting rights to full employment, decent work and social provision for all Americans enjoyed broad support; yet they expired in the New Deal Congress, doomed by the hammer lock that oligarchic Southern lawmakers enjoyed by dint of numbers, seniority and key committee chairs. Southern Democrats joined with conservative Republicans to block a broad social rights agenda, including bills to enact national health insurance, to remedy the many gaps in the 1935 Social Security Act, and to achieve full employment. Thus, at the same moment that Britain was completing construction of its post-war welfare state, the Solid South halted construction of social citizenship in America.

If they had voted the wishes of the region's disenfranchised black and poor white majority, congressional Democrats from the South would have supported these measures. Thus, in terms of constitutional history, the fate of social rights in 1940s America was sealed by the fate of political rights over the previous half century. In the face of the Constitution's bar on race-based disenfranchisement, the Southern state governments in the 1890s and 1900s had disenfranchised black citizens through such racially 'neutral' measures as the poll tax and literacy tests. From the Southern oligarchs' perspective, these had the additional benefit of also disenfranchising a majority of the region's poor whites. And the US Supreme Court, Congress and the Executive acquiesced. The upshot was a reactionary core, the 'Solid South', at the heart of Roosevelt's New Deal coalition.

Hailing from an impoverished region, many southern Democrats in Congress had been staunch supporters of the early New Deal. Even then, however, they insisted on decentralized local administration and local (as opposed to national) standard setting of all labour measures, and they demanded that key bills, including those guaranteeing the right to organize, exclude the main categories of southern labour. By allying with northern Republicans, or by threatening to do so, they stripped all the main pieces of 1930s New Deal legislation of any design or provision that threatened the separate southern labour market and its distinctive meld of class and caste relations, its racial segmentation, and its low wages. Keeping blacks dependent on local labour markets and poor relief was the principal reason for the segmented and caste-ridden system of social provision and labour rights bequeathed by the New Deal.

A quarter-century later, this partial, patchwork system underpinned a fairly robust private welfare state of job security, pensions, and health insurance for organized workers in core sectors of the industrial economy. But that meld of public and private rights excluded most African Americans, whose anger exploded in all the large cities of the North, where millions of southern blacks had moved over the preceding decades to escape Southern apartheid and rural unemployment. For them, public assistance, primarily Aid to Families with Dependent Children (AFDC), stood as the sole federal protection against poverty.

Aid to Families with Dependent Children

Created by the Social Security Act of 1935, originally titled Aid to Dependent Children (ADC) and renamed AFDC in the 1950s, the federal ADC descended from the state-based Mothers' Pensions programmes of the early twentieth century, themselves a modern variant of the age-old practice of giving poor relief to 'deserving widows'.[1] Like the other branches of the Social Security Act, ADC was drafted to propitiate the South. The states could determine AFDC benefits levels, and local administrators enjoyed vast discretion in making eligibility determinations.[2]

Local administrators used that discretion to buttress low-wage labour markets and to exercise other kinds of disciplinary power. In the South, for example, AFDC officials deemed poor black women 'employable mothers', and kept them off the rolls when their labour was needed in the cotton fields.[3] More generally, AFDC payments in the South and elsewhere were kept appreciably below official poverty levels. And throughout the nation, local administrators in the early 1960s still vigorously enforced man-in-the-house rules. Through home visits, unannounced night-time searches, and the like, they removed from the rolls any woman found to be associating with a man, especially if he seemed to live in her house. In this fashion, welfare officers prevented public monies from supporting 'immoral women' and 'unsuitable mothers'; at the same time, they kept poor men from exploiting AFDC to escape any of the rigours of the low-wage labour market.[4] Even for its target universe of impoverished single parent families, AFDC reached a tiny fraction of the whole. Most did not even apply; of those who did, poverty-stricken newcomers to a locale met almost certain rejection. Since colonial times, wayfaring paupers had been 'warned off' and forcibly excluded by the custodians of poor relief. Throughout the country, local custodians of AFDC carried on a modern version of this practice. In New York, for example, the very fact that you applied for welfare was presumptive proof of why you had come to the city. Rejected as ineligible, instead of welfare, you and your offspring got tickets on a Greyhound bus bound for home.[5]

It was this separate, decentralized, and deeply gendered benefits programme, stamped with many of the centuries-old degradations of poor relief, that welfare rights organizers, advocates, and attorneys sought to transform into a dignifying right to a guaranteed income.

The Welfare Rights Movement

Fostered by the War on Poverty, the welfare rights movement of the 1960s was unique in the annals of American reform. Never before had poor African American women formed the rank and file of a nationally organized social movement. The movement departed from the vocabulary of reform bequeathed by earlier movements for social and economic justice. It broke the links these older movements had forged between work and citizenship. Like them, the welfare rights movement claimed decent income as a right; unlike them, it did not tie this right to waged work. Generations of reformers had constructed their ideals of economic justice for the poor and working classes in a gendered fashion, around the workingman/citizen; decent income and social provision belonged, as of right, to (presumptively white male) waged workers, and to their economic dependents. Poor black women had always toiled outside their homes,[6] but they had never been welcomed into the producers' republic of earlier reformers. By the 1960s poor black women had had enough experience in urban labour markets to know that decent jobs were hard to find, and enough experience with workfare programmes to think them coercive and demeaning. Theirs was a consumers' republic.[7] 'Give Us Credit for Being Americans', read the National Welfare Rights Organization's (NWRO) placards demanding Sears credit cards for welfare recipients.[8] For them a guaranteed adequate income was an unconditional citizenship right, essential to equal respect and an appropriate touchstone of equality in an affluent America.

This rupture with the past was both a strength and a limit of the NWRO. It highlighted the coercive and gendered aspects of older employment-based ideals of economic and distributive justice. Gaining welfare as a matter of right would relieve unwarranted suffering and indignity. But it would not do enough to help poor African Americans make their way into a shared social destiny of work and opportunity. Without other enabling rights to – or at least concerted public and private provision for – training, decent work and childcare, welfare rights risked modernizing the badges and incidents of racial and economic subordination instead of abolishing them. Mimicking AFDC also led to the absence of poor men in a movement that claimed to represent the nation's poor and their needs. It led to a rights rhetoric that downplayed the disappearance of decently paid unskilled industrial jobs from the nation's old industrial regions and centre cities.[9] Welfare rights risked saddling poor African Americans with a new variant of the old racist imagery of blacks as idle and dependent.

But the NWRO played the hand that was dealt it. Perhaps only by mimicking AFDC and building on its provisions could a social movement of the poorest, most powerless Americans have been forged. By making AFDC-eligible women the movement's constituents, welfare rights organizers had something to offer the rank and file, and the rank and file developed a sense of efficacy and entitlement by gaining their demands from the local welfare departments. Likewise, AFDC provided a basis for substantial gains through litigation.

Welfare Rights in the Courts

Statutory and Historical Interpretations

American constitutional scholars today remember a handful of constitutional decisions bearing on welfare rights, but we tend to forget the hundreds of statutory cases that dramatically broadened eligibility standards and went a remarkable distance toward transforming a grant-in-aid to the states to be administered as meanly as local officialdom saw fit, into a no-strings and no-stigmas national right to welfare.[10] These cases saw the Supreme Court and the lower federal courts undertake dozens of remarkable doctrinal innovations and boldly revisionist readings of statutory text and history.[11] The whole push of these developments was reflected in the courts' repeated insistence that public assistance for all the nation's needy was, in the Supreme Court's words, a 'basic commitment', not charity or largesse, but a right.

The Court recognized a private right of action against the state welfare agencies that administered AFDC,[12] revising or ignoring jurisdictional rules that seemed to bar the way,[13] and spurning the conventional remedy of federal funding cut-offs in favour of injunctive relief.[14] Above all, the Court shoved aside the view, shared by judges, welfare administrators, and members of Congress alike for the first 30 years of AFDC's existence, that under AFDC the states had authority to run their own programmes, imposing such conditions and standards as they chose, subject only to a handful of limitations listed in the national statute.[15] State and local autonomy over the administration of federal relief had been the southern Democrats' sine qua non, and, as we know, the architects of the 1935 Social Security Act, of which AFDC was a part, had provided it. In place of the wide berth they had left for state discretion, the Court created a new presumption: 'a heavy burden lay on state lawmakers and administrators to justify any exclusion, test or condition that deviated from the principle of "actual need"'.[16] LSO attorneys persuaded the federal courts to embrace this presumption and to wield it against hundreds of state rules excluding would-be AFDC recipients.[17] Within the federal statutory categories, the federal courts in the 1960s and early 1970s proved extraordinarily willing to treat welfare under AFDC as a right of all needy individuals.

The leading statutory case was *King v. Smith*,[18] in which the Supreme Court struck down an Alabama 'man-in-the-house' eligibility rule. Using this rule, Alabama had dropped 16,000 children − 90 per cent of them black − from its welfare rolls. The three-judge court below had invalidated the rule as unconstitutional race discrimination.[19] At oral argument, however, plaintiff's LSO attorney sought a non-constitutional ruling based, instead, on statutory construction. 'If the decision goes off as the lower court's did, then very little will have been accomplished. Even if we win in Alabama, HEW [the US Department of Health, Education and Welfare] will not stop similar practices in other states [where man-in-the-house rules had no such racially discriminatory purpose or effect].'[20] A statutory holding that did not hinge on the constitutional norm of racial equality 'would give us all we wanted',[21] providing 'a way in which the narrowest of rulings would have the broadest of implications ... 'Give us instead',[22] counsel asked the Court speaking for the NWRO rank-and-file, 'a decision interpreting the Social Security Act as having rejected the concept of a worthy and an unworthy poor'.[23]

And the Court did so, giving welfare rights attorneys a reading of the act that would shape AFDC case law for the next two decades.[24] In the face of legislative history that ran almost entirely to the contrary, a unanimous Supreme Court concluded that in 1935 Congress had intended that all 'needy, dependent children' would be entitled to AFDC benefits, and that states and localities could not enforce their own narrower definitions of eligible parents. Thus, Alabama, in dispersing

AFDC, could not decide that Mrs Smith's occasional visitor and lover (a Mr Williams with nine children of his own) was a 'substitute father' and breadwinner whose visits to Mrs Smith disqualified her and her children from the federal entitlement.[25] Chief Justice Warren put aside a wealth of legislative history suggesting that Congress intended precisely to allow states to apply their own standards of 'moral character' and 'suitability' (acquiescing, as we saw, to the southern Democrats' insistence on local control over 'domestic affairs' of race, caste, and the social and economic authority of local white elites). This history might have been relevant at one time, Warren noted, because the 'social context' in 1935 was one in which the distinction between the 'worthy' poor and the 'undeserving' was generally accepted.[26] Now both society and Congress took a different view, 'more sophisticated and enlightened than the "worthy-person" concept of earlier times'.[27] The evidence that the Congresses that enacted the various post-1935 amendments to AFDC shared the Warren Court's enlightened perspective was scant at best.[28] Nonetheless, the chief justice proceeded to read the preamble and statement of purpose of the 1935 Act itself to mean that AFDC 'was designed to meet a need unmet by programs providing employment for breadwinners'.[29] Thus,

> at the same time that it intended to provide programs for the economic security and protection of *all* children ... [Congress surely would not have allowed the states] arbitrarily to leave one class of destitute children entirely without meaningful protection ... Such an interpretation of congressional intent would be most unreasonable, and we decline to adopt it.[30]

Relying on *King v. Smith*,[31] LSO attorneys went on to challenge a wide variety of state practices. The much-resented man-in-the-house rule fell by the wayside, its defeat a victory for the welfare rights movement's vision of woman's autonomy. Other forms of presumed income also were successfully challenged, and the upshot was that courts indirectly increased family's benefits. Few facets of AFDC policy escaped scrutiny in the lower courts. State laws penalizing recipients for fraud, laws and regulations denying benefits to aliens, rules on verification procedure, foster care, and emergency assistance were all struck down.

The US judiciary went a great distance toward transforming a grant-in-aid to the states into a no-strings, no-stigma, national right to welfare. But statutory construction could go only so far. It could not establish a decent social minimum as a floor on welfare benefits, or even prevent the states from diminishing payments as they expanded coverage under judicial nudging.[32] And it could not challenge the exclusions inscribed in the statute's categorical system, forcing Congress to change the system into one embracing all of the nation's poor. If courts were to force these changes, it would be through constitutional adjudication.

At first, LSO relied heavily on constitutional challenges. Residency requirements, as we already have noted, carried forward a centuries-old tradition of localities warning out wayfaring paupers. Nine out of 11 lower courts agreed with welfare rights groups and the LSO that these requirements trenched on the welfare recipient's constitutional right to travel; to be a member of the national community had always included the right freely to travel among the states.[33] In *Shapiro v. Thompson*, the

Supreme Court agreed that the states' residency requirements unconstitutionally burdened poor Americans' enjoyment of that right.[34]

Welfare as a Statutory Entitlement

Eight lower courts also heard LSO challenges to states' summary termination practices, and six held that the due process clause required pre-termination hearings.[35] In 1970, with its decision in *Goldberg v. Kelly*,[36] the Supreme Court upheld the majority view.[37]

Declaring that welfare benefits were 'a matter of statutory entitlement . . . [whose] termination involves state action that adjudicates important rights',[38] *Goldberg* encapsulated the previous five years of federal litigation and decisional law. By recognizing private rights of action, stripping broad swathes of discretionary power from local officials, and eliminating non-need-based eligibility criteria, this new body of law had *made* welfare benefits into just such rights. The Court seemed to go further, stating more fully and forcefully than ever before the premises behind the 'more sophisticated and enlightened' view of welfare it had evoked (and attributed to Congress) in *King*.[39] In a footnote supporting its assertion that welfare benefits were 'a matter of statutory entitlement', the Court observed,

> It may be realistic today to regard welfare entitlements as more like 'property' than a 'gratuity'. Much of the existing wealth in this country takes the form of rights that do not fall within traditional common-law concepts of property. It has been aptly noted that [s]ociety today is built around entitlement . . . Many of the most important of these entitlements now flow from government: subsidies to farmers and businessmen . . . [and] social security pensions for individuals. Such sources of security, whether private or public, are no longer regarded as luxuries or gratuities; to the recipients they are essentials, fully deserved, and in no sense a form of charity. It is only the poor whose entitlements, although recognized by public policy, have not been effectively enforced.[40]

The long quotation was from Yale law professor Charles Reich, whose two enormously influential articles on the 'new property' were published in *Yale Law Journal* in 1964 and 1965.[41] It is an argument about the status of welfare in an era in which 'government largess' takes myriad forms and constitutes so much of individual and corporate wealth. In Reich's account, the welfare recipient belonged to a whole social order of Americans 'liv[ing] on government largess'.[42] 'Social insurance substitutes for savings[, and] a government contract replaces a businessman's customers and goodwill',[43] while in between the new pauper and pensioner and the new businessmen stood petty entrepreneurs and tradesmen, the cab driver dependent on his medallion, the tavern keeper and the hunting guide whose livelihoods hinged on their licenses.[44] In Reich's anxious and nostalgic liberal narrative of American life, political and cultural antagonists, the cab driver or tradesman and the welfare mother, the factory owner and the union worker, were united by their common vulnerability to the state.[45] In fact, precious few of Reich's disparate forms of 'new property' were new.[46] But the assimilation of pauper to tradesman and franchise-holder, the equation of welfare benefits with professional licenses and government contracts, was dramatically new, and this did the important discursive and doctrinal work. The 'new property', unlike the old, was dispensed by the state in 'the form of rights or status rather than of tangible goods'.[47] How, then, Reich asked, can the new property fulfill the social function of the old property? How can it serve as an institution that secures the individual a measure of independence from state domination, when it is itself dispensed by the state?[48] The question sounded in classical liberalism, and so did the answer. If government subsidies, contracts, pensions, and benefits were to serve as a basis for private autonomy and dignified existence, fulfilling the social function of property, then these various forms of largesse must enjoy the same legal protections as traditional common law forms of property.

In particular, the new property, like the old, must be protected against arbitrary deprivations and invasions by the state. What the state gave, the state could not take away – at least not without due process. And, in fact, Reich observed, constitutional due process case law already had begun in the 1950s to establish that the state could not take away such government-granted goods as an occupational license without 'notice and a hearing'.[49] Where the 'freedom to earn a living' was implicated, courts recognized that procedural due process's protections of property applied. But welfare too involved livelihood; like traditional livelihoods, it had the potential to provide 'a secure minimum basis for individual well-being and dignity',[50] but only if the legal order recognized it too as a form of property.

For all its resonance, Reich's argument left many questions dangling, and so did *Goldberg*. First was the question of distributive justice. Conceding that welfare benefits, if recognized as secure legal entitlements, could perform the 'social functions' Reich and the Court claimed for them, why were the poor entitled to them? On what distributive premise did they rest? On the face of it, welfare was not a moral equivalent to a professional license or a pension right in a union contract or even to government-based, but partly contributory, social insurance. Effort and exchange were the ordinary normative bases in liberal legal culture for such 'property' claims. What was the normative argument that made welfare a cognate right, when on the face of it, welfare differed from the others by distributing goods with neither effort nor exchange to underpin the result?

Second was the question of whether the legal/constitutional order's recognition of welfare as a right had only formal and procedural bite. If the social function of welfare as property was to provide 'a secure minimum basis for individual well-being and dignity', then did the entitlement not entail a measure of substantive constitutional protection – say, against lawmakers' decision to repeal the entitlement or to diminish it below the minimum?[51] Or was that kind of recognition of the property-like aspect of welfare strictly a matter of public policy for legislatures to determine?

For Reich the right to welfare seemed to rest on the involuntary nature of individual poverty. 'Today', he wrote in the full text of the passage from which the *Goldberg* Court quoted:

we see poverty as the consequence of large impersonal forces in a complex industrial society ... [Past eras saw poverty as flowing from individual 'idleness' and other moral failings.] It is closer to the truth to say that the poor are affirmative contributors to today's society, for we are so organized as virtually to compel this sacrifice by a segment of the population. Since the enactment of the Social Security Act, we have recognized that they have a right – not a mere privilege – to a minimal share in the commonwealth.[52]

As an assertion about the commitments historically inscribed in the nation's statutes, this is nonsense.[53] As moral reasoning, though, it bears comparison to arguments made in the Britain and Western Europe from the 1980s onward to today on behalf of a 'basic' or 'citizen's income' by Philip Van Parij, Claus Offe and others. Van Parij suggests that we see the basic income as just compensation for those members of society who bear the brunt of our limited supply of good jobs. This would point toward welfare as a kind of just compensation.

Of course, the just compensation clause of the US Constitution is not where the Court looked for constitutional footing. 'From its founding the Nation's basic commitment has been to foster the dignity and well-being of all persons within its borders. We have come to recognize that forces not within the control of the poor contribute to their poverty',[54] the Court observed, citing and paraphrasing Reich:

> Welfare, by meeting the basic demands of subsistence, can help bring within the reach of the poor the same opportunities that are available to others to participate meaningfully in the life of the community . . . Public assistance, then, is not mere charity, but a means to 'promote the general Welfare, and secure the Blessings of Liberty to ourselves and our Posterity'.[55]

So, the Court did not follow Reich in his blunt assertion that welfare was the poor person's just desert as a conscript in the reserve army of the unemployed. It did suggest that because supra-individual, social forces 'contribute' to a person's poverty, welfare should be dignifying and not degrading. Indeed, it implied that assuring that the material bases of 'well-being' were available in a dignifying manner stood as a fundamental or 'founding' national 'commitment'. Reich's bleak quid pro quo rubbed abrasively against the ideal of equal opportunity. That ideal signified bringing the nation's poor into a shared world of work and opportunity, not compensating them for permanent exclusion from it. So, the Court cast welfare not as compensation for the jobless poor's involuntary 'contribution' to the economy, but as a means of bringing within their reach 'opportunities . . . to participate . . . in the life of the community'. Presumably, this meant that without means of subsistence, the poor could not begin to attain education and decent work or to participate in civic life. Participating in these spheres – not welfare as such – is the social basis of equal citizenship, which is why welfare was more the fruit of the New Deal's failure to enact social citizenship than its fulfillment. But here, in a case involving the children and grandchildren of the very Americans the New Deal had excluded, the Court was casting welfare provision, in the words of the Preamble, as a step toward including all Americans in a common framework of 'Liberty' and 'the general welfare'.

With these striking references to the Constitution, the Court seemed to be signaling a willingness to consider whether some constitutional provision might grant a right to welfare for those confronting what the Court called 'brutal need'.[56] As we have seen, this was the push of the Court's remarkable statutory construction cases – that welfare was an individual entitlement and need the only legitimate touchstone of eligibility. The Court's reference to 'the Blessings of Liberty' suggested, in strong echoes of Roosevelt's 'second Bill of Rights', that a measure of economic security was indispensable to freedom and citizenship.[57] Welfare, then, was being cast as a necessary, though not a sufficient, basis of equal citizenship, a step toward including all Americans in a common framework of 'Liberty', a matter of obvious constitutional significance.

Thus, the Court seemed to be verging on judicial recognition of something very much like rights to minimum welfare, education, and other forms of social provision, when the Republican victory in the 1968 presidential election deprived the Court's liberals of the votes they needed to carry the process forward. In 1969, newly elected President Nixon appointed Warren Burger as new chief justice; in 1970, Nixon appointed Harry Blackmun, whose first years on the Court saw him aligned with the fairly conservative new chief; in 1972, he appointed Lewis Powell and William Rehnquist. Few contemporaries would quarrel that four appointments by the 1968 Democratic presidential candidate, old New Dealer Hubert Humphrey, instead of four Nixon appointments, would have made the *Dandridge v. Williams*[58] and *San Antonio Independent School District v. Rodriguez*[59] dissents into majority opinions.

In *Dandridge*, the lower court had built on *Goldberg* and the other welfare rights precedents to strike down Maryland's dollar maximum (of US$250 per month) on welfare grants to poor families. Plaintiffs claimed that the maximum discriminated against poor children in large families, and the court agreed, applying heightened scrutiny to the measure because it affected the constitutionally important interest in welfare, and concluding that the law 'cut too broad a swath on an indiscriminate basis'.[60] Under the new chief justice's leadership, the Supreme Court reversed, announcing that no longer would the Court attend to the details of welfare programmes, even if they appeared discriminatory or made harsh distinctions among people equally in need. Acknowledging that 'administration of public welfare assistance . . . involves the most basic economic needs of impoverished human beings',[61] the Court declared that 'the dramatically real factual difference between [welfare regulation and regulation of business or industry provided] no basis for applying a different constitutional standard'.[62]

In dissent, Justice Marshall assailed 'the Court's emasculation of the Equal Protection clause as a constitutional principle applicable to the area of social welfare administration'.[63] Marshall approvingly invoked the arguments of constitutional scholars on behalf of a substantive right to welfare, as well as Article 25 of the Universal Declaration of Human Rights,[64] which confers just such a right. Thus, he signaled the dissenters' inclination to read the Constitution as conferring something like a right to livelihood. On a Humphrey, rather than a Nixon, Court, the trajectory of constitutional doctrine after *Dandridge* most likely would have been in the direction of ever more exigent signals that Congress and the states must make up shortfalls between statutory offerings and the real world of 'brutal need' and include the statutorily excluded.

Theoretical Underpinnings: Liberal and Republican Perspectives

Frank Michelman's Approach: Equality and Basic Needs

Dandridge, however, lay in the future. In the meantime constitutional law scholars set to work on the unfinished normative underpinnings of constitutional welfare rights. The federal courts had laboured hard to make need the sole criterion for eligibility. But need had never stood on the same plane as effort or exchange in the distributive norms of common law or constitutional doctrine. The concept of a need-based right required a moral and a constitutional argument that extended beyond procedural to distributive justice and addressed the right's substantive reach and bounds. Charles Reich's articles did not provide one.[65] Reich urged courts to attack official arbitrariness and discretion, and the insecurity and indignities they bred. He offered a sociological rationale for treating statutory welfare benefits as rights, but not a moral or constitutional argument as to why courts were obliged to provide for the needy. Frank Michelman, however, did provide such argument.

In 1969 and 1973, respectively, Michelman published two pioneering articles: 'On Protecting the Poor through the Fourteenth Amendment',[66] and 'In Pursuit of Constitutional Welfare Rights: One View of Rawls' Theory of Justice'.[67] 'Protecting the Poor' was an effort to nudge doctrine and doctrinal scholarship toward a theory of judicially enforceable constitutional welfare rights. What, asked Michelman, is 'the role of courts ... [in] the great War'[68] on poverty? The prevailing case law could be read as resting, partly, on a notion of wealth discrimination. Indeed, many lower courts[69] and liberal commentators wishfully read them as signs that the Court might bring the nation's poor into the 'inner circle' of judicially protected classes, along with racial, ethnic and religious minorities.[70] For his part, Michelman read the decisions differently. The Supreme Court, he conceded, was embarking on 'the elaboration of constitutional rights pertaining to the status of being poor',[71] and had clothed the decisions presaging these rights in the 'verbiage of inequality and discrimination'.[72] But the 'inchoate theories of social justice ... at the roots'[73] of these cases was ill expressed in the language of 'equality or evenhandedness'.[74] For the federal courts to begin striking down every state law and policy that falls unequally on the nation's poor would sweep too broadly. Nor does equality offer a plausible benchmark for answering the question of how much protection is 'enough'.

Thus, while inequality and discrimination were the doctrinal notions near at hand, they were misleading. The upsetting feature in the equal protection cases involving poverty was not some odious discrimination that might accompany a poor person's deprivation of a good he could not afford; what was disturbing was the deprivation itself. So, Michelman sought to use the cases as data points from which to infer the outlines of a constitutional universe of 'just wants' or 'basic needs'. Not equal protection, he insisted, but 'minimum protection' was the heart of the matter.[75] Focusing on specific deprivations of basic needs was 'a much more manageable task'[76] for courts.

After the Supreme Court decided the *Dandridge* case, it became clear that most of the Justices on the Burger Court would not compel states or Congress to make up any shortfall between statutory offerings and the real world of 'brutal need', nor continue to subject state laws or practices that fell heavily or arbitrarily on the poor to any exacting constitutional standard. What is important for us about 'Protecting the Poor', however, is not its failed prophecy about doctrinal developments, which, after all, were merely the upshot of Nixon's razor-thin victory in the 1968 presidential election. What matters here is glimpsing the development of social rights ideas among American constitutional thinkers and activists. Inevitably, a constitutional lawyer interested in distributive justice in the 1960s and 1970s would turn to John Rawls, the era's leading liberal moral philosopher.

Rawls's Difference Principle, Civic Republicanism, and the Shape of Social Rights

Of course, what was afoot in the courts shaped the way Michelman and others approached Rawls's epoch-making *A Theory of Justice*, first published in 1971. Thus, when Michelman turned to Rawls, he did so with a mind to asking:

> how ... the book [bore] upon ... legal recognition ... of claimed affirmative rights (let us call them 'welfare rights') to education, shelter, subsistence, health care and the like, or to the money these things cost.[77]

The answer was a vexed one. Michelman rested welfare rights on a distributive principle of 'minimum protection' or 'just wants'; Rawls offered something different. The chief basis for welfare rights in *A Theory of Justice* was Rawls's difference principle.

The difference principle, you will recall, states that institutionalized inequalities must be justified by dint of being in the interests of the least advantaged.[78] Inequalities that do not redound to the benefit of those at the bottom are illegitimate. For Rawls, this principle is not cashed out through income standards or transfer payments alone; it must imbue the general 'organization of the economy', and the distribution of wealth, power and authority as well as income.[79] Because his focus rests on welfare, however, Michelman reads the difference principle with an eye to income and finds it wanting. Rawls seems interested simply in maximizing the income of those at the bottom, irrespective of whether that income is adequate to meeting basic needs,[80] or whether it substantially exceeds that level.[81] Moreover, Michelman finds it difficult to feed the 'primary good of self-respect'[82] into the machinery of the difference principle, because the good of self-respect 'does not seem to fit the difference principle's 'more is better' attitude'.[83] Yet, from the point of view of liberal constitutional theory, the centrality of self-respect and equal respect in Rawls's theory are an important part of his appeal.

Unlike the ''more is better' attitude' of Rawls's difference principle, Michelman's 'just wants' theory provides a touchstone for determining the metes and bounds of welfare provision that seems directly tied to equal respect.[84] Beyond the point at which welfare provides a decent minimum of social goods, it seems wiser to allow considerations of economic incentives and market efficiency to hold sway. As a rational actor behind Rawls's 'veil of ignorance', one might well prefer assurance that one's 'just wants' be satisfied, and for the rest one might prefer to wager that one's individual capacities were at least middling as the market measures things – and choose against the 'more is better' attitude of the difference principle.

However, we risk being misled if we look at the difference principle only from this perspective. From it, we might surmise that what separates Rawls's views about social and economic rights from Michelman's is simply a quarrel over what form of income redistribution to enshrine in the constitution – minimum income pegged to the difference principle, or minimum welfare rights pegged to just wants. In fact, neither of these alternatives captures Rawls's view of how the principles of justice, including the difference principle, bear on constitutional political economy. Rawls devotes great attention in *A Theory of Justice* to just this subject; what he writes makes plain, I think, that he would include constitutional baselines respecting work and participation in the economic order, as well as welfare.

Despite the tension he uncovers between the primary good of self-respect and the 'more is better' attitude of the difference principle applied to income, Michelman is right in suggesting that the difference principle is concerned with the social bases of self-respect and mutual respect. Indeed, it concerns them more than it does the rational actor's calculus of consent regarding income shares. When Rawls writes about consent, he is concerned about what it takes to make each person a consenting member – a charter member – of society. He is concerned not only, or even primarily, with rational choice, but also with contract, undertaking and commitment[85] – more precisely, with consent and commitment to the social enterprise, and, conversely, with the conditions which turn consent and commitment into submission and subjection. This is the problem Rawls dubs the 'strains of commitment'.[86] Under an unjust political economy, such as ours, there are millions of citizens who cannot plausibly see themselves as members of a political community organized in their name to promote their interests and capacities. Instead of supporting their capacities for commitment we have strained them to a breaking point.

What, then, *are* the political-economic bases of consent and commitment? More important, writes Rawls, than 'a high material standard of life'[87] in securing 'a just and good society ... is meaningful work in free association with others, these associations regulating their relations to one another within a framework of just basic institutions'.[88] That is why the difference principle reaches beyond income to the distribution of wealth and power; it concerns shared authority no less than a fair share of goods. This is the key difference between Rawls's constitutional political economy – which he dubs a 'property-owning democracy'[89] – and the political economy of the welfare state. 'In a welfare state', he writes in a 1987 preface to *A Theory of Justice*, 'the aim [of political institutions] is that none should fall below a decent standard of life ... By contrast, in a property-owning democracy the aim is to carry out the idea of society as a fair system of cooperation over time between citizens as free and equal persons'.[90] The 'background institutions of property-owning democracy ... try to disperse the ownership of wealth and capital, and thus to prevent a small part of society from controlling the economy and indirectly political life itself'.[91] 'The idea is not simply to assist those who lose out through accident or misfortune (although this must be done), but instead to put all citizens in a position to manage their own affairs and to take part in social cooperation on a footing of mutual respect.'[92]

In a word, Rawls's precepts for political economy fall squarely within the American social citizenship tradition. His political economy of citizenship bears a strong family resemblance to those of the Populists, Progressives and New Dealers who fashioned the variants of social citizenship thought in America. Like them, he holds that one cannot be a consenting, charter member, a 'citizen', of the national community without decent work, a measure of economic independence, and at least a small share of authority over the governance of one's work and shared economic life.

Whether one rests one's normative claim for welfare rights on some variant of Rawlsian liberalism, or on the civic republican tradition, a key part of the argument for welfare rights is this: These rights are necessary to secure the social bases of self-respect (the main concern in Rawls) and of independence and mutual respect or equal standing (republicanism's primary emphasis). In sum, welfare rights are necessary to a liberal republican (or, if you prefer, a republican liberal) conception of equal citizenship. Yet, plainly the social bases of equal citizenship consist of more than a decent minimum of food, shelter, and other material needs. They also demand a right to earn a livelihood through decent work; they require an opportunity to contribute in some recognized fashion to the social enterprise as well as to civic and political life. This broader view of the material dimensions of constitutional equality has a better mooring in the empirical literature that treats the social and economic underpinnings of self-respect[93] and mutual respect[94] among women and men in today's America – and a better mooring in our constitutional history.

The modern welfare rights claim does not fit well with the republican underpinning constitutional theorists began to assert in the 1980s. Republican maxims hold that a measure of material independence is a necessary basis for political competence and standing. But in the republican outlook, such citizenly standing and competence have always been bound up with the status of one who fulfills some recognized, responsible role in the social enterprise – one who 'earns' his or her measure of material security and 'independence'.[95] We certainly may find, as far back as the seventeenth and eighteenth centuries, support in both 'liberal' and 'republican' texts for the view that the poor have a subsistence claim on society's resources. In truth, that claim was well defended by John Locke; it is there, too, in the writings of Adam Smith.[96] But that is a far cry from making this longstanding claim a basis for citizenship in the sense of full membership in the political community. Neither Locke, nor Smith, nor James Madison and Thomas Jefferson in the 'republican' texts scholars relied on,[97] nor later renderings of liberalism and republicanism – none of these lend support to the idea of making public assistance *simpliciter* the material base of citizenship. That base, that dignifying social minimum, must rest on some socially recognized contribution on a person's part to the common enterprise.

This broader, more participatory conception of social citizenship may not be necessary in every liberal democratic society today to assure a person's standing as an equal participant in civic affairs and community life. But to use a phrase with which Michelman recently has conjured, this account seems firmly embedded in America's 'constitutional identity'.[98] The longstanding links between work, equal respect, and citizenship seem constitutive of 'who we think we are and aim to be as a politically constituted people, [of] where we think we have come from and where we think we are headed'.[99]

The idea that welfare rights fit well with either a liberal or a republican understanding of the material bases of equal citizenship was first forged in the context of
the welfare rights movement. But the movement, like any social movement of subordinate people, was sharply constrained. It played the hand that history and the White
House dealt it. Its programmatic vision, its strategy and goals, all were shaped by the
social provision and institutional resources at hand to address black poverty – AFDC,
LSO, and the Community Action Agencies. But nothing about this conjuncture gave
any assurance that welfare rights were the right solution to the problem of social and
economic exclusion confronting poor black citizens. Black leaders like Martin Luther
King and Bayard Rustin plainly thought otherwise; they called for a 'Negroes' New
Deal' that emphasized decent work. As a normative matter, and as a constitutional
one, I have suggested, they were right.

The vision of citizenship fashioned by the welfare rights movement also was
shaped by the fact that the movement's constituents were women and mothers.
King and Rustin had nothing to say about this fact, and precious little to say about
gender equality in general. But everything we know about welfare and work suggests
that generous and guaranteed welfare provision – however morally imperative it may
be – cannot do the main work of securing gender equality for poor women. That also
demands reconstructing the low wage labour market, striving to assure decent jobs for
women, no less than men, and providing enabling rights, as well, to training and child
care and old-age pensions, as well as provision and incentives that enable and encourage equitable sharing of dependent-care.

A liberal society that prizes the dignity of the individual, if it is an affluent one that
can afford a guaranteed income that protects all against desperate want, must do so.
To refuse is, in Rawls's terms, to put an unbearable and unjust strain on individuals'
commitments to the social compact. But that is not enough. Equal citizenship also
requires social citizenship. Or, as Michelman most recently put the claim on our
joint behalf:

> [We cannot] call on everyone . . . to submit their fates to a democratic-majori-
> tarian lawmaking system, without also committing our society, from the start, to
> run itself in ways designed to constitute and sustain every person as a competent
> and respected contributor to political exchange and contestation and further-
> more to social and economic life at large.[100]

Once one embraces the view that the Constitution must vouchsafe the minimum
social conditions of democratic lawmaking, one cannot leave the question of social
citizenship where Michelman first left it in his Rawlsian and republican arguments.
One cannot leave the work- and economic-independence-and-participation-related
aspects of social citizenship to the give and take of ordinary politics. Specification
of what counts as decent work or recognized but non-waged contribution (such as
child- or elder-care), and how, at a particular time, the nation ought to go about assuring such opportunities to all, of what counts as a decent livelihood at said time, of
what counts as incapacity, and of what quantum of income should separate those,
not incapacitated, who avail themselves of 'welfare' or a guaranteed income versus
those who 'work' – all these issues and more may and, practically, *must* be addressed

through political and market processes. But if social citizenship guarantees are pre-requisites to political equality, then, at the most general level, these commitments must precede ordinary politics; otherwise, a broad swathe of the citizenry would be denied – as today they are denied – a constitutionally fair opportunity to act as citizen-participants in the very debates and decision-making upon which their citizenly standing depends.

The Real Role of Courts: Addressing Problems of Judicial Competence, Democratic Legitimacy, and Normative Indeterminacy

If social citizenship rights are prior to ordinary politics, what happens when ordinary politics gives them short shrift, as it chronically does, nowhere more so, than in these United States? One answer is turning to the courts. But I have just suggested that – quite apart from the current conservative Republican US Supreme Court's deep hostility toward them – constitutional social rights seem to demand political and market-based, as opposed to judicial, elaboration. Let us take a brief look at this dilemma in terms of the practical and the principled problems posed by judicial elab-oration and enforcement of social rights – and in terms of the comparative difficulties produced by different kinds of social rights.

Broadly speaking, the practical problems run to the judiciary's institutional limit-ations in devising complex, choice-laden social policy and, then, in enforcing the often costly and often politically unwelcome implementation of whatever policies it devises. The principled problems go to the way that social rights seem to depart from the traditional model of legal norms as formal, determinate and objective in defi-nition and application, and also to the ways that judicial imposition of social rights seems to preempt wide-open democratic decision-making about social and economic policy.

Certainly, it is true that perplexing questions of economic feasibility may arise with any broad-gauged claim to a social right, whether to housing, education, or employment. A decree fulfilling a claimed right might leave people at the bottom of society worse off than they already are. Likewise, fulfilling any such right, especially in areas like education or employment, involves vitally important subsidi-ary choices and trade-offs which the judiciary lacks all basis for making – and which, as a matter of principle, ought to involve democratic deliberation and decision. However, these considerations do not demand judicial abstention; rather, they may demand that courts not cut social rights out of the whole cloth of moral theory or of the interpretative recollection of extra-judicial constitutional tradition, such as Roosevelt's 'second Bill of Rights'.

Thus, decisions like *King v. Smith*, *Goldberg v. Kelley* and the dissenting opinions in *Dandridge v. Williams*, as well as scores of lower federal courts' welfare rights decisions demonstrate that moral theory and constitutional tradition may inform courts' application of due process and equality guarantees in their formal aspects to statutory materials. Consider the lower courts' pre-*Dandridge* readiness to find in the Fourteenth Amendment's equal protection clause a command to invalidate even seemingly plausible classifications among potential eligibles and generally to put the statutory welfare programmes' limitations, exclusions, and qualifications under strain, in the name of making need alone the constitutionally valid criterion. Likewise, consider statutory cases like *King v. Smith* as studies of how courts can find in statutory welfare rights justice-inspired legislative supplementation of the constitutional catalogue. Unprepared, in the first instance, to declare the existence of a constitutional right to a social minimum (and so openly and irrevocably to constrain Congress), the Court nonetheless was prepared to expand and deepen the limited and qualified commitments Congress had made – and to prod Congress to craft future welfare legislation in keeping with the inclusive commitments the Court attributed to it. Similarly, with other social rights areas, a judiciary mindful of the constitutional dimensions of health care provision or of work and participation has in the past and could in the future nudge state or federal agencies to construe their statutory mandates in ways that lean toward inclusion or actual availability of work opportunities.

But widening the circle of eligibility to, striking down exclusions from, and assuring against arbitrary deprivations of statutory social rights are not the only functions courts can and should perform. The facts that social rights are costly and that implementing them involves complex resource allocations have not prevented many well-respected American state (as opposed to federal) courts from prodding legislatures to ensure that such rights receive a degree of legislative priority. State courts as diverse as New York's, New Jersey's, Texas's and California's have found credible ways to assess claims of glaring failure to fulfill constitutional mandates such as state constitutional rights to education or to housing equity. Mindful that implementing such rights involves resource allocations that should rest in the hands of democratically accountable officials, and also involves creation of new administrative structures and institutional strategies that courts are ill-equipped to design, US and other nations' courts often have responded to these constraints by issuing judicial mandates to legislative, executive, or administrative officers to prepare, submit and carry out corrective plans.

Hammering out such plans to vindicate social rights, in turn, entails political conflicts and accommodations. But constitutional-judicial intervention lends clout in these processes to relatively powerless constituencies, catalyzing new alliances among activists and attorneys, reform-minded lawmakers and bureaucrats, and judicial officials. Often, legislators otherwise reluctant or unwilling to vote in favour of increased education or housing funding prove ready to do so, once they can explain that 'the courts made us do it'. Implementing any social right-inspired plan is also inevitably a protracted process, often entailing substantial trial and error and subject to social and bureaucratic impediments and inertia. Again, there is a virtue here to judicial involvement. Courts can insist on accountability and continued experimentation, even after legislative will flags or fragile bureaucratic coalitions unravel.

Given these considerable judicial virtues in the social rights arena, why is it that many thoughtful social rights advocates nonetheless prefer to put these rights beyond reach of judicial enforcement? Why should a constitutional draftsperson or interpreter prefer instead to dub social rights constitutional 'directive principles', denoting that they belong exclusively to the lawmakers and citizenry to elaborate and enforce?

For my part, I think, courts can play a useful role in promoting some elements of social citizenship far better than others. So, it is worth asking whether there is a case for sorting out social citizenship guarantees into sub-categories of rights and directive principles. Let us return to the contrast between the welfare right to housing or shelter or a social minimum and the right to decent work. The availability of decent work is a state of affairs that may have a uniquely large and disparate set of potential policy levers surrounding it, running to everything from childcare and job training to the prime lending rate, tax and tariff policies, public investments and employment, and beyond. I am hard pressed to say whether anyone, including a court, could say decisively whether a right to decent work is or is not being pursued in earnest. But practical complexity is not all that may importantly distinguish the social citizenship guarantee from welfare rights, like the right to housing.

Practical complexity is linked to complexities of social meaning and of cultural contention and change. What it means to ensure that no member of the community is homeless or without adequate shelter is not self-evident; but the range of plausible meanings is vastly more definite and exigent than what it means to ensure 'decent work' for all.

The crucial difference between welfare rights and the broader right of social citizenship lies not simply along the dimension of practical complexity but also along the intersecting dimension of normative indeterminacy. The normative meaning of the social citizenship guarantee of 'decent work' seems properly subject to a level of good faith disagreement, contestation and change that is quite different from welfare rights to food, clothing, shelter, or even education. In an America constituted by both kinds of guarantees, the response to homelessness, and the incapacitation and indignity it threatens, must be some kind of home; but the response to the marginality and exclusion threatened by joblessness may rightly be more open-ended. It properly entails ongoing revaluation of what we mean by 'full time' and 'work' and 'respected contribution'. And if that is so, then there is good reason to conceptualize welfare rights as rights, and the social citizenship guarantee as a directive principle.

Welfare rights are suited, in ways we have already canvassed, to some non-trivial measure of judicial oversight, even though enforcing them to the hilt is well beyond the courts' domain. Since they are essential to constituting every American as a free and equal member of the polity, it seems folly to forsake the judiciary's contribution. The social citizenship guarantee is no less essential, but because of the wide-open practical and normative choices encircling it, that guarantee presents distinct and intractable justiciability problems. It makes sense, therefore, to deem it a directive principle. If we divvy up the constitutional universe of social rights into rights and directive principles, perhaps, we better serve these competing concerns.

Such a division might help insure against an obvious danger posed by the full-scale morphing of rights into directive principles: while the polity deliberates, and public reason unfolds, people starve. Good faith disagreement shades imperceptibly into dawdling and indifference. And the voices of those at the margins weaken. Judicially cognizable welfare rights might provide a hook and a prod for securing the livelihoods of those at the margins, boosting slightly their ability to participate in the polity's conversations about what it means to sustain everyone as a participant and contributor.

What is more, the simpler we make the judicially cognizable essentials of social citizenship, the more vigorously our constitutional courts might provide stays against political failures.

Conclusion

The rise and fall of constitutional welfare rights in the US Supreme Court seems to confirm the old American adage that the Court 'follows the election returns'. As the national polity shifted rightward, so did the constitutional outlook of newly appointed justices, and so did the Court's welfare rights jurisprudence. In fact, however, many left-liberal constitutional developments of the Warren Court years – in the areas of voting rights, women's equality, and criminal procedure, for example – proved surprisingly durable. Compared to 'welfare rights', these other innovations had stronger bases, in constitutional text and tradition or in the polity at large. The fate of the Warren Court's welfare rights initiatives sprang from the precarious, racialized and marginalized location of 'welfare' in the late twentieth-century United States combined with the lack of any 'social rights' provisions in the US Constitution.

By contrast, of course, the constitutions of most European nations, South Africa, India and many other parts of the democratic world – as well most of the US state constitutions – do contain express social rights. And the present politico-constitutional cultures also contain more robust commitments to social citizenship. Recuperating and reinventing social rights and social citizenship in the United States is not a project to pursue in the present national courts. But in many of our state courts and in courts and constitutional cultures around the globe, opportunities beckon. There, I hope, this brief history may prove suggestive.

NOTES

1. Winifred Bell, *Aid to Dependent Children* (New York: Columbia University Press 1965) (internal quotation omitted), p.9; see Molly Ladd-Taylor, *Mother-Work: Women, Child Welfare, and the State, 1890–1930* (Champaign, IL: University of Illinois Press, 1994), pp.136–66; Sonya Michel, *Children's Interests/Mothers' Rights: The Shaping of America's Child Care Policy* (New Haven, CT: Yale University Press, 1999), pp.424–79; Theda Skocpol, *Protecting Soldiers and Mothers: The Political Origins of Social Policy in the United States* (Cambridge, MA: Harvard University Press, 1992), pp.73–8.
2. Bell (note 1), pp.33–4, 63–5, 76–9, 81–2, 108–109.
3. Ibid. pp.34–5, 42, 55, 79, 83, 130, 138.
4. See ibid., pp.4, 6, 80, 213; R. Shep Melnick, *Between the Lines: Interpreting Welfare Rights* (Washington, DC: Brookings Institute, 1994), pp.57, 85–90, 98, 121–2, 130.
5. See ibid., p.77.
6. See Jacqueline Jones, *Labour of Love, Labour of Sorrow: Black Women, Work, and the Family from Slavery to the Present* (New York: Basic Books, 1985).
7. See William Forbath, 'Constitutional Welfare Rights', *Fordham Law Review*, Vol.69 (April 2001), pp.1850–55.
8. Ibid. p.1851.
9. This was the social fact that civil rights leaders like Martin Luther King and Bayard Rustin highlighted and called on Congress to remedy as a necessary condition for the 'full emancipation and equality of Negroes and the poor'. William Forbath, 'Caste, Class, and Equal Citizenship', *Michigan Law Review*, Vol.98, No.1 (1999), p.87.
10. Forbath (note 7), p.1862.

11. Ibid. p.1863.
12. See Richard B. Stewart and Cass R. Sunstein, 'Public Programs and Private Rights', *Harvard Law Review*, Vol.95, No.6 (1982), pp.1289–90.
13. See e.g. *Hagans v. Lavine*, 415 US 528, 534–5, 537, 541–2 (1974); *King v. Smith*, 392 US 309, 312 (1968).
14. See Melnick (note 4), p.50.
15. See Bell (note 1), p.50; Martha Derthick, *The Influence of Federal Grants: Public Assistance in Massachusetts* (Cambridge, MA and London: Harvard University Press, 1970); Wilbur J. Cohen, 'The Social Security Act of 1935: Reflections Fifty Years Later', in *The Report of the Committee on Economic Security of 1935* (Washington, DC: National Conference. on Social Welfare, 1985), p.3.
16. Forbath (note 7), p.1859.
17. SeeSusan E. Lawrence, *The Poor in Court: The Legal Services Program and Supreme Court Decision Making* (Princeton, NJ: Princeton University Press, 1990), pp.123–48; see generally Martha F. Davis, *Brutal Need: Lawyers and The Welfare Rights Movement, 1960–1973* (New Haven, CT: Yale University Press, 1993).
18. *King v Smith* (note 13).
19. *Smith v. King*, 277 F. Supp.31, 41 (M.D. Ala. 1967).
20. Martin Garbus, *Ready for the Defense* (New York: Farrar, Straus & Giroux, 1971), p.194.
21. Ibid.
22. Ibid. pp.194–5.
23. Ibid. (internal quotations omitted).
24. See *King v Smith* (note 13).
25. Ibid. pp.328–30.
26. Ibid. pp.320, 324–35.
27. Ibid. pp.324–5.
28. The year before, in 1967, Congress had enacted amendments to AFDC that penalized states if they failed to reduce the number of illegitimate children on AFDC. 'Senator Robert Kennedy complained that "the man-in-the-house rule emerges from the conference strengthened rather than weakened" and joined with other liberals in an unsuccessful attempt to kill the conference report'. Melnick (note 4), p.87 (quoting 113 Cong. Rec. 36785 (Dec. 14, 1967)) (internal quotations omitted).
29. *King v Smith* (note 13), p.328.
30. Ibid. p.330.
31. Ibid.
32. See *Rosado v. Wyman*, 397 US 397, 416–17 (1970).
33. Forbath (note 7), p.1862.
34. *Shapiro v. Thompson*, 394 US 618, 629–31 (1969). On the lower court litigation and rulings against residency requirements, see Frank S. Bloch, 'Cooperative Federalism and the Role of Litigation in the Development of Federal AFDC Eligibility Policy', *Wisconsin Law Review*, Vol.1979, No.1 (1979), pp.8–12.
35. Forbath (note 7), p.1863.
36. *Goldberg v. Kelly*, 397 US at 254 (1970).
37. See Bloch (note 34), p.59.
38. *Goldberg v. Kelly*, p.262.
39. *Goldberg v. Kelly*, pp.324–5.
40. *Goldberg v Kelly*, p.262 (quoting Charles A. Reich, 'Individual Rights and Social Welfare: The Emerging Legal Issues', *Yale Law Journal*, Vol.74, No.7 (1965), p.1255).
41. See Reich (note 40); Charles A. Reich, 'The New Property', *Yale Law Journal*, Vol.73, No.5 (1964), p.733.
42. Reich (note 40), p.733.
43. Ibid.
44. See ibid, pp.758–9.
45. Agency discretion wielded 'life and death' power over the livelihoods of one and all. See ibid., p.758.
46. See William J. Novak, *The People's Welfare: Law and Regulation in Nineteenth-Century America* (Chapel Hill, NC: University of North Carolina Press, 1996).
47. See Reich (note 41), p.738.
48. See ibid.
49. Ibid. p.741.
50. Ibid. p.786.
51. Ibid.

52. Reich (note 40), p.1255.
53. In point of fact, the Social Security Act recognized no such right; it provided time-limited unemploy-
    ment insurance and old-age pensions to those who contributed, mothers' pensions (ADC), and public
    assistance for the blind and the elderly poor – those who could not presently or could no longer be
    expected to work, and nothing at all for the 'idle poor'. See Forbath (note 7), pp.68–81.
54. *Goldberg v. Kelly*, pp.264–5.
55. Ibid. p.265 (quoting US Constitution preamble).
56. Ibid. p.261 (quoting *Kelly v. Wyman*, 294 F. Supp.893, 900 (S.D.N.Y. 1968) (quoting Christopher
    May, 'Withdrawal of Public Welfare: The Right to a Prior Hearing', *Yale Law Journal*, Vol.76,
    No.6 (1967), p.1244) (internal quotations omitted).
57. *Goldberg v. Kelly*, p.265.
58. *Dandridge v. Williams* 397 US 471 (1970).
59. *San Antonio Independent School District v. Rodriguez* 411 US 1 (1973).
60. *Dandridge*, p.484 (quoting *Williams v. Dandridge*, 297 F. Supp.450, 469 (D. Md. 1968) (internal quo-
    tations omitted).
61. Ibid. p.485.
62. Ibid.
63. Ibid. p.508 (Marshall and Brennan, JJ, dissenting).
64. Ibid. p.521.
65. The text oversimplifies. Reich, as we saw, did gesture toward a justificatory argument based on com-
    pensation: welfare was just compensation for society's more or less conscious choice of a political
    economy that offered too few decently paid jobs to go around.
66. Frank. I. Michelman, 'Foreword: On Protecting the Poor through the Fourteenth Amendment',
    Harvard Law Review, Vol.83, No.1 (1969), pp. 7–59.
67. Frank I. Michelman, 'In Pursuit of Constitutional Welfare Rights: One View of Rawls's Theory of
    Justice', *University of Pennsylvania Law Review*, Vol.121, No.5 (1973), pp.976–88.
68. See Frank Michelman, 'The Supreme Court 1968 Term-Forward: On Protecting the Poor Through the
    Fourteenth Amendment', *Harvard Law Review*, Vol.83, No.1 (1969), pp.8–9.
69. Thus, the same year as Michelman's 'On Protecting the Poor', a three-judge district court in
    New York enjoined a recent change in the state's welfare regulations, which reduced public assistance
    payments in counties surrounding New York City to levels below those paid to city residents, when
    they had previously been grouped together. *Rothstein v. Wyman*, 303 F. Supp.339 (S.D.N.Y. 1969).
    Applying strict scrutiny to the new classification scheme, the district court wrote, 'Receipt of
    welfare benefits may not at the present time constitute the exercise of a constitutional right'; nonethe-
    less, the court deemed controlling the teaching of *Harper* and *Shapiro*, that classifications creating
    'inequalities affecting the exercise of fundamental or critical personal rights' must be scrutinized
    under 'a more stringent standard'. Ibid., p.346. As in *Harper* and *Shapiro*, so here the court found
    a conjunction of a 'fundamental right' and a 'disadvantaged minority' – only here the right was
    welfare and the minority the poor. While welfare was only an incipient constitutional right, an emer-
    gent fundamental interest, *Shapiro* still seemed to the *Rothstein* court to mark the Supreme Court's
    acknowledgment that 'access to [the] bare necessities of life' was as 'fundamental' as voting. See
    ibid., pp.346–8. And *Douglas v. State of California* 372 U.S. 353 (1963) marked a dawning recog-
    nition of the poor as a protected minority.
70. See John E. Coons *et al.*, 'Educational Opportunity: A Workable Constitutional Test for State Finan-
    cial Structures', *California Law Review*, Vol.57 (1969), p.365; see generally Arthur J. Goldberg,
    'Equality and Governmental Action', *New York University Law Review*, Vol.39 (1964), pp.205–27;
    Lawrence Gene Sager, 'Tight Little Islands: Exclusionary Zoning, Equal Protection, and the Indi-
    gent', *Stanford Law Review*, Vol.21 (April) (1969), pp.767–800.
71. See Michelman (note 68), p.16.
72. See ibid.
73. Ibid. p.10.
74. Ibid.
75. Ibid. pp.13–14.
76. Ibid. p.8.
77. Michelman (note 67), p.962.
78. See John Rawls, *A Theory of Justice* (Cambridge, MA and London: Harvard University Press, 1971),
    pp.100–101; John Rawls, *Political Liberalism* (New York: Columbia University Press, 1996), p.283,
    Michelman (note 67), pp.976–88 explicates and criticizes the difference principle.
79. See Rawls, *A Theory of Justice* (note 78), pp.7–11, 54.

80. A precept for the distribution of material social goods, says Michelman, which ignores claims regarding basic needs as such, and is sensitive only to claims regarding money income, will for many of us seem incomplete and thus not fully in harmony with our considered judgments. Michelman (note 67).

81. Michelman (note 67), p.981, states: 'Income-transfer activity is simply to be intensified just up to the point where any further intensification lowers total output so much that the bottom's absolute income begins to fall even as its relative share of total consumer satisfaction continues to rise. Under the difference principle, that is all there is to it. There can be no implicit insurance-rights package because there is no concern for what the bottom spends (or is able to spend) its income on. Income is income – a primary, an elemental, social good, of which the bottom simply wants and is entitled to as much as it can get'.

82. Ibid. p.983.

83. Ibid.

84. Michelman may have been the first sympathetic critic of Rawls to suggest that the difference principle and the income guarantee it entailed were not the only nor the most compelling principle that could be derived from Rawls's original position. A just wants principle might fit the bill better. For a thoughtful later reading, canvassing the critics and making these points in greater detail, see Jeremy Waldron, *Liberal Rights: Collected Papers 1981–1991* (Cambridge: Cambridge University Press, 1993), pp.250–70.

85. Rawls, *A Theory of Justice* (note 78), p.176 ('When we enter an agreement we must be able to honor it even should the worst possibilities prove to be the case ... Thus the parties must weigh with care whether they will be able to stick by their commitment in all circumstances'.).

86. Ibid. pp.145, 176, 423. For a thoughtful discussion of this theme in Rawls, see Waldron (note 84), pp.259–63.

87. Rawls, *A Theory of Justice* (note 78), p.290.

88. Ibid.

89. John Rawls, 'Preface for the French Edition of 'A Theory of Justice', in Samuel Freeman (ed.), *Collected Papers* (Cambridge, MA and London: Harvard University Press 1999), pp.415, 419.

90. Ibid.

91. Ibid.

92. Ibid.

93. See e.g. William Julius Wilson, *When Work Disappears: The World of the New Urban Poor* (New York: Knopf, 1996); Arthur H. Goldsmith *et al.*, 'The Psychological Impact of Unemployment and Joblessness', *Journal of Socio-Economics*, Vol.25, No.3 (1996), pp.338–58; Amartya Sen, 'The Penalties of Unemployment', *Banca D'Italia Working Paper* No.307 (1997).

94. Of course, complex patterns of respect, deference, and degradation form around class and occupational hierarchies, but all the empirical literature suggests that the most salient border between minimum respect and degradation in today's class structure falls along the line between those who are recognized by organized society as working and providing a decent living for themselves and their families, and those men and women at the bottom of the nation's class hierarchy who are not. See e.g. Joel F. Handler and Yeheskel Hasenfeld, *We the Poor People: Work, Poverty, and Welfare* (New Haven. CT: Yale University Press, 1997); Katherine S. Newman, *No Shame in My Game: The Working Poor in the Inner City* (New York: Knopf, 1999). On the experience of women in regard to the identities of housewife and '[waged] working woman' and the dilemmas of self-respect and social recognition as a full and equal member of American society, see Vicki Schultz, 'Life's Work', *Columbia Law Review*, Vol.100, No.7 (2000), p.1883 (arguing that for women, no less than men, the right to participate in decent work is indispensable to equal citizenship; canvassing empirical literature showing that 'a robust conception of equality [for women] can be best achieved *through* paid work, rather than *despite* it').

95. See William E. Forbath, 'The Ambiguities of Free Labor: Labor and the Law in the Gilded Age', *Wisconsin Law Review*, Vol.1985, No.4 (1985), p.767 (tracing this theme in republican discourse of political and legal elites and labour reformers in US from 1780s to 1880s); Forbath (note 9), pp.13–15, 18–19, 26–51 (same, adding inflections of theme in women's, African American, and agrarian movements, and carrying forward into 1890s–1930s).

96. Regarding Locke, see e.g., John Locke, *Two Treatises of Government*, ed. Peter Laslett (Cambridge: Cambridge University Press, 1960), p.170 (poor man has a right to 'Title to so much out of another's Plenty as will keep him from extream want'); Thomas A. Horne, *Property Rights and Poverty: Political Argument in Britain, 1605–1834* (Chapel Hill, NC: University of North Carolina Press, 1990), pp.48–65; and Richard Ashcraft, 'Liberalism and the Problem of Poverty', *Critical Review*, Vol.6

(1992), p.497 (demonstrating that Locke and classical liberalism emphasize natural right to subsistence; they see 'poor relief [as a] constitutive and necessary feature of *any* legitimate society'). Regarding Smith, see e.g., Adam Smith, *An Inquiry into the Nature and Causes of the Wealth of Nations Vol. 1*, ed. Edwin Cannan, 6th edn. (London: Methuen, 1950), p.80 ('No society can surely be flourishing ... of which the far greater part of the members are poor and miserable'); Istvan Hont and Michael Ignatieff, 'Needs and Justice in the Wealth of Nations: An Introductory Essay', in Istvan Hont and Michael Ignatieff (eds), *Wealth and Virtue: The Shaping of Political Economy in the Scottish Enlightenment* (Cambridge: Cambridge University Press, 1983), p.1 (identifying meeting needs of poor as Smith's theoretical axis for assessing political-economic arrangements).

97. For a Madison or Jefferson, poor relief left paupers still 'dependent' and, therefore, unqualified for citizenship. They favoured ample material opportunities (they even occasionally championed rights to property in 'full and absolute dominion') for all white men willing and able to exploit them, and charity or coercion for the rest. See Forbath (note 9), pp.13–14 (discussing and quoting from the Madison and Jefferson texts relied on by Michelman and other constitutional welfare rights defenders like Sunstein).

98. See Frank I. Michelman, 'Morality, Identity and 'Constitutional Patriotism'', *Denver University of Law Review*, Vol.76, No.4 (1999), p.1025.

99. Ibid.

100. Frank I. Michelman, 'The Constitution, Social Rights and Liberal Political Justification', International Journal of Constitutional Law, Vol.1, No.1 (2003), p.25 (available at <www3.oup.co. ukijclawhdbVolume_01Issue_01pdf010013.pdf>).

Manuscript accepted for publication September 2005.

Address for correspondence: William E. Forbath, School of Law, University of Texas at Austin, 727 E. Dean Keaton Street, Austin, TX 78705, USA. E-mail: <wforbath@mail.law.utexas.edu>.

Democratization Through Law:
Perspectives from Latin America

JULIO FAUNDEZ

Introduction

The process of democratization is today seen as inseparable from the efforts to achieve strong and effective legal systems. Indeed, so close is the relationship between democratization and the quality of legal systems that the notions of democracy and the rule of law have become virtually interchangeable.

The link between democracy and law seems, in general terms, self-evident, since it is difficult to conceive of a truly democratic regime without a legal system that effectively restrains governments, guarantees fundamental rights and fairly and promptly resolves disputes. In practical terms, however, this linkage is problematic. Indeed, most countries currently embarked on transitions to democracy have weak legal systems that are either not respected by the majority of the population or are manipulated by powerful elites to exploit vulnerable groups. Aware of these short-comings, governments in these countries, supported and encouraged by development practitioners, have launched an ambitious crusade to reform legal and judicial systems. Their expectation is that improvements in the quality of legal systems will contribute to the consolidation of democracy. This expectation, however, raises fundamental questions about the relationship between law and democracy. It presupposes that there is a positive correlation between improvements in the quality of legal systems and the quality of democracy. Yet, as an instrument of governance, law serves any type of political regime, including repulsive regimes and detestable dictatorships, as evidenced by the sophisticated legal forms employed by the apartheid system in South Africa[1] and the Pinochet regime in Chile.[2] Many of those involved in the crusade to reform legal systems seem to assume that this type of reform is a purely technical process without any political implications. Accordingly, relying on the experience of legal institutions of Western democracies, they have developed rule of law and governance 'tool-kits' that are meant to serve as blueprints for social engineers involved in the implementation of legal reform.[3] While, undoubtedly, law is a technical device, it is also an elusive and complex mechanism.

Indeed, while most theories about democracy regard the rule of law as an indispensable attribute of democratic regimes, these theories also regard law as an external device to discipline majority rule. The view of law as a tool to restrain democracy is reflected in the modern conception of constitutionalism.[4] Under this conception, the constitution sets the limits of legislative action and assigns to supreme courts or specially constituted constitutional courts the role of enforcing them. But as well as playing a restraining role, law also plays a positive role as guarantor of fundamental rights and as a platform for social and economic empowerment. In this positive role, the rule of law facilitates the smooth functioning of markets, protecting and enforcing property and contractual rights. But the rule of law also purports to be neutral and, as such, does not guarantee equal or fair economic outcomes. It only guarantees formal equality and is unconcerned with prevailing substantive inequalities.[5] As a consequence, many regard the rule of law as an ideology that legitimizes and conceals power relations.[6] Yet such is the power of the notion of the rule of law that even those who endorse social theories that have little regard for it acknowledge that the rule of law is an unqualified human good, despite its shortcomings.[7]

Law is unquestionably an elusive and multifaceted institution. As a consequence, its relationship with democratic institutions is neither simple nor purely technical. The political evolution of countries with a long history of democracy in North America and Europe shows that the process of achieving effective legal systems within a democratic framework is neither smooth nor free of conflict. The expansion of legal rights in those countries was a long-drawn and highly contested process, often violent.[8] Although historians and social theorists disagree over the sequencing of the extension of civil, political and social rights, they nonetheless agree that this process is inseparable from the broader process of democratization.[9] Hence, while legal systems in established democracies are today regarded as neutral frameworks that guarantee that all citizens are treated as equal and enjoy legal security, the process leading to this outcome was neither technical nor neutral. Yet, the expectation of many today is that countries that are building or rebuilding democratic regimes should instantly and effortlessly replicate the legal institutions of older democracies and that they should do this in an orderly manner without political contestation.

Current enthusiasm for the rule of law should not obscure the fact that attempts by most developing and transition countries simultaneously to build strong democratic and legal institutions are fraught with unexpected outcomes that call for reflection and debate. This is especially so in the case of Latin America. The search for democracy in most countries in the region has been long and frustrating. Democratic regimes have generally been short lived. Most countries have been plagued by political instability and a succession of populist and authoritarian regimes. The search for democracy has produced dysfunctional legal systems under which law does not apply equally to rulers and the ruled.[10] While political, economic and social elites behave as if they were above the law, the majority of the people regard law as an instrument of oppression, rather than of empowerment or protection.[11] This popular perception about the law is not surprising in a continent where the richest 10 per cent of the population take 48 per cent of total income, while the poorest 10 per cent have to make do with only 1.6 per cent.[12] Under these circumstances and given that most countries have ruled out policies aimed at equalising incomes, it is difficult to foresee how the current process of democratization can bring about neutral and fair legal systems. More difficult still is to imagine how law and legal institutions could be used by citizens to further the process of democratization.

Yet, the prospects are not altogether gloomy. There are signs that the current wave of democratization is changing the way ordinary citizens relate to public authorities. People are using courts more often than before, human rights commissions are actively denouncing abuses, constitutional charters have empowered indigenous communities, national and international solidarity networks provide support to vulnerable groups, such as poor women and ethnic minorities, and government officials act more cautiously as they become aware that their decisions may be the object of legal and or constitutional challenges. It is, of course, too early to draw unambiguous conclusions about the long-term impact of these developments. Yet, in order to gauge their significance it is important not to lose sight of the obstacles that account for past failures. Since some of these obstacles have deep historical roots they are likely to slow-down the reform efforts. It would be foolhardy if an over-optimistic assessment of the current process of democratization led us to ignore these obstacles.

This analysis is intended as a contribution towards identifying the obstacles, as well as the opportunities, in the current efforts to bring about democratization through law. It does not purport either to resolve the problems or examine in detail the available opportunities. It consists of two sections. The first examines, from a historical perspective, the reasons for the weakness of legal institutions in Latin America, focusing on Chile. The second section examines the experience of constitutional justice in Colombia and reflects upon its impact on the process of democratization.

Markets versus Citizenship – the Case of Chile

Law's Dilemma

The failure of democracy and the weakness of legal institutions in Latin America is often attributed to one or more of the following three factors: the failure of the countries in the region genuinely to embrace the tenets of economic liberalism; excessive state intervention in the economic; and the negative influence of economic imperialism. Jeremy Adelman and Miguel Angel Centeno, a historian and a sociologist respectively, have recently challenged this interpretation.[13] Instead, they argue that the root cause of the problems with Latin American democracy lies in the failure to reconcile market orientated economic policies with systems of political representation. This failing, according to them, has generated a difficult dilemma for law. Market policies, which at different periods in the history of the region have been enthusiastically embraced by local elites, have not been accompanied by policies that effectively recognize the legal equality of citizens. As a consequence, the relationship between markets and legal systems has been explosive, rather than self-reinforcing. Because market-based policies lacked political legitimacy they were short lived and unstable. During the heyday of economic liberalism, in the late nineteenth century and early part of the twentieth century, the elites failed to make the political system more inclusive. Instead of expanding the franchise they either added new legal restrictions or undermined the efficacy of elections through vote-rigging and vote-buying. The elites' greed for profits led them to abandon any attempt systematically to provide public goods, thus further undermining their legitimacy. This policy, characterized by the authors as 'property without representation', brought about a backlash, which between 1930 and the early 1970s was reflected in the emergence of a succession of populist regimes. This populist backlash took many forms, but it is generally identified with the regimes of Getúlio Vargas in Brazil (1930–1945, 1951–1954) and Juán Domingo Perón in Argentina (1946–1955). According to Adelman and Centeno, populist regimes sought to restore the long-forgotten republican tradition of the early days of independence from Spain. They actively incorporated the popular masses into the political system, addressing issues of income distribution and social rights that the advocates of market-based policies had neglected. But populism, in its many guises, also failed to find a proper balance between market-based policies with an expanded notion of citizenship and social equality. This failing brought about, in the 1970s and 1980s, yet another attempt to revive market-based policies, which often required using force to dismantle the social and economic gains achieved by the subordinate classes during the previous period.

The failure to reconcile market policies with political participation generates what Adelman and Centeno characterize as law's dilemma in Latin America: attempts to embrace the market often go together with restrictions of political and social rights; while attempts to expand political and social rights are accompanied by strong state intervention that suffocates the economy. Under these circumstances, the main casualty is the ideal that law should apply equally to all citizens. Instead, what obtains is that one law applies to the rulers and another to the ruled. Law's dilemma is brilliantly captured in the much-quoted statement, attributed to a Brazilian politician: 'for my friends everything, for my enemies the law'.

Chilean Exceptionalism

On the surface, the case of Chile seems to contradict Adelman and Centeno's interpretation. During the nineteenth century, Chile enjoyed long periods of political stability, and in the twentieth century it largely managed to escape the type of populism that affected many of its neighbours.[14] Between 1831 and 1891, presidential and congressional elections under the rule of the constitution were a regular feature of Chilean politics. Although the electorate was small and the electoral process far from perfect, the early adherence to constitutional procedures was not a sham. It contributed to inculcating among the elites respect for formal political processes and brought about an early parliamentarization of politics. Later on, in the first half of the twentieth century, under the rule of the constitution, there took place a major expansion of the franchise along with the acknowledgement of the legitimacy of unions in the manufacturing and mining sectors and the limited extension of social rights to the poor. While there have been three periods of severe crisis and instability – a brief civil war in 1891, an eight-year period of political chaos between 1924 and 1932, and the 17-year long dictatorship of General Augusto Pinochet between 1973 and 1990 – the political system always managed to bounce back to a seemingly orderly form of government under the authority of the constitution. It thus seems that one way or another, Chile largely manages to resolve the dilemma between markets and political representation.

A closer examination of the evolution of the political system suggests, however, that Adelman and Centeno's interpretation also applies to Chile, albeit with qualifications. Indeed, the origins of Chile's most important political crises – the Civil War of 1891 and the military coup of 1973 – can be traced to the tension resulting from the failure to reconcile economic policies with effective civil and political citizenship. The Civil War of 1891 brought to a halt a promising process of political and legal liberalization, and General Augusto Pinochet's dictatorship reversed the process of democratization and crushed hard-won social and economic rights acquired by legal means and through a slow and painful struggle.

In the mid-nineteenth century there was a genuine push towards political liberalization. An alliance was forged between regional economic elites and intellectuals influenced by European libertarian ideas, who pressed for major changes to the political system. The powers of the hitherto authoritarian presidents were drastically reduced, property restrictions to the franchise were eliminated and civil and political liberties, including freedom of assembly and freedom of association, were incorporated into the constitution.[15] These political reforms reinforced the legitimacy of the political regime and were a suitable complement to laissez-faire economic doctrine, which, at the time, was widely endorsed by the elites. Conditions thus seemed ideally suited to bring about a progressive and harmonious process of political and economic liberalization. These auspicious conditions were reinforced, in 1883, by the annexation, through war, of vast nitrate-rich territory hitherto under the sovereignty of Peru and Bolivia. There ensued an export-led boom that stimulated manufacturing industry and expanded the national market for agricultural products. But these favourable economic conditions soon exposed major political disagreements among the elites. What was at stake was whether the state should devote the abundant nitrate revenue to developing and supporting the establishment of a national market through public expenditure in education and infrastructure development, or whether it should refrain from political intervention in the economy, restricting its role to the collection of export duties and the enforcement of law and order to prevent the labour force in mining areas from disrupting the flow of such valuable exports. Failure to resolve this disagreement by political means led, in 1891, to a civil war that lasted nearly a year and resulted in some 6,000 casualties.[16]

The civil war, fought ostensibly over the interpretation of a clause in the constitution, brought about a major change to the political regime. It ushered in a parliamentary regime that enhanced the power of the congress within the political system, but brought to a halt, and in many respects reversed, the process of political liberalization begun in the mid-nineteenth century. Although after the civil war the constitution was promptly restored and elections were regularly held, the majority of the population did not benefit from the prevailing export-driven boom and were excluded from the convoluted and largely sterile congressional debates.[17] While the party system represented a narrow constituency, the power of the law was ruthlessly deployed to repress and contain emerging organisations established by workers, artisans and the urban poor. Thus, while the export-driven economic policy, inspired in the principles of laissez-faire, brought prosperity to a few, the elites showed little interest in implementing liberalism at the political level. Instead, they used the full force of the law to repress those seeking access to justice and political voice. This state of affairs lasted for some 30 years, until the mid-1920s, when international markets for nitrate exports collapsed and the country went into political turmoil for nearly a decade.[18]

The collapse of the political regime did not, however, lead to populism, as was the case in other countries in the region. Instead, what emerged was a stable constitutional government. Despite recurrent economic problems, political institutions seemed to strengthen and to operate in accordance with the standards of developed Western democracies. Between 1932 and 1973, governments were elected at regular intervals following established constitutional procedures, the army accepted the verdict of the polls, political and civil rights were generally respected, the press was free and lively, the judiciary was independent and there were strict financial and legal controls on the activities of the state bureaucracy. These features of the political system suggest that in the late 1930s Chile had found a formula that even today eludes most developing countries. It achieved effective governance within a democratic framework that respected constitutionalism and legality. It also appeared to have avoided the cycle of populism noted by Adelman and Centeno. Yet, on close inspection, the picture that emerges is less rosy. While the democratic achievements were undeniable, the political and legal systems had major flaws that were fully exposed as the regime moved towards more egalitarian policies and began to embrace social and economic rights in favour of the poorest sections of the population.

The stability of the political system in the 1930s and 1940s was largely achieved by making the political system more inclusive. In 1936, an alliance between middle and working-class parties brought into being a Latin American version of the French Popular Front, which gave political voice to an important segment of citizens. The opening of the political system brought about a lively process of coalition politics in which, often, right-wing and Marxist parties were part of the same coalition.[19] But this surprising display of moderation from both sides of the political spectrum was short lived. The political system was progressive, but only up to a point. Women were excluded from the electoral process and agricultural workers – one-third of the workforce – were denied the right to form unions and were kept under the yoke of landowners who continued to enjoy the privileges they had enjoyed during the nineteenth century. In order to sustain this inequitable democratic system a peculiar system of legality evolved, which gave the executive virtually unlimited discretion to use its regulatory powers to resolve urgent economic and political problems and excluded courts from virtually any involvement in controlling acts of the administration. Relying on this type of legality successive governments issued decrees and regulations aimed at controlling prices, securing the distribution of essential consumer goods and ensuring that landlords did not take advantage of the urban poor. But this type of legality also enabled governments to use the full force of the law to repress strikes and contain social protest. In the meantime, courts withdrew into the tranquil area of private law, thus reaffirming both their independence from the government and their irrelevance to the democratic process.

Excessive state intervention in the economy contributed to generating an inflationary process that, in the early 1950s, brought the political system to the brink of collapse. Yet, against the odds, constitutional democracy survived and there began a systematic attempt to embrace market-based policies. Yet, this attempt failed as it was strongly resisted by organized workers, the urban poor, large sectors of the middle classes and even prominent groups within the private sector.[20] Interestingly, however, governments contained social protest through measures of political liberalization, rather than through repression. As a consequence, within a decade the size of the electorate trebled, unions regained their strength, and as centre and left-wing political parties began to compete for the vote of the recently enfranchised, their political programmes became more radical. As this process was taking place, market policies began to lose political credibility so that by the mid 1960s the electorate was offered a choice between two different versions of radical democracy: both peaceful and both decidedly critical of free-market policies [21]

Between 1964 and 1973 two successive administrations – Eduardo Frei (1964– 1970) and Salvador Allende (1970–1973) – attempted to bring about a more radical form of democracy. This attempt was cut short by the military coup of 1973. The failure to shift towards radical democracy led to the collapse of democracy altogether and to the violent pro-market backlash led by General Pinochet with the assistance of homegrown neo-liberal economists. The collapse of democracy opened up an interminable debate among political scientists about the so-called 'lessons of Chile'. Some attribute the collapse either to the malevolence or naiveté of the Marxist parties and the ultra-left, others place the blame on the United States government, while others point out that the root cause of the problem was that political polarization led to the erosion of the spirit of compromise so essential to a democracy.[22] Yet, no one has yet analyzed the role of law and legal institutions in the debacle that brought Pinochet onto the scene. While many have noted that the Supreme Court became heavily involved in the political debate, there has been no attempt to elucidate the wider role of law and legal institutions in this process. It is on this point that Adelman and Centeno's argument about law's dilemma in Latin American becomes pertinent. Indeed, from a legal point of view the collapse of democracy in 1973 stems largely from the fact that, despite the country's exemplary record of political stability, its legal system did not develop in harmony with the process of democratization. The dissonance between legal and political processes was not caused by the traditional detachment of judges from social reality. On the contrary, their detachment was a consequence of the approach to governance initially developed in the 1930s and 1940s and further refined in the following two decades. This approach, as already noted, explicitly excluded courts from key areas of public policy, thus generating a dislocated legal system in which judges were experts in private law matters, but had no experience in resolving issues of public policy.

This politically driven style of governance made courts reluctant to challenge the legislature or the government, even when they committed serious breaches of the constitution. Under this system, citizens affected by arbitrary governmental decisions virtually had no legal remedies and had to rely on political parties, contacts or influence with government officials or members of the legislature to seek redress. Thus, when in the 1960s and early 1970s governments began to use law to promote more egalitarian policies, those who disagreed with these policies sought the support of the courts. However, they soon found out that courts were not their natural allies. Indeed, initially, courts handed down decisions that, on the whole, took the side of the government. As the political confrontation evolved, courts eventually sided with government opponents. Yet, since hitherto courts had consistently refrained from taking sides, the government complained bitterly that courts were in breach of the principle of separation of powers and strongly resisted complying with their orders. Moreover, since courts had no experience resolving issues that involved public policy and public law, their decisions were clumsy and unpersuasive, thus increasing the rage of the government and its supporters, who regarded the courts as instruments of the dominant classes. In the end, neither government nor opposition supporters seriously believed that courts were a neutral arena.

Throughout most of the twentieth century, Chile combined democratic politics with firm adherence to legality. Thus, during this period Chile seemed to have resolved law's dilemma, as characterized by Adelman and Centeno. The foregoing suggests, however, that this was not the case. Indeed, the Achilles' heel of Chile's development has been its failure to secure a balance between legal and political institutions and its inability to reconcile market policies with a reasonable framework of political representation. The institutional consequences of this failing proved fatal to democracy. Courts, though independent, played a marginal role within the political system. They were prevented from effectively protecting the constitutional rights of citizens and were denied any role in major issues of public policy. As long as the political elites were willing to sacrifice their immediate interests for the sake of stability, the system appeared to work well. But when consensus among the elites evaporated and popular demands became more radical, courts proved incapable of playing a constructive role in support of the democratic process.

Constitutional Justice: The Case of Colombia

Judicial Review – Background

Strengthening the institutional capacity of courts is one of the main objectives of contemporary promoters of democracy and legal reform. Their objective is to enable courts to play an active part in restraining arbitrary action by governments and safeguarding constitutional rights. Among the many mechanisms developed to strengthen the political status of judiciaries, none is more important than the power to protect the integrity of the constitution through judicial review of legislation. This mechanism gives courts the power to declare unconstitutional and unenforceable any law or act by a public official inconsistent with the constitution. In recent years judicial review of legislation has spread to all regions of the world and today it is regarded as an essential component of constitution-making.[23] In Latin America, these measures have focused either on attempts to revive the hitherto moribund review powers of Supreme Courts or on the establishment of separate constitutional courts, based on the model used by some European countries.

It is ironic that today, as the notion of judicial review of legislation captures the political imagination of most countries in the world, in the United States – where this mechanism originated – eminent observers are beginning to have second thoughts. They are either re-opening old questions or raising new concerns about the fit between judicial review and democracy. The philosopher Jeremy Waldron, for example, argues that in reasonably democratic societies judicial review of legislation is inappropriate. He characterizes reasonably democratic societies as those that have adequate legislatures and judicial institutions and where its citizens, though disagreeing about rights, are fully committed to the protection of individual and minority rights.[24] This philosophical argument is complemented by a well-known political argument that points out that judicial review is undemocratic as it gives un-elected judges the power to override decisions of democratically elected legislatures.[25] A recent powerful argument along this line challenges the notion of judicial supremacy claiming instead that popular constitutionalism, described as a mechanism that mediates between constitutional law and popular culture, is a more reliable method of resolving disagreements currently settled through judicial review.[26] There is little doubt that the ascent into prominence of judicial review is to some extent attributable to the positive role played by the US Supreme Court in the promotion and defence of civil rights during the 1960s. In recent years, however, even this widely held perception about the role of the Supreme Court has been the object of close scrutiny, as some observers are beginning to question whether the Court does indeed deserve such credit.[27]

Critics of judicial review are, however, a minority. Most academic observers and policy-makers in the United States and Europe fervently support it.[28] Yet not all those who espouse it are necessarily sanguine about its prospects in developing countries. Indeed, Henry Abraham, one of its staunchest advocates, concedes that the successful implementation of judicial review is dependent on some requisites. These requisites include regime stability, a competitive party system, significant horizontal power distribution, a strong tradition of judicial independence and a high degree of political freedom.[29] These requisites presuppose such a high level of political development that it is unlikely that many developing countries in the world today would satisfy them. It is ironic that while Abraham points out that a high level of political development is necessary to ensure the success of judicial review, Waldron argues that societies that have such a high level of development do not need any form of judicial review of legislation.

In Latin America, however, despite theoretical misgivings, judicial review of legislation is a reality.[30] It is perhaps too early to evaluate its impact on the new democracies in the region. It seems, however, that in some countries, Peru, for example, it has not worked very well,[31] while in others, such as Chile, the Supreme Court continues to display considerable reluctance to challenge the constitutionality of legislation.[32] In Brazil, judicial review has been widely used, but it is not yet clear whether this procedure has made a substantial contribution towards improving governance and democracy.[33] Costa Rica and Colombia are two countries where judicial review and constitutional justice appear to be working well. The success of judicial review in Costa Rica is not surprising. Costa Rica, after all, is generally regarded as the country with the most advanced and well-ordered democratic and political system in the region.[34]

Colombia's Constitutional Court

That the experience of constitutional justice in Colombia should be singled out as a source of inspiration for those interested in understanding the link between law and democracy could well be regarded as surprising.[35] Indeed, for four decades, Colombia has been torn by violent conflict and its government has been fighting two firmly entrenched guerrilla movements.[36] In recent years, this conflict has been fuelled by the production and export of illicit drugs, which, in turn, has severely undermined the efficacy and integrity of public institutions. Colombia is one of the most violent countries in Latin America, with one of the highest homicide rates in the world. In 2000, the rate of homicides per 100,000 was 63, while in the same year the Latin American average was 25 and the European average stood at 1.5.[37] Yet despite these problems, the Constitutional Court, established in 1991, has dramatically improved access to justice for ordinary people and has had a decisive impact in shaping and influencing major aspects of public policy.

The resurgence of constitutional justice in Colombia is relatively recent. Prior to 1991, the power to review the constitutionality of legislation was entrusted to the Supreme Court, which, in line with the tradition of similar courts in the region, displayed enormous deference towards the political organs of the state. By the late 1970s, however, the Court began to take its role as guardian of the constitution more seriously. In 1991, the Constituent Assembly established the Constitutional Court and the writ of protection, known in Spanish as *tutela*.[38]

The Constitutional Court has the power to review the constitutionality of legislation and the power to review *tutela* decisions of lower courts. The method established by the constitution for the selection of the members of the Constitutional Court gives its members strong political legitimacy. The Senate elects the nine members of the Court from nominees submitted by the President of the Republic, the Supreme Court and the Council of State (the highest administrative court). As well as enhanced legitimacy, this method of appointment has given members of the Constitutional Court a degree of independence and self-confidence rarely found among members of high courts in Latin America. The Court enjoys 55 per cent approval rate in public opinion polls, a fact that its members undoubtedly relish.

Indeed, as Justice Cepeda-Espinosa notes, when newspapers in Colombia refer to 'the Court', they mean the Constitutional Court, not the Supreme Court.[39]

The *tutela* procedure is a good complement to the Constitutional Court, as it enables individuals to invoke protection from any court in the event that their fundamental rights are threatened or violated either by a public official or, under certain circumstances, by a private party. *Tutelas* can be filed directly by individuals without the assistance of lawyers, and courts are required to respond promptly handing down a decision within ten days. *Tutela* decisions can be appealed, but appeals must be decided within 20 days. If the Constitutional Courts exercises its power to review *tutela* decisions – a power that is discretionary – the court must decide the case within two months. As a mechanism to improve access to justice for ordinary citizens, the *tutela* has been a resounding success. In 1992 the number of *tutelas* decided by all courts in Colombia was just over 10,000. By 1998 this figure increased to 38,000 and by 2002 the number of *tutelas* was just over 141,000. Thus in 10 years, *tutelas* filed before courts in Colombia increased by a factor of 14.[40] These figures suggest that the drafters of the 1991 Constitution correctly detected a hitherto untapped popular demand for justice. On the other hand, they might have unwittingly opened a Pandora's box.

The enormous popularity of *tutelas* is largely due the Constitutional Court's expansive and liberal approach to interpretation. Indeed, in many areas, the decisions of the court are more liberal than those of the most liberal courts in developed countries. The court, for example, has held that in cases of terminally ill patients, society must respect their wishes for a dignified death and that the state should not punish medical doctors that give effect to patients' wishes.[41] It has also declared unconstitutional legislation that criminalized the possession and use of narcotic drugs on the ground that the state can only impose restrictions on behaviour that affects others.[42] The court has also intervened in defence of the right of individuals to determine their personal appearance. These cases generally concern youth who are required by their school to have short hair or who are not allowed to wear make up to school.[43]

The court has also been a reliable guardian of the rights of indigenous peoples, in particular, of their right to administer justice in accordance with their traditions and established practices. Thus, for example, it has held that some forms of traditional punishment, such as administering lashes, are consistent with the constitution and should not be judged exclusively from the perspective of modern Western law.[44] It has also upheld the constitutionality of banishment orders issued by leaders of indigenous communities on the ground that the constitution acknowledges cultural and ethnic diversity.[45]

In cases concerning gender discrimination, the court has almost invariably decided *tutela* cases in favour of women plaintiffs. Thus, it has held that the exclusion of pregnant women from educational establishments, or the exclusion of women generally from night work or from military training schools is unconstitutional.[46] The court has also rejected, as unconstitutional, discrimination on grounds of sexual orientation).[47] In the area of abortion, however, the court has refused to recognise women's right to choose.[48] Likewise, in cases that have raised issues relating to the recognition by the state of property and financial implications of same sex relationships, the position of the court has reflected the traditional conservative views of Colombian society.[49]

The most controversial decisions of the court are those that concern the enforcement of economic and social rights. In this area, although the court concedes that under the constitution the executive and the congress have the power to design and implement economic and social policies, it has held, nonetheless, that in the exercise of this power they are subject to the rules of the constitution. The constitution, according to the court, is not neutral regarding policies that allocate economic and social rights. If these policies have the effect of nullifying a fundamental right, then, by virtue of their impact on such a right, economic and social rights become judicially enforceable. Applying this principle of interpretation, the court has required state agencies in the area of health to provide treatment or medication that the agencies had ruled out on financial grounds. For example, they have been required to provide medication to AIDS patients and treatment for children affected with chronic or serious diseases. In these cases, the fundamental right at issue is the right to life, which according to the court is not merely a right to exist, but a right to a dignified life.[50] The financial consequences of these decisions have been substantial. It has been estimated that in 1998 health state agencies spent US$2 million in excess of its budget to comply with *tutela* decisions. One year later, this figure increased to nearly US$7 million.[51]

In areas of economic policy – such as housing finance and incomes policy – the court has also decided important cases. In three decisions handed down in 1999, the court struck down government regulations, as well as legislation designed to restructure the system of housing finance. The objective sought by the government was to align interest rates on mortgages with market rates. This shift towards the market had the effect of significantly increasing the monthly mortgage repayment bill and placed some 200,000 middle-class homeowners at the risk of losing their homes through re-possession proceedings.[52] The court struck down the regulations on the ground that they made illusory the constitutional right to dignified housing. After rejecting two further schemes proposed by the government the court finally endorsed, in 2000, a new housing-finance scheme on the understanding that the interests charged would not be determined by market forces.[53] The court also scrutinized the legislative provisions that allow the government to set minimum wages for public-sector workers. In a series of cases decided between 1999 and 2001, it held that annual wage increases should never be lower than the anticipated inflation rate for the following year and, accordingly, declared unconstitutional the provisions of the annual budget law on the ground that it did not meet this standard. More recently, however, the court has backtracked, conceding that imposing a rigid judicial standard on incomes policy is not helpful, but has reaffirmed that the government should endeavour to protect the purchasing power of public-sector workers.

The court has also supported the rights of groups that hitherto had no voice in Colombian society. These groups include prison inmates and internally displaced persons. This latter category consists of people who have been forced to flee from their homes and regions as a consequence of the violence that prevails in the countryside. It is estimated that more than three million people have been displaced by violence since 1985.[54] After deciding numerous *tutela* cases brought by prisoners and internally displaced people, the court concluded that both groups were living in sub-human conditions. Thus, in two separate decisions the court characterized the situation of these two groups as 'an unconstitutional state of affairs' and called upon the government promptly to put in place measures to safeguard their right to life, health and dignity. These two decisions prompted the government to launch a US$240 million programme for the modernization of prisons and a US$450 million programme to benefit internally displaced persons.[55]

Given the trend of its decisions, the Constitutional Court's popularity with ordinary citizens is not surprising. It is also unsurprising that, in its relatively short life, the court has attracted criticism from successive governments, from members of the congress and from prominent economists. Even the Supreme Court has joined the rank of critics, as it deeply resents that the Constitutional Court has decided to accept *tutelas* against judicial decisions.[56] There is little doubt that, by the standards of legal reasoning applied by Latin American judiciaries, the court's activist and liberal approach to constitutional interpretation is a breath of fresh air. Instead of automatically deferring to the government or the legislature, the court takes its role as guardian of constitutional rights seriously and, as a consequence, has prompted successive administrations to bring about important changes in many areas of public policy. Its approach to constitutional interpretation is also providing public space to individuals and groups hitherto excluded or marginal to the political system.

While praising the court could well be justified, the question that arises is whether its extraordinary activism is contributing to the process of democratization. This is not an easy question and I will not attempt to offer a definitive answer. There are, however, two dimensions to this question that deserve consideration: one is access to justice and the other is the court's position within the political system. In terms of access to justice, the court has been instrumental in encouraging ordinary citizens to assert their rights and, as a consequence, become aware of the role of the constitution within the political order. Enhanced access to justice also provides individuals and groups with a platform to voice grievances that did not exist before 1991. As well as enhancing citizens' access to justice, the large volume of *tutelas* filed since 1991 is also helping to expose major weakness in the system of governance. Indeed, a recent statistical survey shows that more than 30 per cent of *tutelas* stem from the failure of state agencies to respond in a timely and effective way to complaints and petitions from citizens.[57] A slight improvement in the quality of governance would thus reduce the load of courts and increase the welfare of citizens.

The impact of the Constitutional Court on the political regime is harder to evaluate. At one level, it is difficult to dispute the claim that the court is treading in areas – such as economic or health policies – traditionally reserved for the political organs of the state. It is through political deliberation that policies in these areas should be developed and implemented. From this perspective, it could well be argued that the court is pre-empting political debate, thus confirming the argument of those who regard judicial review as undemocratic. On the other hand, as Justice Cepeda-Espinosa and other local observers note, the court's intervention in this areas of policy is prompted precisely by the weakness of the prevailing democratic structures, manifested mainly by the weakness of the party system and the strong presidential style of government.[58] The weakness of the party system means that politicians do not adequately reflect the concerns and interests of ordinary people, and, even when they do, the strong executive overpowers them. From this perspective, the court's progressive decisions provide a convenient outlet that enables citizens to bring into the public arena issues ignored or neglected by the political system, such as the state of prisons or the plight of internally displaced people. But such easy access to constitutional justice has a downside, as it encourages disgruntled politicians and other individuals to transform political disagreements into issues of constitutional law – such as the debate on housing finance and salary increases – thus undermining the legitimacy and integrity of the political process.

Conclusion

Today there is consensus that the process of democratization cannot be furthered without an effective legal system that restrains governments, guarantees the enjoyment of fundamental rights and resolves disputes without interference either from governments or powerful members of the elites. There is no consensus, however, on how developing and transition countries can get such a legal system. The historical evidence examined in this essay is not entirely promising. Yet the historical evidence also confirms that while there is no clear pathway to achieving democratization through law, legal reform is not altogether futile. Intellectuals and practitioners can make an important contribution towards clarifying how in different contexts law can and does bring about improvements in the process of democratization. But in order to do this they must be willing continuously to question assumptions and prejudices about the role of law in society. In the Latin American context, one such assumption concerns the role of courts.

Courts in Latin America are often criticized because of their indifference to the political consequences of their decisions. Judges respond to this criticism with the familiar argument that their critics miss the point since the problem is not the content of court decisions, but the laws that courts are called upon to interpret. Thus they argue that because courts merely interpret legal rules, critics of judicial decisions should aim their fire at the legislature, rather than courts. Yet, as the case of Chile shows, judges and courts often distance themselves from the consequences of their decisions not because of their adherence to the precepts of legal positivism, but because of the need to survive in hostile political environments. Although this judicial modus vivendi often enables courts formally to safeguard their independence, in the end, it seriously compromises their capacity to play a constructive role within the political system. Against this background, the experience of the Constitutional Court in Colombia is an inspiration to similar courts in Latin America. For in its relentless campaign to persuade Colombian politicians to take the constitution seriously, the court is attempting to resolve the tension between markets and political representation. Its insistence that the constitution is not neutral on matters of economic and social rights is a powerful reminder that, however persuasive the logic of economics may be, it is of no value unless the policies it inspires take into account the needs and interests of all citizens.

NOTES

1. Richard L. Abel, *Politics by Other Means – Law in the Struggle Against Apartheid, 1984–1994* (London: Routledge, 1995).
2. Robert Barros, *Constitutionalism and Dictatorship – Pinochet, the Junta and the 1980 Constitution* (Cambridge: Cambridge University Press, 2002).
3. US Agency for International Development, *Conducting a DG Assessment: A Framework for Strategy Development* (Washington, DC: Centre for Democracy and Governance USAID, 2000).
4. Giovanni Sartori, 'Constitutionalism: A Preliminary Discussion', *American Political Science Review*, Vol.56, No.4 (1962), pp.853–4.
5. F.A. Hayek, *The Constitution of Liberty* (London: Routledge & Kegan Paul, 1960), pp.220–33.
6. Roberto Mangabeira Unger, *The Critical Legal Studies Movement* (Cambridge, MA: Harvard University Press, 1983), pp.5–14.
7. E.P. Thompson, *Whigs and Hunters* (London: Penguin Books, 1975), pp.258–69.
8. Charles Tilly, *Contention and Democracy in Europe 1650–2000* (Cambridge: Cambridge University Press, 2004), pp.1–41, 243–59.
9. Reinhard Bendix, *Nation Building and Citizenship* (Garden City, NY: Anchor Books, 1969), pp.89–126; T.H. Marshall, *Citizenship and Social Class* (Cambridge: Cambridge University Press, 1950), pp.10–27.
10. Juan Méndez, Guillermo O'Donnell and Paulo Sergio Pinheiro (eds), *The (Un)Rule of Law and Democracy in Latin America* (Notre Dame, IN: University of Notre Dame Press, 1998).
11. UNDP, *Report on the Development of Democracy in Latin America* (New York: United Nations, 2004).
12. World Bank, *Inequality in Latin America and the Caribbean: Breaking with History?* (Washington, DC: World Bank Latin Americana and Caribbean Studies, 2003), p.1.
13. Jerry Adelman and Miguel Angel Centeno, 'Between Liberalism and Neoliberalism: Law's Dilemma in Latin America', in Yves Dezalay and Bryant G. Garth, *Global Prescriptions* (Ann Arbor, MI: University of Michigan Press, 2002), pp.139–61.
14. For a general history of Chile, see William F. Sater and Simon Collier, *A History of Chile, 1808–1994* (Cambridge: Cambridge University Press, 1996) and Brian Loveman, *Chile – The Legacy of Hispanic Capitalism* (New York: Oxford University Press, 1979). For a survey of political events during the twentieth century, see Federico G. Gil, *The Political System of Chile* (Boston: Houghton Mifflin Company, 1966) and Julio Faundez, *Marxism and Democracy in Chile: from 1932 to the Fall of Allende* (New Haven, CT: Yale University Press, 1988).
15. Simon Collier, *Chile: The Making of a Republic, 1830–1865* (Cambridge: Cambridge University Press, 2003).
16. Harold Blakemore, 'Chile From the War of the Pacific to the World Depression, 1880–1930', in Leslie Bethell (ed.), *The Cambridge History of Latin America, Volume V* (Cambridge: Cambridge University Press, 1986), pp.499–551; Maurice Zeitlin, *The Civil Wars in Chile* (Princeton, NJ: Princeton University Press, 1984).
17. Karen L. Remmer, *Party Competition in Argentina and Chile – Political Recruitment and Public Policy, 1890–1930* (Lincoln, NE: University of Nebraska Press, 1984).
18. Arnold Bauer 'Industry and the Missing Bourgeoisie: Consumption and Development in Chile, 1850–1950', *Hispanic American Historical Review*, Vol.70, No.2 (1990), pp.227–53.
19. Paul W. Drake, *Socialism and Populism in Chile, 1932–52* (Urbana, IL: University of Illinois Press, 1978).
20. Ricardo Ffrench-Davis, *Las Políticas Económicas en Chile 1952–1970* (Santiago: Ediciones Nueva Universidad, 1973).
21. Atilio Borón, 'Movilización Política y Crisis Política en Chile (1920–1970)' *Aportes*, No.20 (1971), pp.41–69.
22. Julio Faundez, 'The Chilean Road to Socialism', *The Political Quarterly*, July–September (1975), pp.310–25.
23. Tom Ginsburg, *Judicial Review in New Democracies* (Cambridge: Cambridge University Press, 2003).
24. Jeremy Waldron, *The Core Case against Judicial Review* (2005; available at <www.ucl.ac.uk/spp/download/seminars/0405/Waldron-Judicial.pdf>). See also Jeremy Waldron, *Law and Disagreement* (Oxford: Oxford University Press, 1999), pp.209–312.

25. Mark Tushnet, *Taking the Constitution Away from the Courts* (Princeton, NJ: Princeton University Press, 1999). For a recent general critique of judicial review, see Ran Hirschl, *Towards Juristocracy* (Cambridge, MA: Harvard University Press, 2004).
26. Larry D. Kramer, *The People Themselves: Popular Constitutionalism and Judicial Review* (New York: Oxford University Press, 2004).
27. See, for example, Gerald N. Rosenberg, *The Hollow Hope – Can Courts Bring About Social Change?* (Chicago, IL: University of Chicago Press, 1991). See also Michael J. Klarman, *From Jim Crow to Civil Rights: The Supreme Court and the Struggle for Racial Equality* (New York: Oxford University Press, 2004).
28. Aharon Barak, 'Foreword: A Judge on Judging: The Role of the Supreme Court in a Democracy', *Harvard Law Review*, Vol.116 (November 2002), pp.16–162; Mauro Cappelletti, *The Judicial Process in Comparative Perspective* (Oxford: Oxford University Press, 1989); Erwin Chemerinsky, 'In Defense of Judicial Review: The Perils of Popular Constitutionalism', *University of Illinois Law Review*, Vol.2004, No.3, pp.673–90; Ronald Dworkin, *Freedom's Law The Moral Reading of the Constitution* (Oxford: Oxford University Press, 1996), pp.1–38; Robert B. McKay, 'Judicial Review in a Liberal Democracy', in J. Roland Pennock and John W. Chapman (eds), *Nomos 25: Liberal Democracy* (New York: New York University Press, 1983), pp.121–44.
29. Henry J. Abraham, *The Judicial Process*, 3rd ed. (Oxford: Oxford University Press, 1975), p.280.
30. Pilar Domingo, 'Judicialization of Politics or Politicization of the Judiciary? Recent Trends in Latin America', *Democratization*, Vol.11, No.1 (2004), pp.104–26.
31. César Landa, *Tribunal Constitucional y Estado Democrático* (Lima: Pontificia Universidad Católica del Perú, Fondo Editorial, 1999).
32. Javier A. Couso, 'The Politics of Judicial Review in Chile in the Era of Democratic Transition, 1990–2002', *Democratization*, Vol.10, No.4 (2003), pp.70–91.
33. Keith S. Rosenn, 'Judicial Review in Brazil: Developments Under the 1988 Constitution', *Southwestern Journal of Law and Trade in the Americas*, Vol.7 (Fall 2000), pp.291–319.
34. Robert S. Barker, 'Judicial Review in Costa Rica: Evolution and Recent Developments', *Southwestern Journal of Law and Trade in the Americas*, Vol.7 (Fall 2000), pp.267–90; Bruce M. Wilson and Roger Handberg, 'From Judicial Passivity to Judicial Activism: Explaining the Change Within Costa Rica's Supreme Court', *NAFTA: Law and Business Review of the Americas* Vol.5 (Autumn 1999), pp.522–43; and Bruce M. Wilson, 'Changing Dynamics: The Political Impact of Costa Rica's Constitutional Court', in Alan Angell, Rachel Sieder and Line Schjolden (eds), *The Judicialization of Politics in Latin America* (Basingstoke: Palgrave Macmillan, 2005).
35. For a critical overview of law in Colombia, see Boaventura de Sousa Santos and Mauricio García, 'Colombia: El Revés del Contrato Social de la Modernidad', in Boaventura de Sousa Santos and Mauricio García (eds), *El Caleidoscopio de las Justicias en Colombia* (Tomo I) (Bogotá: Colciencias, 2001), pp.11–84.
36. Daniel Pécaut, 'Presente, Pasado y Futuro de la Violencia', in Jean-Michel Blanquer and Christian Gros (eds), *Las Dos Colombias* (Bogotá: Grupo Editorial Norma, 2002), pp.19–79.
37. UNDP (note 11), Table 29.
38. On the role of the Supreme Court before 1991, see Rodrigo Uprimny, 'Las Transformaciones de la Administración de Justicia en Colombia', in Boaventura de Sousa Santos and Mauricio García (eds), *El Caleidoscopio de las Justicias en Colombia* (Tomo I) (Bogotá: Colciencias, 2001), pp.261–308; Manuel José Cepeda-Espinosa, 'Judicial Activism in a Violent Context: The Origin, Role, and Impact of the Colombian Constitutional Court', *Washington University Global Studies Review*, Vol.3 (Special Issue, 2004), pp.529–697. See also Mauricio García, 'La Acción de Tutela', in Boaventura de Sousa Santos and Mauricio García (eds), *El Caleidoscopio de las Justicias en Colombia* (Tomo I) (Bogotá: Colciencias, 2001), pp.423–54.
39. Manuel José Cepeda-Espinosa, 'Judicialization of Politics in Colombia: The Old and the New', in Angell, Sieder and Schjolden (note 34).
40. Catalina Botero, *Justicia Constitucional en Iberoamérica: Colombia* (available at <www.uc3m.es/uc3m/inst/MGP/JCI/02-colombia.htm>; accessed 27 July 2005).
41. Cepeda-Espinosa, 'Judicial Activism' (note 38), p.580.
42. Ibid. p.579.
43. Ibid. p.582.
44. Ibid. p.624. See also Ricardo Peñaranda, 'Los Nuevos Ciudadanos: Las Organizaciones Indígenas en el Sistema Político Colombiano', in Francisco Gutiérrez *et al., Degradación o Cambio, Evolución del Sistema Político Colombiano* (Bogotá: Grupo Editorial Norma, 2001), pp.131–81.

45. Esther Sánchez Botero, *Justicia y Pueblos Indígenas en Colombia* (Bogotá: Universidad Nacional, 1998), p.328.
46. Cepeda-Espinosa, 'Judicial Activism' (note 38), p.600. See also Martha I. Morgan, 'Taking Machismo to Court: The Gender Jurisprudence of the Colombian Constitutional Court', *University of Miami Inter-American Law Review*, Vol.30 (Summer 1998), pp.253–342.
47. Ibid. p.604.
48. Ibid. p.587.
49. Ibid. p.604.
50. Ibid. pp.580–81.
51. Rodrigo Uprimny, 'The Judicial Protection of Social Rights by the Colombian Constitutional Court: Cases and Debate' (manuscript on file with the author). It must be noted that the approach of the Constitutional Court in the area of health is not altogether different from the response of courts in South Africa; see Heinz Klug, 'Five Years On: How Relevant is the Constitution to the New South Africa?', *Vermont Law Review*, Vol.26, No.4 (2004), pp.803–19.
52. Uprimny (note 51).
53. Cepeda-Espinosa, 'Judicial Activism' (note 38), p.644.
54. On internally displaced persons in Colombia, see Global IDP, *Colombia: Government Response to IDPs Under Fire as Conflict Worsens*, 27 May 2005 (available at <http://www.db.idpproject.org/Sites/IdpProjectDb/idpSurvey.nsf/wViewSingleEnv/ColombiaProfile + Summary>).
55. Uprimny (note 51).
56. Silvio Fernando Trejos Bueno, 'Declaración de la Corte Suprema de Justicia', *Corte Suprema de Justicia Revista 18*, October (2004), pp.81–4.
57. Mauricio García, César Rodríguez and Rodrigo Uprimny, 'Justice and Society in Colombia: A Sociological Analysis of Colombian Courts', in Lawrence Friedman and Rogelio Pérez-Perdomo (eds), *Legal Culture in the Age of Globalization* (Stanford, CA: Stanford University Press, 2003).
58. Eduardo Pizarro Leongómez, 'La Atomización Partidista en Colombia: el fenómeno de las microempresas electorales', in Francisco Gutiérrez *et al.*, *Degradación o Cambio, Evolución del Sistema Político Colombiano* (Bogotá: Grupo Editorial Norma, 2001), pp.357–401.

Manuscript accepted for publication August 2005.

Address for correspondence: Julio Faundez, School of Law, University of Warwick, Coventry, Warwickshire, CV4 7AL, UK. E-mail: <J.faundez@warwick.ac.uk>.

Political Security and Democratic Rights

JOHN F. McELDOWNEY

Introduction

Political security underlines many of the freedoms enjoyed by democratic societies. To many in society the fear of a breakdown in law and order through civil disturbance threatens the basis of society itself. The right of the state to protect itself is therefore used as a means of securing stability in society. Many lawyers and political scientists view debates about law and order as, in reality, about controls on political protest and public order. In British history, there are many instances where popular protest only became effective when it challenged the state. The abolition of slavery, repeal of the 1815 Corn Laws in 1846, the legality of trade unions, the suffragette movement, and other popular and political causes all endured conflict with the state and state authorities on the road to eventual recognition. Legislation was often the response of the authorities to popular protest such as the Public Meeting Act 1908, passed to prevent disruption at political meetings. The two world wars had an impact on the range of emergency powers available to the state. The rise in Irish nationalism and the development of the fascist movement threatened the political security of the UK that required special powers and exceptional measures.

The focus of this study is an assessment of the impact on democracy and civil rights of measures taken to combat terrorism.[1] It is timely to consider the impact of terrorism on democracy, in the light of recent judicial decisions in the highest courts of the UK when considering challenges to the legality of some of the anti-terrorist legislation. In the aftermath of terrorist events in the United States on 11 September 2001, most Western democracies, led by the United States and the UK, responded with tougher terrorism laws than hitherto. One of the themes in this essay is the developing nature of anti-terrorist legislation and the ratchet effect it has on the operation of the ordinary criminal justice system. The use of extreme measures, such as detention without trial, may have a salutary short-term impact but may prove counter-productive for democracies engaged in long-term governance building.

The effect of anti-terrorist laws in their long-term use may result in incremental creep in executive power and a diminution in the protection afforded to civil liberties. The complexities of finding a sensible balance between effective anti-terrorist laws and maintaining civil liberties is a core element in strategic planning. Democracy and anti-terrorist laws are difficult to reconcile. There is also the international perspective of the world order harnessing the common interests with other states, securing credible support from international organizations and recognizing and obeying international law.

The account addresses the main underlying focus of how anti-terrorist laws impact on political and civil rights as follows. First, there is an attempt to explain the values that underpin a democratic society and governance, followed by an explanation of the main elements in anti-terrorist legislation with particular attention to the lessons drawn from Northern Ireland, as a case study. The role of the judiciary is analysed in the light of landmark decisions in the courts in the UK. Finally, conclusions are drawn that set out the stress points between upholding democratic rights and achieving political security of the state.

Democratic Fundamentals: Defining and Combating Terrorism

Democracy and Constitutional Protection

Democracy and the protection of civil liberties appear in different forms under a country's constitutional arrangements. In Britain, great emphasis is given to elected government that is representative and accountable to the electorate and through ministerial accountability to Parliament. The absence of a formal written constitution in the UK and the pre-eminence of the sovereignty of Parliament have the potential effect that civil liberties are vulnerable to parliamentary interference in the hands of the executive. The norms of the constitution are unwritten and depend on observance of the rule of law and trust in the institutions of Parliament to act as a check on arbitrary power. More generally, the reality is that democracies are likely to be more vulnerable to terrorism than authoritarian systems. Equally there are tendencies within democratic systems that allow for the accretion of power to the executive. In reality elections that occur usually once every five years may prove ineffective in holding government to account, especially if they secure large majorities for a single party.

In the UK, the common law is often seen as a source of individual protection, but even Albert Venn Dicey (1835–1922),[2] the leading constitutional lawyer of his period, and its fervent exponent, admitted that the rule of law enshrined in the common law tradition could be exposed as weak and ineffective, especially at times of emergency. Further suspicion about the effectiveness of the rule of law is found in the patchy framework of judicial decisions it relies upon. In fact political and economic rights were won through political battles and ultimately through political power rather than judicial decision-making. The test of legality, as defined in many judicial decisions, appears to be too narrow and circumscribed to provide a reliable or substantive protection. Judicial cases are too random and decisions too pragmatic, to provide a reliable protection of fundamental rights.[3]

In the end, it is clear that healthy political systems, strengthened and supported by international and national law, provide an important component in the checks and balances against arbitrary or authoritarian power. Popular protest, political unrest and public order issues have helped shape the main case law in areas such as the right to demonstrate, freedom of assembly and the law of public meetings. What emerges is that, invariably, property rights were better protected at common law than political liberties. In a number of important cases[4] involving various popular causes and political movements, including trade unions, the suffragette movement, as well political groupings such as the Communist Party, the rise in fascism and from various workers' movements, including Irish nationalist causes, there was conflict with the public authorities, usually the police. In such instances, the courts felt constrained to uphold the interests of the state. As a result, judicial discretion, whenever it was possible, was narrowly interpreted and showed a degree of reluctance to encourage civil liberties or advance judicial protection. The struggle for civil liberties brought the judiciary into contact with a variety of political movements for which they had little sympathy. Opposition to the state from an internal threat such as a political group or organization was treated as a 'public order' issue that threatened the internal security of the state. The public interest required protection.

The history of republican movements abroad resulting in the removal of the monarchy in many countries during the eighteenth century was a living legacy and engendered fear of how internal revolt or rebellion might threaten the survival of the UK.[5] The need for exceptional measures to keep the peace and preserve law and order became a regular occurrence. The statute book contained many examples of exceptional powers needed to meet the perceived threat from internal opposition. The UK grew its legal system on the twin-track basis that ordinary law might be supplemented by additional legal powers to meet an ongoing emergency.

Even in constitutional systems, such as the United States,[6] that favour a written code of entrenched rights, it is not always predictable to guarantee liberty. Paradoxically, it is when democracy is under threat that democracies seem most casual about the protections democracies have characteristically cherished. Dicey, the great believer in the common law tradition and the protection of the rule of law, was prepared to suspend jury trial and abrogate rights when Ireland faced a state of emergency in the 1880s.

Terrorism and its Impact on the State

Democracy and political systems are particularly sensitive to terrorism. As Gearty has noted, 'paradoxically, acts of terror thrive in the relative freedom offered by mature democracies'.[7] Defining terrorism is important in understanding its essentials. Terrorism is not a recent occurrence. Broadly defined as the use of violence for political ends, terrrorism represents a recurrent threat to political security. From the time of the French Revolution, state action was used against terrorist activities. Since then, it has remained a constant threat. The term 'terrorist' is emotive because it contains a threat to democratic rights, as it may allow disaffected minorities a disproportionate influence over the conduct of the state. Responses to terrorism may attack the foundations of democracy by subverting democratic rights. The threat against society is such that many of the normal rules of democratic society such as the trial and custody of suspects are abridged to fit an emergency or civil disorder. For example, in Britain Section 1 of the Terrorism Act 2000 has a wide definition including 'the use of violence for political ends' or 'any use of violence for the purpose of putting the public, or any section of the public in fear'. Political demands drive the use of violence, fear, extreme anxiety and instability as a means of achieving the political demands of the perpetrators.[8] Significantly, the Terrorism Act also includes religious or ideological purposes and applies to both national and international terrorism.

It is clear that terrorism takes many forms, and its label may be applied to many different activities. What is striking is that there is a remarkable similarity in the fear of terrorism today, the 'war against terror', in the minds of most Western governments with the fear of communism before its decline in Eastern Europe in the 1980s. Terrorism is viewed as a new threat, that raises profound ideological differences between Western and Eastern religions and helps underline the ideological nature of terrorism in defining philosophical and religious differences. Muslim and Christian societies appear in opposition to each other; Western attitudes often engender perceptions that are anti-Islamic and anti-Arab; non-conforming Eastern states appear in opposition to the mature Western democracies and sit as an alternative to Western values. Islamic religious beliefs in its wide variety of forms seem to stand in opposition to the values of Christianity. Such states that belong to the Arab and Muslim worlds may have authoritarian or totalitarian regimes in control. This raises difficulty about the role of opposition and whether it is justifiable to use violence under such circumstances.

The term 'terrorism' offers a convenient one-size label that has the potential to fit all forms of opposition. In a generic way, the term 'terrorist' may be found in the vocabulary of politicians and is given added provenance by the issuing of a 'war on terror'. Defining terrorism and finding it in the language of opposition to Western governments or values provides a convenient counter-terrorism culture. The fact that terrorism may cover many diverse activities and also different degrees of involvement in terrorist movements is an illustration of the difficulty and complexity of the subject. The terrorist label may be recalibrated in the light of historical events. In South Africa the African National Congress (ANC) was considered terrorist in the old days of apartheid, but today it forms the government of the new South Africa. Converting or changing terrorism from violent means to political non-violent activities must surely lie at the heart of any anti-terrorist strategy.

Terrorism has become a propaganda weapon in the hands of rival groups that manipulate violence for political ends. It is in addressing the problems of terrorism that mature democracies are most vulnerable, requiring a careful balance in developing responses that are not disproportionate and counter-productive. The fact that terrorism threatens the ordinary lives of many people through its random use of violence brings its greatest potency. Equally, terrorism impacts on how civil liberties are treated and there are many examples where counter-terrorism becomes a self-fulfilling prophecy.

Political security has a long history in Britain with profound political change and transformation coming about through political pressure. Consequently, in Britain, the struggle for civil liberties may be recounted in historical periods, each notable for the powers of the state to protect itself against external attack during war. In recent times, the First World War and the Defence of the Realm Act 1914 are good examples of the extent of state power based on the necessity of war. Far-reaching restrictions included the prolongation of the life of Parliament during the war,[9] restrictions on movement, compulsory military service and immigration controls and restrictions.[10] The Second World War[11] provided even more generally drawn powers that allowed government to rule by executive order. The Emergency Powers (Defence) Act 1939 provided broadly based executive law-making powers covering all aspects of life and commercial activity of the nation. The justification for such measures came when the nation faced external threat and the war against Nazism. The habit of legislation took hold and the unbridled scope of executive powers during war-time has had an impact on how emergency legislation may ultimately change the culture of government itself. The judicial supervision of executive power was sporadic and unpredictable.[12] The steady and incremental growth of executive powers in the hands of the prime minister may be traced back to these war-time measures and this legacy is one that remains.

The Northern Ireland emergency from the late 1960s also defined the extent of state power in terms of civil emergency where the threat came from within the country in the form of terrorism. When this spilled over to the UK after the Birmingham pub bombings, Parliament passed the Prevention of Terrorism (Temporary Provisions) Act in 1973, followed by annual renewal until 1996. The Northern Ireland example is illustrative of the features of terrorism with a political aim that is linked to political movements. Northern Ireland is given a fuller discussion below because it provides such a good case study of the variety of responses used by British and Irish governments, with the support of the United States, to end violence and build new structures for the region. Northern Ireland had its impact on the UK before the events of 11 September 2001. In the UK, the enactment of the Terrorism Act 2000 was significant in breaking the mould of operating distinct legal regimes designed to deal with terrorism in Northern Ireland and the rest of the UK. The Terrorism Act 2000 is sourced from laws that applied to Northern Ireland in the decade after the 1970s because of terrorist violence. It sits in a long line of anti-terrorist laws that may be traced back over previous centuries to medieval times.

The 2000 Act provides a number of measures to combat terrorism throughout the UK and retains certain additional powers for Northern Ireland. The nature of the terrorist threat in the UK as a whole comes from a series of different sources linked to international terrorism.

The events of 11 September led to the speedy enactment in the UK Parliament of the Anti-Terrorism, Crime and Security Act 2001, providing additional powers for detention and arrest of terrorist suspects.[13] Specifically, Part 4 of the 2001 Act allows for the continued detention of international terrorists, without reasons being given and for unlimited duration. As Part 4 is contrary to Article 5(1) of the European Convention on Human Rights (ECHR), Article 15 of the ECHR was invoked with the intention of allowing the government powers to derogate from the various articles of the ECHR 'in time of war or other public emergency threatening the life of the nation'. The justification for derogation from Article (5) is currently the subject of review by the European Court of Human Rights at Strasbourg.

In the UK's parliamentary system, a government with a large parliamentary majority supported by opposition Members of Parliament (MPs) had no difficulty enacting such draconian legislation. Concerns about civil liberties and the breadth of powers granted to the authorities were met with arguments about the threat to the state and the need to uphold the public interest. Political power dissipated through political parties exerted an unstoppable momentum over the delicate (and often unwritten) checks and balances in the British constitution against arbitrary power. This steady incremental growth in executive power continued in the hands of successive prime ministers with large majorities, and only appears to face review through the pragmatic operation of judicial review and the occasional defeat in the House of Lords or muted opposition from back-bench MPs.

The experience of the UK is particularly relevant with its post-colonial knowledge of anti-terrorism laws, and more recently its experience in operations in Northern Ireland. As McCrudden has observed:

> An important theme running through British legal thought concentrates on history and tradition, when evaluating the processes by which political and legal decisions are made. The results of these processes are assessed pragmatically. Problems are solved, in this empiricist tradition, on the basis of experience. Solutions are what works and what lasts. Institutions should therefore operate flexibly, learn from the past, and develop to suit the conditions of their time. This is the essence of a common-law approach in which principle is often sacrificed to pragmatism.[14]

McCrudden also acknowledges that equally important is the development of 'ideological constitutionalism'. This idea is drawn from the United States ideals of a liberal constitution. It places a strong emphasis on building democratic institutions and creating the right political conditions by integrating diverse and disparate groups into the core values of society. Participatory democracy is therefore a means of institution building and this, in turn, includes good governance and techniques of strategic management. Paradoxically, in a time of heightened terrorist activities the UK government has been actively engaged in modernizing the constitution.

In the United States,[15] a military holding camp was established at the Guantanamo Bay Naval Base, Cuba, where up to 1,000 detainees were held under indefinite detention.[16] For both the United States and the UK, the use of military rule in Iraq has spilled over into how combatants are treated. Both countries have had their military reputation severely dented by accusations of torture and inhuman treatment.[17] A small number of military personnel face disciplinary charges for mistreatment of prisoners. More troubling is the view advanced in their defence that they were following superior orders and that such mistreatment was sanctioned implicitly in the war against terrorism. In general terms, it would appear that the justification advanced by the United States and the UK for the use of force and the war against terrorism is to advance democracy and democratic institutions in countries where human-rights abuses and the absence of rights are prevalent.[18] Democracy is said to provide the main bulwark against authoritarian regimes and abuse, yet it is democracy that seems incapable of restraining the continued accretion of executive power in the UK and the United States. Indeed, the abuse of many prisoners raises issues about the means used and whether the ends justify such methods.

Terrorism and the UK: The Northern Ireland Experience

The UK approach to terrorism has developed along two distinctive paths. First, there is the British constitutional tradition which has shaped much of the pragmatic empiricist approach indicative of the way the UK approach has evolved. McCrudden argues that:

> several of the principles which are said to describe, inform, and underpin the British Constitution, such as majoritarian democracy, parliamentary supremacy and constitutional conventions may be seen as the embodiment of this tradition, concentrating as they do on the authority of experience and the continuity of practice and ensuring the flexibility of the process by which decisions are made. In this tradition, authoritative constitutional structures are thought to *evolve*; they are seldom *made*.[19]

The first pragmatic approach has given rise to both authoritarian tendencies in support of the sovereignty of Parliament and also to distinct periods of liberalism. Northern Ireland provides a useful case study. In Northern Ireland, detention without trial could be justified in order to support the rule of law through military intervention calculated to build political agreement. The second approach draws from constitutional idealism that is found in the values of due process, the democratic process and notions of justice and equality that enhance the protection of minorities against arbitrary decision-making by the majority.

The Northern Ireland example is one where the entity itself was created with an inbuilt majority, Unionists, mainly Protestant and in favour of union with the UK, while the Nationalist, mainly Catholic minority favoured unification with the rest of Ireland. The majoritarian ideals underpinning British approaches to sovereignty and Parliamentary decision-making led to political polarisation and the seeds of discontent fuelled terrorist activity to bring about re-unification with Ireland. Opposing any re-unification are terrorist groups that believed in the maintenance of the Union. Circumventing majority democratic controls led to creating novel constitutional frameworks including inter-governmental talks between the British and Irish governments. Inventing new institutions and processes became part of a peace process to end the use of violence by terrorists. Thus constitutional innovation and idealism were brought to bear on terrorism. This had at least three strands.

First, was the separation of the active terrorist groups from their supporters, which required differentiation of those who were engaged in political discussion from those engaged in criminal activities and acts of terrorism. Second, was provision of sufficiently strong laws to reduce the terrorist threat and allow police and military to infiltrate terrorist groups. In that context, the system of jury trial for serious offences was replaced by scheduled offences tried by a single judge sitting alone without a jury.[20] Rules of evidence were suitably adjusted to allow evidence to be presented before the court. The use of internment without trial was particularly controversial.

Third, having made it possible to secure terrorist convictions, it was considered necessary to attempt to balance the interests of justice with the needs of protecting communities through counter-surveillance operations. The needs of the security forces were set in balance against the needs of developing political dialogue. This called for innovative constitutional reforms, including new power-sharing systems of government, a Human Rights Commission, reforms to the police service and radical changes to the law on equality in terms of employment, sexual relations and laws against religious discrimination.

The Northern Ireland courts had few opportunities to go beyond a narrow interpretation of the law[21] on issues surrounding the grounds of suspicion for membership of proscribed organizations. Anti-Religious Discriminatory provisions of Northern Ireland's 1920 constitution were given limited interpretation by the courts and rarely used to challenge public bodies.[22] Hesitation to use or develop a litigation strategy[23] did not appear until the late 1970s and this had limited success.[24]

Many of the lessons gained from Northern Ireland have informed similar or closely related examples in South Africa and in Canada. Northern Ireland provides object lessons in terms of building a strategy against terrorism.

Terrorism and its Impact on Democracy

The advent of tough new terrorism laws has seen the gradual accretion of powers to the executive. In addition, the 'normal rules' of criminal justice have been gradually eroded in terms of protection for the accused through increasing pressures to increase efficiency in the criminal justice system. A crime-control model is increasing in prevalence, with minor indiscretions and serious crimes becoming subject to similar procedures and practices. Anti-terrorist laws have a ratchet effect on the operation of the criminal justice system. This is seen in the erosion of the privilege against self-incrimination, the role of jury trial and the use of Anti-Social Behaviour Orders (ASBOs) and Acceptable Behaviour Contracts. From 1972 it was possible for the jury to draw adverse inferences from a failure of a suspect to answer questions from the police.[25] In 1981, the Royal Commission on Criminal Procedure took the next step to allow inferences to be drawn from such silence, even if adverse to the accused. In Northern Ireland in 1988, the Criminal Evidence (Northern Ireland) Order 1988 provided that a trial court[26] could draw such inferences as seem proper from a suspect's failure to mention a fact which he could be reasonably expected to mention and which he might rely on at his trial. Effectively, the same law became law in England and Wales through the Criminal Justice and Public Order Act 1994. Thus, the absolute right to remain silent under police questioning was restricted. This includes defendants at trial where adverse inferences may be drawn if the defendant refused to give evidence.

Jury trial was abandoned in Northern Ireland for the trial of terrorist offences that fell within the category of scheduled offences.[27] There is considerable pressure on jury trial, and successive governments have expressed concerns about the ability of juries to handle serious frauds, corruption and other cases. There is steady pressure on expanding the role of the magistrate courts to reduce the use of jury trial, even in some theft cases where dishonesty is a component.

Aside from trial procedures and practices, there has been an increasing use of a wide range of measures to combat fairly minor offences, such as graffiti, abusive language, excessive noise, litter on the streets and drunken behaviour. Section 1 of the Crime and Disorder Act 1998 created a wide category of misdemeanour that became subject to the use of an ASBO. From 1999, when they were introduced, there has been a steady increase in the use of ASBOs. Primarily based on civil law procedures (where the standard of proof is less than in criminal cases), ASBOs provide the courts with a discretion to set very wide restrictions on an individual's movement and lifestyle.

In March 2003, the government White Paper on *Respect and Responsibility – Taking A Stand Against Anti- Social Behaviour* was published, containing detailed powers for the police to deal with serious anti-social behaviour. The Anti-Social Behaviour Act 2003 contains widely drawn powers covering public nuisance to anti-social behaviour in public places, including local authority powers to tackle anti-social problems in the community. There are powers to tackle areas where drug use may be occurring to problems with high hedges, graffiti and fly-posting, and including waste and litter and noisy premises. At the heart of the act is the continued use of ASBOs, civil orders setting restrictions on a persons' movement for a minimum of two years. Breach of such an order can bring the young person into serious conflict with the criminal law and sanctions such as imprisonment are available for persistent offenders.

Judicial Oversight of Executive Power

Judicial responses to emergency powers or extraordinary powers taken by the state to counter-terrorism provide evidence of pragmatism in judicial decision-making. The famous dissent of Lord Atkin in *Liversidge v Anderson*[28] is indicative of judicial vacillation in war-time Britain; by a majority of four to one, the House of Lords refused to require an affidavit to satisfy the Secretary of State's actions under

Regulation 18B. Objective evidence was not required as a subjective test of what the Secretary of State believed was sufficient. Judicial discretion was prepared to accept the absolute powers of the Secretary of State. From the modest dissent of Lord Atkin, judicial power since the 1960s has become more sceptical of executive powers as the practice of judicial review has developed.

In Northern Ireland, the Government of Ireland Act 1920, a UK Act of Parliament, on the face of it provided the means to review legislation passed by the Northern Ireland Parliament, a subordinate legislature. The Northern Ireland government took special powers under the Civil Authorities (Special Powers) Act 1922, an act subject to annual renewal and then given permanency. Attempts to challenge the legality of the special powers under the 1922 Act were limited[29] as the Northern Ireland courts upheld the validity of the act on the basis of presuming that the executive would only exercise powers that they lawfully assumed they had, through invoking the saving doctrine of 'police power' drawn from US jurisprudence.[30] However, in *R. v Londonderry Justices ex parte Hume et al.*[31] Lord Lowry, then lord chief justice, held that certain specific powers under the Special Powers Act could not be used by the military as limitations under section 4(1) of the Government of Ireland Act 1920 applied to the Northern Ireland Parliament in respect of Her Majesty's armed forces. The result of striking down part of the special powers legislation led the UK Parliament to pass the Northern Ireland Act 1972, retrospectively reversing the effect of the *Hume* decision.

Security measures in the UK continued to contain terrorist activities arising out of the security problems in Northern Ireland. Concern about the use of lethal force by the security forces led to the setting up of an inquiry led by senior police officer John Stalker and later Colin Sampson into the allegations that there was a directed policy by the security services of 'shoot to kill'. Inevitably, this did not curtail controversy. Renewed concern came after the shooting of three members of the Irish Republican Army (IRA) in Gibraltar. This led to civil proceedings against the Ministry of Defence, and eventually to a claim to the European Court of Human Rights about the denial of rights to the deceased. Those matters were refused before the court as inadmissible. However, on a very narrow ground that the rights of the deceased were violated; the court criticised the authorities.[32] Article 2 rights have been at the forefront of a number of applications made to the court arising out of shootings by the security forces and the adequacy of the investigations before and after the event. In many instances, the court made findings criticising the authorities.[33] In October 1988, the home secretary decided to ban IRA spokespersons from broadcasting interviews on television or radio. The ban was challenged by a number of journalists under Article 10 of the European Convention on Human Rights and on grounds that the ban was discriminatory under Section 19(1) of the Northern Ireland Constitution Act 1973. The ban was upheld as legal by the House of Lords.[34]

There are a number of examples where the judiciary became directly involved in the steps taken to address terrorism. In both Ireland and Northern Ireland, internment without trial has been used. The use of extended periods of unlimited detention received heavy criticism. In 1975 the Gardiner Committee reviewed the use of extraordinary powers of internment and concluded that their effectiveness could be for only a limited time. The Committee concluded:

> After long and anxious consideration, we are of the opinion that detention cannot remain a long-term policy. In the short term, it may be an effective means of containing violence, but the prolonged effects of the use of detention are ultimately inimical to community life, fan a widespread sense of grievance and injustice, and obstruct those elements in Northern Ireland society which could lead to reconciliation. Detention can only be tolerated in a democratic society in the most extreme circumstances; it must be used with the utmost restraint and retained only as long as it is strictly necessary.[35]

From 1972 to 1975, there was a problematic form of review through a quasi-judicial procedure. This was replaced by a Detention Advisory Board. The last interned suspects were released in December 1975 and the policy was abandoned in Northern Ireland. Internment powers when exercised inevitably led to interrogation of suspects.

The abandonment of internment led to the setting up of the non-jury Diplock courts and indirectly placed the judiciary in the frontline in the measures taken by the government against terrorists. The so-called Diplock courts, where the accused was charged with terrorist offences before a single judge and without a jury, were named after Lord Diplock, the judge responsible for their introduction. The Diplock courts provided the accused many of the protections available to criminals before the ordinary courts, with the major exception that the jury was not present. This gave rise to concerns about 'case hardening' by the judiciary and low acquittal rates. The evidence for case hardening is not conclusive but it raised fears that the judiciary were succumbing to the prosecution view of the trial system. Attempts to modify the Diplock court system of trial by a single judge into trial by three judges were rejected.[36] However, interrogation of suspects under detention awaiting trial gave rise to questions about the legality of questioning.

Generally, the methods and techniques for the treatment of suspects under detention in Northern Ireland were found to be in breach of human rights. In *R. v McCormick*[37] the trial judge, Lord Justice McGonigal, accepted that under emergency powers the interviewer could use 'a moderate degree of physical maltreatment for the purpose of inducing a person to make a statement'. This interpretation of Article 3 of the European Convention on Human Rights proved controversial. Lord Lowry in a later case took a different approach, arguing that any assault in the form of physical violence would raise a doubt in the interpretation of any statement made by the accused.[38] The law operated on the basis that once a prima facie case was made out that there was some ill treatment, then the Crown had the onus of rebuttal to establish that any admissions, beyond a reasonable doubt, were obtained voluntarily. In addition, the court had an overriding discretion as part of the common law to exclude evidence if its prejudicial weight outweighed its probative value. Police powers under terrorist legislation appear to have expanded in response to the changes in criminal activity. In those circumstances, the judiciary provided a minimum set of safeguards to protect civil liberties. The Northern Ireland law has influenced the law in the UK.[39] The ordinary law in the UK under the Police and Criminal Evidence Act (PACE) 1984 and later, in Northern Ireland, the PACE (Northern Ireland) Order 1989, while setting more demanding standards than the terrorist law, is nevertheless closely related to following the case law as to what is or is not permitted.

An illustration of the potential for judicial oversight of emergency powers arose in the case of trials involving the use of informers or 'super-grasses'. This category included large trials, usually with multiple defendants charged with a large number of inter-connected terrorist offences. The main evidence rested on accomplices who were either paid police informers or active participants who became police informants in return for a new identity, financial remuneration and anonymity. Often, the evidence given was uncorroborated and this led to the Northern Ireland Court of Appeal[40] quashing the convictions in a number of cases. As a result, the use of 'super-grass' trials effectively came to an end.

Greater opportunities for an expanded judicial role came from changes in Northern Ireland's Constitution[41] and also from the European Court of Human Rights. This coincided with the development of judicial review and the growth in a rights culture in terms of civil rights.

In *Ireland v United Kingdom*,[42] various techniques of interrogation were found to be in breach of the European Convention on Human Rights, after the Irish Republic's government took the British government to the European Court of Human Rights in Strasbourg. This proved to be an influential decision in terms of changing the attitude towards interrogation techniques.[43]

Terrorism and Human Rights

The terrorism debate and its impact on democracy have taken a new direction with the decision to go to war in Iraq to topple Saddam Hussein. This has proved controversial in terms of the legality of the war, the role of international law and the legitimacy of any action against terrorism. Coinciding with this discussion is the development of a human rights strategy. The implementation of the Human Rights Act 1998 has an added dimension to the discussion of terrorism, given the necessity of the UK to derogate from Convention rights. As the threat of terrorism is at the heart of the rationale for going to war, the treatment of the war is an important consideration[44] because this involved the detention without trial of a number of terrorist suspects under the provisions of the Terrorism Act 2000 as well as under additional powers made under Section 21 of the Anti-terrorism, Crime and Security Act 2001. Particularly sensitive are the use of such powers against non-British nationals and the use of the Human Rights Act 1998 (Designed Derogation) Order 2001, purporting to review the protection of human rights under the European Convention on Human Rights.

In the case of detention for non-nationals, the earlier case law of the UK adopted a number of protections, namely, that such detention should be for a limited time and only for such time as was reasonably necessary.[45] The question is how might the courts interpret both the derogation order and also the question of the rights of non-British national detainees? Both questions came before the House of Lords in a landmark decision on the government's approach to terrorism and how it should exercise its legal powers in respect of terrorist suspects.[46]

The challenge was based on whether the detention of nine non-British nationals was in breach of the convention and not on the grounds of whether they were unlawfully detained under domestic law. The majority of the House of Lords ruled that indefinite detention of foreign nationals was contrary to human rights protection and against long-standing common law protections. Seven of their Lordships gave specific objection to the fact that the detention powers were discriminatory because similar detention powers were not available to non-British nationals. Less clear is the question of whether such a detention might be lawful if the law applied in the same way to British and non-British nationals. There was also the question of whether the UK was entitled to derogate from its convention rights responsibilities. This latter point was fudged by many of their Lordships' speeches. The majority held that it was possible for the government to justify a public emergency that threatened the life of the nation. However the derogation under Article 5 and the indefinite detention of non-British nationals was disproportionate and discriminatory.

The government's response to the House of Lords decision took at least three forms. First, the Home Secretary decided that new executive control orders might be issued covering both British and non-British nationals suspected of terrorism.

Second, these control orders might take different forms, such as restrictions on movement and access to communications equipment. In line with the use of ASBOs, discussed above, the control orders might take the form of a curfew or electronic tagging, forcing the suspect to be under house arrest at home. In common with detention without trial there will be no time limit on a control order and such a control order may be varied to take account of changing circumstances. Also in common with unlimited detention without trial, there will be the reliance on information from the security forces. Forms of surveillance, such as close-circuit television (CCTV) will also be used and restrictions on visitors might also apply. In effect, the government believes, unlike the law lords, that detention without trial is justified, and this form of house arrest is seen as preferable to detention.

Third, a new Anti-Terrorism Bill 2005 was drawn up. This bill has become law as the Prevention of Terrorism Act 2005 and the act attempts to address the problems raised by the judges in the recent House of Lords decision discussed above. Before the act was passed, arrangements for review of detention powers were limited. Detainees were able to appeal on the reasonableness of their detention to the Special Immigration Appeals Committee (SIAC). In such reviews, detainees were unable to procure the details of the evidence against them, and representation by their lawyers were limited because of the difficulty of not having details of the evidence against the detainee. Advocates appointed to help test the evidence were pre-vetted by the security services. The hearings were held in secret, were limited in scope and operated without the benefit of external assessment or public scrutiny. Advocates were unable to discuss the details of any evidence they discovered with the detainee.

The result of the House of Lords decision was that suspects detained for over three years at Belmarsh Prison under the 2001 Act were released on bail and immediately placed under the new non-derogating control orders after the 2005 Act received the royal assent on 12 March 2005.

The 2005 Act is the result of much debate, all-night sittings in the House of Lords and, in the end, compromises offered by the government in the face of further delay and a threatened back-bench revolt by Labour Members of Parliament. The act has a limited life expectancy because the government has agreed to publish a draft counter-terrorism bill in autumn 2005 and promised to bring forward a bill containing new anti-terrorist powers after the annual review of the existing legislation undertaken in January 2006. Review of the new procedures under the 2005 Act comes from a three-monthly report to Parliament to be made by the Home Secretary.

The 2005 Act has incorporated some distinct features, built on the use of ASBOs mentioned above, into the anti-terrorist strategy that are to be called control orders. Such orders replace the severely criticised unlimited prison detention without trial. The orders are available in two forms. The first, the derogating control order, is the most severe as it specifically requires derogation from the European Convention on Human Rights and may only be validly made if both Houses of Parliament have passed a resolution approving the derogation. Derogating control orders can be made only by the high court on the application of the home secretary. This concession was made by the government after serious objections were made to the arbitrary nature of such powers if wholly vested in the government of the day. The test is on the balance of probabilities that the suspect was involved in terrorism-related activities – a broad and ill-defined catch-all category. The use of a derogating control order is effectively house arrest and places severe restrictions on the activities of the suspect.

The second form of control order is the non-derogating control order which allegedly fall short of infringing the Convention's rights protections. However, its remit is broad and includes restrictions on the suspects' activities, contact with others and co-operation in arrangements for the monitoring of activities. In common use, this means electronic tagging. It is questionable, given the extent of the restrictions that may be imposed, whether such orders are compatible with convention rights, though they do not require specific derogation. There is limited review of non-derogation control orders through judicial review, and the threshold is less than the balance of probabilities required for derogating orders. Such orders are in the power of the home secretary and the courts are limited to considering whether the Home Secretary's decision was 'flawed'. Non-derogating control orders that are made by the Home Secretary are made on the basis of his having reasonable grounds to believe that a suspect was involved in terrorism-related activities, and that in the public interest, such an order is necessary. There are severe restrictions on what evidence is allowed to be seen by the courts, thus increasing the executive nature of such orders. There are also accompanying powers of arrest and investigation given to the police.

The proposed use of control orders extends the breadth of executive powers. Seen as preferable to institutional detention, it may, in fact, broaden the use of executive powers. It is clear that this may have long-term implications for the detainee's family and relatives including children. The outcome may be to castigate a community where the detainee is living with the suspicion of wrongdoing where none may be proven and, indeed, taint many innocent people with the stigma of the detainee.

The result may be counter-productive to the aims of the legislation by making suspected terrorists become the 'victims' of executive power. Given the absence of any specified time limits, this may provide cohesion and sympathy for the causes that may offer tacit support to terrorism without any active engagement. This may result in many idealists opposed to terrorism laws being recruited into the terrorist cause. Finally, in the UK, the use of control orders continues a trend where anti-terrorist laws and laws against non-terrorist offences form a homogenised whole in terms of techniques and methods. This is a worrying trend where there is insufficient separation between the degrees and gravity of offenders or suspects. The Council of Europe Commissioner for Human Rights in his recent report[47] questioned whether the use of non-derogating control orders was compatible with human rights contained in the ECHR. More generally, he hoped for a greater sensitivity to the potential abuse of human rights under any proposed strengthening of the law.

Conclusion

Political security and democratic rights are often in conflict when confronted with the phenomenon of terrorism. Terrorism is a broadly defined and value-laden term that seeks to stigmatise all forms of subversion, including violence. The value of such a broad definition is that it allows equally broad and ill-defined ways to define counter-terrorism. While this may be self-defeating, it is a seductive pathway for democratic governments to take when faced with violent attacks on the state. The precise impact on democratic government is hard to calculate. One lesson is that harsh and unjust use of violence permeates the responses, official and unofficial, of democratic governments when confronted with the public interest and the necessity to curtail spiralling violence.

Particularly important are the lessons from Northern Ireland in the UK's strategy against terrorism. In the main, British perceptions about building political security and democratic rights to counter-terrorism come from a post-colonial approach that has benefited from that experience. A balance needs to be struck between the competing claims of addressing terrorism and building democratic institutions.

The role of international organizations is an important dimension to any discussion. The enthusiasm for international law diminished as the United States has taken policy stances, often in opposition to decisions taken by international organizations. The aftermath of the war in Iraq[48] has many implications for building political systems through democratic processes and underpinning such processes through international recognition. The result is to place the future of international cooperation in doubt and ultimately weaken national government responses.

While there is no single model or approach to terrorism, there are common threads that run through attempts to address terrorism while at the same time seeking to facilitate democratic principles, such as unimpeded and corruption-free elections and respect for the rule of law. In the latter, the judiciary have a pivotal role in reviewing the balance between the measures necessary to combat terrorism and those needed to protect human rights. The performance of the judiciary is examined in the light of recently decided cases. Although judicial decision-making is often pragmatic and difficult to predict, it is argued that the judiciary must act to prevent arbitrariness and abuse. The international dimension is important as a means of influencing rights. In the UK example, the role of the European Court of Human Rights was influential in providing a standard for human rights for the UK's courts. The role of international law should not be discounted. Differences in perception about the centrality of the rule of law should not obscure the ultimate authority of the rule of law over political pragmatism. In conclusion it may be argued that the UK government responses to terrorism have to be considered in the light of judicial interpretation and analysis. Terrorism laws need to be tailored to the particular norms and understandings of a community in the specific context of the culture and society of the country where the laws apply.

NOTES

1. See Alberto Abadie, *Poverty, Political Freedom and the Roots of Terrorism* (Cambridge, MA: Harvard University and NBER, 2004).
2. See John F. McEldowney, 'Dicey in Historical Perspective – A Review Essay', in Patrick McAuslan and John McEldowney (eds), *Law Legitimacy and the Constitution* (London: Sweet & Maxwell, 1985), pp.39–61.
3. See K.D. Ewing and C.A Gearty, *The Struggle for Civil Liberties* (Oxford: Clarendon Press, 2000).
4. *Beatty v Gillbanks* (1882) 9 QBD 308, *Duncan v Jones* [1936] 1KB 218, *Elias v Pasmore* [1934] 2 KB 621.
5. See *Thomas v Sawkins* [1935] 2 KB 249.
6. S. Walker, *In Defence of American Liberties: A History of the ACLU* (Oxford: Oxford University Press, 1990).
7. Ibid., p.1.
8. G. Gearty, *Terror* (London: Faber & Faber, 1991).
9. Parliament and Registration Act 1916, Section 1, amended Section 7 of the Parliament Act 1911 and the Parliament and Local Elections Act 1917 and 1918 requiring elections.
10. The Aliens Restrictions Act 1914, the Military Service Act 1916.
11. N.Stammers, *Civil Liberties in Britain during the Second World War: A Political Study* (London: Croom Helm, 1983).
12. G.J.Alexander, 'The Illusory Protection of Human Rights by National Courts during Periods of Emergency' *Human Rights Law Journal*, Vol.5, No.1 (1984). Also see: P. Wilkinson, *Terrorism and the Liberal State*, 2nd ed. (London: Macmillan, 1986).
13. The international dimension is to be found in the Crime (International Co-operation) Act 2003.
14. C. McCrudden, 'Northern Ireland, The Belfast Agreement, and the British Constitution', in D. Oliver and J. Jowell (eds), *The Changing Constitution*, 5th ed. (Oxford: Oxford University Press, 2004), pp.195–236.
15. Specific powers were granted in the United States, to hold special military trials with Congressional approval through a joint resolution authorizing the use of necessary force.
16. Ronald Dworkin, 'The Threat to Patriotism', *The New York Review of Books*, 28 February 2002.
17. See: Karen J. Greenberg and Joshua L. Dratel, *The Torture Papers* (Cambridge: Cambridge University Press, 2005); Mark Danner, *Torture and Truth* (Cambridge: Granta, 2005), Steven Strasser, *The Abu Ghraib Investigations* (New York: Public Affairs Reports, 2005).
18. See the attorney general's advice to the prime minister on 7 March 2003 before war was announced (available at <www.number-10.gov.uk>).
19. McCrudden (note 14), p.197.
20. *The Diplock Commission Report*, Cmnd. 5185 (London: HMSO, 1972), chaired by Lord Diplock, Northern Ireland (Emergency Provisions) Act 1973 amended in 1975, 1978, 1987, 1991,1996 and 1998.
21. See *McEldowney v Forde* [1971] AC 632.
22. *Londonderry CC v McGlade* [1925] NI 47.
23. *Purvis v Magherafelt District Council* [1978] NI 26.

24. See Claire Palley, 'The Evolution, Disintegration and Possible Reconstruction of the Northern Ireland Constitution', *Anglo-American Law Review*, Vol.368 (1972), C. Palley, 'Constitutional Solutions to the Irish Problem', *Current Legal Problems*, Vol.121 (1980).
25. Criminal Law Revision Committee, *11th Report Evidence (General)* Cmnd.4991 (London: HMSO, 1972).
26. *Murray v DPP* [1994] 1 WLR 97.
27. See *Diplock Report*, Cmnd. 5185 (1972).
28. [1942] AC 206.
29. *McEldowney v Forde* [1971] AC 632.
30. *O.D. Cars Ltd v Belfast Corporation* [1959] NI 62
31. [1971] NI 23
32. *McCann v United Kingdom* (1995) 21 EHRR 97.
33. See *Jordan v UK* (Application No. 24746/94), *McKerr v UK* (Application No. 28883/95), *Kelly v UK* (Application No. 30054/96), *Shanaghan v UK* (Application No. 37715/97), *McShane v UK* (Application No. 43290/98).
34. R. v Secretary of State for the Home Department ex parte Brind [1991] 1AC 696.
35. The Gardiner Committee para. 175, cited in S.H.Bailey, D.J Harris and D.C. Ormerod, *Civil Liberties Cases and Materials* (London: Butterworths, 2001), p.616.
36. S. Greer and A. White, *Abolishing the Diplock Courts* (Belfast: Cobden Trust, 1986).
37. [1977] NI 105
38. *R. v O'Halloran* [1979] NI 45.
39. Section 76 of the Terrorist Act 2000 is drawn from Section 12 of the Emergency Provisions Act 1996.
40. See *R. v McCormack* [1984] NI 50, *R. v Gibney* [1986] 4 NIJB 1.
41. Northern Ireland Constitution Act 1973 made void any legislation that purported to discriminate against any person or class of person. The Northern Ireland Act 1998 introduced a new form of devolution, maintained the anti-discrimination tradition set under the 1973 Act.
42. European Court of Human Rights Series B Vol. 23-1 (1972), also see K. Boyle and H. Hannum, 'Ireland in Strasbourg', *Irish Jurist*, Vol. 243 (1976). Also see W. D. Carrol, 'The Search for Justice in Northern Ireland', *New York University Journal of International Law and Politics*, Vol.6, No.49 (1973).
43. In *Rasul v Bush*, the Supreme Court reviewed the regime of detention and imprisonment without charge at Guantánamo Bay and held that detainees were entitled to have their captivity reviewed in the United States federal courts.
44. See Claire Taylor and Tim Youngs, 'The Conflict in Iraq House of Commons', Research Paper 03/05 23 May 2003 (available at <www.parliament.uk>). Also see Philip Giddings, 'To War or Not to War: That is the Question', in P. Giddings (ed.), *The Future of Parliament* (London: Macmillan Press, 2005), pp.187–200.
45. See *R. v Governor of Durham Prison ex p Hardial Singh* [1984] 1 WLR 704, the Privy Council decision of *Tan Te Lam v Superintendent of Tai A Chau Detention Centre* [1997] AC 97.
46. See *A and Others v Secretary of State for the Home Department* [2004] UKHL 56 (16 December 2004).
47. Report by Mr Alvaro Gil-Robles, Commissioner for Human Rights, on his visit to the United Kingdom 4–12 November 2004 Comm DH(2005)6, paras.18–20.
48. Thomas M. Franck, 'What Happens Now? The United Nations After Iraq', *The American Journal of International Law*, Vol.97 No.3 (2003), pp.607–20.

Manuscript accepted for publication August 2005.

Address for correspondence: John F. McEldowney, School of Law, University of Warwick, Coventry, Warwickshire CV4 7AL, UK. E-mail: <J.F.McEldowney@warwick.ac.uk>.

Democratizing Democracy: Feminist Perspectives

ANDREA CORNWALL and ANNE MARIE GOETZ

Introduction

As the numbers of women in politics increase in many parts of the world, it has become more evident than ever that the strategy of getting female bodies into formal political spaces is only part of what it takes to 'engender' democracy. Much of the focus in the debate on 'engendering' democracy has been on how to insert women into existing democratic structures, with an emphasis primarily on formal political institutions. Yet, taken literally, the idea of 'engendering democracy' might be read in a rather different way: as concerned with bringing about changes in political systems that make them genuinely inclusive, *democratizing* democracy. This article begins from the observation that while representative democratic arenas have received the lion's share of attention, understanding women's political engagement requires that we pay closer attention to the other spaces – 'new' democratic spaces as well as more 'traditional' arenas outside the domain of formal politics – in which women participate as political and social actors, and to their pathways into politics.

The analysis begins with questions that have dominated the debate on women's political representation. It proceeds to examine the extent to which new democratic spaces – from civil-society organizations to interface institutions that mediate the administration of state policies – offer new opportunities for creating more inclusive democratic practices, as well as at some of the potential costs of inclusion for groups contesting the gendered status quo. The final part discusses the implications of this analysis for the strategic engagement and articulation of feminist agendas within and across different democratic arenas, and for democratizing democratic practice.

Beyond Numbers

Efforts to enhance women's political participation have gained new urgency with the designation of numbers of women in politics as an indicator of women's empowerment, as enshrined in the third United Nations' Millennium Development Goal (MDG). Yet there is no straightforward equation between getting women into political office and the pursuit of policies of gender equality by these same women. Measures to build women's presence in public office have been advocated by women's movements around the world for some time. Affirmative action measures to increase the numbers of women participating as public representatives in political institutions, such as quotas of women candidates or reserved seats in legislatures, have returned a growing number of women to public office. The global average has increased, though not spectacularly, from less than 9 per cent in 1987 to 15.9 per cent in 2004. In some cases, quotas have been more successful than expected. In Iraq's elections for the Interim National Assembly in January 2005, for instance, the 25 per cent quota requirement was exceeded, producing 86 women winners out of 275, or 31 per cent of the assembly.

There are staunch defenders of the idea that women's descriptive or numerical representation produces changes in their substantive representation, particularly after a critical threshold has been passed so that women are no longer a token minority – usually this threshold is more than 30 per cent of seats.[1] Yet observers of decision making in countries with legislatures in which more than 15 per cent of politicians are women have argued that the gradual feminization of legislatures does not necessarily produce major changes in what parties and governments actually do.[2] Women in office do not necessarily defend a feminist position on policies. Indeed for some women, winning and keeping office can be contingent upon *downplaying* feminist sympathies.

The assumption that democracy can be made more inclusive by adding women tends to advantage sex difference relative to other factors shaping interests, political skills and accountability relationships – notably, political party affiliation. One of the blind spots of this position is to the possibility that sex may be less determinant of a representative's political interests and aptitudes than their 'political apprenticeship': the routes via which representatives enter and engage in political activity, and which influence how they define and acquire the arts and activities of politics, and negotiate the boundaries of the political.

Defenders of the 'numbers' position point out that it is far too early to expect women in office to have an impact on decision making. Even in most of the 16 countries where, by 2004, women had captured 30 per cent or more of legislative seats,[3] women are simply too new to office necessarily to have made a tangible difference. The sense that women representatives *ought* to be representative of women's interests (regardless of their party affiliation) and have an additional task of accountability to a female constituency is quite widespread in public perceptions (and probably serves to undermine their perceived legitimacy as public representatives in the eyes of some of their male colleagues). But conventional political accountability – the constituencies to which representatives answer and the means of making them do so – makes rather different demands of these representatives. Like male politicians, women representatives must balance obligations to follow the party line with their commitment to their constituents. The affirmative action measures to usher more women into politics neither make parties more responsive to gender equality issues, nor do they help to construct electoral constituencies with an interest in gender equality.

Quotas: A Shot in the Dark?

Most women enter office through methods which do not base the selection of women politicians on the preferences of women as an electoral constituency. In most countries, affirmative action to feminize legislatures is pursued through voluntary or imposed quotas – political parties must front women candidates for a proportion of the seats they contest.[4] Quotas are widely seen as a legitimate means of remedying women's under-representation precisely because they acknowledge that women do not constitute a politically distinct group with interests limited to gender-related concerns. Gender does not map onto distinct geographic areas or constituencies in the way that ethnic or racial differences can do. Quotas enable women to participate in political parties, but those parties' agendas represent a range of often competing perspectives. As Anne Phillips points out, if the parties that women join do not advocate 'an explicitly woman-friendly programme (which men might claim they were equally capable of pursuing) there *is* no guarantee that women will represent women's interests': 'gender parity is in this sense a shot in the dark'.[5]

Available measures to enable group-specific representation for women include reservations systems, such as those used to address the under-representation of ethnic or other minorities which can involve the creation of special electoral districts limiting competition to group members, or provisions for direct appointment to reserved seats in the legislature. Reservations are intended to recognize the autonomy of particular political communities and give them a share of power independently of existing political parties. Yet they have run into a number of problems when used to boost women's political presence, not least because women do not operate as a distinct political community. For several decades, for instance, Tanzania, Pakistan and Bangladesh have filled seats for women in parliament by assigning seats for parties' own female nominees in proportion to the seats they have won. These reserved seats have simply been a way of further boosting government majorities, not connecting women representatives to a political community organized around interests *as women*.

Reservations have been used in Uganda since the late 1980s to ensure that at least one member of parliament (MP) from every district in the country is a woman. As detailed by Sylvia Tamale, it has never been clear just what constituencies these Women District Representatives are meant to represent. Representatives of other categories of people for whom seats are reserved, such as youth, workers, and disabled people are chosen directly by national organizations that bring together relevant associations and non-governmental organizations (NGOs), but reserved seats for women are filled by a special electoral college composed of heads of local government councils. Affirmative action seats for youth, the disabled, the army, and workers, are described in Uganda's constitution as being for people who will be 'representatives *of*' these special interests. Women District Representatives, in contrast, are not described as representatives *of women*, but as women representatives *for* each district. Women running for these seats must appeal to a narrow electoral college of mostly male heads of local councils in the district, not the local population or the female voters of the area.[6] Inevitably, this selection process favours elite and socially conservative candidates; professing a commitment to women's rights might well virtually disqualify a candidate in the eyes of this electoral college.

Experiments with affirmative action to feminize legislatures, and their unsurprisingly less-than-dramatic impact in terms of bringing feminist perspectives to politics remind us that the interests represented in public office are those that are well prepared in organizations backing each politician – in the political parties and lobby groups providing policy development and resources to advance particular issues. Accountability systems also, of course, provide incentives to politicians to promote some interests over others and electoral system design will help determine to whom public actors feel they must answer, explain their actions, and from whom they can expect sanctions should they fail. As Phillips notes:

> In what sense can we say that the women produced through (party-contested elections) carry an additional responsibility to represent women? In the absence of mechanisms to establish accountability, the equation of more women with more adequate representation of women's interests looks suspiciously undemocratic. How do the women elected know what the women who elected them want? By what right do they claim responsibility to represent women's concerns?[7]

The expectation that the sex of representatives determines their interests undermines ideas about the accountability of politicians to party programmes. It also introduces essentialist equations between sex and interests that obscure the multiplicity of women's perspectives and interests, and disregard the fact that many men can adopt feminist positions on public policy. Indeed, if social justice concerns seeking to redress gender inequity are to make it into public policy they need precisely to garner broader-based political appeal and support.

Feminizing Legislatures: Advancing Gender Equality?

Clearly, if the concern is to bring gender equality perspectives into politics and public policy, a focus on packing public space with female bodies is misplaced unless supported by efforts to bring gender issues into the many other spaces where political interests are formed. Worse, it may actually undermine the project of enhancing gender equality. The 31 per cent female occupancy of assembly seats in Iraq, for instance, offers no protection against the conservative Islamist assault on the country's Ba'ath-era secular family law. A significant proportion of women in the assembly belong to the Islamist Shia list, and are at the forefront of calls to reinstate Sharia law in personal relationships. As Iraq's minister of women's affairs, the Sunni Kurd Narmeen Othman despairs: 'It is very difficult to fight this when their women politicians are advocating Sharia. The men say: "See you are wrong because even these women are supporting us."'[8]

Feminizing legislative delegations may have other undesirable effects. It may erode the quality of democracy and public deliberation where reservations have been a means of reinforcing the ruling party's position with female party 'hacks' unwilling to question authoritarian and highly centralized party leadership – as many claim is the case in Rwanda[9] and South Africa.[10] Women may lack experience of public debate, opposition or deal-making, stemming from their shallow or skewed political apprenticeship, and this may make them ineffective legislators, or legislators who are easy to manipulate. Denise Walsh describes how gender differences in debating styles, and the lack of training in preparing women for the formal culture of parliamentary work, create real obstacles to women being taken seriously in the South African legislature. She cites Mahau Phekoe of the Women's National Coalition: 'At the last budget speech, three women commented on the budget. One read a speech written in English. She struggled with what she had to say ... Comments were made on her bad delivery. The other two had done no research. This discredited these women.'[11]

Of course, getting more women into public office has always been connected to a wider project of deepening democracy. In this broader democratic project, a challenge for feminists has been to develop a distinct political community of women, and to articulate interest in and around gender-based injustices. Indeed, part of this project has been the recognition that the pursuit of equality and social justice calls not only for broader-based representation of women in formal political arenas, but also for the democratization of other domains and institutions, including the private sphere. It is precisely here that the limits of the feminist project have been most acutely felt, when it became evident that large numbers of women in public office may perform an important role-modelling effect, but beyond that, few feminists make it into or survive in formal politics, and it is enormously difficult for them to have a tangible impact on policy-making.

Two issues arise here that deserve further attention. The first is the question of *how* women enter politics. What are women's pathways into political office? How and where do women learn the arts and activities of politics? How is political apprenticeship itself gendered? The second relates to the nature of the public sphere institutions in which women *do* participate, in the wake of waves of governance reform over the course of the last decades. To what extent have democratic reforms provided new opportunities to address issues of gender justice? We address each of these issues in turn.

Women's Political and Democratic Apprenticeship

Political participation matters a great deal for women. It does so not only because of the potential gains of successful protest, mobilization around collective interests, advocacy or engagement in policy processes. It also offers women a form of political apprenticeship that enables them to recognize and articulate interests, build alliances, broker differences and learn modes of cooperation and consensus-building to advance common projects. In addition, for participation to yield influence, to sway others in deliberative processes, an apprenticeship in *democratic* practices is useful – a training in the ability to mount an argument and to debate effectively, to tolerate opposition and to accept setbacks and failure. The political arts learnt through these forms of participation can be applied by women who move on to formal political arenas.

Looking at women's pathways into politics, however, making that transition appears far from straightforward. There is no shortage of women's activity – and indeed leadership – in civil society and community activism. Why, then, do these spaces produce so few feminist leaders able to make the transition into formal representative politics and be effective in influencing policy? The traditional incubators of political leaders have been trade unions, campus politics and political parties. They are also the crucibles in which interests are identified, debated, aggregated and promoted. These arenas foster styles of politics and forms of political apprenticeship that can exclude and silence women. Though women participate, they have often found themselves relegated to lower levels in hierarchies and to community mobilization work. Political parties in particular have rarely assigned priority to gender issues or promoted women as candidates for office without being formally obliged to do so. Women in many countries form the bulk of the 'foot soldiers' in campaigning and fund-raising, but parties the world over appear hostile to women's engagement in decision-making, especially at top leadership levels.

Proof of the stubborn resistance of parties to women's leadership is their unwillingness to introduce internal leadership quotas. In Africa, only the African National Congress (ANC) has a quota for women in its National Executive Committee. Four parties in Brazil have internal quotas, and these remain the only ones to have more than 10 per cent of women in their leadership. Even then, quotas are treated as strict ceilings, not entry points. The Partido dos Trabalhadores (PT) in Brazil, for instance, has filled, exactly, but never surpassed its 30 per cent quota of women in the national executive for over 10 years.

What matters for *what* issues are represented is *how* women get selected for these leadership positions and for participation at other levels, and the uses to which they hope to put this participation. Where resources, candidacies and positions in parties are determined by patronage, where there is no transparency or internal accountability in decisions about who leads and what policies are promoted, we ought not to expect women leaders, if they emerge, to be connected to gender equality concerns. Parties organized on the basis of patronage, or indeed a kleptocratic operation of a single powerful family, are often found in developing-country contexts. Such parties often have highly personalized leadership systems based on family dynasties, and decision making is not open to internal challenge. Women's political apprenticeship within such systems involve exploiting kinship connections. Where a woman has gained position within a party via such a route, there is less chance that she will seek connections with organized feminism or other expressions of women's concerns in civil society, or challenge the masculine party hierarchy by supporting gender causes.

'Women's wings' of political parties have rarely provided the essential incubating ground for women leaders, for female solidarity in parties, and for feminist policy proposals. Instead, women's wings are commonly captured by the spouses of male leaders and have developed a species of female sycophancy.[12] In west and east African countries, women's wings in dominant parties have sought to control and contain the wider women's movement, harnessing women's energies to support the president. Nana Konadu Agyeman Rawlings's 31 December Women's Movement in Ghana was a notorious example, but similar efforts by political spouses to monopolize international resources for women's development and to limit women's independent associational activity has rightly made women wary of engagement with politics and parties.[13]

Expanding Democratic Space: New Possibilities for Women?

Liberalization and governance reforms have cut into old political institutions and fostered the growth of diverse new democratic spaces for participation in governance. This reconfiguration of the landscape of governance is potentially significant for the representation of traditionally marginalized political actors. Pathways into politics were once clearly defined and largely excluded women. New [democratic] spaces offer a variety of sites for learning and networking that might serve to generate new leadership, and alternative entry routes into politics. In what follows, we look first at the opportunities and costs of donor enthusiasm for spreading 'democracy' through support to 'civil society'. We turn from this to look at some of the new democratic spaces that have been created, especially at local government level, and ask: What impact has all of this had on women's representation? In particular, does influence in, and access to, one set of deliberative spaces offer the potential for leverage in others?

The turn to 'strengthening civil society' in the 1990s good governance agenda sought the expansion of the public sphere through fostering the creation of social actors who would both serve as representatives of diverse interest groups and work to hold the state to account. The exponential growth of 'civil society organizations', together with the new political spaces opened by waves of democratization, has offered women's organizations and movements the possibility of exerting influence on the policy process from outside formal political institutions. The unrelentingly positive image that 'civil society' has come to have in donor discourse is at odds, however, with the rather more dissonant and complex reality of the sheer diversity of organizations captured in this category – including those that may serve as much to domesticate, and even repress, the political agency of marginalized interests as to champion their concerns.

Amid this plurality of organizations, women's movements appear the most promising candidates to further the project of 'engendering democracy'. Yet these, too, are as diversely constituted and motivated as they are different across cultures and political contexts. One obvious contribution they might be seen to make is in incubating political leaders. Yet this has come under scrutiny, precisely because success in grass-roots mobilization, in service provision and survival activities, in mobilization to end authoritarianism (such as in Chile and Argentina), or in fighting social ills such as male alcoholism (such as in Andhra Pradesh in India), often fails to move to a further stage with women activists taking charge of the formal governance institutions that follow. Questions arise about the extent to which these institutional forms provide alternative democratic spaces for women's participation, and opportunities for the kinds of political apprenticeship that can equip women to contend with the masculinism of formal political arenas. Yet feminist non-governmental organizations (NGOs) continue to play critical roles in creating what Nancy Fraser terms 'subaltern counterpublics' which constitute 'parallel discursive arenas' in which marginalised groups can find voice, by fostering spaces outside the formal political arena for political learning.[14] One such initiative is a recent project initiated by a consortium of north-eastern Brazilian feminist NGOs. Their *escolas feministas* (literally 'feminist schools') seek precisely to address the question of women's political apprenticeship, using popular education to create spaces for potential political candidates and women in public office to discuss feminist theory and share tactics for engagement.[15]

External support to feminist NGOs and movements has enabled them to expand their scope and range of engagement. Yet it has not come without costs. One consequence that has been highlighted by a number of commentators is professionalization – 'NGO-ization'[16] – of women's movements, with implications both for internal democracy and the political potential of such organizations for promoting broader processes of democratization. Silliman, for example, argues that the expansion of civil society has, paradoxically, served to contract *political* spaces, diminishing the potential of such organizations to take on a more radical redistributive political project.[17] The roles NGOs have come to play in welfare functions formerly performed by the state has also served in some contexts, notably in Latin America, to supplant advocacy with provisioning and produced a shift from horizontal face-to-face relationships to professionalized project administration hierarchies.[18] This has resulted, in some contexts, in a deepening of old cleavages within the women's movement, especially around issues of class. As Schild comments for Chile, 'the clientization of some poor and working-class women, carried out by others in the name of advancing the cause of women, is in effect undermining the possibility that poor and working-class women will come together to articulate their own needs'.[19]

Procedural requirements and competition for funds act as a further constraint. Jenkins cites the director of a Peruvian NGO that evolved with donor funding from origins as a grass-roots feminist organization to a nationally-renowned NGO: 'You win some and you lose some with donor involvement. Perhaps the worst thing that happens is the bureaucratization, and maybe a bit of domestication as well.'[20]

The rosy democratizing ideals associated with civil society sit awkwardly with the realities of NGOs' permeability to, and indeed reproduction of, existing political culture. Jad, for example, cites Shalabi's observations that the internal governance of Palestinian NGOs simply mirrored 'the Palestinian political system based on individual decision-making, patronage and clientelism'.[21] And far from conforming to the neo-Tocquevillian role (after Alexis de Tocqueville's *Democracy in America*) that is marked out for them in contemporary governance policies, dense relationships of mutual dependency can come to characterize a brake on their political efficacy. In the absence of strong membership organizations and where resources are scarce, Jaquette points out, 'relations between civil society and the state can easily be distorted into forms of clientelism that are weakly democratic at best'.[22] The issues raised here pose acute political dilemmas for feminist organizations: from the hazards of inclusion to the alienation of potential alliances across class and other differences that have cost feminism so dear in the past.

Constituting 'Women'

What of other 'civil society' spaces beyond those associated with feminist movements and NGOs? How do they constitute 'women' as an interest group – and what kinds of interests do they bring into the public arena? In *Crazy for Democracy* (1997), Temma Kaplan argues that traditional conceptions of politics fail to pay attention to the significance of grass roots community mobilization in the United States and South Africa as sites for women's political participation – just as those who participate in these activities may resist regarding what they do as 'politics', and their own politics as 'feminist'. Instead, women often mobilize at the grass-roots around identifications that appear at first sight to reinforce sex stereotypes: as mothers, and guardians of community welfare.[23]

Yet such identities are far from fixed. Indeed, their political salience lies precisely in their malleability. Citing studies that explore how, in the aftermath of economic crisis in 1980s Latin America, women mobilizing around basic needs created institutions that evolved over time to take on a more directly political character, Stromquist shows how the subject position that had provided the basis for mobilization – that of mother – underwent substantive shifts. In the process, maternal identifications were reconstituted and relocated within the public sphere. Competing views exist on whether engagement in these kinds of institutions enables women to exercise greater autonomy in their everyday lives. Yet, as Stromquist argues, they provide important sites for political learning. Exposure to new decision-making and leadership practices can have potentially transformative effects in providing opportunities for the kind of apprenticeship we suggest is vital for women to pursue political careers.[24]

Two questions arise. The first is when – and how – does this kind of political learning carry over into the spheres of formal politics? And, the second, given the non-democratic character of many community-level organizations – whether due to the styles of founder-leaders or the lack of democratic procedures for accountability and decision-making – is what *kind* of political learning do they foster?

One obvious limitation of community-level institutions as 'micro-democracies' is that female identifications reinforced within them may offer women little scope to develop their political agency.[25] Different kinds of organizations foster a range of different – often competing – identifications. A diversity of female subject-positions comes into play as the basis for the construction of group-based interests. Faith-based organizations, for example, can be important sites for women's identification with other women, and social and business networks built in these domains can enable women to 'empower' themselves as individuals.[26] Yet faith-based constructions of the category 'woman' often offer a limited and stereotyped repertoire of subject-positions with which women are identified and come to identify themselves. By domesticating and naturalizing women's grievances, normalizing acquiescence to male authority, and excluding women from positions of leadership,[27] such organizations can work to naturalize the very unequal privileges that feminist organizations seek to redress. As workers of a Brazilian feminist NGO observed, with some frustration, their work involves a constant struggle with the identifications promoted by the evangelical church in which 'there are no rights and there is no citizenship ... and women are told to endure their husbands, rather than to question why they are being treated in this way'.[28]

Informal associations, self-help groups and organized grass-roots women's groups are other sites in which women may gain experience of collective action. A key question for feminist analysis has been to what extent, when this is based on identification with traditional notions of womanhood, does this bring about broader shifts in women's consciousness and mobilization around issues of gender and social justice? The instrumentality with which these institutions have been fostered by development agencies, whether through state-sponsored programmes or the efforts of international NGOs, points to a rather different set of potential outcomes. Von Bulow shows how income-generating groups in Tanzania contain elements of 'empowerment', but are also avenues for individual accumulation strategies for better-off women.[29] Batliwala and Dhanraj paint a depressing picture of the extent to which such self-help groups strip away women's political agency. Drawing on observations from the same area of India that was once the site for large-scale women's political mobilization and is now home to myriad self-help groups, they conclude:

> The neo-liberal rules for the new woman citizen ... are quite clear: improve your household's economic condition, participate in local community development (if you have time), help build and run local (apolitical) institutions like the self-help group; by then you should have no political or physical energy left to challenge this paradigm.[30]

As this example illustrates, it is vital to understand the historical contingencies of women's mobilization against a broader backdrop of changing political configurations and opportunities.

New Democratic Spaces

As governments have pluralized sites for citizen engagement with policy institutions, whether in the form of deliberative councils or Participatory Poverty Assessments – often at the behest of donors or banks – the interface between 'civil society' and the state has been recast to reflect an ever-closer working relationship, and mutual dependency. At the same time, as claims are made about the extent to which these new democratic spaces offer greater scope for inclusion of diverse voices and interests,[31] questions arise about the extent to which participation and deliberation in these arenas can serve to advance issues of gender justice.[32]

The political logic that accompanied the fostering of civil society organizations in the development process has recast these institutions as *partners*, reconfiguring governance as a collaborative endeavour rather than a terrain of contestation. Civil society organizations have come to 'stand for'[33] the interest groups that development agencies 'target', taking on roles as spokespeople for 'the poor', 'women' and other social groups, with legitimacy claims ranging from proximity to descriptive representation.[34]

The expansion of these 'invited spaces'[35] arguably affords a new set of actors the opportunity to exercise leverage and to develop and advance new forms of representation. The normative basis of these institutions and the forms of conduct that they promote ought to be good for any traditionally marginalized actors. Such institutions have been seen as offering a particularly important opportunity for women to expand their political skills and to improve the quality of public decision making by introducing their views. As the means of entry into many of these new democratic spaces is mediated by civil society organizations, rather than traditional political institutions, they ought in theory to offer greater scope for *feminist* social actors to gain political space.

In some parts of the world, notably in Africa where women have successfully mobilized across older divides, the politicization of women's organizations, as they have evolved from responding to needs of engagement in agenda setting and mobilization around women's demands, would seem to favour the possibilities for exercising substantive voice in these new democratic arenas.[36] Evidence suggests that it is precisely where politicized feminist organizations have built skills for engagement that women have been able to exercise voice most effectively.[37] In the northeastern Brazilian state of Pernambuco, for example, the feminist movement has successfully occupied spaces within deliberative councils and articulated with other movements to pursue political projects within these spaces.[38] Yet in the absence of organizations such as these, women face considerable difficulties in overcoming cultural obstacles to substantive inclusion.

Despite the promise of deliberative institutions as more inclusive and participatory, the challenges faced by women are effectively little different to those in more formal arenas. Gender-based inequalities are embedded even in the range of permissible subjects for deliberation and the language and culture of public debate.[39] Indeed, women may be at a *disadvantage* in deliberative forums, where the onus is on participants to demonstrate altruism and to reach consensus, especially since women may be socialized into a surrender of self-interest. Assumptions about the nature of deliberation in democratic forums, about the ways interests are debated, represented, challenged and changed and about fair and equal participation in deliberation, are no less problematic than those that associate the sex of a representative with their political perspectives.

Young insists on the compatibility between deliberative democracy and guarantees of group representation.[40] But if women fail to gain respect for their methods of articulation, or if the very deliberation of the issues they wish to raise is placed in question, then group representation becomes essential. As Jane Mansbridge points out, it is precisely in situations marked by histories of distrust and where interests are uncrystallized that descriptive representation matters. The conditions that enhance deliberation and consensus may not achieve fair distribution between groups that are in conflict: 'laboratories' for interest articulation are needed, she argues, institutions that are based primarily on self-interest.[41]

But group representation *as women* is not in itself the solution. As Molyneux points out, the sheer diversity of women's interests works against any simple translation of sexual difference with perceived commonalities. Where women's representation in these institutions is through reserved seats, however, it is on the basis of sexual difference.[42] And, unsurprisingly, a similar set of obstacles arise as in the formal political arena. Once again, the lack of opportunities for political apprenticeship for women and for acquiring alternative models of leadership and the exercise of power means that political learning in these arenas may hardly lend itself to the practice of participatory or deliberative democracy. Batliwala and Dhanraj suggest for India's *panchayats*:

> We find that since most women have entered these institutions without any kind of political or ideological training, skills or experience – they have not been members of a political party or cadre, for example – or have only the limited apolitical experience of their participation in a village self-help group, they are forced to learn and acquire these skills in the most arduous ways and at great cost.[43]

Some women are able to find the means for political agency through this kind of engagement, but success stories are overshadowed by a more gloomy picture of women being installed by families and husbands, and remaining silent so as to preserve their reputations. Indeed, women who are included simply to fulfil quota requirements can end up absent from debates altogether, called upon merely to perform certain formalities. In another part of India, Rajasthan, Ranjita Mohanty shows how social provisions guaranteeing women's participation in watershed committees have led to a situation where a woman's signature – rather than her presence – marks her value to the process. Those women who are vocal about their rights and actively claim inclusion risk being labelled as troublesome and ostracized. Mohanty cites an activist, Nirmala, who says:

> Few women here have the awareness about their rights. Some of us who are educated and are aware about our rights, we are seen as a 'nuisance' and a constant threat within the village. Hence, while women who are silent and docile will be called to meetings, we will deliberately be kept outside.[44]

Mohanty argues that while state-created spaces might appear to promote inclusion, the reproduction of stereotyped assumptions about women serve to make women subject to 'multiple doses of humiliation, discrimination and exclusion'.[45]

The reconfiguration of the terrain of governance with the expansion of 'invited spaces' has further consequences for women's political engagement. As co-governance institutions multiply, women who, like Nirmala, are regarded as a 'nuisance' can find older channels for expressing dissent ever more illegitimate. Engagement has other costs, especially for those whose time poverty already presents constraints. There is a very real danger that enlistment in 'participatory' institutions effectively keeps women 'busy and out of harm's way, distracted from wider political considerations and submerged within the minutiae of issues in their own backyard'.[46] The effects of this, as Batliwala and Dhanraj so powerfully illustrate, are not lost on right-wing groups who are able to step into the political void and actively mobilize women. Indeed, as Mouffe argues, 'when these parties are the only ones offering an outlet for political passions their claims to offer an alternative can be seductive'.[47] And the effects involve not only the depoliticization of such organizations, but the de-naturing of the concept of citizenship itself. Batliwala and Dhanraj contend:

> If we combine the mobilizations of women by the fundamentalist agenda, the depoliticized forms of collective action promoted by state-sponsored micro-credit programmes, and the subversion of agency of elected women in *panchayats*, what emerges is a deeply problematic and bounded construct of women's citizenship – a construct that must be seriously analyzed, challenged and re-framed.[48]

Add Women and Stir?

The basic assumptions that lie behind efforts to increase the numbers of women in political office are that the inclusion of women leads to better, fairer and more responsive government. But in contexts in which women continue to have tenuous purchase on basic citizenship rights, and where masculinist political cultures mediate participation in the public sphere, 'democratizing democracy' raises complex challenges.

For many women, available spaces for political learning are patriarchal and traditional institutions (family, community), often apolitical women's associations or informal associations that either assign women to the tea-making brigade (women's wings of parties) or make women's ascent to leadership positions contingent on patronage from a top male leader. In the first case, women receive little training for *democratic* participation. In the second, there is often too weak a foundation to back political interests with constituency support and resources for formal politics. In the third, women leaders are cut off from a constituency base that might enable them to question party leadership and bring women's interests on to party agendas.

Pluralizing democratic institutions has offered significant spaces for mobilization around issues of gender inequality. Yet creating new democratic spaces is not in itself enough to erase embedded cultural dispositions and styles of politics that are often as inimical to women's participation as those in the formal political arena. Ewig argues that the political efficacy of feminist NGOs ultimately depends on 'the cyclical nature of the democratic state, with its shifting politics and priorities'.[49] The issues at stake here go to the very heart of the ambivalent relationship between feminism and

democracy that is mediated through the state. A deeper and more widespread democratic project may not necessarily result in greater social and political legitimacy for
feminist projects. On the contrary, feminist ambitions for social transformation are so
profoundly counter-cultural, that new democratic spaces may end up shepherding in
stronger controls over women and limitations on their rights.

Different as their political logics and procedural norms might be, when they are
viewed through a gender lens, traditional and new democratic spaces have significant
similarities in failing to redress gender injustice and inequality. Why is this the case?
The answers may lie less in institutional design or even in styles of politics, and more
in the contentious nature of feminist political concerns. With agendas that are often
radically redistributive in terms of resources and relations of power, such concerns
are only ever likely to be able to win over a minority of supporters within the political
arena, whether it is in terms of votes or the possibility of securing consensus. Where
redistributive policies have been successfully pursued, it has often been due to *other*
political configurations – notably through alliances with progressive bureaucrats and
legislators. Yet the very strategies that enable organizations to get a foot in the policy
process door may undermine their prospects for pushing radically redistributive
agendas. Indeed, Marian Sawer comments, the very delinking of democratization
from issues of redistribution may reduce the project of 'engendering democracy' to
'making democracy safe for the free market, with women's presence providing an
alibi for cuts to welfare'.[50]

Given that pressures for democratization almost always arise from civil society
opposition, Dryzek notes, a shift from opposition to engagement can lead to the
reduction of the prospects for further democratization. Unless directly connected
with state imperatives, the democratic gains of incorporation are questionable:

> To the extent that public policy remains under the sway of state imperatives,
> groups whose inclusion coincides with no imperative will not easily acquire
> the tangible goods they value. They may be allowed to participate in the policy-
> making process, but outcomes will be systematically skewed against them ... A
> high price will be paid by any group included on this basis... Inclusion in
> the life of the state is, then, bought at the expense of relatively unrestricted
> democratic interplay in the oppositional public sphere.[51]

Further concerns about the terms for inclusion in contemporary democratic politics are posed by Chantal Mouffe, who argues that neo-liberalism and the conflation of
politics with morality in the turn to deliberative democratic mechanisms signals 'the
retreat of the political'.[52] She contends that:

> the political is from the outset concerned with collective forms of identification;
> the political always has to do with the formation of an 'Us' as opposed to a
> 'Them', with conflict and antagonism ... the very condition of possibility of
> the formation of political identities is at the same time the impossibility of a
> society from which antagonism has been eliminated.[53]

Both the aggregative and deliberative models of democratic political theory, she
argues, 'leave aside the central role of 'passions' in the creation of collective political

identities'.[54] Crucial to democratic politics, she argues, is how the establishment of an 'Us' can be compatible with pluralism: this, she contends, requires the transformation of antagonism into agonism:

> In the agonistic model, the prime task of democratic politics is neither to eliminate passions nor to relegate them to the private sphere in order to establish a rational consensus in the public sphere; it is, rather, to 'tame' these passions by mobilizing them for democratic ends and by creating collective forms of identification around democratic objectives.[55]

Democratizing Democracy

What prospects, then, are there for the projects of 'engendering democracy' with which we began this paper? As our analysis suggests, the boundaries between political spaces are far more blurred than political theory would have us believe. Similarities between constraints to women's political influence in both traditional and 'new democratic spaces' draw attention to the need to facilitate opportunities for political apprenticeship alongside that of creating the conditions for the effective articulation of positions that challenge the status quo. Recognizing that 'invited spaces' may serve as much to divert and dissipate social and political energy as provide productive spaces for engagement calls for circumspection by international donor agencies. That is to say, should their enthusiasm for creating spaces for institutionalized participation be tempered in the light of the evident reproduction of existing political culture and constraints to inclusion within many such spaces?[56]

Feminist organizations have a key role to play in broadening opportunities for the articulation of gender-transformative agendas in both traditional and 'new democratic spaces'. Yet, time-consuming and inflexible donor procedures and the dampening effects of projectization of funding create significant obstacles. Where feminist movements or NGOs strategize across projectized initiatives, they may be able to overcome some of these obstacles; but the amount of effort absorbed in meeting the demands of donors and shoe-horning projects to fit their funding categories can work to undermine the political agency and efficacy of such organizations. Less structured support given in solidarity rather than in response to LogFramed project proposals could make a broader difference to the democratizing potential of these kinds of organizations.

Lastly, our analysis has highlighted the significance of other spaces outside the formal political or deliberative arenas which can incubate leaders, and in which women can formulate positions, exchange perspectives and hone political skills.[57] There are important lessons to be learnt from initiatives such as Brazil's *escolas feministas* that seek to work with women within public office as well as to build the capabilities as *feminists* of would-be politicians and women representatives in other democratic spaces. Yet for these spaces to produce political actors who are effective within the political arenas described in this account, it is vital that such 'laboratories' move beyond the conflation of identity with identification. This calls for what Katherine Adams describes as a new politics of 'self-interest', one that borrows from Arendt's notion of 'inter-est' as that 'which lies between people and *therefore can relate and bind them together*.[58] Such sites would serve 'not merely to articulate different identities and agendas, but to instrumentalize those differences towards the formulation of new identities, new agendas, new alliances, and new political forms'.[59] It is in the use of these spaces to develop bridges into the political arena – developing the bases for new alliances, as well as offering opportunities for political learning – that the challenges of *democratizing* democracy, can perhaps begin to be addressed.

ACKNOWLEDGEMENTS

We would like to thank John Gaventa for the financial support given by the Development Research Centre on Citizenship, Participation and Accountability for writing this paper, Kirsty Milward for her editorial assistance and Julio Faundez for commissioning this paper and for helpful comments on an earlier draft.

NOTES

1. Karen Beckwith, 'The Substantive Representation of Women: Newness, Numbers, and Models of Representation', paper presented at the Annual Meetings of the American Political Science Association, Boston, 29 August 2002. Drude Dahlerup, *The New Women's Movement. Feminism and Political Power in Europe and the USA* (London: Sage, 1986)

2. Jane Jenson and Celia Valiente, 'Comparing Two Movements for Gender Parity: France and Spain', in Lee Ann Banaszak, Karen Beckwith and Dieter Rucht (eds), *Women's Movements Facing the Reconfigured State* (New York: Cambridge University Press, 2003). Mala Htun and Mark Jones, 'Engendering the Right to Participate in Decision-making: Electoral Quotas and Women's Leadership in Latin America', in Nikki Craske and Maxine Molyneux (eds), *Gender and the Politics of Rights and Democracy in Latin America* (London: Palgrave, 2002).

3. These countries are: Rwanda (48.8 per cent), Sweden (45.3 per cent), Denmark (38 per cent); Finland (37.5 per cent), the Netherlands (36.7 per cent), Norway (36.4 per cent), Cuba (36 per cent), Spain (36 per cent), Belgium (35.3 per cent), Costa Rica (35.1 per cent), Argentina (34 per cent), Austria (33.9 per cent), Germany (32.2 per cent), Iceland (30.2 per cent), Mozambique (30 per cent), South Africa (30 per cent) (UNRISD 2005). The global average proportion of parliaments that are female was 15.9 per cent in 2004. This is up from nine per cent in 1987, a rate of increase (at just 0.36 per cent per annum) which is nothing to get excited about: if growth at this level is maintained, a simple linear projection shows that women will not achieve parity with men until the turn of the twenty-second century. See Pippa Norris and Ronald Inglehart, *Cultural Barriers to Women's Leadership: A Worldwide Comparison* (Quebec City: International Political Science Association World Congress, 2000), p.2.

4. See Mala Htun, 'Is Gender like Ethnicity? The Political Representation of Identity Groups', *Perspectives on Politics*,Vol.2, No.3 (2004), pp.439–58 for a list of countries using gender quotas at national and local levels, and countries using reservations.

5. Anne Phillips, *The Politics of Presence* (Oxford: Clarendon Press, 1995), pp.157–8.

6. Sylvia Tamale, *When Hens Begin to Crow: Gender and Parliamentary Politics in Uganda* (Kampala: Fountain Publishers, 1999).

7. Anne Phillips, 'Democracy and Representation: Or, Why Should it Matter Who our Representatives Are?', in Anne Phillips (ed.), *Feminism and Politics* (Oxford: Oxford University Press, 1998), p.235.

8. *The Wall Street Journal*, 9 March 2005.

9. 'Women's Voices Rise as Rwanda Reinvents Itself', *The New York Times*, 26 February 2005.

10. Shireen Hassim, 'Representation, Participation and Democratic Effectiveness: Feminist Challenges to Representative Democracy in South Africa', in Anne Marie Goetz and Shireen Hassim (eds), *No Shortcuts to Power: African Women in Politics and Policy-Making* (London: Zed Books, 2003).

11. Denise Walsh, 'The Liberal Moment: Women and Just Debate in South Africa 1994–1996', paper presented at the 2002 Midwest Political Science Association Conference, 2002, p.13 citing Shamim Meer, *Women Speak: Reflections on Our Struggles 1982–1997* (Kwela Books/Oxfam GB, 1998), p.163.

12. Dzodzi Tsikata, *National Machineries for the Advancement of Women in Africa: Are they Transforming Gender Relations?* (Ghana: Third World Network-Africa, 2001).
13. Aili Mari Tripp, 'New Trends in Women's Political Participation in Africa' (University of Wisconsin, Madison, 1999) (available at <http://democracy.stanford.edu/Seminar/AiliTripp.pdf>).
14. Nancy Fraser, 'Rethinking the Public Sphere: A Contribution to the Critique of Actually Existing Democracy', in Craig Calhoun (ed.), *Habermas and the Public Sphere* (Cambridge, MA: MIT Press, 1992), p123.
15. Silvia Cordeiro, personal communication. For further details on *Projeto Mulher e Democracia*, see <www.cmnmulheredemocracia.org.br>.
16. Sonia Alvarez, 'Advocating Feminism: The Latin American Feminist NGO "Boom"', *International Feminist Journal of Politics*, Vol.1, No.2 (1999), pp.181–209.
17. Jael Silliman, 'Expanding Civil Society: Shrinking Political Spaces – The Case of Women's Non-governmental Organisations', *Social Politics*, Vol.6, No.1 (1999), pp.23–53.
18. Christina Ewig, 'The Strengths and Limits of the NGO Women's Movement Model: Shaping Nicaragua's Democratic Institutions', *Latin America Research Review*, Vol.34, No.3 (1999), pp.75–102. Islah Jad, 'The NGO-ization of Arab Women's Movements', *IDS Bulletin*, Vol.35 No.4 (2004), pp.34–42.
19. Veronica Schild, 'New Subjects of Rights? Women's Movements and the Construction of Citizenship in the 'New Democracies'', in Sonia Alvarez, Evelina Dagnino and Arturo Escobar (eds), *Cultures of Politics/Politics of Cultures* (Boulder, CO: Westview Press, 1998), pp.93–116.
20. Katy Jenkins, 'Feminist NGOs: Promoting Development Alternatives at the Grassroots?', paper presented at conference on "Reclaiming Development? Assessing the Contributions of Non-Governmental Organisations to Development Alternatives", Manchester, 27–29 June 2005, p.9.
21. Jad (note 18), p.39.
22. Jane Jaquette, 'Women and Democracy: Regional Differences and Contrasting Views', *Journal of Democracy*, Vol.12, No.3 (2001), pp.111–25.
23. Temma Kaplan, *Crazy for Democracy: Women in Grassroots Movements* (London: Routledge, 1997).
24. Nelly Stromquist, 'The Political Experience of Women: Linking Micro and Macro Democracies', *La Educación*, Vol.37, No.116 (1993), pp.541–59.
25. Ibid.
26. Anne Motley Hallam, 'Taking Stock and Building Bridges: Feminism, Women's Movements and Pentecostalism in Latin America', *Latin American Research Review*, Vol.38, No.1 (2003), pp.169–86.
27. Karen Beckwith, 'Beyond Compare? Women's Movements in Comparative Perspective', *European Journal of Political Research*, Vol.37 (2000), pp.431–68.
28. Andrea Cornwall, field notes.
29. Dorthe von Bulow, *Power, Prestige and Respectability: Women's Groups in Kilimanjaro, Tanzania*, Centre for Development Research Working Paper, 95.11 (Copenhagen: Centre for Development Research, 1995).
30. Srilatha Batliwala and Deepa Dhanraj, 'Gender Myths than Instrumentalise Women: A View from the Indian Frontline', *IDS Bulletin*, Vol.35, No.4 (2004), pp.11–18.
31. Iris Marion Young, *Inclusion and Democracy* (Oxford: Oxford University Press, 2000); John Gaventa, 'Deepening the Deepening Democracy Debate', mimeo (Brighton: Institute of Development Studies, 2004).
32. This has been the subject of an extensive debate among political theorists, to which Iris Marion Young, Nancy Fraser, Anne Phillips and Jane Mansbridge have been key contributors.
33. Hannah Fenichel Pitkin, *The Concept of Representation* (Berkeley, CA: University of California Press, 1967).
34. Adrian Lavalle, Peter Houtzager and Graziella Castello, *In Whose Name? Political Representation and Civil Organisations in Brazil*, IDS Working Paper 249 (Brighton: Institute of Development Studies, 2005).
35. Andrea Cornwall, 'Locating Citizen Participation', *IDS Bulletin*, Vol.33, No.2 (2002), pp.49–58; Gaventa (note 31).
36. Tripp (note 13).
37. B. Agarwal, 'Re-sounding the Alert: Gender, Resources and Community Action', *World Development*, Vol.25, No.9 (1997), pp.1373–80; M. Mukhopadhyay and S. Meer, *Creating Voice and Carving Space: Redefining Governance from a Gender Perspective* (Amsterdam: KIT, 2004).
38. Andrea Cornwall, fieldnotes.
39. M. Kohn, 'Language, Power and Persuasion: Toward a Critique of Deliberative Democracy', *Constellations*, Vol.7, No.3 (2000), pp.408–29.

40. Young (note 31).
41. Jane Mansbridge, 'What Does a Representative do? Descriptive Representation in Communicative Set-tings of Distrust, Uncrystallized Interests and Historically Denigrated Status', in W. Kymlicka and W. Norman (eds), *Citizenship in Diverse Societies* (Oxford: Oxford University Press, 2000), p.154.
42. Maxine Molyneux, 'Mobilization without Emancipation? Women's Interests, the State and Revolution in Nicaragua', *Feminist Studies*, Vol.11, No.2 (1985), pp.227–54.
43. Batliwala and Dhanraj (note 30), p.16.
44. Ranjita Mohanty, 'Gendered Subjects, State and Participatory Spaces: The Politics of Domesticating Participation' in Andrea Cornwall and Vera Coelho (eds), *Spaces for Change? The Politics of Partici-pation in New Democratic Arenas* (London: Zed Books, 2006).
45. Ibid.
46. D. Taylor, 'Citizenship and Social Power', in D. Taylor (ed.), *Critical Social Policy: A Reader* (London: Sage, 1996), p.785.
47. Chantal Mouffe, *Politics and Passions: The Stakes of Democracy* (London: Centre for the Study of Democracy, 2002), p.13.
48. Batliwala and Dhanraj (note 30), p.17.
49. Ewig (note 18), p.98.
50. M. Sawer, 'Constructing Democracy', *International Feminist Journal of Politics*, Vol.5, No.3 (2002), pp.361–5.
51. John Dryzek, 'Political Inclusion and the Dynamics of Democratization', *The American Political Science Review*, Vol.90, No.3 (1996), pp.475–87.
52. Mouffe (note 47), p.3.
53. Ibid. pp.5, 7.
54. Ibid. p.8.
55. Ibid. p.9.
56. Andrea Cornwall, 'New Democratic Spaces? The Politics and Dynamics of Institutionalised Partici-pation', *IDS Bulletin*, Vol.35, No.2 (2004), pp.1–10.
57. As do Margaret Kohn and Nancy Fraser, among others.
58. Hannah Arendt, *The Human Condition* (Chicago, IL: University of Chicago Press, 1958) cited in Katherine Adams, 'At the Table with Arendt: Towards a Self-Interested Practice of Coalition Dis-course', *Hypatia*, Vol.17, No.1 (2002), pp.1–33.
59. Adams (note 58), p.2.

Manuscript accepted for publication August 2005.

Address for correspondence: Andrea Cornwall; Anne Marie Goetz, both Institute of Development Studies, University of Sussex, Brighton, East Sussex, BN1 9RE. E-mail: <A.Cornwall@ids.ac.uk; anne-marie.goetz@ids.ac.uk>.

Democratic Thought and Practice in Rural China

SUSANNE BRANDTSTÄDTER and GUNTER SCHUBERT

There can be no democracy without a sense of belonging to a political collectivity. In most cases, the collectivity is a nation, but it also could be a township, a region ... Democracy is based on the responsibilities of the citizens of a country. If those citizens do not feel responsible for their government because it exercises its powers in a territorial space that seems to them artificial or foreign, their leaders cannot be representative and the ruled cannot be free to choose their rulers.[1]

Introduction: Contextualizing Democracy

More than 20 years after China embarked on a path of gradual 'reform and opening up' (*gaige kaifang*), the country has witnessed unprecedented change in all areas of social, economic and cultural life: the rise of a powerful market economy, an unprecedented social and geographical mobility, the emergence of a small middle class in the larger cities, the total reconstruction of many urban and rural areas, a consumer revolution, the construction of a new legal system, and the emergence of public debates, on issues ranging from the Cultural Revolution to foreign policy and domestic problems. Against all these changes, the communist party-state has stood out as the pillar of stability and national continuity, a political apparatus that has proved uniquely resilient and able to rise to new political challenges. Since the 1989 Tiananmen Square incident, the symbol of brutally crushed hopes for democracy in China, two collections of state of the art scholarship attest little prospect for a democratization of the existing political system, with the second collection concluding on an even more pessimistic tone than the first.[2] Strikingly, shortly after Tiananmen, the well-known China scholar Merle Goldman still had hopes that an emerging urban intellectual culture could form the 'sprouts of democracy' in China – a hope she grounded in the Confucian legacy of intellectuals as critics of oppressive or immoral governments.[3] As the 1990s unfolded and China's liberal intellectuals were sidelined by a more conservative and nationalist mainstream, this hope evaporated. At the turn of the millennium, China's intellectual sphere has been split into two – the world of the so-called neoliberals and the world of new leftists who debate forcefully about China's future by aptly avoiding pinpointing the one-party-state as the source of the problems facing the country.[4]

This study will look for 'sprouts of democracy'[5] at the other end of the political and social spectrum: in the countryside, within so-called 'peasant' China and local forms of collectivity.[6] Chinese peasants are the only part of the population which have, for nearly 20 years now, attained some experience with formal democratic procedures on a small scale.[7] With the dismantling of the Maoist communes, brigades and production teams in the mid-1980s, Chinese villages officially became the 'villagers' self-governing organisations' (cunmin zizhi zuzhi). While self-governing initially stood for *economic* self-governing (as the planned economy was being replaced by the market), rising local dissatisfaction with local leaders and the centre's fear of losing control at the grass roots led to the promulgation of the Organic Law of Villager Committees on an experimental basis in 1987. The new law stipulated that village committees (cunmin weiyuanhui) – local representatives who are charged with 'running' the village on a daily basis – should be elected by all villagers above the age of 18, for a term of three years. Despite the fact that the party secretary (shuji) – the official who in most of the cases still exerts the greatest influence over village politics in contemporary China – is not directly elected,[8] the new 'grass-roots democracy' (jiceng minzhu) is officially being praised as genuine village self-government.

Political planners in Beijing, however, conceived local elections primarily as a more effective tool of governance, as a way to bind peasants as loyal subjects to state institutions and state policies, and not as a way to expand the political and civil rights of peasants against the state.[9] The institution of village elections must be seen here in the wider context of government efforts to introduce 'rule by law' (fazhi) in the post-Maoist period. Fazhi (a term that does not distinguish between rule *by* law and rule *of* law) has been a central part of the government's efforts to promote the country's 'development' (fazhan) through increasing 'material' and 'spiritual civilization' (*wuzhi/jingsheng wenming*). On the one hand, *fazhi* was aimed at supporting China's new market economy by standardizing practices across China's vastly different regions, creating a more attractive environment for international investment, and also meeting the requirements of international organizations such as the World Trade Organization (WTO). On the other hand, *fazhi* was central to the government's efforts to create a new 'model citizen' as the standard-bearer of the reforms: a mobile, law-abiding and self-disciplining citizen in place of the immobile Maoist mass-citizen under direct political and ideological control by local cadres. As Mechthild Exner points out, the reform state's five-year campaign to spread legal knowledge was first and foremost a means to affect ideological transformation with the help of the state's still formidable propaganda apparatus. The campaign aimed at promoting compliance with the law, social stability, economic development and adherence to the continuing authority of the Communist Party, rather than inculcating the concept of the 'rightful' citizen and the rule *of* law in China.[10]

Peasants in contemporary China are viewed by the country's elites and a majority of the urban population as the epitome of all that is 'backward' (*luohuo*): collective, brutish, uneducated and local, and therefore in particular need of outside intervention to 'develop' and to 'civilize'. 'Grass-roots democracy' was part of this mission to transform the peasant into a 'civil' subject through the introduction of a set of modern state institutions; a subject that is politically empowered but that remains very different from the democratic, 'civic' subject constituted in inalienable rights as defined by Alain Touraine.[11] In spite of this, scholars like Li Lianjiang and Kevin O'Brien have documented an emergent civic or rights consciousness in the countryside, which expresses itself most vividly in new forms of collective action and social protest, demanding from local governments an adherence to the law by evoking the language of democracy and citizen rights.[12] As the authors observe, in these instances of 'rightful resistance', peasants frequently behave as if they have the right to due process, reinterpreting *fazhi* as rule *of* law and claiming their civil rights against (local) governments. In other words, a national discourse on law, citizenship and democracy – terms used within the context of development (*fazhan*), civilization (*wenming*) and population quality (*suzhi*) – is appropriated and reinterpreted by peasant society in terms of political and civil rights.

Our account starts from the premise that – aside from those very few cases in which it has been successfully 'exported' after the Second World War – democracy can never be simply 'imposed' from the outside, but must always emerge from already existing practices, in interaction with larger structural changes. We therefore also eschew typical discussions about the 'compatibility' of local societies with democratic institutions. As Alain Touraine writes, democratization is a process through which a community is 'transformed into a society governed by laws, and a state into both a representative of society and a power that is limited by basic rights';[13] a process that transforms community membership into citizenship defined through inalienable rights. This definition implies that democratic rights evolve out of entitlements held by community members; that inalienable entitlements held as collective *insiders* are being transformed into the inalienable *rights* of citizens. As part of processes of state-formation, democratization thus might involve a hybridization of abstract principles and procedures inherent in the state sphere with the entitlements and claims that define membership in local communities, and, as a consequence, the legal expansion of the democratic capacity rooted in such membership.

Especially in the context of an authoritarian state, however, 'sprouts of democracy' are often not found in the immediate political sphere, but emerge from the *synergy* between changes in the 'system world', in Habermasian terms, and processes that reproduce entitlements or claims, social integration and trust within local 'life worlds'; processes which constitute a civil society in the wider sense as suggested by Chris Hann.[14] Peasant China's democratic 'potential' here lies in the fact that the village collective remains the most important source and distributor of social and political rights in contemporary China. As an administrative unit of the state, and as unique, localized communities formed in historical relations of shared property, kinship and worship, Chinese villages constitute 'contact zones' in Sally Merry's sense:[15] places where the production of 'civil' citizens and legitimate authority in the context of state institutions comes into contact with processes in which rightful *bendiren* (locals, literally 'own-soil-people'), local identities and communities of solidarity are being created.

In the following section, we will use the term 'moral economy' to denote these local processes that produce collectivity in rural China. Moral economy here signifies a complex interaction of individual and collective entitlements and obligations which establish a basic equality of 'insiders', enable meaningful participation in the local collective and shape local notions of a 'collective good', and thereby, also concepts of good leadership and legitimate authority.[16] We will argue that processes of active appropriation of state categories by 'peasants' and their reinterpretation in the light of claims and entitlements derived from the local moral economy are central to democratization in China. As active local appropriations, these processes of hybridization not only 'charge' the concept of the citizen with the notion of rights by reinterpreting civil as civic – therefore transgressing into the sphere of the state – they also act on local society by reinterpreting membership in local communities through the prism of 'rights'. Our article shows that democratic practice and thought in rural China develops the concept of a 'moral contract' within society and between the society and the authorities.[17] This concept emerges from the moral economy that constitutes the village as a social and political community, but has taken on aspects of contractual thinking and of a national rights discourse linking it to the nation-state.

Identifying Modes and Patterns of 'Peasant Democracy'

Peasants in China operate in a context where an official national discourse about 'socialist democracy' (*shehui minzhu*), political system reforms (*zhengzhi tizhi gaige*) as well as 'human rights' (*renquan*) has gained considerable momentum since the mid-1990s, that is, since the reconsolidation of communist rule in the aftermath of the 1989 Tiananmen suppression. The new discourse reflects China's post-Tiananmen aspirations to become a full member of the international community in which these terms denote development and modernity. It also points to the country's offensive against international criticisms of its human rights record. At the same time, the concept of democracy has had its own historical trajectory in China, where it took on different meanings, most of which are widely different from academic definitions of democracy known in the West. More than 100 years ago, the concept of *minzhu* ('the rule of/by the people') was employed by Chinese republicans and nationalists eager to create a unified 'Chinese people' from a population they likened to a 'loose sheet of sand', disconnected, dispersed and parochial, and lacking any national consciousness.

Under Mao, *minzhu* became associated with the 'socialist democratic dictatorship of the people', a rarely utilized term which was, nevertheless, the most important metaphor for the enduring legitimacy of communist one-party rule. Democracy was now thought as the dialectic unity between the (peasant) masses and the party, as captured in the slogan 'from the masses, to the masses'; as economic equality, collective ownership and the absence of private property; as the selfless devotion of both cadres and masses to the building of a great socialist society; and as the ideological right of the masses to 'struggle against' the cadres who had strayed from the 'right path' to communism and who no longer 'serve the people' (*wei renmin fuwu*).[18] Maoist notions of *minzhu*, though having the peasant as its standard-bearer, were directed against the institutions of the 'ancient regime': first and foremost, against the corporate kinship groups and local temples, which, to nation-building Maoists, symbolized the parochialism, factionalism and superstition that had kept the peasant class divided and exploited.[19] They were to be replaced by production brigades and teams as new socialist collectives; collectives that would realize *minzhu* by making all entitlements and political power derivative from the socialist state and local communities its elementary units.

With the beginning of the Reform period in 1978–79, and, in particular, after Tiananmen, democracy (as the 'rule of law') came to be closely associated with the 'developedness' (*fada*) of the country and with 'advanced culture' (*xianjin wenhua*). As heirs to Maoism, Deng Xiaoping and his followers maintained that the new national goal of material development and increasing 'civilization' could only be achieved by a transformation of society and self under the firm leadership of the vanguard party. But their strategy was experimental and reform-oriented rather than revolutionary. Deng's discourse on political reforms gave shape to 'socialist democracy' as the guiding idea for market transformation under one-party rule. Under Jiang Zemin, who recentralized the political system and brought technocratic leadership to the party apparatus, 'socialist democracy' was then reduced to economic performance and the containment of personality rule at the top of the ruling party.[20] With the promulgation of the Organic Law of Villager Committees and the implementation of rural elections, democracy then took on the new meaning of 'village democracy' in the countryside, emphasizing fair electoral procedures and 'governing through law' (*fazhi*). However, as an ideal *minzhu* is being constructed in opposition to the contemporary stereotypes of peasants, who are, today, not only connected with 'feudal superstitions' (*fengjian mixin*), but further delegitimized by their association with Maoism. In popular opinion, thus, *minzhu* and *fazhi* are to be developed from outside *and against* peasant culture. Even liberals and neo-leftist intellectuals much inspired by the Maoist era rarely include peasants in their conceptions of a democratic China.[21] But what does democracy mean in the country-side, where the phenomenon of 'rightful resistance' developed? How do local villagers practice democracy and what notions of democracy do they hold; how have they appropriated and reinterpreted political innovations from above?

From Civil to Civic: Village Democracy and Local Moral Economies

In rural Fujian, one of the provinces in south and south-eastern China that the reforms allowed to 'get rich first', villagers view increasing democracy (*minzhu*) as part of the overall policy of 'reform and opening up' (*gaige kaifang*), as an important step on the country's path to 'developedness', civilization and modernity. Our own research focused on three villages in southern Fujian, located between the Xiamen Special Economic Zone and the old port city Quanzhou to the north, which were each visited for several months between 1994 and 2002. In all three places, *minzhu* was one important yardstick against which villagers judged not only changes in the relations between peasants and cadres, but also more generally the degree of 'developedness' (*fada*) that state and society had achieved. Local discourses on 'democracy' reflected also more immediately the shifting currents of the larger political discourse.

In 1994 and 1995, not long after Tiananmen, elderly villagers, especially, often used the term *minzhu* to point out to the foreign observer the many advances in personal freedom the Reform Era had brought them, in comparison to the 'total' control they had experienced under Mao. In these discourses, *minzhu* meant that local people were now able to make many important decisions without state interference, especially decisions concerning economic or family matters. Villagers would also frequently point out that they could now criticize the local government in private, without the fear of being reported to the authorities by fellow villagers and then suffering political retribution. In the early 2000s, in contrast, *minzhu* was used in the context of other reforms in state-society relations that were commonly regarded as positive: villagers no longer mentioned advances in basic personal freedoms, but used 'democracy' to point to a substantial curtailing of cadre power, especially in relation to prohibiting the arbitrary confiscation of property and arbitrary arrests of fellow villagers. Once again, this was closely linked to the 'developedness' of the region: places where village cadres still defined local law, some villagers pointed out, were 'backward' (*luohuo*) or 'developing more slowly' (*fazhan bijiao man*), and were usually located in China's interior. At the same time, however, there was a critical counter-discourse that referred to 'democracy' to highlight serious flaws in 'real-existing' cadre-peasant relations. In all three villages, local governments were criticized as corrupt, self-interested and incompetent, and thus of 'no use' (*mei you yong*) in relation to village development. Another frequent complaint was that candidates for village committees had been pre-selected by the township government and thus represented township interests, or they were linked to competitive factions in the village, and favoured their kin over other villagers. For some villagers, democracy in China was 'lacking' (*cha*) or even 'non-existent' (*bu minzhu*) in comparison to neighbouring Taiwan or other 'more developed' countries. This was because villagers had no voice in important decisions on local development made at the township level or above, and because higher-level cadres protected corrupt village cadres with whom they had built 'good relations' (*hao guanxi*).

Not surprisingly, village elections has a similarly ambivalent status in these *minzhu* discourses. Villagers cherished local elections as a democratic achievement, which expressed to them the ideal of popular sovereignty, government accountability and civilizational progress. The 'Organic Law' was interpreted as an invitation to peasants, by the central government, to participate politically, control 'wayward cadres' and share responsibility. There was generally much less enthusiasm in all villages, however, about the reality of local elections. People complained that elections were being manipulated by higher-level governments, rigged through vote-buying, dominated by powerful factions in the village, and used by local strongmen to reassert their control over economic, social and political resources. Village elections were thus not perceived as instances of genuine village democracy, but as moments when a democratic ideal clashed with an undemocratic reality; procedures that revealed an existing democratic deficit and a deficit in the 'quality' (*suzhi*) of local governments *and* local society. Villagers, like the state authorities, thus linked the realization of 'true' democracy to a civilizational state not yet attained in China; that is, as people were still trapped in short-sighted self-interest and irrational behaviour, they were unable to advance the common good.

In spite of the wide-spread disenchantment with the practice of village democracy in Fujian, however, there were virtually no local demands to abolish elections, nor any voices regarding elections as the *source* of an 'evil' factionalism which undermined village solidarity, nor claims that peasant culture was principally incompatible with competitive elections or disadvantageous for the villages' social integration – all views that are common among a substantial group of Chinese political scientists.[22] To the contrary: elections only reconfirmed and made visible problems that were already in existence; at the same time underlining the idea of the village collective as electorate, audience and public 'referee' for leaders. Here we find an important local re-interpretation of village democracy: from a tool of more effective governance and for the creation of 'civil' subjects, to an institution that emphasizes a public and civic role for peasants. Most local discourses about democracy, furthermore, linked it closely to the idea of equality – which was no longer perceived as economic equality, but as an equality of chances which left different individual abilities or skills as the only acceptable source of differences in wealth and power. In an ideal village democracy, a village leader would thus be a person elected for leadership qualities (*you nengli*), fairness (*gongping*), relevant knowledge (*renshi shi*), education/culture (*you wenhua*) and 'care' (*guan*) for the village as a whole; a *primus inter pares* whose power over fellow villagers should by definition be limited to preserving the collective good and leading the way of development.

In these discourses, we find strong echoes of Maoist discourses on the political role of peasants and of the Maoist ideal of a 'selfless or complete altruism'[23] that demanded from both leaders and the masses to serve the people (*wei renmin fuwu*); a negation of individual interest and a total personal devotion to the greater common good, as defined by Mao's teachings. Today, to act on *individual* interests in elections, against the interest of the collective good, is considered selfish and essentially 'undeveloped' (*bu fada*). In contrast to the Maoist era, however, local discourses strongly emphasised that *personal* rights should place limits on political power; rights that were understood first and foremost as the right to partake in development and basic personal freedoms. Moreover, these villagers in Fujian defined the ideal of democratic leadership first and foremost in terms of 'local loyalties':[24] elected village representatives should be accountable to villagers *and should not* work as agents of the township government or to pursue individual interests. They should advance the collective good of the village, *and not* undermine it by siding with township or factional interests. Therefore, villagers saw a conflict both between local interests and the local state, and between local interests and 'selfish' interests.

But what did villagers mean when they said 'we'? How did they define the *rightful* collective? In all three Fujian villages, the reform period has seen the reconstruction of 'traditional' institutions such as temples and ancestral halls, which in pre-revolutionary times were not only centres of political power, but also represented the village as a community of kinship and worship.[25] In pre-revolutionary China, the centrality of these 'collective' institutions in village life often demanded from local leaders substantive donations in exchange for legitimate authority. Society or collectivity was here produced in relations of shared property and gift exchange; a local moral economy that organised the entitlements and obligations of insiders, and that defined the village as 'local moral world'.[26]

As Stephan Feuchtwang's comparative analysis shows, these local institutions were reconstructed in particular in communities that had little or no income from collective enterprises; and here they often regained considerable political influence on village affairs through the assembling of new 'collective' funds.[27] In the south Fujian villages researched here, these institutions had assembled funds from donations and 'incense money' (*xianghuo qian*), which were not only spent on annual collective rituals, but also increasingly on the construction of village roads, village beautification, old people's homes and 'prizes' for local students – on projects that would, in local understanding, enhance village development and further 'public welfare' (*gongyi*).[28] In this context, it is not surprising that villagers re-interpreted the 'abstract' Maoist masses as the village community, and the (national) common good as the (local) collective good, emphasising a separation between the interests of the local state and those of the village.

Local democracy discourses emphasized popular sovereignty, development, 'governing through law', equality and 'serving the people' – all elements of different state discourses – but they hybridized them with notions of legitimate leadership and of the collective entitlements of insiders (*bendiren*), and thus with a local moral economy that again defined the collective 'we' in the village.[29] From a local perspective, village democracy (defined in terms of the loyalty of local leaders and local definitions of the collective good) was thus not so much sustained by public deliberation or state institutions but by the 'silent practices' that create local identifications and rightful 'insiders', and that turned cadres into village patrons.[30]

The term patron makes the ambivalence of such ties evident: a patron can use his personal influence to advance public welfare, or he can dispense favours, increase inequalities and personal power, and damage the collective good. Elite discourses depict peasant culture as prone to such factionalism and therefore sometimes view elections as counter-productive in terms of social stability and development. In contrast, villagers often blame local factionalism and corruption on an environment where access to resources is dependent on the 'pulling of connections' (la guanxi) and the using of back-doors (houmen). From the villagers' 'bottom-up' perspective, thus, the evils of corruption and factionalism are not simply rooted in 'peasant culture', but are results of a wider environment (represented by the local state and market) which corrupts relations within the community and relations between cadres and peasants. In contrast, temples and/or ancestral halls were thought to further an ideal of collective welfare (gongyi) tied very closely into the larger national project on development, modernity and democracy.[31]

In his article on peasants and democracy in China, Stephan Feuchtwang advances the argument that many practices associated with the governing of local temples could be called democratic, such as the annual elections of leaders through the throwing of divination blocks, the praxis of office rotation, and existent forms of 'exit' and 'voice'.[32] From the perspective of this study, however, the democratic relevance of these institutions lies not in that they are 'compatible' with modern democracy (which is Feuchtwang's point, as he argues against a common opinion held among Chinese intellectuals). Rather, it lies in the collective entitlements that they stand for, which are translated into rights against elected village leaders in the context of village democracy and the 'state collective'. It also rests on the fact that one can read 'democracy' into these 'traditional' institutions (which is what Feuchtwang actually demonstrates in his article). Villagers in Fujian frequently undertook such 'readings' by way of comparisons: the village government is corrupt (fubai), but the leaders of local religious associations would not dare (bu gan) to embezzle collective properties; the village government is broke and does nothing for collective welfare (gongyi), but the temple builds streets, schools and old people's homes; the village government's accounting practices are obscure, while ancestral halls and temples make theirs public. Local institutions thus form a space from which to think 'good government'[33] while official elections render these values public and reveal the village's right to be electorate, sovereign, and public 'referee' of local leaders. In these processes of transplantation, hybridization and cultural appropriation and re-appropriation, local 'moral worlds' are themselves being changed. The adoption of discourses on citizenship, modernity and the nation tie local processes of producing bendiren to national citizenship regimes, while notions of contract, inherent to the spheres of the state and the market, transform existing social entitlements increasingly into the direction of rights.

Guo Yuhua has demonstrated this development on the case of 'filial piety', probably the most lastingly important aspect of Chinese family ethics.[34] Relationships between parents and children in pre-revolutionary China had been shaped by steep status hierarchies, which demanded 'total' devotion, support and obedience towards parents from children; while parents only had the (non-enforceable) duty to further the welfare of the family, arrange marriages for children, and not squander family property. Today, as Guo Yuhua writes, young people often see no reason to fulfil their part of the generational contract (for example, to support aging parents financially) when members of the older generations do not *act* as parents or grandparents (for example, when they fail to look after grandchildren). Similarly, relations within 'traditional' institutions have changed. Although control over localized lineages, for example, often remained in the hands of the most influential members of the lineage (generally also those who have donated most to the reconstruction of the ancestral hall), these now often have 'management committees' or 'work groups' that are elected by the heads of households for a certain number of years,[35] rather than being institutions represented by lineage elders and controlled by local power-holders.

Furthermore, although official positions remain largely restricted to men, women seem to identify increasingly with, and regard themselves as, members of, these formerly male-dominated institutions. In one place, for example, women, who had left to work or marry out, returned to the village to participate in, and financially contribute to, a festival of 'their' ancestral hall. In another village, the head of the temple committee was an elderly woman, whose son lived in Hong Kong and had donated a considerable amount of money to the reconstruction of the temple. Although his mother obviously 'stood in' for him, the presence of women in temple committees is, in itself, a novelty. What is obvious in these changes is that local moral economies play not only an important role in the emergence of a 'civic' consciousness and the emerging citizen in rural China, but that they are also being transformed themselves through the integration of notions of citizenship and equality emanating from the state sphere. Both in relations within society, and between society and the state, we observe a move towards a more contractual understanding of political and social relations, and a gradual shift from an older notion of entitlements to the more explicit notion of rights.

Participation, Trust and 'Rightful Resistance'

The introduction of direct elections as an effort of the central state to enhance cadre efficiency and rural stability in the countryside had an impact on power relations that can hardly be overlooked. One of the most debated issues related to this impact is the rise of 'policy-based' or 'rightful' resistance. Rightful resisters (*diaomin*) fight collectively against corrupt local cadres and rigged elections by appealing to written laws and regulations passed down from higher administrative levels (or the central state) to protect – as it is seen by villagers – the peasants' democratic rights. As Li Lianjiang and Kevin O'Brien note, peasants

> seem to view taxes, fees, and other demands in terms of exchanges that imply mutual obligations. They see their relationship with cadres partly in terms of enforceable contracts and fulfil their responsibilities so long as rural cadres treat them as equals and deliver on promises made by officials at higher levels.[36]

Constitutive for this relationship are duties defined in terms of local loyalties, a fair distribution of economic chances and reciprocal socio-political equality all firmly entrenched in the village's moral economy and now guaranteed by the Organic Law on Villager Committees.

In that sense, *rightful* resistance informs the idea of a moral contract with authority. It is therefore embedded in the local moral economy, which allows resistance in the case of a violation of the moral dimension of authority that makes hierarchy acceptable. Village elections bring to the fore and render visible this moral contract with authority. The peasants who engage in rightful resistance against the local cadre bureaucracy claim rights and may even consider violent action as legal, though what they mean in the first place is that such action is morally legitimate or just. At the same time, they consciously partake in the national discourse on village self-government that de-localizes their claims and entitlements and transforms the peasants' political awareness. Fair elections are gradually assumed as entitlements granted by the state which peasants defend ever more vigorously against the local cadres when they feel deprived of them. As O'Brien has remarked, they act like citizens before they have become true citizens.[37]

In more recent fieldwork in Hunan province, Li and O'Brien have come across coordinated peasant organisation beyond the village level and rightful resisters who even now ground their claims and entitlements on constitutional principles, such as popular sovereignty, the rule of law and citizenship.[38] This suggests that they could soon cross their local boundaries and enter the national stage of demanding abstract citizenship, not moral 'redemption' in a primarily local context. However, the overall majority of China's peasants are still far away from such a step, as they still cling to their belief in the trustworthiness of the central government in providing for protection against local cadre abuse and corruption.

Besides engendering rightful resistance, however, village elections have led to very different results in terms of implementation, participation and cadre accountability. The reasons for this variety of outcomes are manifold, although ultimately, they all boil down to the local cadres' response to village elections. Although the direct ballot has given significant power to peasants which they had never enjoyed before, elections have rarely changed the established power structure in the locality. As has been widely reported from all over the country, village party secretaries and township governments continue to dominate most of rural China, although there have been some important adjustments. For instance, elected village heads now may challenge the authority of non-elected party secretaries in intra-village disputes, leading to paralyzing stand-offs or new modes of power-sharing.[39] In poorer parts of China, on the other hand, elections are often badly implemented and do not receive any significant attention by the peasants, who are too preoccupied with their daily struggle for survival. For the same reason, elections can still be easily manipulated and controlled by local cadres. In very rich areas like the Shenzhen Special Economic Zone, elections are often 'captured' by influential village cadres who control a prosperous local economy, allowing them to distribute sufficient benefits to 'buy the peasants off' and, consequently, to sidestep any meaningful control by elections.[40] Generally speaking, where local cadre corruption and malfeasance are not rampant and do not induce peasants to revolt, engage in *shang-fang* (the state-sanctioned practice of officially complaining at some higher level) or even turn to rightful resistance, direct elections do not affect the life of peasants too much.

In north-eastern Jilin Province, however, where village elections were introduced early on and gained national fame as showcases of rigorous and successful implementation, we came across an interesting phenomenon: peasants in two villages in Lishu County felt genuinely empowered by their right to vote although they hardly saw a reason to contact the elected village committee after an election, challenge the non-elected party secretary or demand an extension of the direct ballot to the township level. The turnover of elected village cadres had been comparatively low over the years. Furthermore, although the dominance of the party secretary was evident and the village committee staffed with long-term office-holders who apparently had no fear of electoral defeat, the peasants did not complain but displayed much satisfaction with their local leaders. The seeming paradox to be found here is that even if elections are fulfilling what one may expect of them, that is, to nurture a belief among peasants that the direct ballot makes a fundamental difference in their lives, the peasants would not use this new right to challenge the established village power hierarchies. How can this be explained?

Obviously, in moderately developed north-eastern Jilin, these peasants could not be simply 'bought off', while at the same time, economic development and cadre performance were obviously sufficiently good for the villagers. Still, there was something more to be factored in: all cadres who we met at the village, township and county levels were extremely proud and motivated to perpetuate Lishu's reputation as a national model of grass-roots democracy. They insisted that the villagers' rights and the obligation of the local cadres to serve the people had to be honoured, that deficient cadre behaviour should be punished by the villagers through the direct ballot, and that strictly abiding to the law had to be one of the evaluation criteria of cadres besides their administrative efficiency. The peasants, for their part, recognized the efforts made by the village cadres to fulfil these duties. Complaints were made, but the overall assessment of their work was positive. As it turned out, the peasants felt taken seriously by the cadres, and responded with surprising disinterest in overturning the established village order.

It was not a successful deceit of peasants – how could they be deceived in the local microcosm of a village? – by clever cadres that came to the fore here, but proto-citizenship linked to political trust based on the above-mentioned contractual thinking in the context of the local moral economy. Trust, a concept that originates from the early Western debate on civic culture and system legitimacy, can be generally defined as citizens' belief or confidence that the government or political system will produce outcomes that match their expectations.[41] Clearly, trust has always played a major role in China's moral economy where a complex system of mutual obligations and status hierarchies produced certainty and reliability in all social relations. Arguably, village elections in Lishu have renewed the moral contract between the peasants and the local power-holders. Cadres may now enjoy substantial legitimacy as long as they respect the peasants' right to vote them out of office, while the latter acquiesce in the privilege of (cadre) power that, certainly enough, only good cadres can claim. What we might be facing here are 'trust villages' in which the established order is perpetuated by instilling it with a new brand of legitimacy attached to older values rooted in the village's moral economy. As long as the cadres respect the peasants, they can live on their trust and may even be protected from low economic performance (though not from corruption). Once again, it becomes clear that village elections are contextualized and appropriated by local traditions of legitimizing power and authority. The right to vote may change these traditions, but not in a fundamental sense. Power and authority are redefined by drawing on a national discourse (here on village elections and rural self-government), but their context remains – at least for the time being – local in the first place: As *rightful resistance* is directed to the good centre, *trust* affirms cadre leadership as long as it is *just*.

The Village, the State and the Collective Good

All modern types of state-building seek to transform the relations between citizens and the state in a way that it becomes primarily the latter and its policies, and no longer the local community, that shapes identity-construction and the formation of a national body, including the political system. Socialist China, while sharing the same aspirations to integrate and appropriate 'the local' as all modern states, underwent a very particular form of state-building, in which not the individual citizen but the localised collective became the elementary unit of the state. This collective – most prominently the urban 'unit' (*danwei*) and the rural production brigades and teams (*shengchan dadui and shengchan dui*) – built on existing structures of local community, but redefined them as a product of the state. It is in this sense that villages became 'contact zones': places, in which existent forms of community reproduction where appropriated and integrated into local forms of state-building.[42] Socialist state-building thereby grounded on a necessary opening up of national horizons and, at the same time, effected an increasing restriction and localization of rural life as part of the planned economy.[43] Furthermore, because the 'other' of the state was not the individual citizen but the collective, the central tension in Maoist China was not one between the state rationality and individual interests, but between the local state and the localized collective, a tension that centred on economic rights.[44] As Western states 'resolve' *their* tension through transforming the individual into a citizen, Maoist China 'solved' this problem by transforming local communities into production brigades and production teams.

With the end of the planned economy, and the erosion of the socialist collective, the village community emerged from 'under' the state: in a process of re-appropriating 'the local', spearheaded by the reconstructed ancestral halls and local temples,[45] and by the revitalized lineage and temple politics. This re-localization also revealed the (formerly politically-obscured) antagonism between the village collectives and higher levels of local governments, the ambivalent position of village cadres as members of both 'state' and 'civil society', and the essential absence of rights against the state. The antagonism is evident when, in the name of 'development', township governments simply appropriate resources formerly held by local collectives,[46] make decisions that hurt village interests, and manipulate village elections or bribe village cadres into siding with township interests. In this context, the essential ingredient of any Western definition of democracy, the separation of state and civil society, has anti-democratic connotations: it does not stand for a civil society insulated from (and thus protected against) state power, but for a village community without meaningful influence over its political elites.[47] What appears today from the state's perspective as a growing problem of parochialism among cadres and of rural governance in many localities,[48] are the effects of 'silent practices' that aim at reintegrating village cadres into their local collective. The importance of the local moral economy for village democracy is intrinsically linked to the absence of political rights against the state and – at least in many cases – to the failure of state institutions to enforce a new normative, rule-based consensus between cadres and peasants.[49]

When peasants today evoke central tenets of Maoism – that cadres should 'serve the people' (*wei renmin fuwu*), or the peasants' right to 'correct' corrupt cadres – the meaning of this discourse must be sought in the contemporary political context and not in a nostalgia for the years between 1949 and 1978. With the erosion of the socialist collectives and the concomitant re-localization processes described above, slogans of Maoist 'direct democracy' invoke the new ideal of 'true' village democracy; they represent the demand for popular sovereignty at the village level and for the accountability of power holders towards their electorate. The above-mentioned new normative consensus is indeed being manufactured locally, as Isabelle Thireau and Hua Linshan argue, often in informal processes of dispute mediation in the villages.[50] However, because local 'normative struggles' assume and recycle many elements of the national discourse on democracy, citizenship and development, the re-emergence of local identities and their 'traditional' key symbols does not necessarily lead to a closure against the state and wider society. By trying to ensure a new 'selflessness' in local cadres, peasants see themselves in many ways doing the work of the central government, whose introduction of village elections and intention to 'govern through/according to law' (*fazhi*) has aimed at reducing the arbitrary use of power and at increasing political accountability at the local level.[51] For the time being, the centre is widely trusted as the ultimate guardian of the collective good which must therefore be supported or helped against corrupt cadres at lower levels.[52]

A local closure – a destruction of trust in the central state – is most likely to arise from two scenarios: first, when the state destroys, for example, in the name of 'development', local collectives and the rights and entitlements derived from membership in these collectives without replacing them with genuine citizenship rights; and second, when state agents without any interest to 'selflessly work for the collective maintain control over key resources, and use this control to advance their own individual interests at the expense of a majority of villagers and without any redeeming response from the central state. In this situation, clientelism and factionalism become endemic, forcing 'ordinary villagers' to choose sides and thus undermine the collective basis of a village. Lineages can then have a very negative impact on social integration. In the mid-1980s, when cadres in southern China still retained a considerable control over essential resources, lineage or clan structures experienced a revival in many places, sometimes causing the outbreak of collective-based violence that had already shaped the region before the Revolution.[53] But lineages are not simply clientelist structures that are always causing friction and division in a village. The lineage also stands for the idea of a unified group of essentially equal brothers, an idea instituted in collective property and social reciprocity to which legitimate leaders must contribute. Lineage formations can thus be part of a civilizing process in Norbert Elias's sense, through which arbitrary power is restrained.[54]

Bringing About Democracy by Defending the Collective Good?

Can the idea of a moral contract with authority and with society, a contractual thinking that is the result of local appropriations and reinterpretations of a national discourse on law and democracy, ensure that local cadres respect and advance the collective good, thereby stabilizing the countryside and even redefining the current regime in more democratic terms? Can it eventually transform a 'community' structured around entitlements into a local 'society' structured through rights, thus creating genuine forms of democracy in rural China, which restrict the power of local leaders through the internalization of a concept of citizen rights? Can such a development even expand beyond the local sphere and prepare the ground for democratic reforms at the national level? Even if we take into account the above-mentioned case of Jilin province and similar positive experiences in other parts of China, the institutional innovation of direct elections itself has so far produced mixed results at best in terms of true 'village democracy' and a possible 'bottom-up' development.[55] Although peasants value the idea of elections as a democratic achievement, running for office is often not considered a democratic exercise, but seen as a way to gain privileged access to collective resources. Consequently, elections often result in bitter infighting and the election of leaders who are not necessarily recognized as the best choice for the 'collective good'. Local party branches and the township government aggravate this situation by blocking the election of 'non-conformist' cadres to ensure continuing influence and control over village assets.

The negative assessment of 'local self-government' as rigged by power-mongering and corrupted by self-interested cadres clearly contrasts evaluations of 'local self-government' in villages that centre on a temple community. While temple elections *via* divination are formally less democratic than village elections (because it is the local deity who elects), villagers in Fujian today often think them to be *more* so – because the temple belongs to local people (*bendiren*), and because the god's decision, as local guardian and representative of the 'ideal' village, is made in the best interests of the community (in a form of transcendent Habermasian 'deliberation'), and thus advances the collective good. To further this metaphor, it is, as villagers say, because the collective property of the temple belongs to the temple god – that is, under collective control backed up by a transcendent power – that temple leaders 'do not dare' to embezzle temple funds. *Vice versa*, because village collective property is controlled by cadres who do not have to fear state retribution, corruption is rampant in local governments, 'evil' factionalism destroys local communities and the collective good of the village is slandered.

Interestingly, in our research sites in Jilin the practice of village elections seems to have translated into a moral contract that binds the cadres to the collective good in much the same way that temple leaders are said to be bound to it. This example shows that contractual thinking is effective through both old and new institutions in contemporary village China. It becomes openly manifest in both rightful resistance and trust (read local), depending on the peasants' evaluation of local cadres – an assessment which is itself determined by the moral contract between them. By engaging in upper-level *shangfang* and protest in the cities, peasants demonstrate that their collective good must be protected by the central state against the local cadres. It can be assumed that when they – by way of 'rightful resistance' – oppose the latter for their breach of the moral contract in the villages and remind the centre of its own obligations to ensure the peasants' well-being, they arguably contribute significantly to the ongoing transformation of China's multiple local communities into a coherent society governed by laws, and to the rise of a state limited by individual civil rights. Thus, by invoking the ideal of the collective good and the idea of a moral contract between themselves and the state (central and local), peasants are an important agent of China's future democratization. The gradual 'nationalization' of reciprocity, solidarity, trust and moral duty may soon result in the constitution of the peasant citizen who may still be predominantly oriented towards the collective good in the village, but at the same time 'generalizes' it by thinking (and acting) beyond the village boundaries. If then the state can or does not want to provide what the peasants claim for preserving the collective good in their localities, it may soon be confronted with a powerful group that challenges the existing order by fighting for their collective good now turned national and by using a language that has turned moral entitlements into abstract rights.

ACKNOWLEDGMENTS

The authors would like to thank Kevin O'Brien and Julio Faundez for their comments on an earlier draft of this paper.

NOTES

1. Alain Touraine, *What is Democracy* (Boulder, CO: Westview Press, 1998), p.64.
2. See *Journal of Democracy*, Vol.9, No.1 (1998) and Vol.14, No.1 (2003). Andrew Nathan's article 'Authoritarian Resilience' (pp.6–17) set the tone for the second collection's discussion on China's political future, pointing at two contending 'schools' in the China studies field: while some scholars find the People's Republic of China (PRC)'s regime more stable and even legitimate today, others would rather predict imminent implosion because of rapidly falling degrees of state capacity.
3. Merle Goldman, 'China's Sprouts of Democracy', *Ethics and International Affairs*, No.4 (February 1990), pp.70–90.
4. See Zhang Xudong, *Whither China: Intellectual Politics in Contemporary China* (Durham, NC and London: Duke University Press, 2001).
5. We use this phrase in a slightly ironic way. 'Sprout watching' could be called a typical profession of contemporary China scholars trying to understand China's unique path of development while looking for similarities with the 'West' (as in 'the sprouts of capitalism'). The 'sprouts' metaphor is appropriate, however, in the sense that it supports our argument that democracy 'grows out' of entitlements and claims that define membership in local communities.
6. We use the term 'peasant' (*nongmin*) for those Chinese who hold a 'peasant household register' (*nongmin hukou*) and are thus classified peasants by the state, irrespectively of whether they still work the land. *Nongmin* is, furthermore, an important political category in China: under Mao, *nongmin* were the standard-bearer of the revolution; the revolutionary masses the party claimed to be 'one' with in the 'democratic dictatorship of the people'. In the reform era, peasants have

become the 'peasant problem' (*nongmin wenti*) of China's modernity, a group of people regarded as backward (*luohuo*) and as 'undercivilized' (*bu wenming*), and thus as an obstacle to national development and modernization.

7. However, recent experiments with (more or less) direct elections in urban neighbourhoods may have paved the way for comparable experiences in the coming years in China's cities. See Li Fan, *Zhongguo jiceng minzhu fazhan baogao (Report on China's Grassroot's Democracy Development) 2003* (Beijing: Falü, 2004).

8. However, according to a 2002 guideline issued by the party headquarters, party secretaries in villages must face 'recommendation votes'. In these instances, all villagers are given the opportunity to vote on a candidate. However, the result is non-binding for the village party committee which would have the final say (while being supervised by township party authorities).

9. Daniel Kelliher, 'The Chinese Debate over Village Self-Government', *China Journal*, No. 37 (January 1997), pp.63–86; Kevin O'Brien and Li Lianjiang, 'Accommodating "Democracy" in a One-Party State: Introducing Village Elections in China', *China Quarterly*, No.162 (June 2000), pp.465–89.

10. Mechthild Exner, 'The Convergence of Ideology and the Law: The Functions of the Legal Education Campaign in Building a Chinese Legal System', *Issues and Studies*,Vol.31, No.8 (1995), pp.68–102.

11. Touraine (note 1), pp.124–8.

12. Kevin O'Brien, 'Rightful Resistance', *World Politics*, No.49 (October 1996), pp.31–55; Li Lianjiang, 'Elections and Popular Resistance in Rural China', *China Information*, Vol.15, No.2 (2001), pp.1–19; Kevin O'Brien, 'Villagers, Elections, and Citizenship in Contemporary China', *Modern China*, Vol.27, No.4 (October 2001), pp.407–35; Kevin O'Brien and Li Lianjiang, *Rightful Resistance in Rural China* (forthcoming, 2006).

13. Touraine (note 1), p.66.

14. Chris Hann 'Introduction. Political Society and Civil Anthropology', in Chris Hann and Elizabeth Dunn (eds), *Civil Society: Challenging Western Models* (New York and London: Routledge, 1996), pp.1–26.

15. Sally Engle Merry, *Colonizing Hawai'i: The Cultural Power of Law* (Princeton, NJ: Princeton University Press, 1999), pp.28–9, uses the term 'contact zone' to denote a zone between complex social fields where cultural production involves hybridization and processes of cultural appropriation and re-appropriation. As she shows, these processes take often place in relations of domination and subordination, such as colonialism. The socialist state in China can be said to have colonized the 'cultural world' of rural China through turning local communities into socialist collectives.

16. We use a notion of moral economy that is slightly different of James Scott's famous formulation of 'the moral economy of the peasant'. Moral economy in Scott's sense describes a set of economic practices which follow a 'subsistence ethic' rather than a logic of profit-maximizing, and which are embedded in social institutions that help to spread economic risk. We expand the notion of economy to look at processes that produce collectivity, local identities and entitlements in rural China. These are, however, centrally rooted in reciprocal relations of shared property and exchange in a rural gift economy, which places emphasis on a fundamental equality of insiders and on the responsibility of local leaders towards their collective. Cf. James Scott, *The Moral Economy of the Peasant. Rebellion and Subsistence in Southeast Asia* (New Haven, CT: Yale University Press, 1976).

17. See John Flower and Pamela Leonard, 'Community and State in Sichuan', in Chris Hann and Elizabeth Dunn (eds), *Civil Society: Challenging Western Models* (New York and London: Routledge, 1996), pp.199–221. Flower and Leonard write of a 'moral equilibrium of mutual obligation' that from the villagers' point of view should define interactions both within the community and between peasants and the state. They regard this notion as an important element in the formation of civil society in China; a civil society in which the state, and its local representatives, are part of a local moral order.

18. See James Townsend, 'Chinese Nationalism', in Jonathan Unger (ed.), *Chinese Nationalism* (Armonk, NY: M.E. Sharpe, 1996), pp.1–30; Gunter Schubert, *Chinas Kampf um die Nation (China's Struggle for Nationhood)* (Hamburg: Institute of Asian Affairs, 2002); Suisheng Zhao, *A Nation-State by Construction* (Stanford, CA: Stanford University Press, 2004).

19. See Jack M. Potter and Shulamith Heins Potter, *China's Peasants. The Anthropology of a Revolution* (Cambridge: Cambridge University Press, 1990), p.255.

20. Joseph Y.S. Cheng (ed.), *China in the Post-Deng Era* (Hong Kong: Chinese University Press, 1998); Lowell Dittmer, 'Three Visions of Chinese Political Reform', *Journal of Asian and African Studies*, Vol.38, No.4–5 (2003), pp.347–76.

21. Claudia Derichs, Thomas Heberer and Nora Sausmikat, *Why Ideas do Matter: Ideen und Diskurse in der Politik Chinas, Japans und Malaysia (Ideas and Discourses in the Politics of China, Japan, and Malaysia)* (Hamburg: Institute of Asian Affairs, 2004).

22. Quite prominently among this group figures the concept of *shehui guanlian*, 'social (inter)connected-ness', which describes the complex structure of personal networks within a village as an asset for soli-darity and development, now severely menaced by a decontextualized implementation of elections which follows a logic of individual interest-seeking. See Tong Zhihui, *Xuanju shijian yu cunzhuang zhengzhi (Election Incidents and Village Politics)* (Beijing: Zhongguo shehui kexue, 2004).

23. On the shifts in the make-up of the good citizen from the collective and altruistic mass citizen to the individual and entrepreneurial citizen in the reform era, see Michael Keane, 'Re-defining Chinese Citizenship', *Economy and Society*, Vol.30, No.1 (2001), pp.1–17.

24. See Stephan Feuchtwang, 'Peasants, Democracy and Anthropology. Questions of Local Loyalty', *Critique of Anthropology*, Vol.23, No.1 (2003), pp.93–120.

25. See Stephan Feuchtwang, 'What is a Village', in Eduard B. Vermeer, Frank N. Pieke and Woei Lien Chong (eds), *Cooperative and Collective in China's Rural Development. Between State and Private Interests* (Armonk, NY: M.E. Sharpe, 1998), pp.46–74.

26. See Yan Yunxiang, *The Flow of Gifts. Reciprocity and Social Network in a Chinese Village* (Stanford. CA: Stanford University Press, 1996).

27. Feuchtwang, 'What is a Village' (note 25), pp.68–9.

28. Susanne Brandtstädter, 'Re-defining Place in Southern Fujian: How Overseas Mansions and Ancestral Halls Re-appropriate the Local from the State', Max Planck Institute For Social Anthropology Working Papers No.30 (2001), (available at <www.eth.mpg.de>); see also Lily Lee Tsai, 'Cadres, Temple and Lineage Institutions, and Governance in Rural China', *The China Journal*, Vol.48 (July 2002), pp.1–27; Feuchtwang, 'What is a Village' (note 25).

29. Brandtstädter (note 28), Feuchtwang, 'What is a Village' (note 25).

30. See Flower and Leonard (note 17).

31. See Brandtstädter (note 28); John Flower, 'A Road is Made: Roads, Temples, and Historical Memory in Ya'an Country, Sichuan', *The Journal of Asian Studies*, Vol.63, No.3 (2004), pp.649–86; Stephan Feuchtwang, 'Religion as Resistance', in Elizabeth.J. Perry and Mark Selden (eds), *Chinese Society: Change, Conflict, and Resistance*, 2nd ed. (London: Routledge, 2003), pp.173–4.

32. Feuchtwang, 'Peasants, Democracy and Anthropology' (note 24).

33. Feuchtwang, 'Religion as Resistance' (note 31), pp.173–4; also see John Flower and Pamela Leonard, 'Definining Cultural Life in the Chinese Countryside. The Case of the Chuan Zhu Temple', in Eduard B. Vermeer, Frank N. Piek and Woei Lien Chong (eds), *Cooperative and Collective in China's Rural Development. Between State and Private Interests* (Armonk, NY:M.E. Sharpe, 1998), pp.273-290.

34. Guo Yuhua, 'D'une forme de réciprocité à l'autre', in Isabelle Thireau and Wang Hansheng (eds), *Disputes au village chinois. Formes de juste et recompositions locales des espaces normatifs* (Paris: Éditions de la maison des science de l'homme, 2001), pp.39–77.

35. As is argued, for example, by Xiao Tangbiao, whose description clearly shows the influence of 'village democracy': 'The clan's "working leaders" have a modern spirit. Among the Xiao clan the village leader's working group is made up of the village leader, deputy village leader, accountant and cashier. Apart from the cashier role – which is performed in rotation by family heads from the minor hall – the other personnel are elected annually by the village's households – one vote per house-hold. In the last ten years, these working group members have all been young men from the minor hall, and no member of the senior hall has taken part. Because of the limitations brought by the one year term of office – since 1998 – the lineage has extended the term of the village leader's working group to three years. The mode by which this working group is constituted clearly shows the modern spirit of demo-cracy and equality.' 'Rural China Entering the 21st Century – Clans and Lineages', China Research Papers Online, Universities Service Center, Chinese University of Hong Kong (available at <www.usc.cuhk.edu.hk/wk_wzdetails.asp?id=1594>, accessed 21 July 2005).

36. Li Lianjiang and Kevin O'Brien, 'Villagers and Popular Resistance in Contemporary China', *Modern China*, Vol.22, No.1 (1996), p.42.

37. O'Brien, 'Villagers, Elections, and Citizenship' (note 12), p.59.

38. O'Brien and Lianjiang (note 12).

39. Guo Zhenlin and Thomas P.Bernstein, 'The Impact of Elections on the Village Structure of Power: the Relations Between the Village Committees and the Party Branches', *Journal of Contemporary China*, Vol.13, No.39 (2004), pp.257–75.

40. Richard Levy, 'The Village Self-Government Movement: Elections, Democracy, the Party, and Anti-corruption – Developments in Guangdong', *China Information*, Vol.17, No.1 (2003), pp.28–65.

41. Certainly enough, this comes close to the concept of legitimacy. However, trust should be analytically distinguished from legitimacy as it lays the ground for the latter and is also a result of legitimacy. While trust is based on reasonable expectations, legitimacy stems from factual knowledge.

42. See also Feuchtwang, 'What is a Village' (note 25), p.68.
43. Vivienne Shue, *The Reach of the State: Sketches of the Chinese Body Politic* (Stanford, CA: Stanford University Press, 1988).
44. Jean Oi has called this tension 'the struggle over the harvest'. See Jean Oi, *State and Peasant in Contemporary China: The Political Economy of Contemporary Village Government* (Berkeley, CA: University of California Press, 1992).
45. Brandtstädter, 'Redefining Place' (note 28).
46. A good recent example is the urbanization of villages by administrative decree (*chengshihua*) in China's big cities with the effect that control of the local land is taken away from the village committees and transferred to the district governments. This measure is strongly resented by the new urbanites who believe to be unjustly deprived of the right to further develop their respective communities.
47. See Flower and Leonard (note 17).
48. See Elizabeth Perry, 'Rural Violence in Socialist China', *The China Quarterly*, Vol.103 (1985), pp.414–40.
49. See Susanne Brandtstädter, 'With Elias in China. Civilizing Process, Local Restorations and Power in Contemporary Rural China', *Anthropological Theory*, Vol.3, No.1 (2003), pp.87–105.
50. Isabelle Thireau, Hua Linshan, 'Du présent au passé: Accords et désaccords concernant les affaires communes villageoises', in Isabelle Thireau/Wang Hansheng, pp.79–124.
51. See Kevin J. O'Brien, and Lianjiang Li, 'Selective Policy Implementation in Rural China', *Comparative Politics*, Vol.31, No.2 (1999), p.180.
52. Li Lianjiang, 'Political Trust in Rural China', *Modern China*, Vol.30, No.2 (2004), pp.228–258.
53. See Perry (note 48).
54. Brandtstädter, 'With Elias in China' (note 49).This is the position of Tong Zhihui and He Xuefeng, who suggest that lineages contribute positively to the social integration of a village, something that village elections may destroy by fostering interest fragmentation. See Tong, *Xuanju shijian yu cunzhuang zhengzhi; He Xuefeng, Xiangcun zhili de shehui jichu (The Social Basis of Village Governance)* (Beijing: Zhongguo shehui kexuan, 2003).
55. For a more recent comprehensive account of the state of Chinese village elections see Li Lianjing, Guo Zhenlin and Xiao Tangbiao, *Xuanju guancha (Observing Elections)* (Tianjin: Tianjin renmin, 2001).

Manuscript accepted for publication August 2005.

Address for correspondence: Susanne Brandtstädter, Dept. of Anthropology, University of Manchester, Manchester, UK. E-mail: <Susanne.brandtstadter@manchester.ac.uk>. Gunter Schubert, Institute for Chinese and Korean Studies, University of Tübingen, Tübingen, Germany. E-mail: <gunter.schubert@uni-tuebingen.de>.

Building Inclusive Democracies: Indigenous Peoples and Ethnic Minorities in Latin America

DONNA LEE VAN COTT

Indigenous Peoples, Ethnic Minorities and Democratization

Hostility among peoples of diverse ethnic and cultural backgrounds, whether rooted in generations of conflict or precipitated by recent events, is one of the most serious challenges to the survival and quality of democracy. Even where relatively free and fair multi-party elections are regularly held, governments violating the rights of ethnic minorities and indigenous peoples, or failing to constrain dominant groups from oppressing and exploiting others, prevent their citizens from enjoying democratic rights and political freedoms. Discrimination and oppression erode the values of equality and solidarity, and reduce the quality of public trust that democratic culture requires. In many cases, cultural difference itself impedes equitable access to democratic institutions and fosters political exclusion. In the face of oppression or exclusion, minority groups may opt to carve out a space of protection and autonomy for themselves and, thus, opt out of participation in the larger state and society, with negative effects on national unity. It is, thus, no accident that the most successful cases of democratization in Latin America and post-communist Europe occurred in the least ethnically-diverse states – such as Hungary, Poland, Costa Rica, Uruguay – while the most ethnically diverse states are having a harder time constructing democratic institutions, for example Romania, Ukraine, Guatemala and Peru.[1]

By the 1990s, public opinion in the advanced industrialized democracies had shifted from the view that policies favouring ethnic minorities are the stuff of discretionary public policy to the view that ethnic minorities have rights and that these rights protect the basic dignity of human beings.[2] As a result, most countries have codified minority rights in national political constitutions and many international organizations have developed norms for protecting minority, immigrant and indigenous peoples' rights. Once the discretionary concern of national governments, the question of minority rights has become internationalized and states increasingly are pressured to adopt as a minimum these international standards in exchange for recognition and access to trade and financial aid.[3] European organizations in particular have established a strong regime of minority-rights norms and condition admission to institutions, such as the European Union and North Atlantic Treaty Organization (NATO), on the adoption of these standards. The Council of Europe and the Organization for Security and Cooperation in Europe have even mediated ethnic disputes in post-communist Europe.[4]

However, although international standards for the treatment of ethnic minorities and indigenous peoples provide useful guidelines for societies wishing to address the problems that ethnic conflict and inequality create for democracy, they alone cannot resolve ethnic tensions. Such standards must be accepted and embraced by political elites and mass publics – a difficult prospect, particularly in poor and newly democratic countries, where cultural lines tend to be drawn around socio-economic classes. And Western democracies and international organizations must be willing to pursue enforcement, something that they have tended to subordinate to overriding security and political concerns.[5] Even in Europe, where minority-rights norms are most developed, the substance of the minimal standard for minority rights remains unclear, given the diversity of norms and their uneven application. Western countries have been reluctant to force the issue on their eastern neighbours as this could lead to further tensions or result in an examination of their own minority-rights regimes, and post-communist countries have rejected the favoured approaches to moderating ethno-national conflict adopted in the West. In fact, since the fall of communism, in many post-communist countries minorities actually have fewer rights, since eastern European elites largely perceive minorities to be a serious security threat.[6]

This inquiry surveys the main approaches that scholars and policy-makers use to construct democratic institutions in ethnically diverse and divided societies. It then focuses on particular cases of ethnic accommodation in Latin America. In the Latin American context, this almost always concerns indigenous peoples, the descendants of the inhabitants of the Americas at the time of the arrival of Europeans in the sixteenth century. Although there is no widely accepted definition of indigenous peoples, partly due to indigenous activists' insistence that they retain the right to define themselves, they are comparable to national minorities, in that they exist as distinct cultural and political systems within modern states, and that they aspire to self-government. Kymlicka argues that, whereas national minorities lost the battle to establish themselves as the dominant group within a modern state, indigenous peoples were isolated from the processes of nation-building and state-building entirely.[7] This distinction may hold up in Europe, but it fails in the American context, where nation-building was undertaken through the destruction and subordination of indigenous cultures and authorities. It is the process of economic modernization, rather than nation-building, from which indigenous peoples have been relatively more isolated. Finally, the account evaluates efforts by democracies in that region to implement institutional solutions for managing ethnic conflict and offers practical recommendations for policy-makers.

Conceptual Issues and Approaches

Notwithstanding the intellectual convergence on the idea that ethnic minority and indigenous rights should be protected, debate persists over how liberal-democratic institutions can best protect minorities while promoting values and practices essential to democracy. How should liberalism – which developed in a context of relative ethnic homogeneity – be interpreted in a context of ethnically diverse societies, particularly in those lacking a liberal-democratic philosophico-cultural tradition? Does the recognition of distinct national minority groups destroy the cohesion and collective identity necessary for democratic nationhood, or is that recognition required to uphold basic liberal principles? How can minority cultures be respected and protected from the intrusion of dominant cultures, while protecting individual members of minority cultures from violations of their right to express a version of their culture that may diverge from that of their cultural authorities? Should the liberal-democratic state aim to express complete neutrality with respect to culture and ethnicity or, since all states implicitly favour the dominant culture and attempt to build a cohesive nation around this model, should they aim to reflect all cultures explicitly and equally? Does the equality of universal political institutions better promote democratic values and practices than the asymmetry of 'special' autonomous regions and political rights?

Within political philosophy a consensus has emerged around 'liberal culturalism', which Kymlicka defines as

> the view that liberal states should not only uphold the familiar set of individual civil and political rights which are protected in all democracies, but should also adopt various group-specific rights and policies which are intended to recognize and accommodate the distinctive identities and needs of ethnic cultural groups.[8]

In practice this means that the state may need to intervene to protect individuals from restrictions against their individual rights imposed by ethnic group members, and that the state should protect minority cultures against the intrusion of more dominant groups in society.

State practice, however, demonstrates neither convergence nor consistency. Among those who design policies for states a key debate concerns the question of whether or not ethnicity should be 'politicized'. Arend Lijphart is the most renowned proponent of the view that ethnically divided societies must design institutions that explicitly recognize ethnic identity in order to promote power-sharing (also called 'consociationalism') and group autonomy. In power-sharing systems, leaders of explicitly identified communal groups participate in a 'grand coalition' government, in which each group receives a proportional share of state resources, maintains autonomy over sensitive cultural issues, and reserves the right to veto policies concerning cultural rights, that is, policies pertaining to language, education and religion.[9] 'Quasi-power-sharing' arrangements reserve seats in government for minority groups in order to ensure their participation and, thus, their loyalty to the political system. For example, the legislatures in India and Iran reserve seats for lower-caste groups and religious minorities, respectively, and American policy-makers, prior to the January 2004 elections in Iraq, had suggested that seats be reserved for Sunnis, who make up 20 per cent of the population, to avoid their domination by Shiites and Kurds.[10] The model is based on the successful experiences of Belgium and the Netherlands and, to a lesser extent, Austria and Switzerland.

Although Lijphart endorses power-sharing for all societies, the model has failed to succeed in developing countries. Among the most important reasons for failure are: (1) the presence of significant group-based economic and social inequality, political instability and societal violence; (2) the resultant scarcity of inter-ethnic trust and shared elite values and interests in developing as opposed to advanced industrialized societies; as well as (3) varying birth rates among ethnic groups, which require difficult, periodic adjustments in the distribution of power and resources. Moreover, the approach tends to reduce the fluidity of communal identities and to reduce the scope of choice for voters. Thus, power-sharing is best used where cultural and economic differences are not great and democratic values are strong.

Donald L. Horowitz offers a distinct approach that promotes the careful design of institutions to diminish the political salience of ethnic and other communal identities in order to discourage the adoption of stable communal identities and to create incentives for inter-ethnic elite cooperation. The approach relies mainly on electoral laws that punish extremism and reward political moderation and preelectoral inter-ethnic coalition building.[11] The difficulty is that it is impossible for such laws to promote all democratic values at once. For example, laws that increase the accountability of politicians directly to constituents and promote durable government coalitions may reduce the proportionality of representation and even exclude small minorities. Laws that explicitly promote the proportional representation of minorities in office may discourage inter-ethnic cooperation by fragmenting the party system and legislative bodies.[12] Moreover, it is difficult to convince societies that are accustomed to certain institutions to adopt new ones with which they lack cultural affinity. Generations of failed presidentialism have yet to convince Latin Americans that they should try parliamentary systems, which may produce more stable and effective governments and allow executives to govern with legislative support.[13]

It is difficult to know beforehand how electoral laws developed in the West will affect political outcomes in different cultural contexts.[14] It is equally plausible that more ethnically homogeneous electoral districts will promote inter-ethnic cooperation by satisfying ethnic elites' hunger for government jobs and their constituents' quest for 'authentic' representation, as it is that ethnically heterogeneous districts will promote inter-ethnic cooperation by encouraging more moderate political views. The only pattern discernible is that Western democracies have been relatively successful at designing policies that harmonize the twin goals of (1) building national unity and collective identity, and (2) protecting minority rights. These policies have tended to promote greater equality among groups and, thus, to reduce incidences of conflict derived from fears of domination. This typically is accomplished through a combination of federalism – the devolution of executive, legislative, and judicial powers, resources, and responsibilities to sub-national levels of government[15] – and 'multicultural policies' targeted at ethnically distinct immigrant groups, which typically protect (and sometimes publicly fund) their distinct justice, religious and educational institutions. Shifting powers to local or regional levels where national minorities and indigenous peoples constitute majorities enables them to freely develop their cultures without interference and to exercise powers of self-government that reduce the feeling of domination by the majority.[16] Where federalism is inappropriate or lacks public support, quasi-federal arrangements provide some autonomy for distinct groups. Examples of such arrangements include the establishment of legislatures for Scotland and Wales within Great Britain, and the relationship of Puerto Rico and the Aaland Islands to the United States and Finland, respectively.[17]

Federalism has been most successful where all sub-units of the state have relatively equal powers. Switzerland and India are good examples of successful federalism, representing the wealthy industrialized and poor industrializing worlds, respectively. Typically, however, a country has one or a few regions where national minorities are concentrated and seek autonomous self-governing rights, while the remainder of the country is divided into units based upon region rather than ethnicity. For example, Canada's federal system and Spain's system of autonomous communities were constructed in order to satisfy autonomy claims from the province of Québec and the Catalan, Basque and Galician communities, respectively. Asymmetric federalism, however, establishes a tension between minority ethnic groups, who seek special autonomy rights that regionally defined units lack, and the majority, which seeks to prevent any region from acquiring greater rights than those enjoyed by all units in order to uphold the principle of equality.[18] Although instituted in order to reduce demands for secession, asymmetric federalism may increase such demands, as autonomous peoples come to view themselves as capable of going it alone.

Federalism does not always produce the desired result. When federal sub-units are drawn around territorially concentrated ethnic groups identities tend to become rigid and power is typically seized by more extreme members of the ethnic elite in each subunit, reducing the choices of citizens to candidates and platforms proposed by this ethnic elite.[19] In the post-communist and developing worlds federal systems have proved to be extremely vulnerable to collapse and secession: the Soviet Union, Yugoslavia (neither of them true federations) and Czechoslovakia barely survived the fall of communism, and separatist movements continue to agitate in Russia, India, Nigeria and Ethiopia. In democratizing countries, societies often lack the abundant goodwill necessary for successful territorial power-sharing. The failure of federalism in post-communist Europe largely is attributable to the lack of a democratic context for its operation and the simultaneous oppression of minorities within the system. This legacy has made the federalism option anathema among leaders in ethnically diverse eastern and central European countries, who view it as encouraging 'disloyalty' and even secession among minorities. Such leaders find the spectre of their minorities seeking to secede and join ethnic kin in neighbouring countries particularly threatening.[20]

A situation somewhat comparable to asymmetric federalism exists in industrialized countries that create self-governing reserves for indigenous peoples, who typically receive distinct treatment under national and international law compared to ethnic minorities. Indigenous peoples have been relatively more isolated – geographically, politically and economically – from the process of economic and political modernization, and their cultures are relatively less similar to the dominant culture in the state in which they reside. The greater vulnerability of indigenous groups, their relatively small numbers compared to the total population, and widespread sympathy for the justice of their rights claims have led to relatively generous regimes of autonomous rights in advanced industrialized democracies, including Canada, Sweden, New Zealand and the United States. Autonomous reserves remove indigenous cultures from specific aspects of the jurisdiction of national and sub-national governments – whether federal or unitary – and confer special powers which allow indigenous authorities to control access to indigenous culture and territory by outsiders and to apply culturally appropriate means of conflict resolution and rule adjudication. For example, in the United States, Native American reservations are exempt from state law and have their own tribal courts and police, and Canada's Inuit have governed an autonomous territory called Nunuvut since 1999. New Zealand and the Scandinavian countries have established autonomous territorial rights for the Maori and the Sami, respectively.

In contrast to the success of liberal culturalism in wealthy democracies, institutions in developing countries designed to protect ethnic minorities and indigenous peoples' rights have had more limited results. A key obstacle is the far higher degree of inequality in developing areas, which typically corresponds to ethnic differences. Developing countries lack the economic resources, and usually the political will, to rapidly ameliorate inter-group inequalities. Many indigenous and ethnic groups' claims are essentially redistributive and poor, developing countries, having fewer resources and less economic autonomy relative to international financial institutions and markets, find redistribution to be more challenging. In addition, developing countries often contain what Amy Chua calls 'market-dominant minorities': ethnically distinct groups that monopolize economic and financial resources and access to international markets, while widespread poverty afflicts an ethnically distinct majority. As Chua observes, many contemporary ethnic conflicts consist of the efforts of market-dominant minorities to maintain their dominance in the face of intense resentment expressed by impoverished and excluded majorities. Contemporary efforts to open markets to international commerce tend to exacerbate existing inequalities, since market-dominant minorities benefit disproportionately.[21]

The Latin American Experience

Latin America is an interesting region for the discussion of approaches to ethnic accommodation in democratizing countries. Ethnic conflict in the region mainly concerns the longstanding inequalities among the region's three main ethno-racial groups: the descendants of the original inhabitants, 'indigenous peoples' or 'Indians'; the descendants of European conquerors and immigrants, 'whites' or '*criollos*'; and the descendants of African slaves, 'Afro-descendants' or 'blacks'.

Indigenous peoples constitute approximately 40 million individuals, or roughly ten per cent of Latin America's population, with large concentrations in Bolivia, Chile, Ecuador, Guatemala, Mexico, and Peru.[22] Contemporary indigenous social movements formed in the 1960s and 1970s to demand bilingual education and collective land rights. These movements gained strength and public recognition in the 1980s and became important collective political actors in Bolivia, Chile, Colombia, Ecuador and Mexico. By the 1990s, extensive and persistent interaction with neighbouring movements generated a common, cohesive set of indigenous rights claims associated with the right to self-determination, or the right to freely develop their cultures, forms of production, and traditional modes of political organization.[23]

The Afro-descendant population is estimated at 120–150 million, or roughly 30 per cent of the region's population, with high concentrations in the circum-Caribbean and Brazil.[24] Most blacks live in urban areas and do not identify themselves as members of a distinct ethnic group. In the 1970s urban intellectuals inspired by the American Black Power movement tried to organize national movements for racial equality, but these have failed to gain momentum, since most Afro-descendants do not identify themselves as such but have, rather, assimilated into the national or a regional culture. In contrast, there are Afro-descendant communities in geographically remote areas that runaway slaves established in the sixteenth and seventeenth centuries. Geographic isolation enabled these communities to develop and maintain distinct cultures derived from their African ancestry. Afro-descendant political mobilization was delayed until the late 1980s, and has been most active in Brazil, Colombia, Ecuador, Honduras and Peru. The principal demands expressed are for collective land rights for rural communities – on which Afro-descendants often have a common cause with their indigenous neighbours – and an affirmative action agenda to acknowledge and to remediate the markedly lower socio-economic status of blacks. Afro-descendant organizations are far weaker and less cohesive than their indigenous counterparts and, thus, far less effective. They have achieved policy goals mainly in alliance with stronger indigenous organizations and, in some countries like Bolivia and Honduras, they have a similar legal status as indigenous peoples.[25]

In Latin America, we see some of the tension and conflict that Chua attributes to the existence of market-dominant minorities: in this case, the light-skinned economic and political elite of European descent and, to lesser degree, successful immigrant communities from Lebanon, China and elsewhere. Whites dominate politics and the military, and enjoy preferential access to economic opportunities and resources, while a majority of indigenous and Afro-descendant Latin Americans live in poverty. A large proportion of the most violent episodes of conflict witnessed in Latin America in the last decade is attributable to popular backlash against efforts by the light-skinned elite to undertake neo-liberal reforms that would improve their own market position, but would harm indigenous and Afro-descendant communities and economies. Examples are the 1994 Zapatista uprising in Chiapas, Mexico, and the 2003 'Gas War' that toppled Bolivian President Gonzalo Sánchez de Lozada. Inter-ethnic relations are complicated by the great extent of racial mixing, which has created a numerically dominant *mestizo* or mixed-race group. Individuals can achieve limited upward mobility by migrating from rural indigenous or Afro-descendant communities to urban centres and adopting the cultural habits of the Europhile elite.

Since independence in the nineteenth century, and for most of the region's history, Latin American states have attempted to destroy indigenous languages and cultures and to forcibly assimilate the indigenous population. The liberal reforms of the late nineteenth and early twentieth centuries dismembered much of the collective territorial base upon which indigenous cultures depended for their existence. In the 1930s 'indigenist' policies emphasized Spanish-language education and the integration of distinct indigenous cultures into national life. These policies persisted into the 1960s and 1970s in most countries. In the last 15 years, however, the region has become a laboratory for the design and implementation of 'liberal culturalist' policies, particularly with respect to indigenous rights, autonomous regimes and affirmative action.

The Constitutional Reform Wave

A wave of constitutional reform followed the region's return to elected, civilian rule in the 1980s. By the 1990s, almost all Latin American countries had undertaken major reforms or wholesale replacements of their constitutions in an effort to modernize the state and the economy, to establish regimes of human-rights protection that would prevent a return to military-style, authoritarian rule, and to resolve institutional problems related to the hyper-centralization of public administration, judicial weakness and the exaggerated powers of the executive relative to the legislature.[26] Indigenous peoples' organizations throughout the hemisphere had achieved a high level of political organization and mobilization by this time and many were able to insert their rights claims into the new constitutions by linking them to elite goals. For example, indigenous peoples' organizations promoted decentralization as a means to create a territorial system amenable to constructing self-governing autonomous reserves. They joined forces with liberal elites and their allies in international financial institutions seeking to decentralize administrative and political powers and resources in order to create a more efficient, responsive and accountable state. Indigenous organizations promoted the recognition of indigenous customary law and institutions of self-government as a means to fortify spheres of territorial autonomy with meaningful jurisdictional powers and, thus, end local elites' domination of indigenous peoples. They joined forces with political elites seeking to increase the coverage and quality of the rule of law in rural areas, where ordinary courts and police had been unable to establish order in the face of guerrilla violence and criminal activity.[27]

Contemporary Latin American constitutions vary considerably in the kind and number of indigenous rights provisions they encompass. Table 1 illustrates the

TABLE 1

MULTI-CULTURAL RIGHTS FOR INDIGENOUS PEOPLES IN LATIN AMERICA

Country	Date of constitution/ recognition	Collective land rights	Self-government rights	Cultural rights	Customary law	Representation/ consultation in government	Rhetorical affirmation of distinct status	Ratification of ILO 169
Argentina	1994	+		+	+		+	2000
Belize	1981							
Bolivia	1995	+	+ for limited purposes	+	+		+	1991
Brazil	1988	+		+			+	2002
Chile	1993 by statute				+ limited			
Colombia	1991	+	+	+	+	+	+	1991
Costa Rica	Laws passed in 1977/1993/1999	+		+	+			1993
Ecuador	1998	+	+	+	+	+	+	1998
El Salvador	1983/1991–92	+						
Guatemala	1986	+		+	+		+	1996
Guyana	1980/1996	+						
Honduras	1982	+		+	+			1995
Mexico	1917/1992/2001	+	+	+	+		+	1990
Nicaragua	1987/1995	+	+	+	+		+	
Panamá	1972/1983/1993–94	+	+	+	+	+	+	
Paraguay	1992	+	+	+	+		+	1993
Peru	1993/2003–04	+ weakened in 1993	+	+	+		+	1994
Suriname	1987							
Venezuela	1999	+	+	+	+	+	+	2002

distribution of the most common types of constitutional rights accorded to indigenous peoples: collective land rights; self-governing rights; cultural rights, which typically refer to official status for language and/or the right to bilingual education; the right to practice customary law; reserved seats in legislative bodies; and the rhetorical recognition of a distinct status. The last column indicates whether the country has ratified International Labour Organization (ILO) Convention 169 (1989) Concerning Tribal and Indigenous Peoples in Independent Countries. Such countries recognize indigenous peoples' right to hold land collectively, govern themselves, exercise customary law and to receive some type of language recognition and an appropriate educational policy.

Two trends are discernible with respect to the codification of indigenous rights in Latin America. Firstly, over time, countries tended to expand and deepen indigenous rights regimes as these were adopted in neighbouring countries and received support from international actors. Colombia, the first country to adopt a significant regime of indigenous constitutional rights, inspired Bolivia, Argentina, Ecuador and, subsequently, Venezuela to adopt similar rights. Secondly, countries with smaller indigenous populations tended to adopt more generous and meaningful indigenous rights regimes. The most important autonomous regimes established for indigenous peoples are located in Colombia, Nicaragua and Panama, where indigenous populations constitute ten per cent or less of the total population. Panama, where indigenous peoples constitute 8.4 per cent of the population, contains the region's oldest indigenous self-governing reserves, called *comarcas*. The Kuna secured theirs in the 1920s following a long-running war with the state, and with support from the United States government.[28] Similarly, only in Colombia and Venezuela, where indigenous peoples constitute less than three per cent of the population, have indigenous seats been reserved in legislatures. In 1991, two seats were reserved for indigenous senators in the Colombian National Senate and five seats were reserved in the Chamber of Deputies for indigenous peoples, Afro-Colombians and Colombians living abroad. In 1999, three indigenous seats were reserved in the single-chamber Venezuelan National Assembly and a seat is reserved in municipal and state assemblies where indigenous populations are present. The measures automatically provided political representation and a platform for public voice to an excluded sector of society. Moreover, indigenous organizations have used the reserved seats and the resources accruing to them to launch successful electoral vehicles that are competing with surprising success in general elections at all levels of government. For example, in 2000 a Venezuelan indigenous political party won the governorship of the state of Amazonas, elected a representative to the National Assembly (in addition to the three indigenous legislators required by law), and elected mayors for three of the state's seven municipalities.[29]

Elites in countries with significant indigenous populations, fearing the dramatic implications of a shift of power in favour of a large excluded group, have tended to adopt more restrictive multi-cultural policies and have avoided granting territorial autonomy or guaranteeing access to the formal political system. Elites in these countries have, traditionally, united to prevent the incorporation of the indigenous majority (or significant minority), and created institutions designed to exclude the poor, dark-skinned majority. The relatively poor quality of democracy in such countries gave indigenous social movements relatively less leverage for alliance formation and political action.

Weak movements in favour of the cultural and territorial rights of isolated, riverine black communities in the Pacific Coast region emerged in Colombia and Ecuador in the late 1980s and made claims based on historic continuity as distinct cultures dating back hundreds of years. They emulated the successful discourses and strategies of indigenous organizations. As a result, Latin Americans of African descent have received some modest constitutional rights in both countries. Colombia was the first country to recognize Afro-descendants as a distinct ethnic group deserving of special rights. It did so at the insistence of indigenous delegates participating in the 1991 National Constituent Assembly. Implemented through Law 70 (1993), Afro-Colombian rights include collective land rights, support for culture and education, and the creation of a reserved seat for an Afro-Colombian representative in the national Chamber of Deputies. Although these rights originally were targeted toward the descendants of black slaves living in traditional, riverine communities in the Pacific Coast region, Colombia's Constitutional Court subsequently interpreted the subject of Afro-Colombian rights more broadly, opening up the possibility that blacks elsewhere in the country might develop distinct cultures requiring state protection.[30]

Afro-Ecuadorians gained constitutional rights in the 1998 Constitution. As in Colombia, these resulted largely from alliances with stronger indigenous peoples' organizations and are noticeably weaker than those accorded to indigenous peoples, who are considered in both countries to have stronger cultural identities and more legitimate claims to territorial and political sovereignty. Afro-Ecuadorian constitutional rights also are more vague. Apart from the recognition of collective land rights, the applicability of indigenous constitutional rights to Afro-Ecuadorians is to be 'determined by law'. The process of negotiation between black activists and the state over this legislation has enabled incipient black rights movements in Colombia and Ecuador to grow. Thus, perhaps the most important impact of constitutional recognition was the public legitimation of Afro-descendant identity and culture, which encouraged more Colombians and Ecuadorians to identify themselves as black.[31]

Brazil, Honduras and Nicaragua also recognize some limited collective land rights for descendants of escaped slave communities.[32] Honduras and Peru have established official agencies to address the needs of black populations, but they have little legal authority or resources.[33] Elsewhere, recognition of black rights takes the form of programmes to remediate racial discrimination. In Brazil, which has the largest black population outside Nigeria, the Fernando Henrique Cardoso administration in October 2001 enacted a variety of affirmative action policies for blacks, including 20 per cent hiring quotas in three ministries, an effort to improve the performance of blacks on the entrance exam for the diplomatic corps, and a 40 per cent admission quota for universities in three states. By December 2001, quotas had been established for blacks in television programmes and advertisements and 14 distinct quota proposals awaited congressional action. Many state and municipal governments were considering similar policies. In 2002 President Cardoso issued a decree establishing a National Affirmative Action Program.[34] According to Htun, this remarkable change of policy in Brazil – where elites have long denied the existence of racial discrimination – partly is attributable to soul-searching provoked by preparations for the September 2001 World Conference on Racism. In the months leading up to the conference, black legislators met to demand attention to the problem of racial equality and the new policies fulfil pledges made at the conference.[35] Thus, in the same way that international activism around the ratification of ILO Convention 169 put pressure on states to address indigenous rights, international activity surrounding the racism conference helped to forge a consensus in Brazil that something must be done, even though the conference itself may be deemed a failure.[36] The left-leaning Luis Inacio da Silva administration subsequently established a Ministry for the Promotion of Racial Equality and, in 2004, the Federal University of São Paulo adopted a quota system for black, mixed-race and indigenous applicants, reserving 10 per cent of new openings for these populations.[37]

'Liberal Culturalism' in Practice

The simultaneous adoption of European-style mechanisms for the enforcement of human rights – such as the Swedish Human Rights Ombudsperson, the Western European Constitutional Court, and the office of the Prosecutor General, which holds government officials accountable to the law – provided tools for disadvantaged groups to petition the government for redress when their rights are violated. In some cases, these mechanisms have enabled indigenous and Afro-descendant organizations to force the implementation of constitutional rights that had been stalled by legislative inaction or obstruction. For example, Colombia's 1991 constitution established a Constitutional Tribunal to protect citizens' constitutional rights from violations by the state and private actors. The tribunal has adjudicated dozens of *tutelas* (writs of protection) that indigenous and, to a lesser extent, Afro-descendant individuals and communities, have brought before it. The majority of these have been decided in favour of ethnic minorities and, in several important cases, the tribunal has actually expanded and deepened the implications of the rights in question.[38]

Nevertheless, serious challenges impede the implementation of indigenous and Afro-descendant rights in Latin America. A high level of structural inequality and poverty that is closely associated with ethnicity exacerbates conflicts among ethnic groups, while sustained economic crisis since the early 1980s reduces state resources for redistribution and poverty alleviation. Throughout the region, particularly in Guatemala, Colombia, Brazil and Peru, rural violence against indigenous and Afro-descendant peoples inhibits the exercise of existing rights, particularly land rights, and the weakness of the rule of law provides inadequate recourse to protection. For various reasons, the most difficult right to implement has been collective land rights.

First, in Latin America the state retains subsoil rights and can exploit such resources or sell them to private corporations. It has been particularly difficult for indigenous peoples to protect collective land rights where petroleum and other precious natural resources are located and, in fact, a significant portion of unexploited natural resources in Latin America is located on indigenous land.[39] Secondly, conservative political elites, who often are over-represented in legislatures, have prevented the passage of legislation implementing territorial rights, since such rights conflict with their interests in expanding the agricultural, grazing and extractive frontiers.

Thirdly, and this affects all constitutional rights, many Latin American countries have experienced extreme political instability and party system fragmentation since the adoption of new constitutions, rendering legislatures incapable of passing all but the most routine legislation. This problem has been particularly marked in Ecuador, where the indigenous and Afro-Ecuadorian self-governing regimes have awaited implementation since 1998.

According to an analyst for the Inter-American Development Bank, the main reason for the slow progress of implementation is that governments lack sufficient financial resources, staff with expertise in indigenous public policy, and mechanisms for the state and ethnic minorities to hold each other accountable. It is rare that ethnic minorities serve in positions of authority in state agencies working with ethnic minorities.[40] This situation has improved somewhat since the late 1990s, when indigenous peoples entered national legislatures, often with indigenous movement-based political parties, notably Bolivia, Colombia and Ecuador. In the absence of effective formal political representation, policies are most likely to be implemented where ethnic minorities are well organized into a single, coherent social movement that is able to apply sustained pressure. Unfortunately, implementation is a frustrating Catch-22 situation: elite consensus and political stability is required for effective legislative and executive action, but such conditions tend not to lead to the adoption of generous ethnic rights regimes. They are more likely to facilitate a more incremental approach that is unlikely to satisfy extremely disadvantaged groups.

Attention to the needs of ethnic minorities also is impeded by widespread resistance to the idea that racial and ethnic difference and inequality exist in Latin America. This has changed somewhat since the consciousness-raising efforts surrounding the 1992 marking of the quincentenary (the 500th anniversary of Columbus' voyage to the Americas). But many Latin Americans prefer to reduce race- and ethnicity-based inequality to class and to deny the extent of racial discrimination. Even states that recognize a generous regime of rights for indigenous peoples tend to focus on cultural differences and avoid discussion of race, preferring to promote the myth of the racially neutral state.[41]

Nevertheless, the symbolic recognition gained in these constitutions has helped to revive indigenous and Afro-descendant cultures and to inspire identity-based social movements to mobilize politically to realize and expand their new rights. Improvements in the quality of democracy in the region have opened space for these movements, whose effective representation of once-excluded sectors of society, in turn, enhances the quality of democracy. Although critics of these reforms argue that symbolic recognition means nothing, particularly in a context in which it has been difficult to fully implement more substantive ethnic rights, symbolic recognition after centuries of humiliation and domination is enormously important to Latin America's indigenous peoples, whose struggle is as much for substantive rights as it is for dignity and recognition of their status as *peoples* existing prior to the Latin American state and, thus, entitled to a special place in political institutions. Symbolic recognition was crucial to the revitalization of Afro-descendant identity in South America. As Kymlicka and Norman argue, 'symbolic gestures granting or denying recognition can have profound and continuing effects within a political culture in ways that directly affect the well-being and self-respect of citizens of minority cultures, as well as their enthusiasm to participate in the political life of a larger state'.[42] Horowitz concurs that such recognition is of great importance in democratizing multi-ethnic societies because it explicitly includes threatened, non-dominant minorities in the future of the political project. More practically, indigenous organizations have used symbolic constitutional language to argue claims before constitutional courts and to oppose legislation proposed by national parliaments.

The multi-cultural rights discussed above represent a common approach in Latin America to addressing longstanding political, economic and social exclusion of indigenous peoples and, in a few cases, Afro-descendants. Countries recognizing 'strong' regimes of multi-cultural rights – Colombia, Ecuador, Venezuela and certain states within Mexico, such as Oaxaca – base these regimes on a federal or quasi-federal politico-territorial organization that supports ethnically defined electoral districts and self-governing autonomous reserves, municipalities or regions, where land is held collectively, indigenous customary law is practiced and authorities are chosen through customary means.[43] This represents the 'territorial power-sharing' approach that Kymlicka advocates. In two countries – Colombia and Venezuela – this approach is combined with aspects of group-based power-sharing, in that seats are reserved for indigenous and, in Colombia, Afro-descendant minorities in legislative bodies. Only in Peru do we see the adoption of Horowitz's advice to design electoral rules that encourage inter-ethnic electoral alliances. In 2002, the Peruvian government adopted legislation requiring political parties in certain Amazonian electoral districts to place indigenous peoples in 15 per cent of the slots on their candidate lists.[44]

Conclusion: Implications for Scholars and Policy-makers

The political mobilization of indigenous peoples, ethnic minorities and oppressed majorities has presented challenges to democratizing countries. Although in other regions of the world this has fostered anti-democratic tendencies, in Latin America, on balance, it has improved the quality of democracy by placing new issues and values – justice, equality, tolerance of difference – on the political agenda and by presenting a model of policy-making in which citizens have a central role. Indigenous movements have forced governments to take into account the impact of public policy on society's most vulnerable. They have been less effective in achieving the implementation of existing rights and in facilitating the design and adoption of alternative forms of inter-ethnic governance.

What, then, can be done to enable ethnic minorities, excluded and oppressed majorities, and indigenous peoples to enjoy the benefits of democracy? What lessons does the Latin American experience offer?

First, ethnic political mobilization is more effective when combined with international pressure, particularly from international financial institutions and aid organizations willing to require sensitivity to ethnic claims in exchange for granting to states access to financial assistance. Western democracies and the multilateral institutions that they support must establish clear, consistent standards with respect to minority rights and these standards must be vigorously and consistently enforced.

Second, external aid agencies and governments should invest in the organizational and technical capacity of disadvantaged ethnic minorities and indigenous organizations and professionals. Where these entities are strong, positive policy outcomes are more likely.[45]

Third, as the case of Colombia and its activist Constitutional Court demonstrates, strong judicial institutions are crucial for the protection of the rights of vulnerable groups, particularly in the face of resistance on the part of dominant groups. Individuals and organizations representing ethnic minorities and indigenous peoples must have easy access to credible, efficient judicial mechanisms for asserting and protecting their rights. Even where they are relatively cohesive and well organized, organizations representing oppressed groups require a strong legal system to ensure the existence of a democratic public space in which to make claims and to participate in formal and informal politics. This is even more important in developing regions, such as Latin America, where economic inequalities correspond to ethnic identity and significantly impair access to justice. A strong rule of law and strong judicial institutions are as vital to the quality of ethnic relations as they have been proven to be vital to the quality of democracy.[46]

Fourth, where ethnic identity is a proxy for economic status, states must undertake significant programmes of redistribution in order to reduce the economic basis of ethnic inequality. As Chua observes, this requires redistributive tax systems. Such systems, however, are weak in the developing world, since governments generally are too weak to force privileged minorities to pay their share, let alone more than their share. Redistributive policies should include public funding for the fledgling political parties of oppressed ethnic minorities and indigenous peoples to reduce the significant disadvantage they face in competition against well-funded dominant groups.[47] No real progress can be made, however, until privileged ethnic minorities voluntarily contribute to the reduction of inequality. Given the violent backlash against market-dominant, light-skinned elites and foreigners, the time may be coming when such elites understand it is in their best interest to address the basic needs of the impoverished majority.[48]

Finally, governments must be flexible. They must try new ideas and tailor well-known conflict resolution mechanisms and institutional designs to the particular circumstances in their own societies. Such circumstances change over time, often quickly, and require constant vigilance, a disposition to negotiate, and a commitment to inter-ethnic cohabitation. Policy-makers, committed as they are to producing measurable, substantive results, should not underestimate the importance of symbolic gestures and the act of talking, both of which send signals to excluded ethnic minorities and indigenous peoples, and to members of dominant groups, that a process of accommodation is underway.

NOTES

1. Will Kymlicka, 'Western Political Theory and Ethnic Relations in Eastern Europe', in Will Kymlicka and Magda Opalski (eds), *Can Liberal Pluralism be Exported?: Western Political Theory and Ethnic Relations in Eastern Europe* (London: Oxford University Press, 2001), p.3.
2. Will Kymlicka, *Politics in the Vernacular: Nationalism, Multiculturalism, and Citizenship* (Oxford: Oxford University Press, 2001), p.6.

3. The most important global standard is the 1992 United Nations Declaration of the Rights of Persons Belonging to National or Ethnic, Religious and Linguistic Minorities. With respect to indigenous peoples, International Labour Organization Convention 169 Concerning Indigenous and Tribal Peoples in Independent States (1989), and the United Nations Draft Declaration on the Rights of Indigenous Peoples, are the most relevant norms.

4. See Kymlicka, *Politics in the Vernacular* (note 2), pp.6–7; Graham Smith, 'Sustainable Federalism, Democratization, and Distributive Justice', in Will Kymlicka and Wayne Norman (eds), *Citizenship in Diverse Societies* (Oxford: Oxford University Press, 2000), p.345.

5. Will Kymlicka, 'Reply and Conclusion', in Kymlicka and Opalski (note 1), pp.369–87.

6. See Kymlicka, 'Western Political Theory' (note 1), and 'Reply and Conclusion' (note 5). See also Jon Elster, Claus Offe and Ulrich K. Preuss, *Institutional Design in Post-communist Societies: Rebuilding the Ship at Sea* (Cambridge: Cambridge University Press, 1998), pp.247–60. The most important European norms are the Organization for Security and Cooperation in Europe's 1990 Copenhagen Declaration on the Rights of National Minorities, and the weaker Council of Europe 1995 Framework Convention for Protection of National Minorities.

7. Kymlicka, 'Western Political Theory' (note 1), p.24.

8. Kymlicka, *Politics in the Vernacular* (note 2), p.9; for a complete statement of this approach, see Will Kymlicka, *Multicultural Citizenship: A Liberal Theory of Minority Rights* (Oxford: Oxford University Press, 1995).

9. Arend Lijphart, 'Constitutional Design for Divided Societies', *Journal of Democracy* Vol.15, No.3 (April 2004), pp.96–109.

10. Steven R. Weisman, 'U.S. Is Suggesting Guaranteed Role for Iraq's Sunnis', *The New York Times*, 26 December 2004, online edition.

11. See Donald L. Horowitz, 'Electoral Systems: A Primer for Decision Makers', *Journal of Democracy* Vol.14, No.4 (2003), pp.115–27; Benjamin Reilly, *Democracy in Divided Societies: Electoral Engineering for Conflict Management* (Cambridge: Cambridge University Press, 2001).

12. Larry Diamond and Leonardo Morlino, 'The Quality of Democracy: An Overview', *Journal of Democracy* Vol.15, No.4 (October 2004), p.21; Horowitz, 'Electoral Systems' (note 11).

13. Juan J. Linz and Arturo Valenzuela (eds), *The Failure of Presidential Democracy: The Case of Latin America*, Vol.2 (Baltimore, MD: Johns Hopkins University Press, 1994).

14. Horowitz, 'Electoral Systems' (note 11); Donald L. Horowitz, *Ethnic Groups in Conflict* (Berkeley, CA: University of California Press, 1985).

15. On the topic of federalism and autonomy, see Yash Ghai, *Autonomy and Ethnicity: Negotiating Competing Claims in Multi-Ethnic States* (Cambridge: Cambridge University Press, 2000); Hurst Hannum, *Autonomy, Sovereignty, and Self-Determination: The Accommodation of Conflicting Rights*, rev. ed. (Philadelphia, PA: University of Pennsylvania Press, 1990); Ruth Lapidoth, *Autonomy: Flexible Solutions to Ethnic Conflicts* (Washington, DC: United States Institute of Peace Press, 1997).

16. Kymlicka, *Politics in the Vernacular* (note 2), pp.3, 95.

17. Kymlicka, 'Western Political Theory' (note 1), p.30.

18. Kymlicka, *Politics in the Vernacular* (note 2), p.105.

19. Graham Smith, 'Sustainable Federalism, Democratization, and Distributive Justice', in Will Kymlicka and Wayne Norman (eds), *Citizenship in Diverse Societies* (Oxford: Oxford University Press, 2000), p.345.

20. Kymlicka, 'Reply and Conclusion' (note 5).

21. Amy Chua, *World on Fire: How Exporting Free Market Democracy Breeds Ethnic Hatred and Global Instability* (New York: Anchor Books, 2004).

22. Cletus Gregor Barie, *Pueblos Indígenas y Derechos Constitucionales en America Latina: Un Panorama*, 2nd ed. (Mexico: Comisión Nacional para el Desarrollo de los Pueblos Indígenas, Abya Yala, 2003), pull-out chart.

23. This literature is vast. Among the most cited general and comparative works are Alison Brysk, *From Tribal Village to Global Village: Indian Rights and International Relations in Latin America* (Stanford, CA: Stanford University Press, 2000); David Maybury-Lewis (ed.), *The Politics of Ethnicity: Indigenous Peoples and Latin American States* (Cambridge, MA: Harvard University Press, 2002); Rodolfo Stavenhagen, 'Indigenous Rights: Some Conceptual Problems', in Elizabeth Jelin and Eric Hershberg (eds), *Constructing Democracy: Human Rights, Citizenship, and Society in Latin America* (Boulder, CO: Westview Press, 1996), pp.141–60; Kay Warren and Jean Jackson (eds), *Indigenous Movements, Self-Representation, and the State in Latin America* (Austin, TX: University of Texas Press, 2002); and Deborah J. Yashar, 'Contesting Citizenship: Indigenous Movements and Democracy in Latin America', *Comparative Politics*, Vol.31, No.1 (Oct. 1998), pp.23–42.

24. Inter-American Dialogue, *Race Report* (Washington, DC: Inter-American Dialogue, 2003); World Bank, <www.worldbank.org/afrolatin>.
25. Eva T. Thorne, 'Ethnic and Race-based Political Organization and Mobilization in Latin America: Lessons for Public Policy', paper prepared for the Inter-American Development Bank, p.18.
26. For a discussion of these reforms, see Julio Faúndez, 'Constitutionalism: A Timely Revival', in Douglas Greenberg *et al.* (eds), *Constitutionalism and Democracy: Transitions in the Contemporary World* (New York: Oxford University Press, 1993), pp.354–60; César Landa and Julio Faúndez (eds), *Contemporary Constitutional Challenges* (Lima: Pontificia Universidad Católica del Perú, Fondo Editorial, 1996).
27. On this process, see Willem Assies *et al.* (eds), *The Challenge of Diversity: Indigenous Peoples and Reform of the State in Latin America* (Amsterdam: Thela Thesis, 2000); Barie (note 22); Rachel Sieder (ed.), *Multiculturalism in Latin America: Indigenous Rights, Diversity and Democracy* (London: Palgrave Macmillan, 2002); Donna Lee Van Cott, *The Friendly Liquidation of the Past: The Politics of Diversity in Latin America* (Pittsburgh, PA: University of Pittsburgh Press, 2000).
28. The Embera-Wounaan obtained their *comarca* in 1993, followed by the Ngobe-Bugle in 1997. Although Panamanian Indians enjoy considerable autonomy within these reserves, conflict continues over the presence of non-Indians within the comarcas and over the unresolved issue of access to and ownership of natural resources. Thorne (note 25), p.21
29. See Donna Lee Van Cott, *From Movements to Parties in Latin America: The Evolution of Ethnic Politics* (New York: Cambridge University Press, 2005); Venezuelan electoral results at <www.cne.cantv.net>.
30. See Jaime Arocha, Nina S. de Friedemann, 'Marco de Referencia Histórico-Cultural para la ley Sobre Derechos Etnicos de las Comunidades Negras en Colombia', *América Negra* Vol.3 (June 1992), pp.39–54; Libia Grueso, Carlos Rosero and Arturo Escobar, 'The Process of Community Organizing in the Southern Pacific Coast Region of Colombia', in Sonia Alvarez *et al.* (eds), *Cultures of Politics/ Politics of Cultures: Revisioning Latin American Social Movements in* (Boulder, CO: Westview Press, 1998), pp.196–219; Van Cott (note 27); Peter Wade, *Blackness and Race Mixture: The Dynamics of Racial Identity in Colombia* (Baltimore, MD: Johns Hopkins University Press, 1993).
31. Grueso, Rosero and Escobar (note 30); Van Cott (note 27), pp.97–8; Wade (note 30), pp.182, 356–8; author interview, Pablo de la Torre, 28 July 1999.
32. Thorne (note 25), p.6.
33. Inter-American Dialogue, *Race Report 2004.*
34. Mala Htun, 'From "Racial Democracy" To Affirmative Action: Changing State Policy on Race in Brazil', *Latin American Research Review* Vol.39, No.1 (2004), pp.61–71.
35. The full name of the conference was: World Conference Against Racism, Racial and Ethnic Discrimination, Xenophobia And Related Intolerance. Htun (note 34), pp.61–2.
36. Anti-Israeli and anti-Semitic groups seeking to make Palestinian rights the dominant issue repeatedly disrupted the conference. The issue of reparations for colonization and slavery also impeded the creation of governmental consensus and a plan of action. Natalie Steinberg, 'Background Paper on the World Conference against Racism, Racial and Ethnic Discrimination, Xenophobia and Related Intolerance', November 2001, available at <www.wfm.org/ACTION/racismconf1101.html>.
37. Htun (note 34), pp.61–2; Thorne (note 35), p.23; 'UNIFESP to Adopt Quota System for Black Students', 1 September 2004, translated and reprinted in *The Black Americas* Issue 8 (September 2004), p.2.
38. For example, the tribunal affirmed the right of indigenous peoples to exercise their customary dispute resolution mechanisms even when these violate ordinary legislation and constitutional rights of lower rank than the right to cultural and ethnic diversity. Van Cott(note 27), pp.112–18; Donna Lee Van Cott, 'A Political Analysis of Legal Pluralism in Bolivia and Colombia', *Journal of Latin American Studies* Vol.32, No.1 (February 2000), pp.207–34.
39. Juan Houghton and Beverly Bell, 'Indigenous Movements and Globalization in Latin America', *Native Americas* (Spring 2004), pp.11–19.
40. Thorne (note 25), p.2.
41. Htun (note 34); Thorne (note 25), p.3.
42. Will Kymlicka and Wayne Norman, 'Citizenship in Culturally Diverse Societies: Issues, Contexts, Concepts', in Will Kymlicka and Wayne Norman (eds), *Citizenship in Diverse Societies* (Oxford: Oxford University Press, 2000), p.29.
43. On territorial autonomy in Latin America, see Héctor Díaz Polanco, *Autonomía Regional: La autodeterminación de los pueblos indios* (Mexico: Siglo veintiuno editores, 1991); Donna Lee Van Cott, 'Explaining Ethnic Autonomy Regimes in Latin America', *Studies in Comparative International*

Development Vol.5, No.4 (Winter 2001), pp.30–58. On experiments with autonomy in Mexico, see Aracely Burguete Cal y Mayor, coord., *Mexico: Experiencias de Autonomía Indígena* (Copenhagen: International Work Group on Indigenous Affairs, 1999).
44. Van Cott (note 29), ch.5.
45. Thorne (note 25), pp.26-30.
46. Diamond and Morlino (note 12), pp.23, 26; see also Juan Méndez, Guillermo O'Donnell and Paulo Sérgio Pinheiro (eds), *The (Un)Rule of Law and the Underprivileged in Latin America* (Notre Dame, IN: University of Notre Dame Press, 1999); Guillermo O'Donnell, 'The State, Democratization, and Some Conceptual Problems', in William C. Smith *et al.* (eds), *Latin American Political Economy in the Age of Neoliberal Reform* (Miami, FL: North–South Center, 1994), pp.157–80.
47. Diamond and Morlino (note 12), p.24.
48. Chua (note 21), pp. 267–79.

Maunuscript accepted for publication August 2005.

Address for correspondence: Donna Lee Van Cott, Department of Political Science, Tulane University, 316 Norman Mayer Hall, New Orleans, LA 70118, USA. E-mail: <dvancott@tulane.edu>.

Index